SACRED TATTOOS OF THAILAND

Exploring the Magic, Masters and Mystery of *Sak Yan*

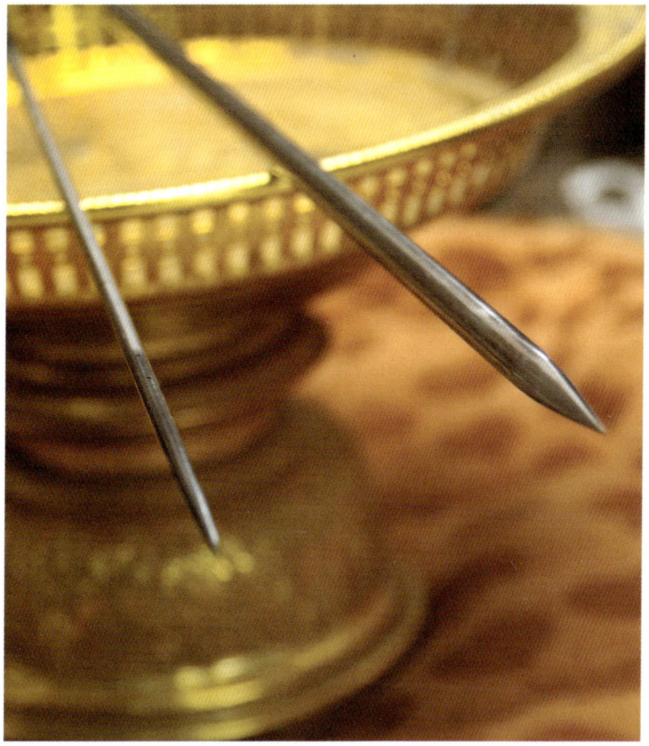

Text by Joe Cummings
Photography by Dan White

Marshall Cavendish Editions

Project Editors: Greg Lowe (Thailand), Melvin Neo & Stephanie Yeo (Singapore)
Design: Mark Soo/Shy Designs & Benson Tan/MCIA

All photos by Dan White except pages 18 & 55 (Amy Gold), page 57 (John LaFortune Collection), page 118 (Pratch Siridhara), pages 83 & 198–199 (Joe Cummings), page 172 (Paula Neudorf & Oliver Bjerrehus) & page 174 (Sacha Rovinski)

Published by Marshall Cavendish Editions
An imprint of Marshall Cavendish International (Asia) Private Limited
A member of Times Publishing Limited

Other Marshall Cavendish Offices
Marshall Cavendish International. PO Box 65829, London EC1P 1NY, UK • Marshall Cavendish Corporation. 99 White Plains Road, Tarrytown NY 10591-9001, USA • Marshall Cavendish International (Thailand) Co Ltd. 253 Asoke, 12th Flr, Sukhumvit 21 Road, Klongtoey Nua, Wattana, Bangkok 10110, Thailand • Marshall Cavendish (Malaysia) Sdn Bhd, Times Subang, Lot 46, Subang Hi-Tech Industrial Park, Batu Tiga, 40000 Shah Alam, Selangor Darul Ehsan, Malaysia

National Library Board Singapore Cataloguing in Publication Data

Cummings, Joe, 1952-
Sacred tattoos of Thailand : exploring the magic, masters and mystery of sak yan / text by Joe Cummings ; photography by Dan White. – Singapore : Marshall Cavendish Editions, c2012.
p. cm.
ISBN : 978-981-4302-54-8

1. Tattooing – Thailand. 2. Tattooing – Thailand – Religious aspects – Buddhism.
3. Tattooing – Social aspects – Thailand. 4. Tattooing – Thailand – Pictorial works.
5. Body marking – Thailand – Religious aspects – Buddhism.
I. White, Dan, 1965- II. Title.

GT2346
391.6509593 -- dc22 OCN751807568

Printed in Singapore by Fabulous Printers Pte Ltd

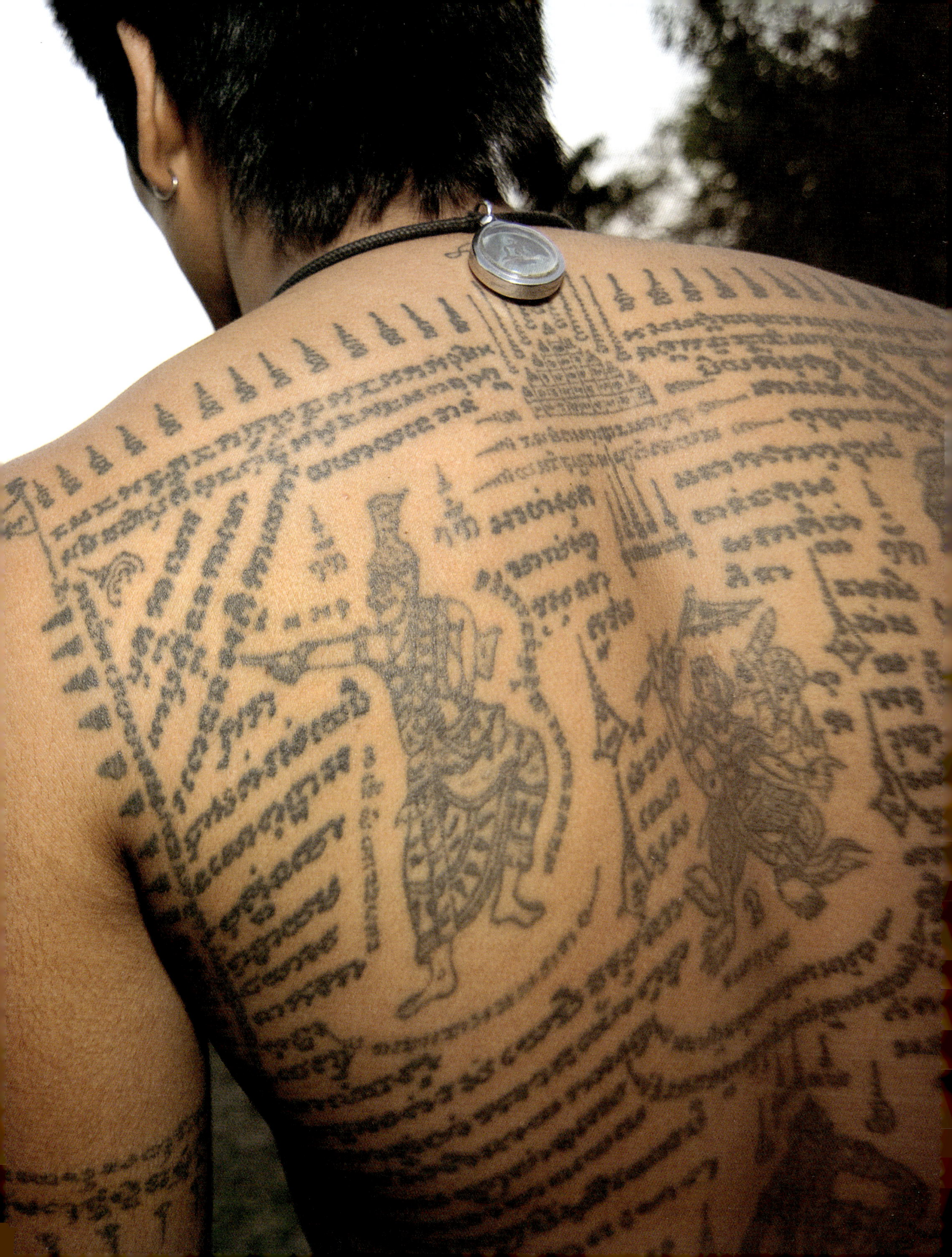

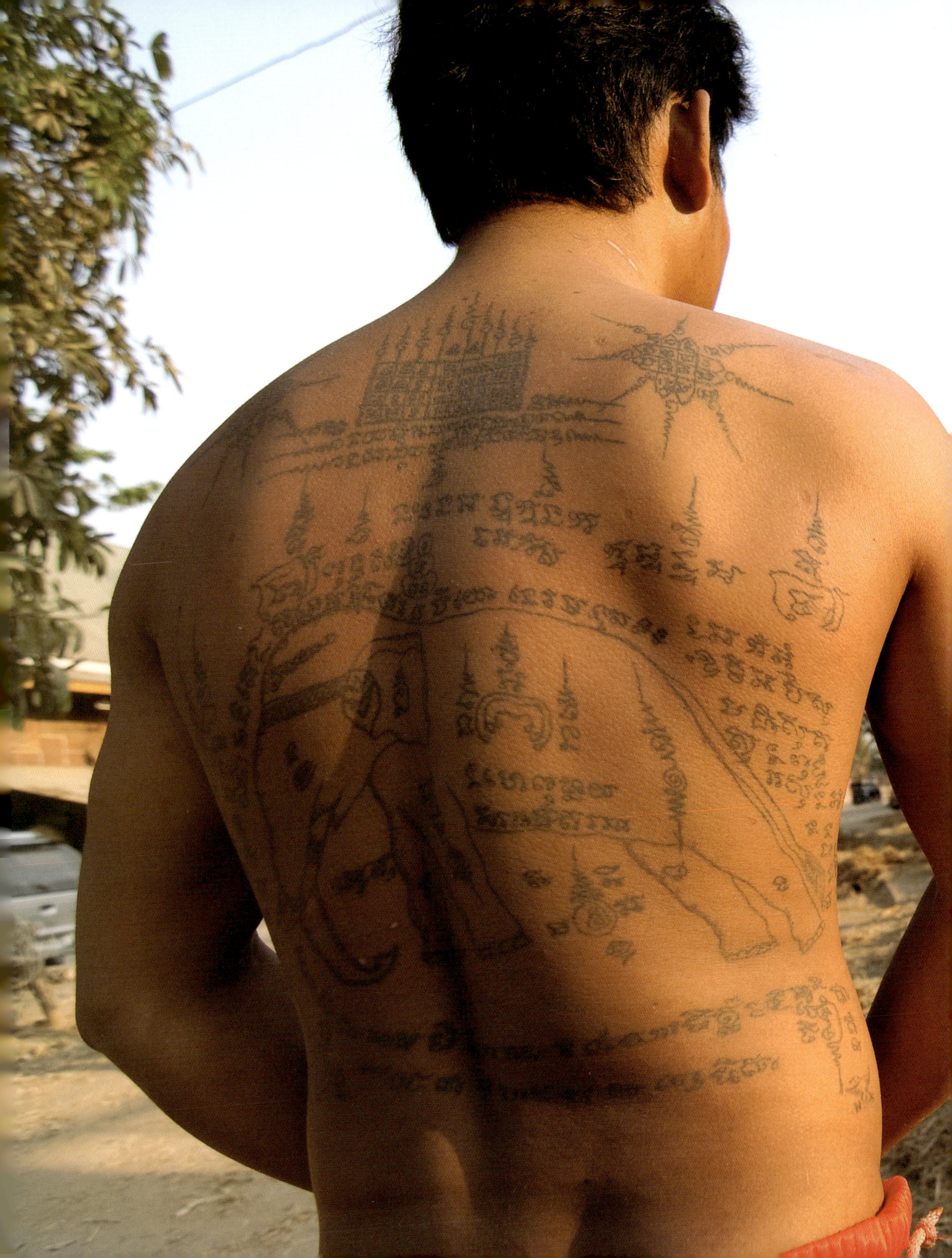

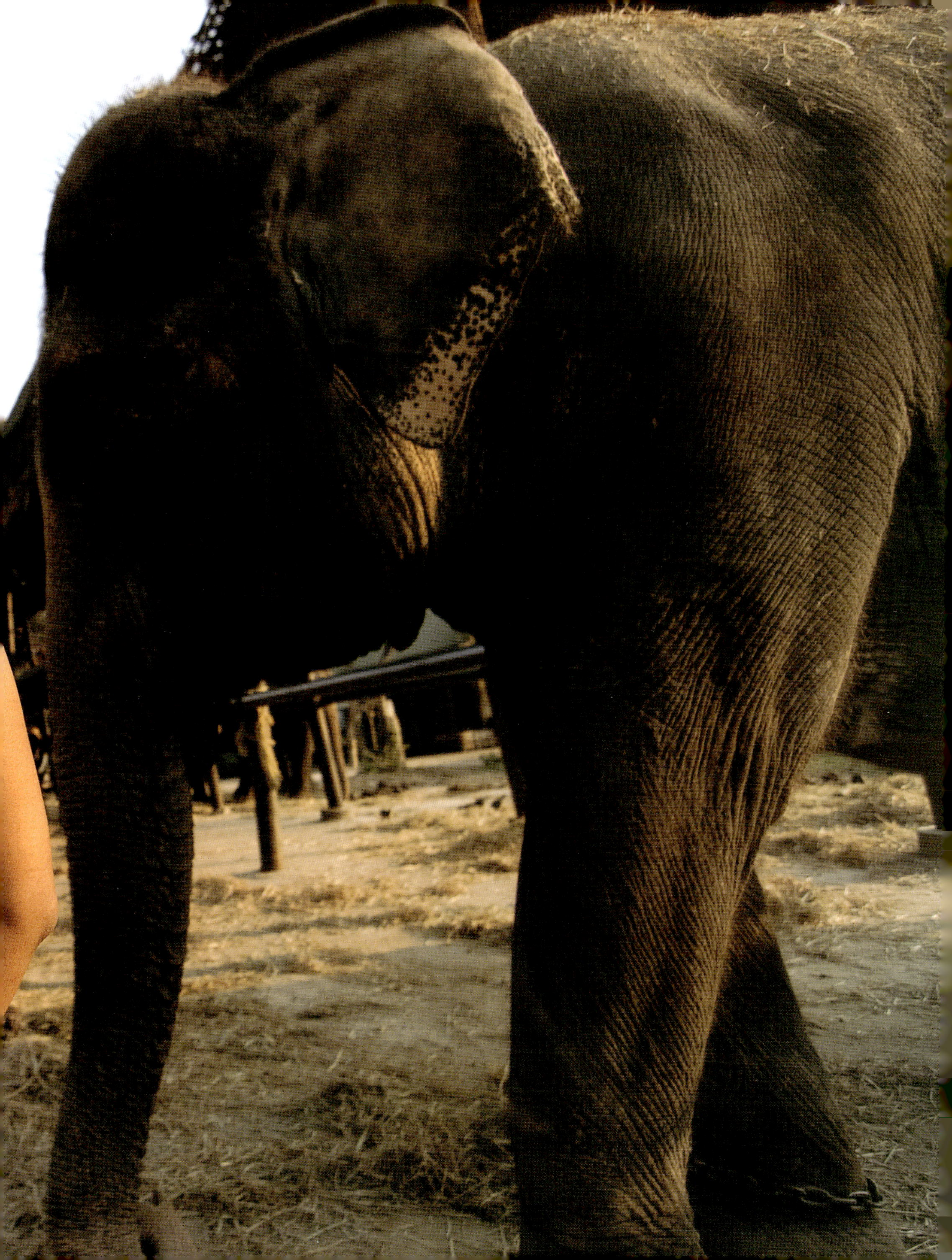

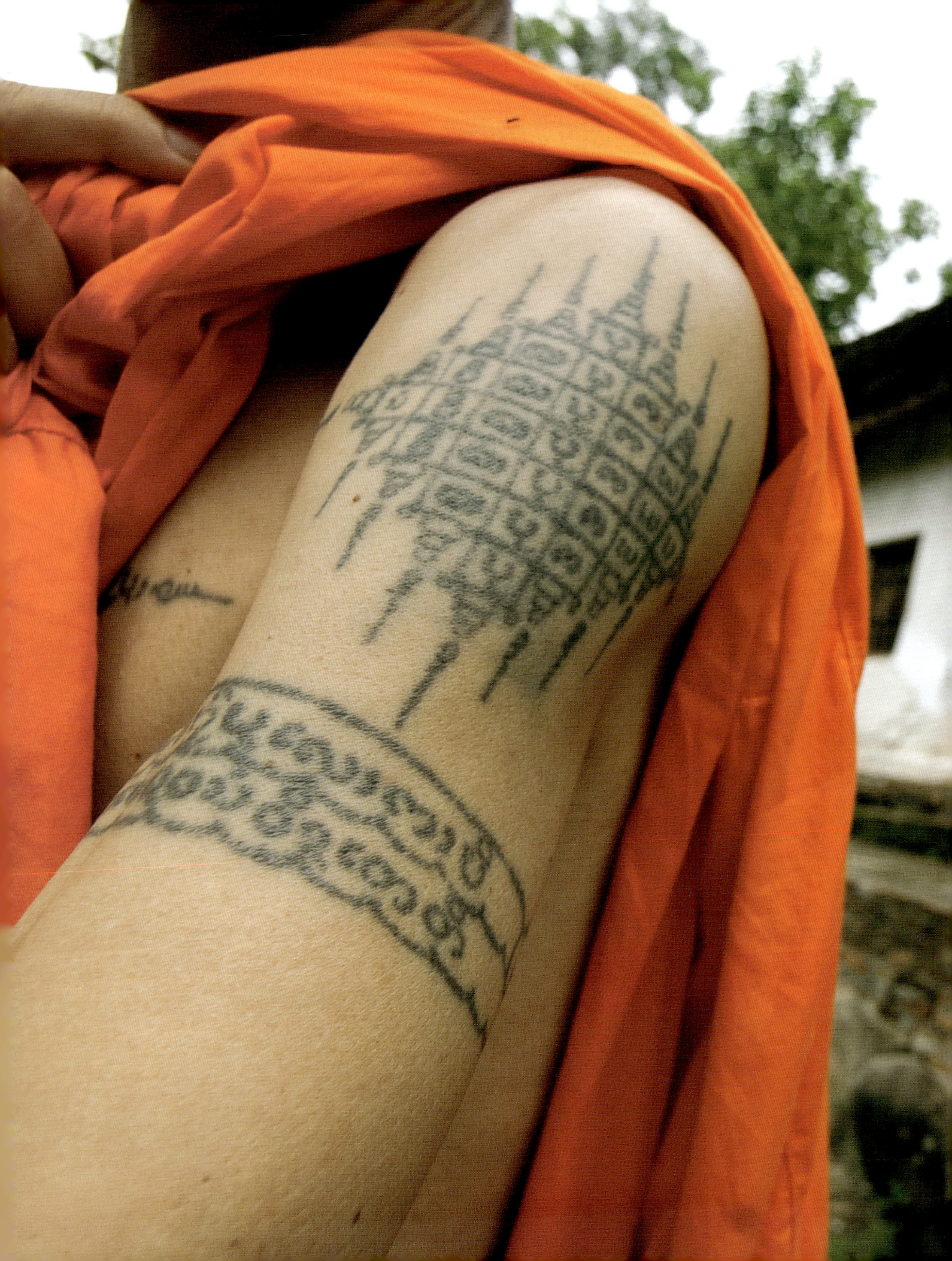

CONTENTS

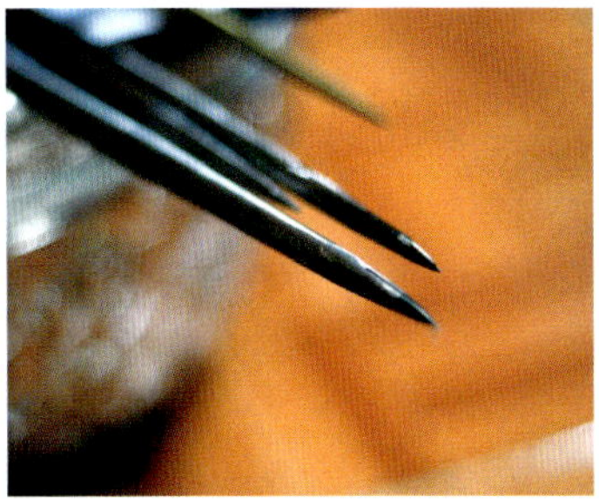

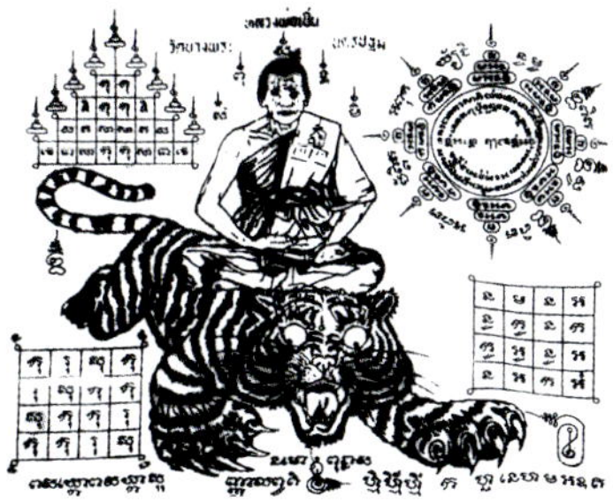

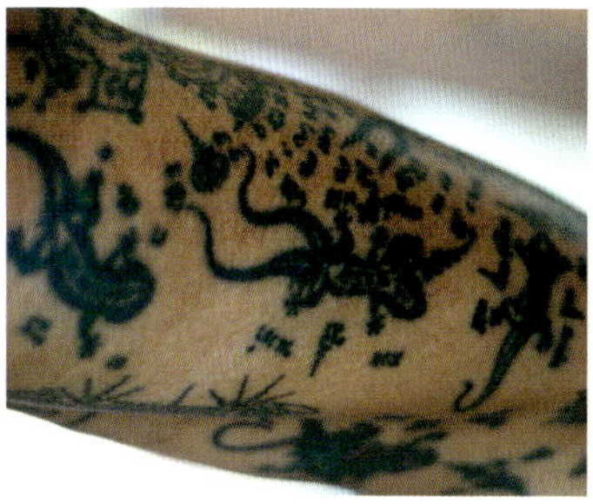

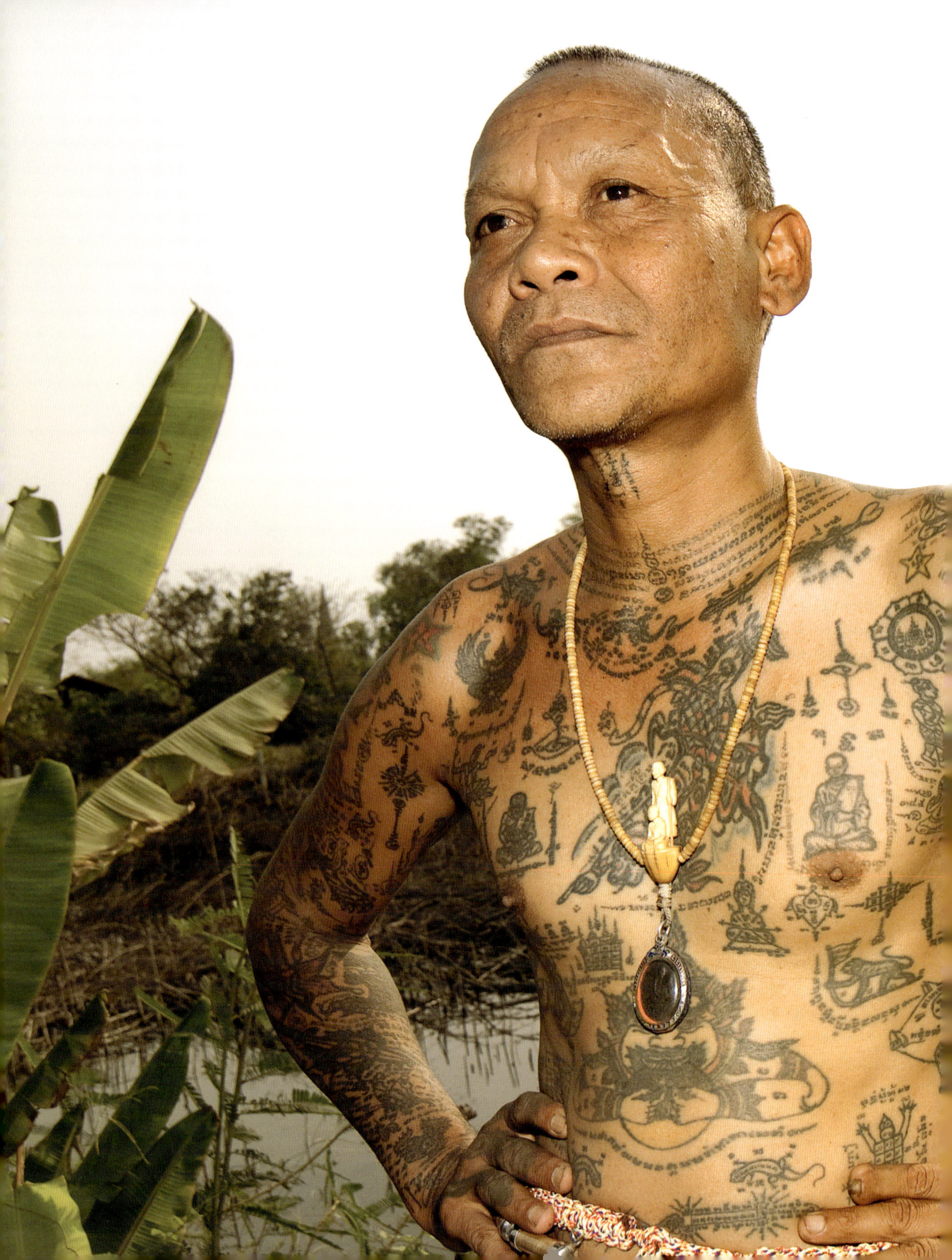

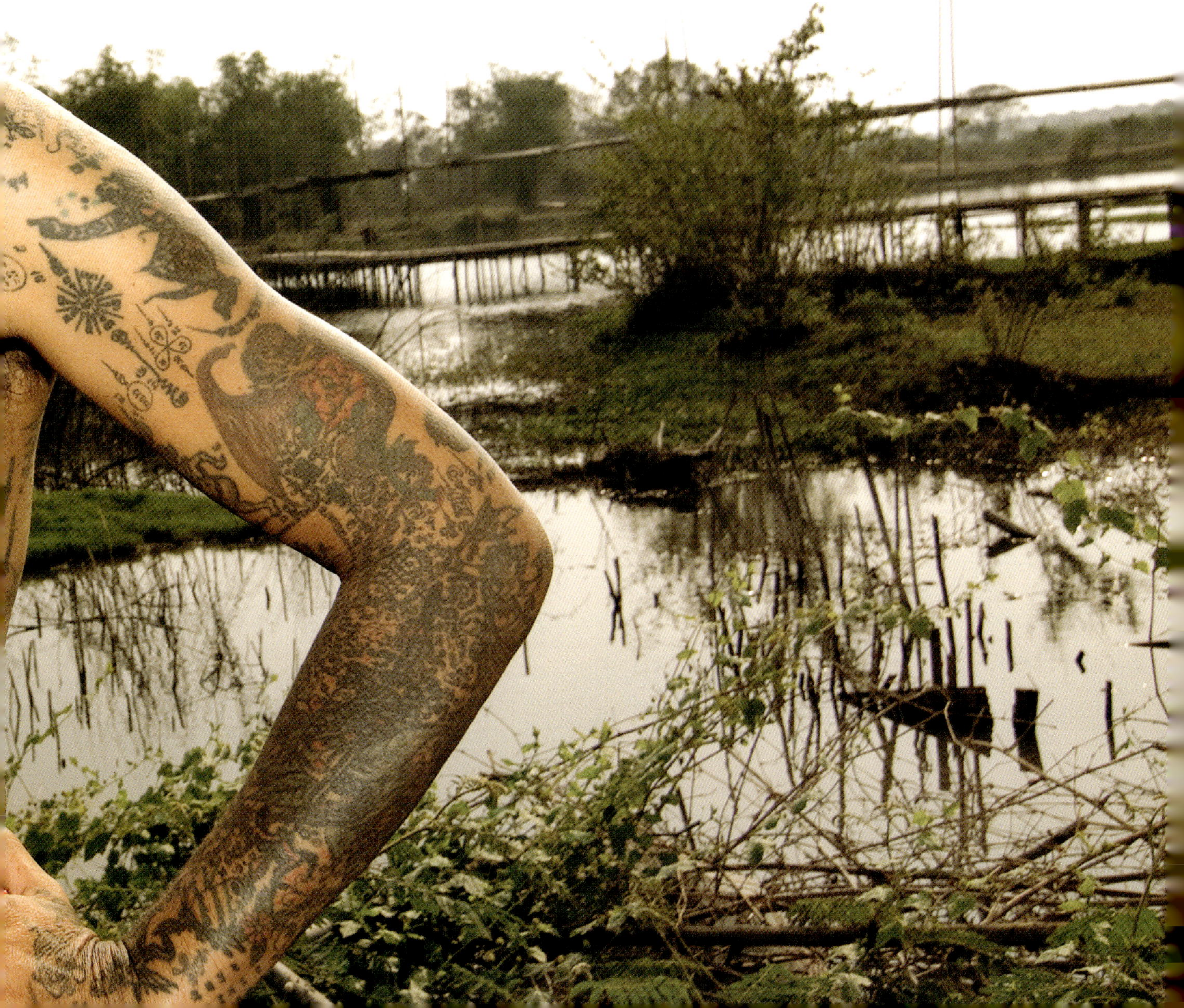

FOREWORD: JOE CUMMINGS

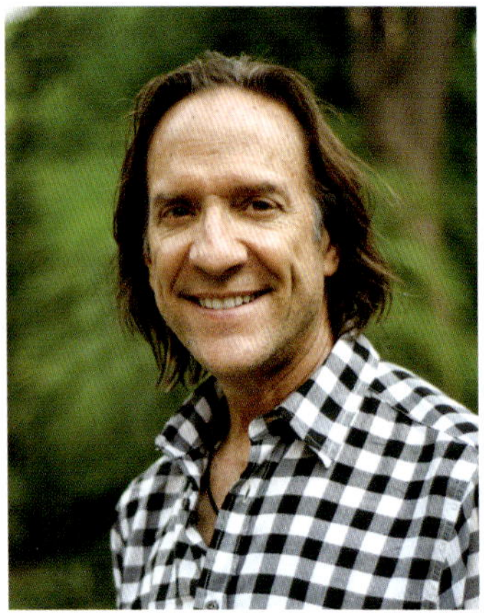

The masters often work in isolation or only among masters of the same lineage, each forming their own analysis of *sak yan* iconography and the cosmology behind it.

Before I came to Thailand, my impressions of Buddhism were scattered and abstract, borne of reading Schopenhauer, Jack Kerouac and a few Zen poems. In Thailand I found something different altogether, a unique fusion of magic, mysticism and morality.

I came across one of the more colourful fruits of this fusion one warm evening on the veranda of a Thai friend's house in Khon Kaen. A nephew visiting from out of town removed his shirt for relief from the heat, revealing the most amazing tattoo I'd ever seen. It was a boldly-inked tiger, leaping diagonally across his muscular chest and surrounded by a halo of mysterious alphabetic characters. The nephew explained that it was *sak yan* – a sacred *yantra* tattoo – inked by hand by an accomplished master in order to boost his strength and courage in kickboxing matches.

Researching and writing this book offered a rare opportunity to go deeper into the subject. I read every Thai-language book I could find on the *sak yan* theme. Fewer than a dozen have been published, most written in sensationalistic, tabloid style and cleaving to the point of view of a particular master or lineage. An integrated explanation had yet to be written.

Interviews with *sak yan* masters came next. As it turned out, the world of *sak yan* is so esoteric and guarded that there was no definitive theory to be had from any one master or disciple immersed in the tradition. The masters often work in isolation or only among masters of the same lineage, each forming their own analysis of *sak yan* iconography and the cosmology behind it. Sources contradicted each other; everyone seemed to have a different set of ideas about how it all worked.

Photographer Dan White and I made field trips around Thailand, Cambodia and Laos sporadically over a span of 18 months to find out what all these disparate sources had in common, and how they differed. It has been a journey that has not only taught me about the sacred tattoo arts, but has transformed the way I think about Thai Buddhism.

FOREWORD: DAN WHITE

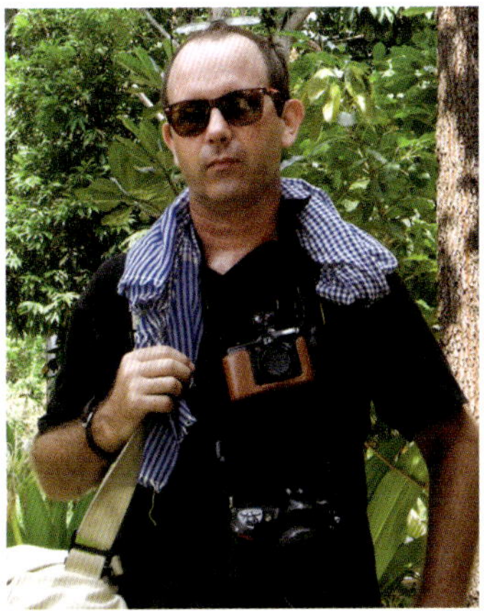

The *samnaks* are focused places where the masters work in an atmosphere of devotional clutter, dim lighting and milling crowds.

In Thailand and the surrounding countries, a parallel realm of the spirits provide powerful, everyday companions to mortal man. The symbols of *sak yan* serve as a key to a door and a means of influencing this parallel world that invests those who create them with enormous mystique. The history of the pre-Buddhist mythology winds its way back to India in a hotchpotch of Hindu, Buddhist and animist iconography.

Photographing this fascinating world comes with challenges. The first challenge is to track down the masters. Hidden behind mountain temples, in shacks down rural winding lanes and in crowded corners of urban slums, the *samnaks* of the *sak yan* Ajarns are often pokey and cluttered, lit by harsh florescent tubes, if lit at all. Once the *samnak* is found, gaining the trust of the master and his followers is a delicate process. The author on this project, Thailand and Laos expert, Joe Cummings, made that side of things a lot easier. His complete command of the language and his obvious respect for and knowledge of customs and beliefs very quickly put our subjects at their ease. Once they realised he was not only knowledgeable, but keen to strip away the sensationalised hyperbole that often surrounds the media portrayal of *sak yan*, people became positively effusive in their efforts to help me. Sessions were usually conducted with that combination of grace and humour that so often personifies interaction with Thai people. The *samnaks* are focused places where the masters work in an atmosphere of devotional clutter, dim lighting and milling crowds. They are also very unpredictable as the spirits take control and, out of the blue, drama unfolds.

Photographing *Sacred Tattoos of Thailand* was never easy in logistical, technical and physical terms, but it has been incredibly rewarding to have myself and Joe so warmly welcomed by these fascinating and respected men. I hope the pictures do justice to the warmth and kindness they showed us.

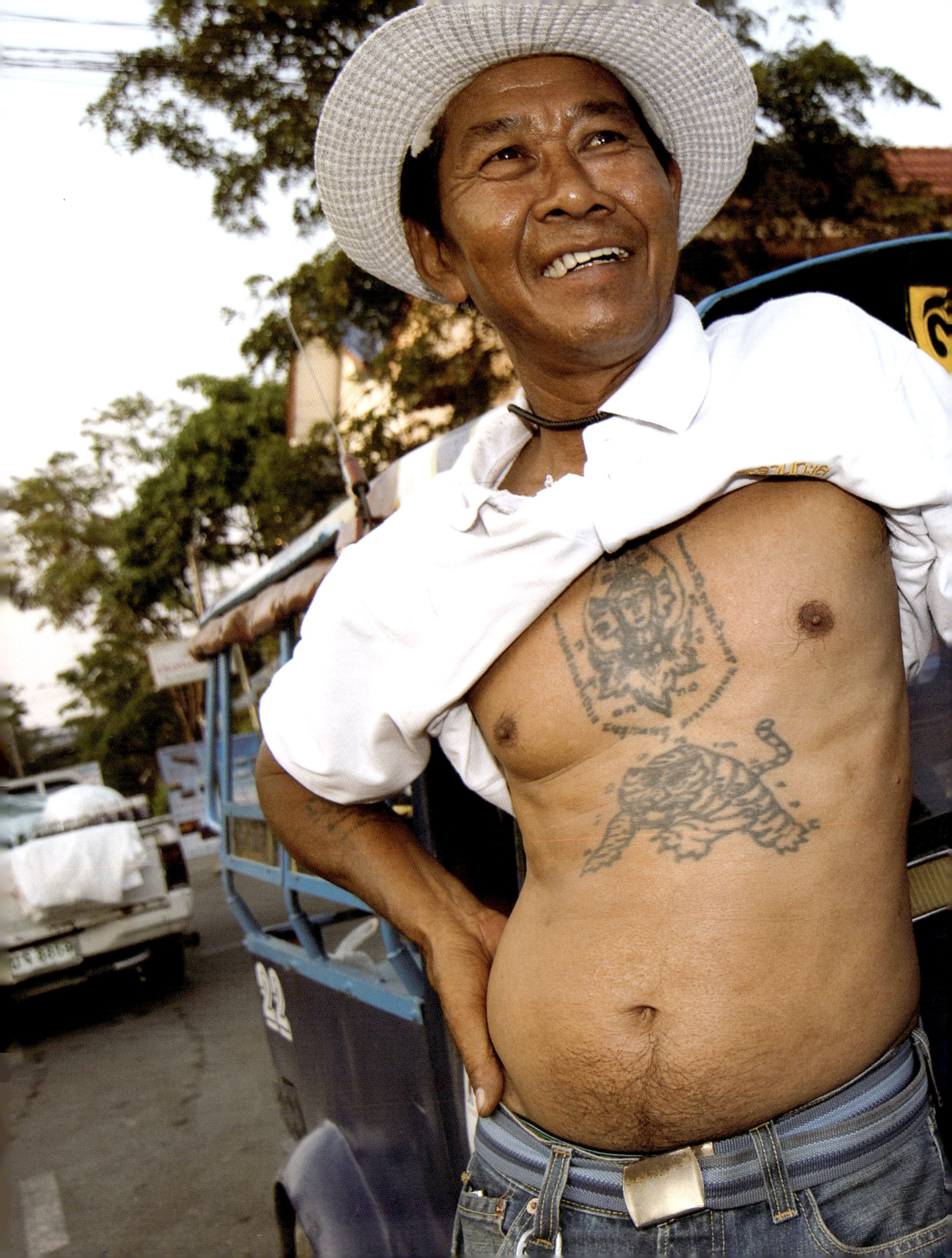
22

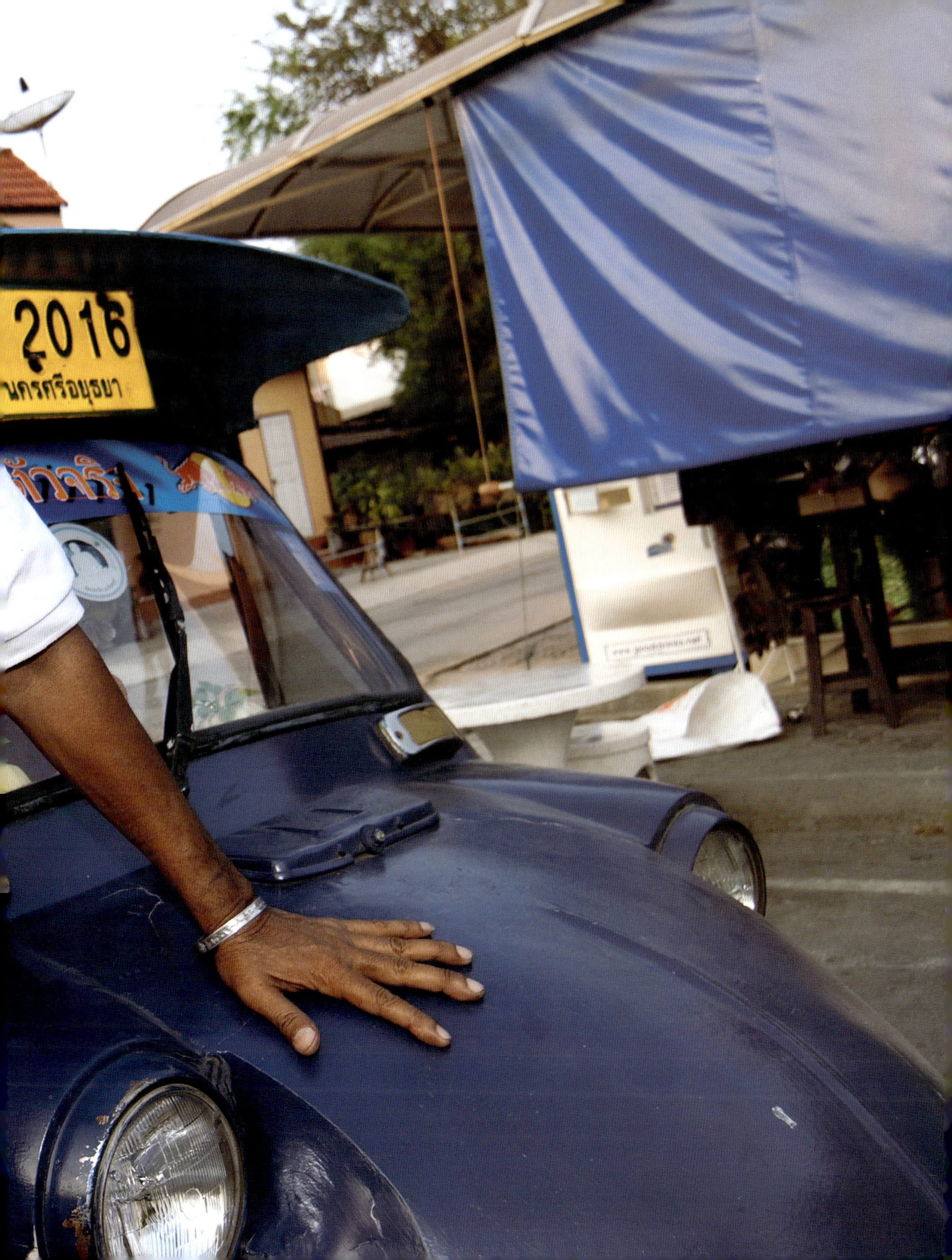
2016
นครศรีอยุธยา

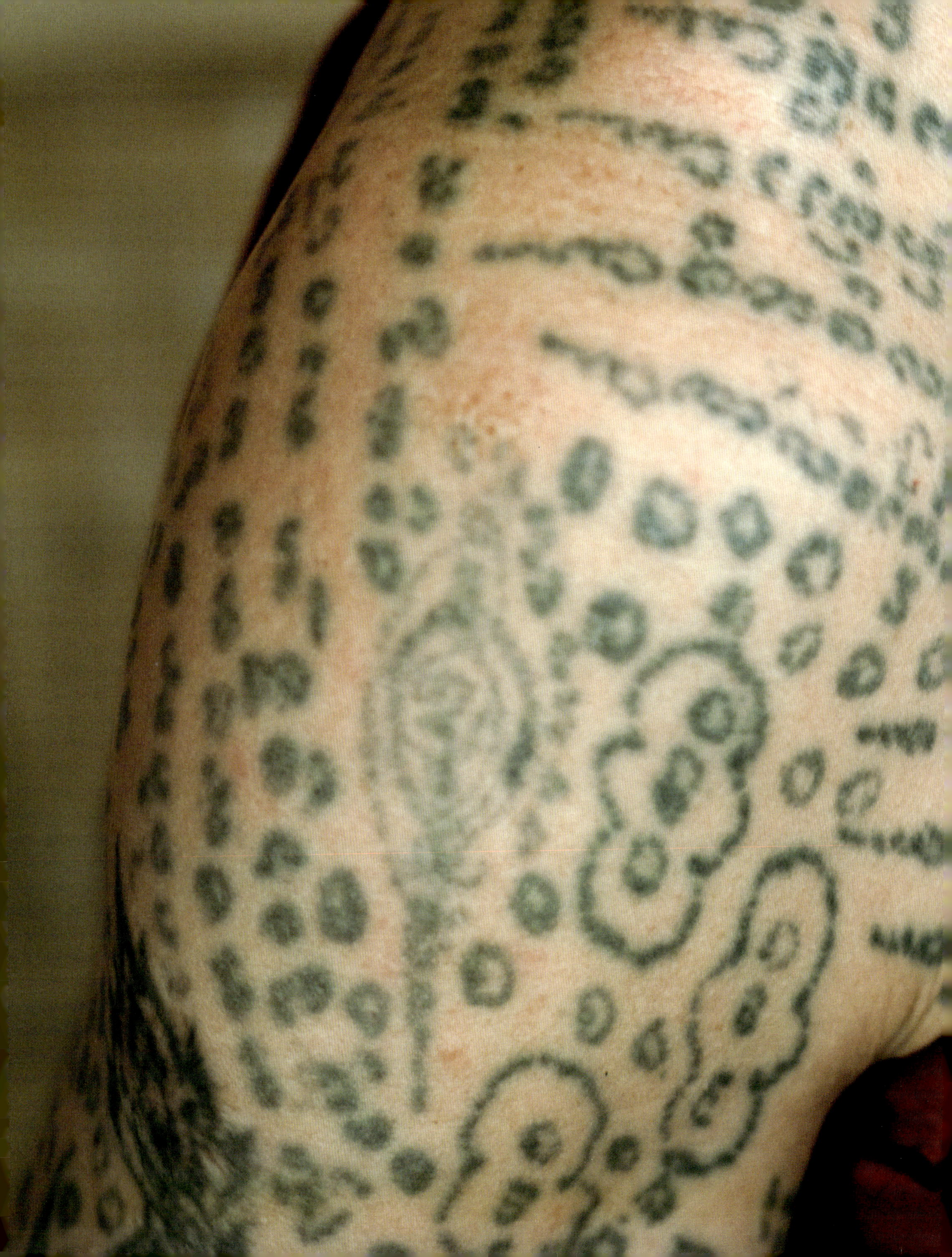

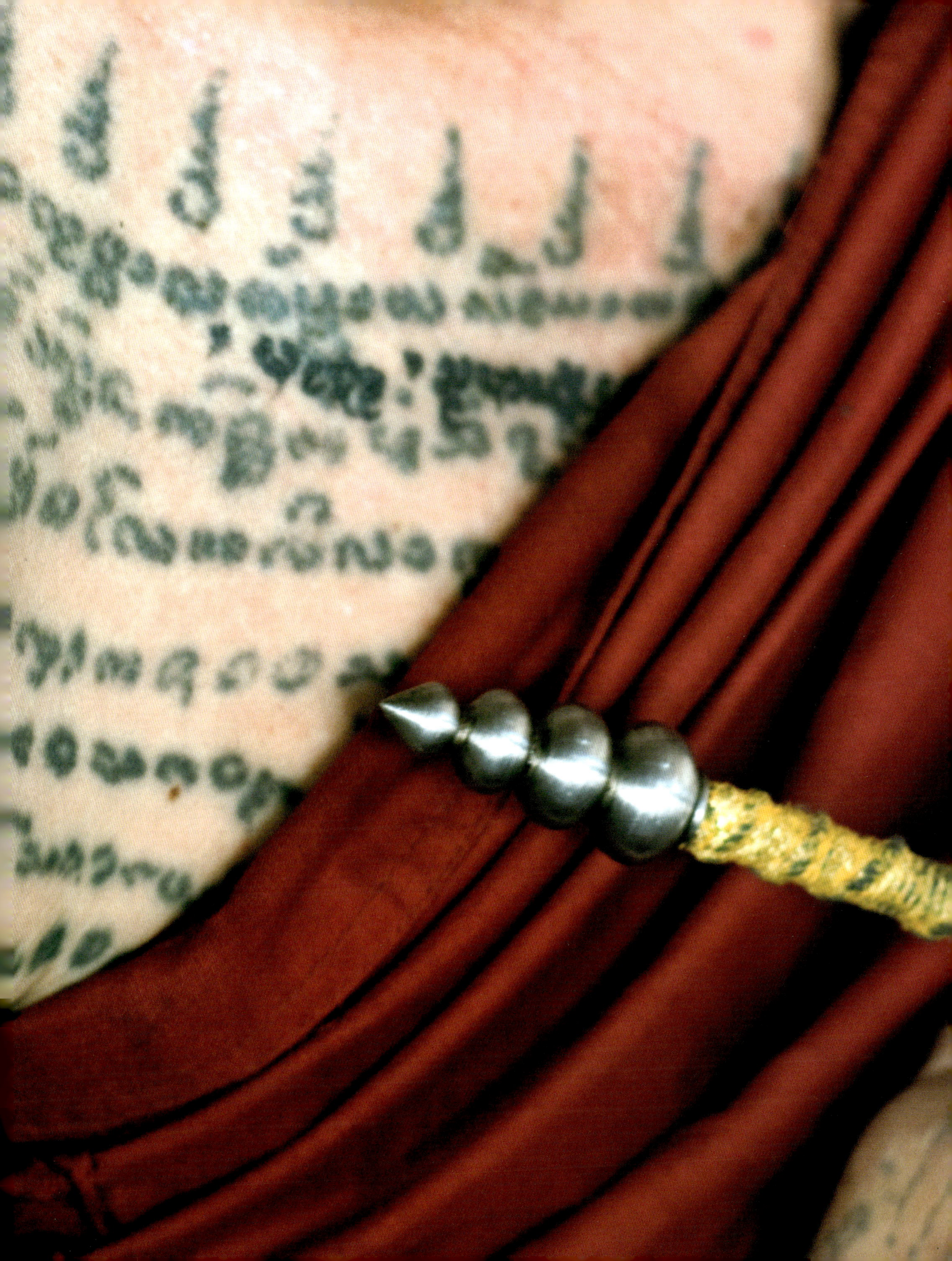

OUT OF THE PAST

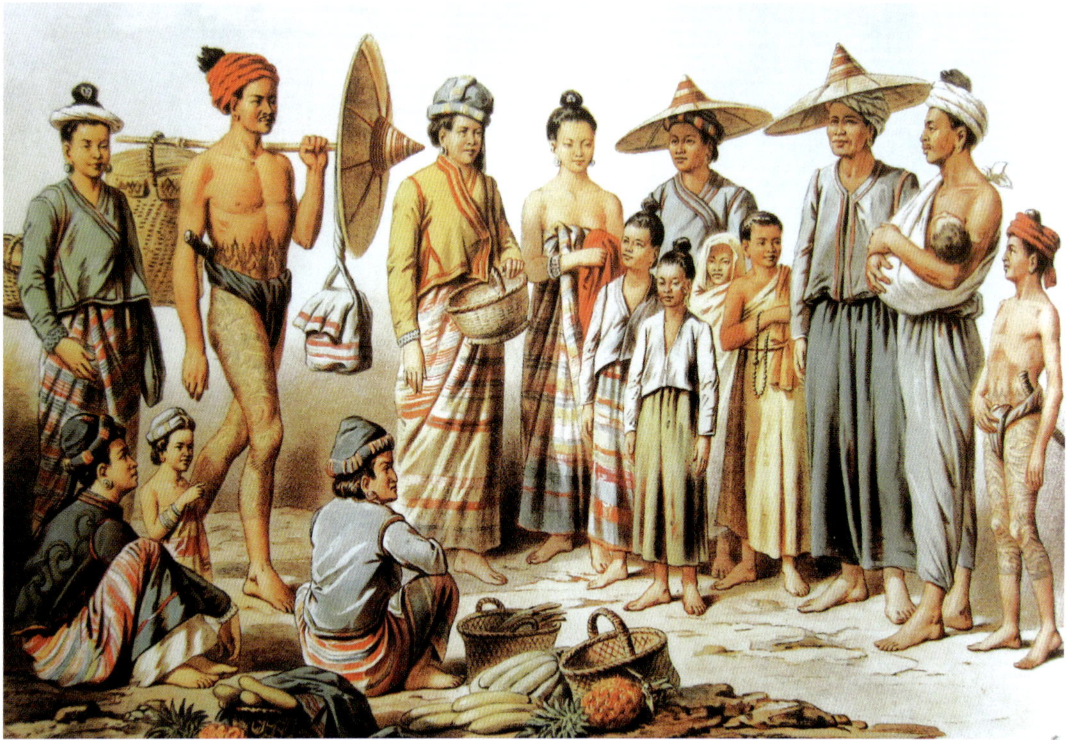

Above: A scene in 19th-century rural Laos as painted by Louis Delaporte.

It is believed that the first tattoos were inspired millenniums ago when early man saw how rubbing soot into minor wounds to sterilise them often left permanent markings on the skin. Alongside other body modifications such as skin piercing, body painting, body binding and hair design, tattoos eventually became a regular part of the "magic kit" that many societies employed to cope with the spirit world and mark rites of passage. Experts on tattoo history have established that as recently as 500 years ago virtually every major society had a sacred tattoo culture, including in Europe, Japan, the Americas, Africa, Polynesia and Oceania.

French explorers and colonials in the Americas noted in the 18th century that all the Amerindian tribes had active tattoo traditions. French soldiers and forest runners even began tattooing themselves using Amerindian designs, both to increase their power in relation to the natives, and to mark the fact that their expatriate community was autochthonous from French society back home.

In Borneo, the Philippines and Indonesia, several tribes maintain traditions of spiritual tattoos. "A man without tattoos is invisible to the gods," says an Iban proverb in Borneo.

The application of magic tattoos in the Mekong region was practised in very early times. Records from China's Qin dynasty (221–206 BC) describe how men of the Lue and Yue tribes living in areas near the Mekong were tattooed from waist to ankle with designs of "demons" and "water serpents" (the legendary naga perhaps) to ward off evil spirits. Archaeological surveys suggest that their kingdom, known as Van Lang (Land of the Tattooed), dated back to 2879 BC.

Scholars believe the Lue/Yue were ancestral to the earliest Proto-Tai speaking groups, who appeared about 2000 years ago in the Tonkin Valley region on the border of north Vietnam and Laos, and also to the Tai-speaking populations of southwestern China, including the Tai Lü, Tai Neua, Tong, Shui, Bu Yi and the Zhuang (today China's largest official minority).

> "A man without tattoos is invisible to the gods," says an Iban proverb in Borneo.

Just as the English word "tattoo" comes from the Samoan *tatau*, meaning to mark or strike twice, the Tai word *sak* means "prick" or "jab," as with a needle. The term has been traced to Proto-Zhuang-Tai languages of southern China and northern Vietnam (where Tai tribes originated) and is today the word for "tattoo" in Thai, Lao, Shan, Lü and other related languages. The word *sak* has been borrowed by the Khmer language as well.

The linguistic evidence, along with Chinese chronicles mentioning tattoo customs, suggests that the tradition moved south-southwest from southwestern China and northern Vietnam into what is today Thailand, Laos and Cambodia. Although they may have held much in common in general design and motif, each area developed its own specific style of sacred tattoo based on different scripts.

Because most *sak yan* in central Thailand today use Khmer script, many people have assumed that the tradition came from Cambodia. In fact it is more likely that only after they conquered the Angkor Empire in the 15th century did the central Thais begin using Khmer script in tattoos. Khmer script was common in Pali manuscripts, and many Khmer words also began entering central Thai vocabulary at this time.

Until a half century ago, many Shan men bore elaborate full-body designs. Meanwhile, Lanna and Tai Lü men were tattooed from the waist to the knees to give them power for work and for civil defence, and to bolster virility. The applying of tattoo "shorts" was performed either by Buddhist monks or by village shamans, and the ritual could last many days, during which the devotee might be sedated with opium. Most men also wore a less dense matrix of tattoos on their chest, back and arms. In those days it was said that a man without tattoos was "undressed" or "raw".

Soot or powdered charcoal, mixed with binding agents such as gum arabic or animal glue, remained the main blackening ingredient for tattoo ink worldwide until relatively recently, when it was replaced by metal agents such as nickel.

Although *sak yan* are today associated with Buddhism, the tradition in fact presents an integrated blend of animism, Brahmanism and Buddhism. Long before Buddhism and Brahmanism came to them from India and Sri Lanka, the inhabitants of Southeast Asia held the conviction that the world was occupied by nature spirits who, if properly placated or petitioned, might protect and serve, but who, if improperly treated or alienated, might harm them. Animism no doubt dominated most of the early tattoo traditions, and it remains an important element today.

Indian traders and missionaries brought Brahmanism to mainland Southeast Asia during the

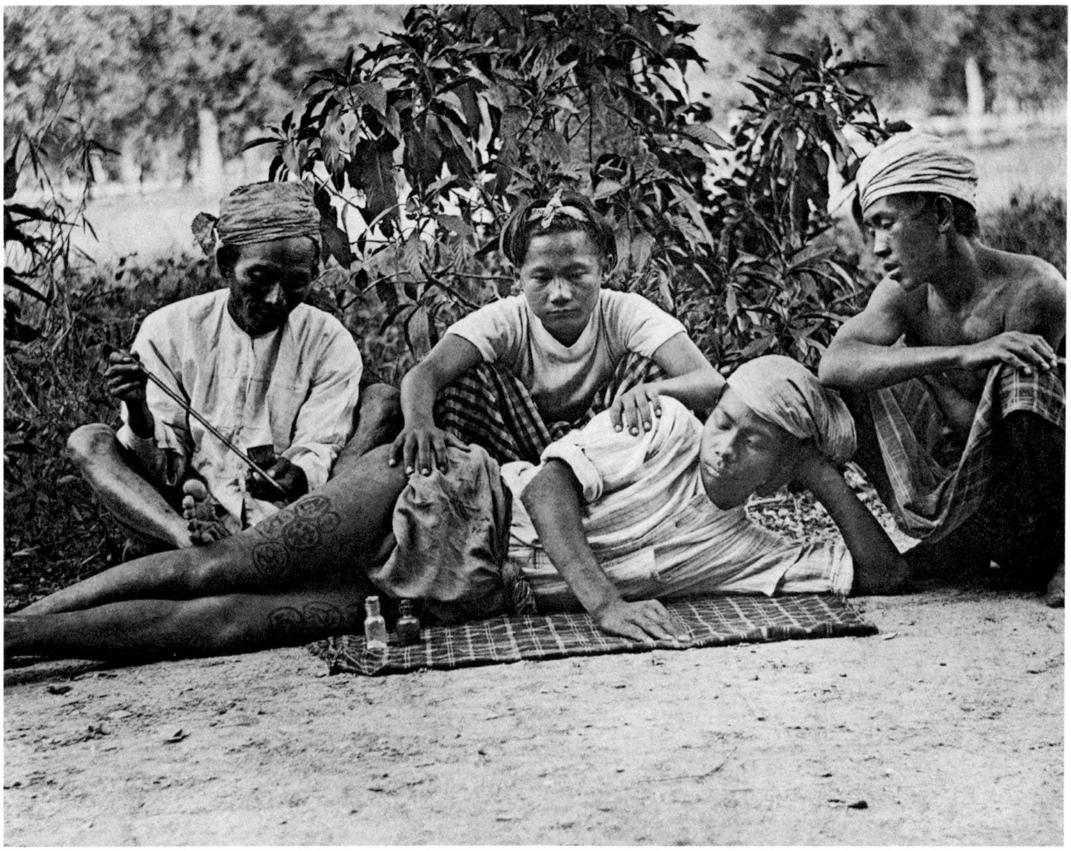

Photo by Amy Gold

Above: Tattoo 'shorts' were common in northern Thailand, northern Laos and northeastern Myanmar until the 1960s.

first half of the first millennium, including devotion to Vishnu, Garuda, Hanuman and Ganesha, all common elements in present-day *sak yan* design. Brahmanism may have furthered the concept of magic tattoo designs as a means for changing an individual's destiny with the introduction of the *yantra* (geometric designs imbued with spiritual power) to Southeast Asia cultures.

In India, however, the *yantra* more commonly appears as a geometric design drawn or painted on flat surfaces such as stone, paper and wood, rather than tattooed on skin. Many Brahmanic castes forbid tattoos, although they are not uncommon in lower caste and outcast Indian society.

Buddhism arrived in what is today Thailand around the 6th century AD and established a moral code that forms the basic tenets of Thai Buddhism today. Just as the artistic and iconographical elements of a Thai Buddhist monastery are not restricted to Buddhist origins, the art and iconography of *sak yan* are saturated with complex beliefs relating to all three historic systems – animism, Brahmanism and Buddhism – combining the magical, the theistic and the philosophical.

The arrival of Europeans on Southeast Asian soil in the 17th century, and Americans in the 19th century, played a significant role in the evolution of the Tai tattoo tradition. Impressed by Western technological superiority, Southeast Asian rulers invited Westerners to counsel them on modernisation. Bangkok royals also sent many of their offspring to study in Victorian England, where they were influenced by Western notions of modesty. Through such contact, the predominant Western religion, Christianity – both indirect (by example) and direct (in the case of evangelism) – gradually brought about less favourable attitudes towards tattoos. Missionaries exhorted men to wear shirts to cover their tattoos, and a royal decree in Chiang Mai in the early 20th century ordered women to cover their breasts and men to cover their tattoos.

The once-ubiquitous secular Western notion that tattoos were for convicts and outcasts also made headway into Southeast Asian society. By the 1960s, most urban, educated Thais would not think of getting *sak yan*. The tradition remained popular in rural areas, but much less so than in pre-WWII days. Oil tattoos, which do not leave any permanent markings, gained in popularity over ink tattoos.

Certain sectors of society continued to believe in the power and significance of *sak yan* regardless of contemporary social mores. Thai soldiers who participated in the Second Indochina War in Vietnam and Laos often protected themselves with tattoos, for example. Many Buddhist monks, especially those who travelled alone as *phra thudong* (wandering ascetic monks), availed themselves of the tradition to ward off malevolent spirits in the forest. *Sak yan* have also remained popular among Thai royals. It is said that virtually every male member of the Chakri dynasty, including Thailand's current monarch, King Bhumibol, has received *sak yan*.

Western influence recently played a role again in shaping attitudes, this time spurring the revival of *sak yan* in Thailand. After screen star Angelina Jolie received a *sak yan* from Ajahn Noo Ganpai in 2003, to be followed by a second, larger one the following year, vast numbers of Thais renewed their interest in the tradition. Although it had never died out in Thailand, and one could find tattoo masters in almost every province even "pre-Angelina", today the *sak yan* tradition is thriving. In particular more Thai women than ever are choosing ink tattoos over oil tattoos.

Similar revivals have yet to reach neighbouring Cambodia and Laos, where only a handful of masters and disciples keep the tradition alive.

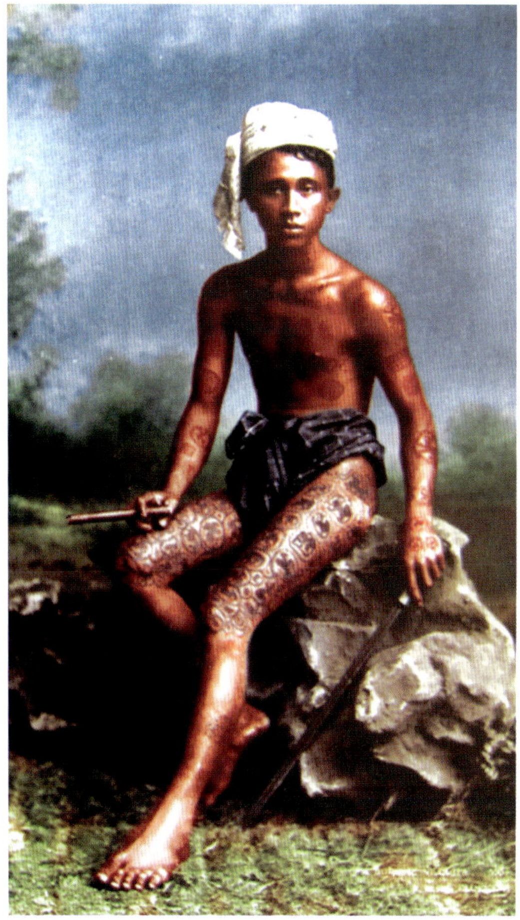

Above: Tattoo 'shorts' were common in northern Thailand, northern Laos and northeastern Myanmar until a half century ago.

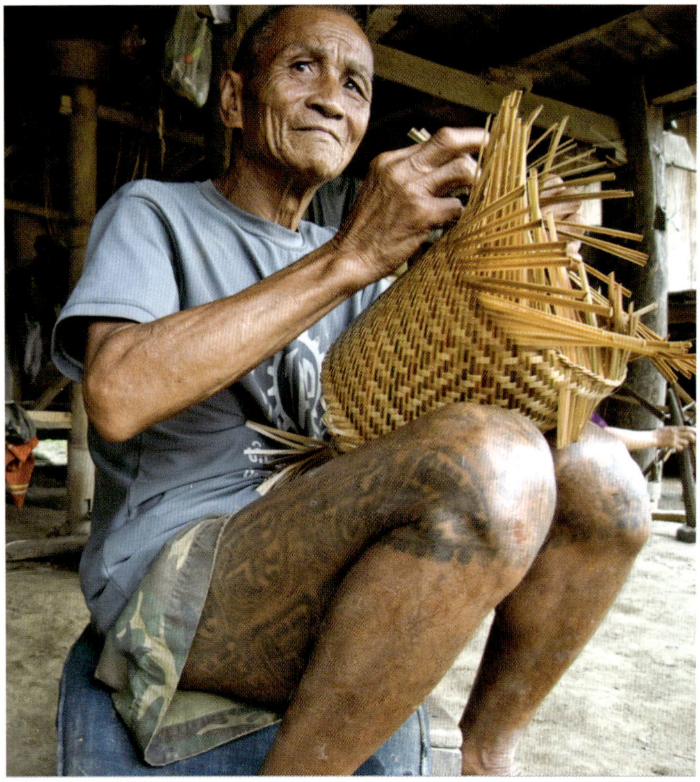

Above: A tattooed Tai Lü man weaves a basket in the shad of his traditional stilted home.

Right: A Tai Lü man in northern Laos has script on his arms and animals on his legs, folllowing tradition.

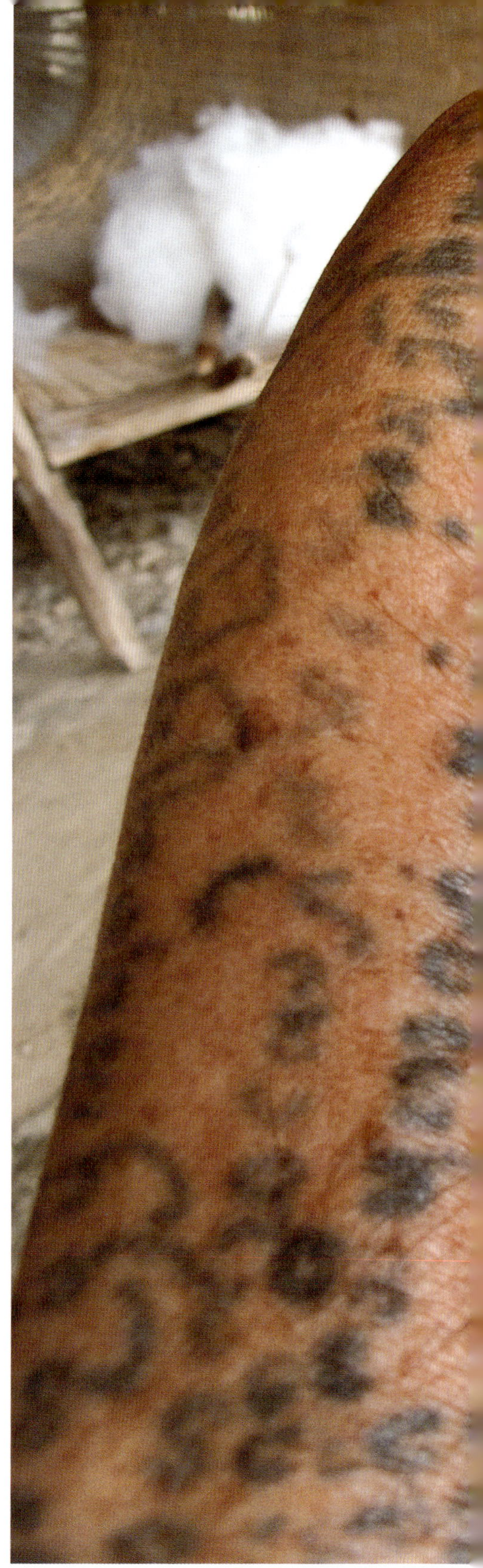

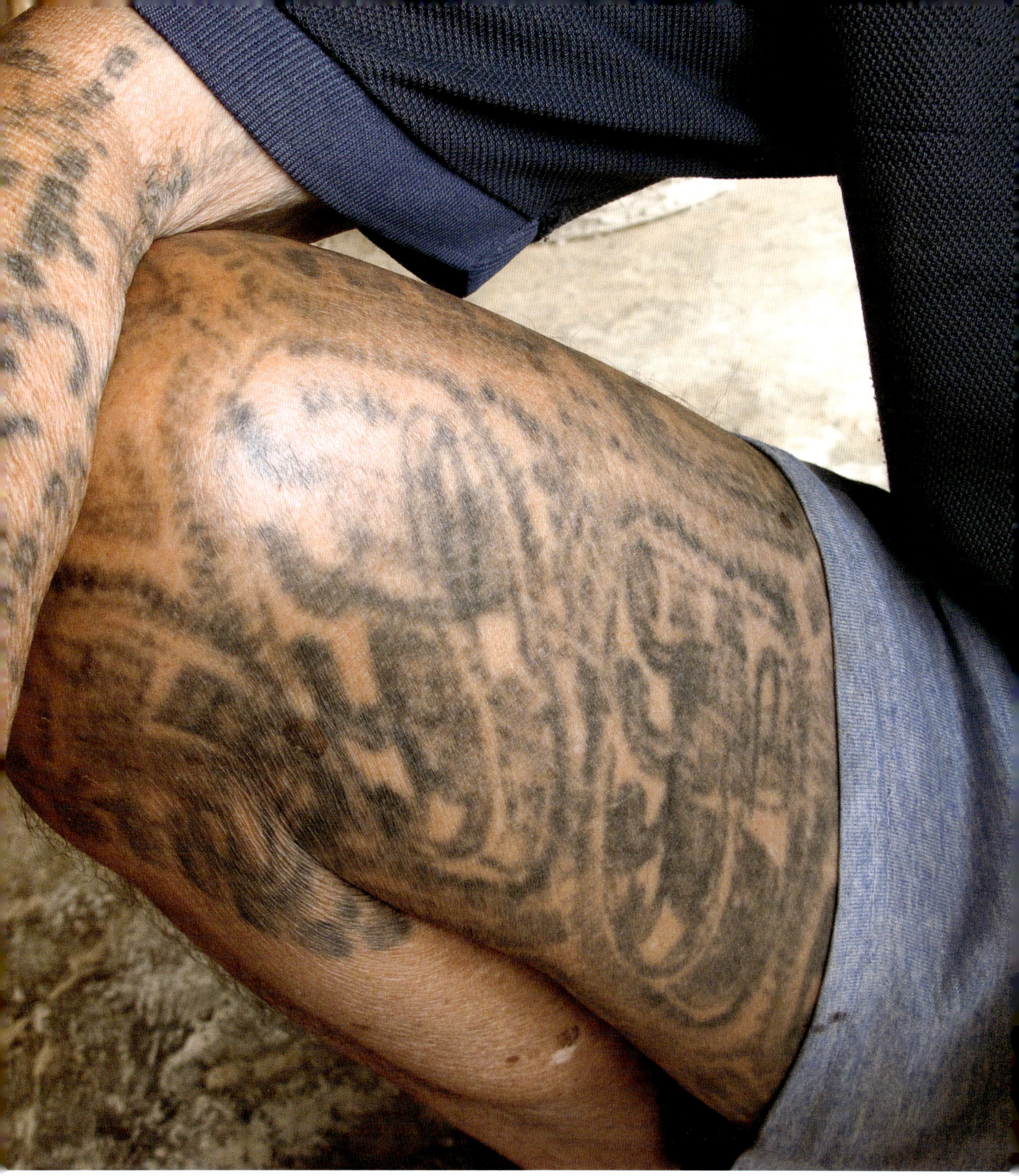

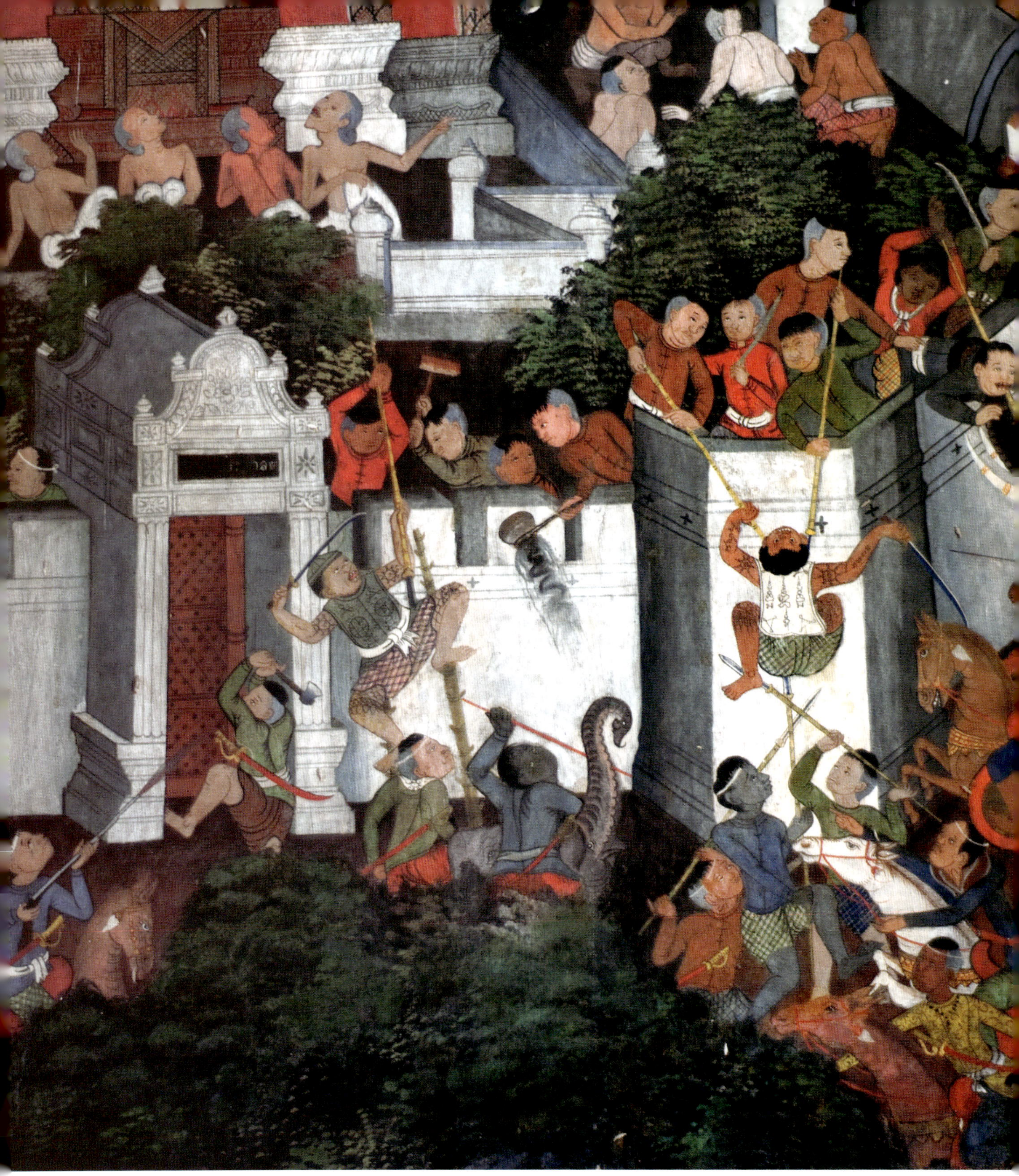

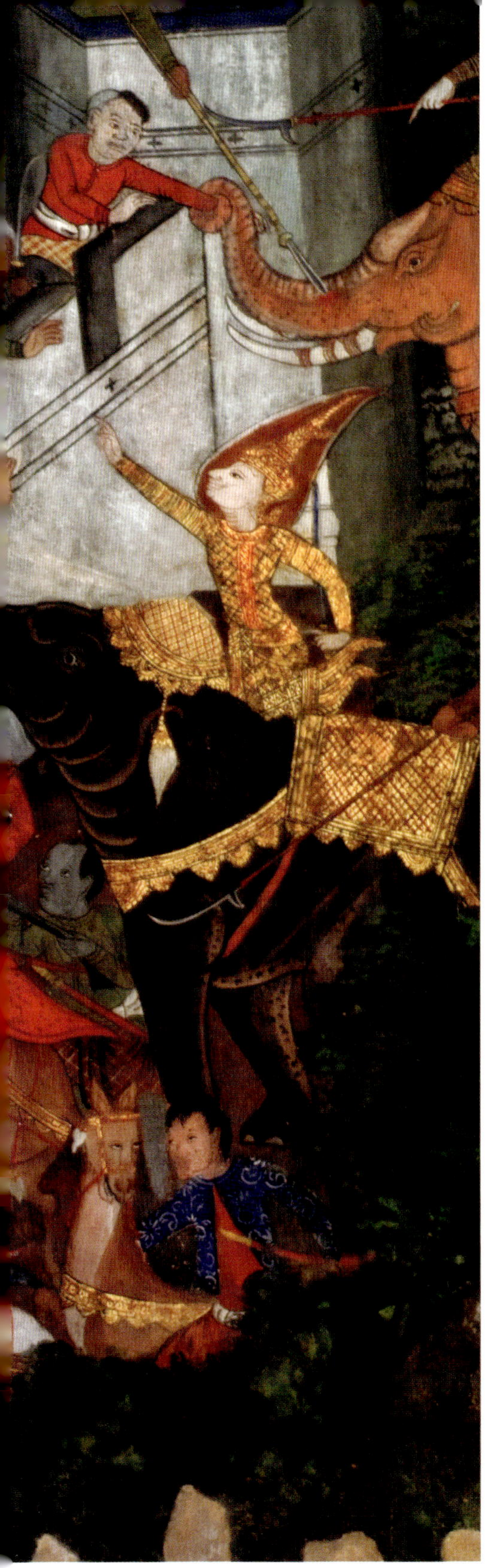

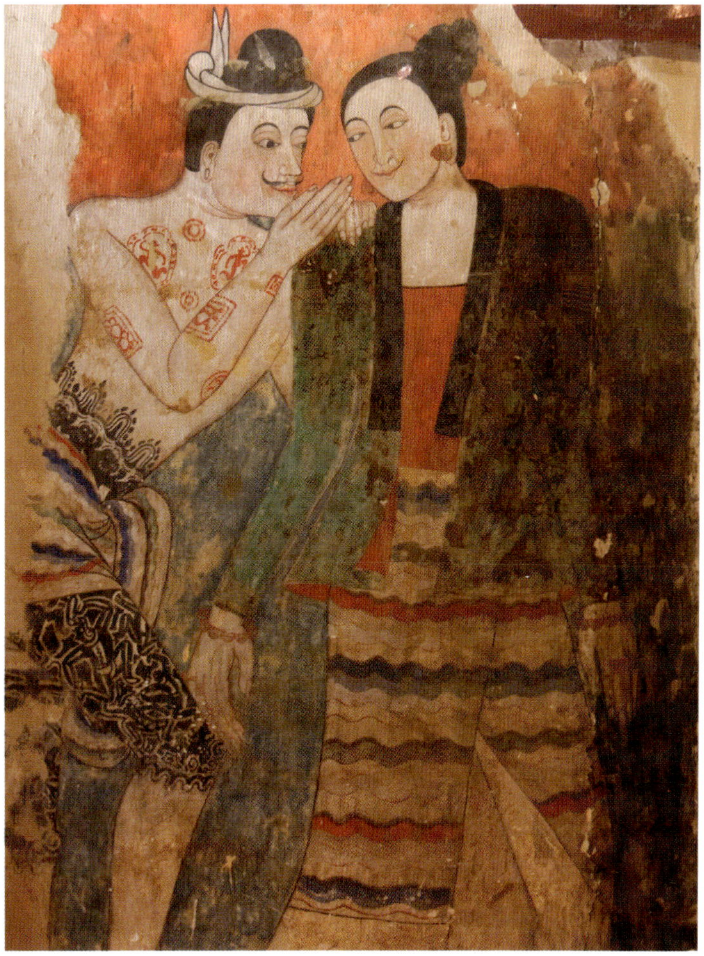

Left: Tattooed warriors wearing *sak yan* shirts scale palace walls in a temple mural at Wat Nairong, Thonburi.

Above: In this famous mural inside Wat Phumin, Nan, Thailand, a man wears black-inked power tattoos on his thighs and red-inked *yantra* for blessings and good fortune on his chest and arms.

THE SAK YAN TRADITION IN THAILAND

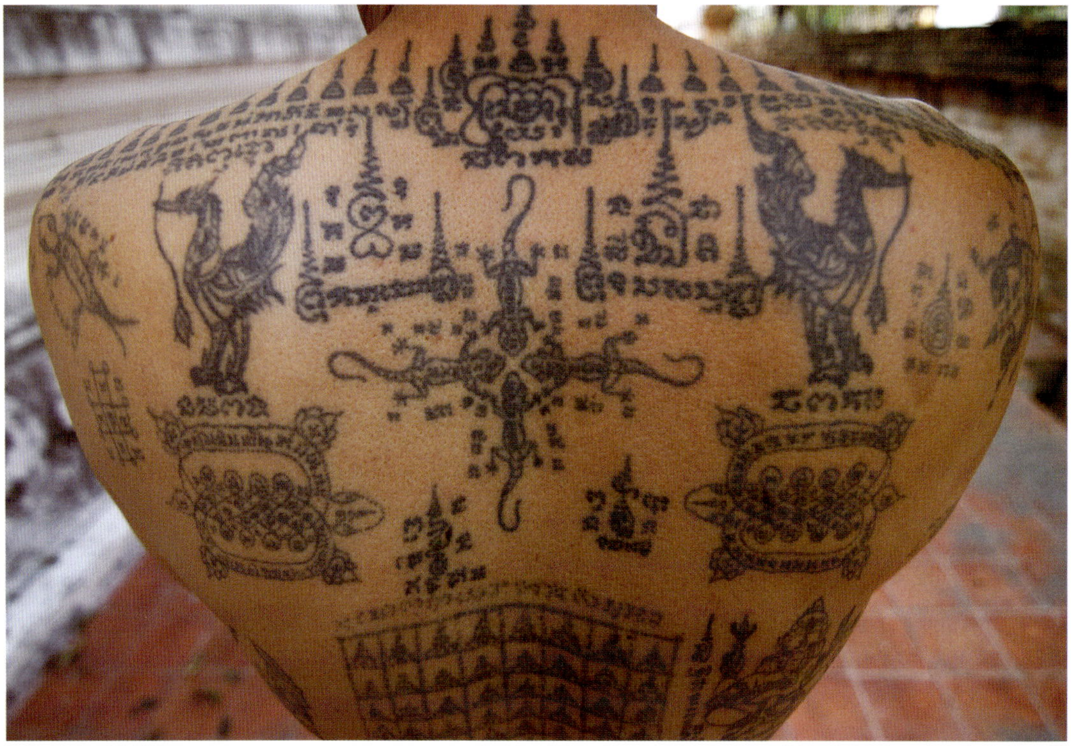

Above: This monk from Ayuthaya is visiting Wat Bang Phra to pay respects to the spirit of the late Luang Pho Poen, who inked these *sak yan* while still alive.

Anyone who has spent time in Thailand has likely caught glimpses of exotic, fine-lined black-ink tattoos, whether emblazoned across a kickboxer's chest at Lumpini Stadium or decorating the bare shoulder of a woman on a motorcycle. These intricate designs, all but incomprehensible to the non-Thai eye, belong to the historic *sak yan* (*yantra* tattoo) tradition.

As elegant and eye-catching as the art may be, it is intended as far more than simple decoration or cosmetic enhancement. Each design represents a specific magico-religious purpose, served not only by the design itself, but by the *khru sak* (tattoo master) who applied the tattoo and, just as importantly, by the self-discipline and morality of the wearer.

SAK YAN

Sak yan typically feature a combination of alphabetic syllables and geometric designs. Some may also depict deities, sacred animals or mythical creatures from the Hindu-Buddhist tradition. When the alphabetic syllables appear in short, telegraphic clusters they are called *mon* in Thai (from the Pali-Sanskrit mantra), and when they include longer phrases or verse, *khaathaa* (from the Pali-Sanskrit term *gatha*, meaning spoken word). Some tattoos

SAK YAN

Sak is the Thai word for "tattoo". *Yan* is the Thai pronunciation of the Pali-Sanskrit *yantra*, meaning "sacred (or magic) design". Some English-language transliterations of the word appear as "yant", although the "t" or the "-tra" is never pronounced in the Thai version of the word.

may consist entirely of *khaathaa*, in which case they are called *sak khaathaa* rather than *sak yan*. The alphabets themselves are called *akkhara*, and tattooed syllables may be referred to by the same term.

The *akkhara* are written in a variety of alphabets: Khmer script throughout central Thailand as well as in other parts of the country (although usually applied by masters from central Thailand), and in Cambodia, where the tradition has almost disappeared; Shan and Lanna script in northern Thailand; Tai Lü in some parts of northern Thailand and northern Laos; and Lao Tham in northeastern Thailand and in central and southern Laos.

The thousands of designs – no one knows exactly how many are in common use – are meant to serve a variety of purposes. Many people who approach tattoo masters for *sak yan* work in risky occupations, including police, soldiers, truck drivers, elephant trainers and *muay thai* (Thai martial arts) fighters. Such clients typically seek protection from physical danger, whether accidents or acts of aggression. They may also desire physical and mental power to help them survive, and in the case of soldiers and fighters, to triumph over their opponents.

Men and women who work as office managers, salespeople and civil servants may seek bureaucratic power, successful promotions and pay raises. Yet others would like to bolster their romantic charisma, or compel forgiveness from their peers for past wrong-doings. There are also many general-purpose designs for good fortune and wealth.

For each of these purposes, the designs may be partly or mostly geometric – combining squares, circles, triangles and rectangles with *na* (curlicue designs) and *akkhara* (syllables) – or they may include deities, Buddha images or animal designs. In the latter case the animals depicted come from the Himaphan (a Thai word derived from "Himalaya") mountains of Jambudvipa, a divine realm described in early Indian literature. These include a range of mythical animals that resemble the lions, rhinos, tigers, deer, horses, elephants, birds and monkeys of our world, as well as more fantastical beasts such as the *kilen*, said to have the head of a dragon, the body of a deer, the scales of a snake, the tail of an ox and horse-like hooves.

The most common part of the body to receive *sak yan* is the upper back, followed by the chest, arms, lower back and thighs. Occasionally a disciple may be tattooed on the hands, throat or top of the head, but such choices are atypical.

As elegant and eye-catching as the art may be, it is intended as far more than simple decoration or cosmetic enhancement.

KHRU SAK

The magical power of Thai *sak yan* begins first and foremost with the power of the tattoo master *(khru sak)*. While some foreigners harbour the impression that Thai tattoo masters are always Buddhist monks (hence the popular nickname "temple tattoos"), there are in fact as many laymen applying *sak yan* as there are monks involved in the practice. What both usually have in common is a long

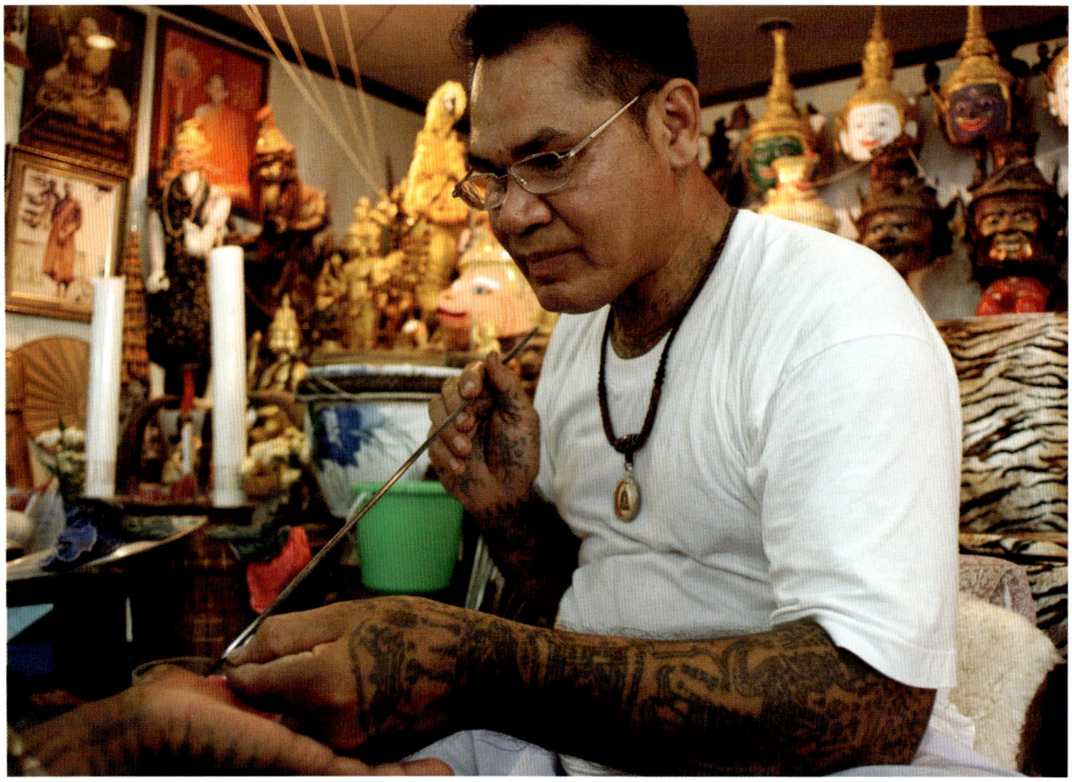

Above: Ajahn Somchat, Nonthaburi. Right: Ajahn Nuad, Wat Bang Phra.

apprenticeship under an older *khru sak*, whether monk or layperson. The apprenticeship is deemed complete when the master feels that his apprentice has fully absorbed the master's *weechaa* (magical knowledge) and is fully capable of tattooing on his own. When the apprenticeship has been completed, the master is considered to have completely transferred – *thaai thaut* in Thai – his knowledge and skill to his disciple. There are no female tattoo masters in the *sak yan* world. It is generally believed that only men may engender the special powers required for the role.

In some quarters, monks are forbidden from tattooing animal *yantras* because of their potential to provoke aggressive behaviour. Instead they focus on *sak yan* that bring *metta* (loving kindness) and other Buddhist virtues. Laymen have no such restrictions. The master can choose to limit the power of a tattoo by shortening the tail of an animal, or omitting one of the *akkhara* letters, if he feels that the disciple may not be capable of handling the full power of the tattoo.

The broad range of knowledge to be absorbed includes, at a minimum:

1. Ability to read and write the *akkhara* (script), whether Khmer, Lao Tham, Tai Lü, Mon, Lanna or Shan.
2. Ability to perform empowerment rituals to awaken the power of the designs once they have been tattooed.
3. Ability to select the proper *khaathaa* and *yantra* for each individual, based on their needs.

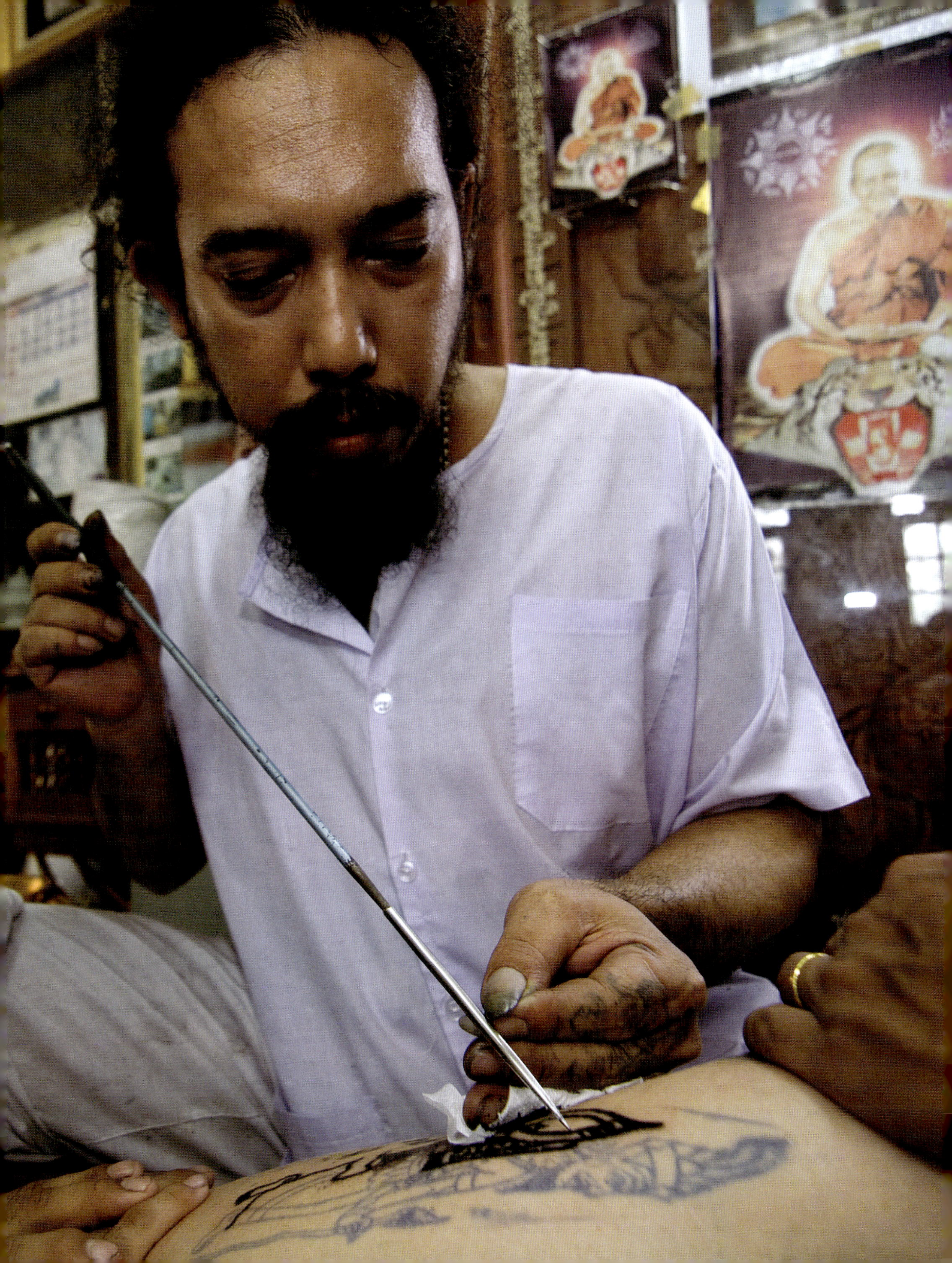

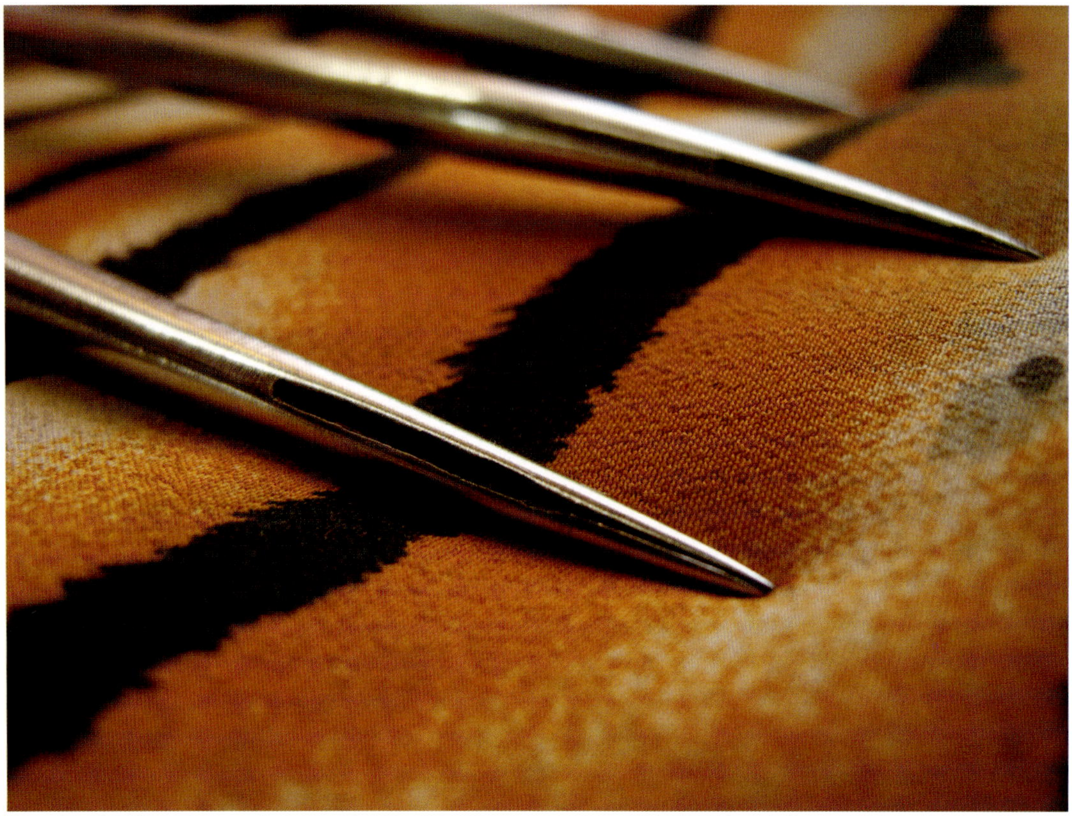

Above: Needles resting on imitation tiger skin.

4. Proficiency in perfectly imitating the designs as taught by the master.
5. A long-term and abiding acquaintance with Buddhism, including meditation.
6. Following behavioural codes prescribed by the master, beginning with the five precepts of Theravada Buddhism and extending to precepts that preserve the power of the tattoos, and protect both master and disciple from harm.

A *khru sak* is held to high moral standards by the local community. For monks, this means staying true to the Vinaya (227 precepts of the Theravada Buddhist monastic discipline). For laymen it means living a chaste life or, if married, remaining loyal to one's wife and family, and refraining from intoxication.

To represent this higher moral standard, many non-monastic *khru sak* wear white clothing while practising their occupation. A few masters don tiger-print tunics, representing the garb of the *reu-see* (from the Pali-Sanskrit *rishi*) or forest hermit. Presumably in the past real tiger skins were worn, although the more recent inspiration for such costuming comes from paintings and statues of Pho Kae (Old Father), a legendary forest hermit who is believed by most Thais to have been Southeast Asia's first *sak yan* master. Several tattoo masters in Thailand today claim to trace back all the way to this semi-mythical figure, who some say once lived in Phetchabun province and was associated with Si Thep, a Dvaravati Buddhist site which appears to have been built on an earlier Khmer temple dedicated to Shiva. Apocryphal or not, the character may be inspired by the Hindu *rishi* tradition associated with Shiva worship.

Properly trained and morally fit, the *khru sak* bears the title *ajahn* (master or scholar) and will be addressed as such. A master named Somchai, for example, will always be called "Ajahn Somchai". Monks will be addressed by the monastic honorifics that go with their clerical status, such as *luang phee* (great elder brother), *luang pho* (great father) or *luang poo* (great grandfather).

The *khru sak* is qualified to tattoo all of the designs he learned from his mentor. A few daring masters have added to the repertoire of designs handed down to them through generations, usually inspired by visions that appeared during meditation.

NEEDLE TO SKIN

Traditionally the *khru sak* chooses both the design and the placement of the tattoo, based on the client's desired result. Some masters prescribe a single initiatory *khru yan* (master *yantra*) for all new applicants, such as the common *kao yaut* (nine peaks) design as described later in this book.

Once a design has been agreed upon, the disciple must make an offering to the master at the main altar in the *samnak sak yan*, the consecrated

SAFETY

Scientific data on infection rates from *sak yan* is virtually non-existent, but with reference to tattooing in general, not a single case of HIV infection has ever been recorded anywhere in the world. Anecdotal evidence indicates that infections of any kind are rare, despite the fact that relatively little sterilisation is used before, during or after applying *sak yan* in the traditional manner.

Most masters soak their needles in alcohol between clients. As mentioned above, the typical penetration of *sak yan* is noticeably less extensive than for machine tattoos, hence there is little or no contact with blood. This also makes the potential risk of infection lower for *sak yan* than for machine tattoos, given the same general levels of hygiene.

Of more concern to some recipients is the ink used for *sak yan*. A few masters use a fresh jar of ink for each client but this is quite rare. Many pigments used in tattoo inks are not approved for skin contact by such organisations as the FDA. Some are industrial grade colours that are suitable for printers' ink or automobile paint. Although allergic reactions to tattoo pigments are rare, when they occur they may be particularly troublesome because the pigments can be hard to remove. Occasionally, people develop an allergic reaction to tattoos they have had for years.

Another concern is the variety of substances added to the ink. While *waan* root is said to be an antiseptic, other herbs and roots may be added for fragrance, for consistency and for magical properties. A common tale in Thailand claims that some *khru sak yan* in the past used the chin fat from the corpse of a woman who died in pregnancy to add power to the ink. The tale is often embellished with descriptions of the collection process, in a temple graveyard in the middle of the night. However, we could find no master anywhere in our travels who condoned such practices. Many masters use ink without any additives at all.

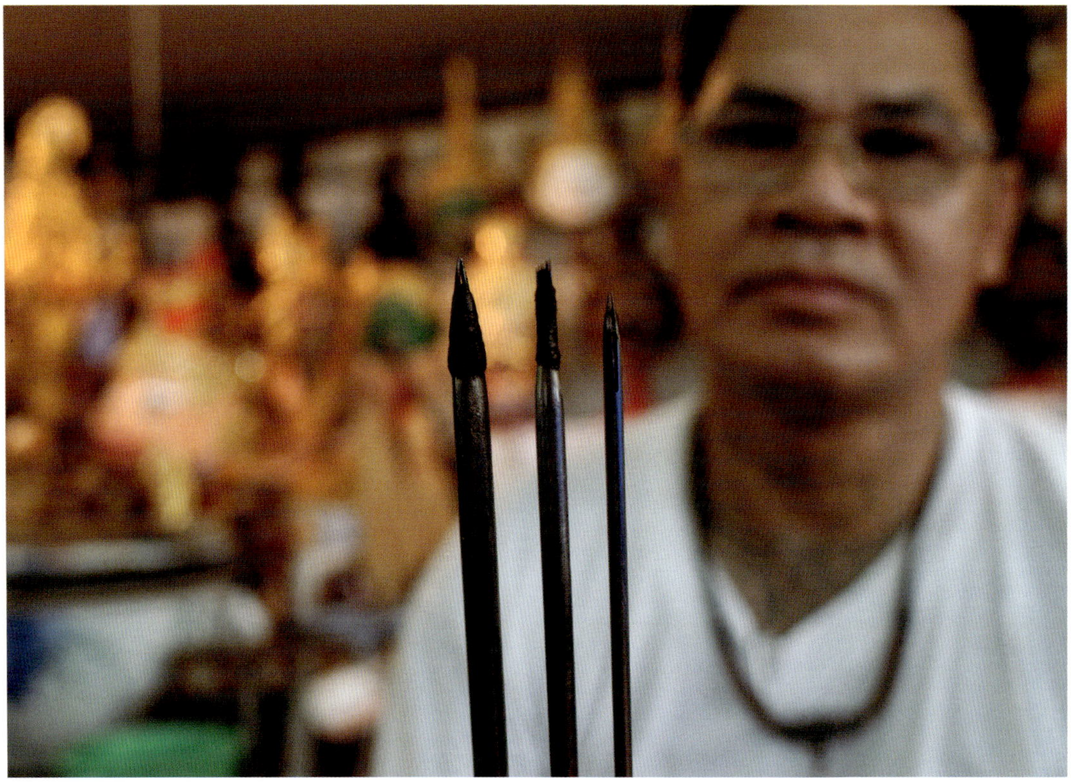

Above: Three sizes of *khem sak*. The heavier ones are less commonly used nowadays.
Right: Ajahn Gop, at his *samnak* in Ayuthaya, Thailand, displays the fine-line work he is known for.

tattoo room. The altar can be relatively small or a large and elaborate affair, displaying Buddha images, portraits of deceased tattoo masters, portraits of the Thai royal family and statues of Pho Kae. While holding the offerings on a metal platter the disciple kneels before the altar. The offerings typically include candles, flowers and incense, as a tribute to Buddhism, along with a cash donation for the master. Offerings may also include a pack of cigarettes, betelnut and alcohol to appease any spirits in the vicinity, and, for more elaborate tattoo designs, a boiled pig's head.

Once the offerings have been made, the *khru sak* takes a *mai sak* (tattoo rod), dips it into a small saucer of ink, and begins tapping the design into the outer layer of the skin. The master's right hand moves the tattoo rod back and forth, using the weight of the needle and shaft to break the skin and deposit ink beneath the epidermis. The thumb and index finger of the left hand are used to guide the needle itself.

At regular intervals of several taps, the stylus is dipped back into the ink reservoir to capture a new dab of ink. The traditional method calls for tapping to create a series of dotted lines, called *khai plaa* (fish eggs). Nowadays many masters place the taps so closely together that a continuous line results. The number of strikes per tattoo varies greatly depending on the size of the designs, but one estimate suggests that 3000 strikes is an overall average number.

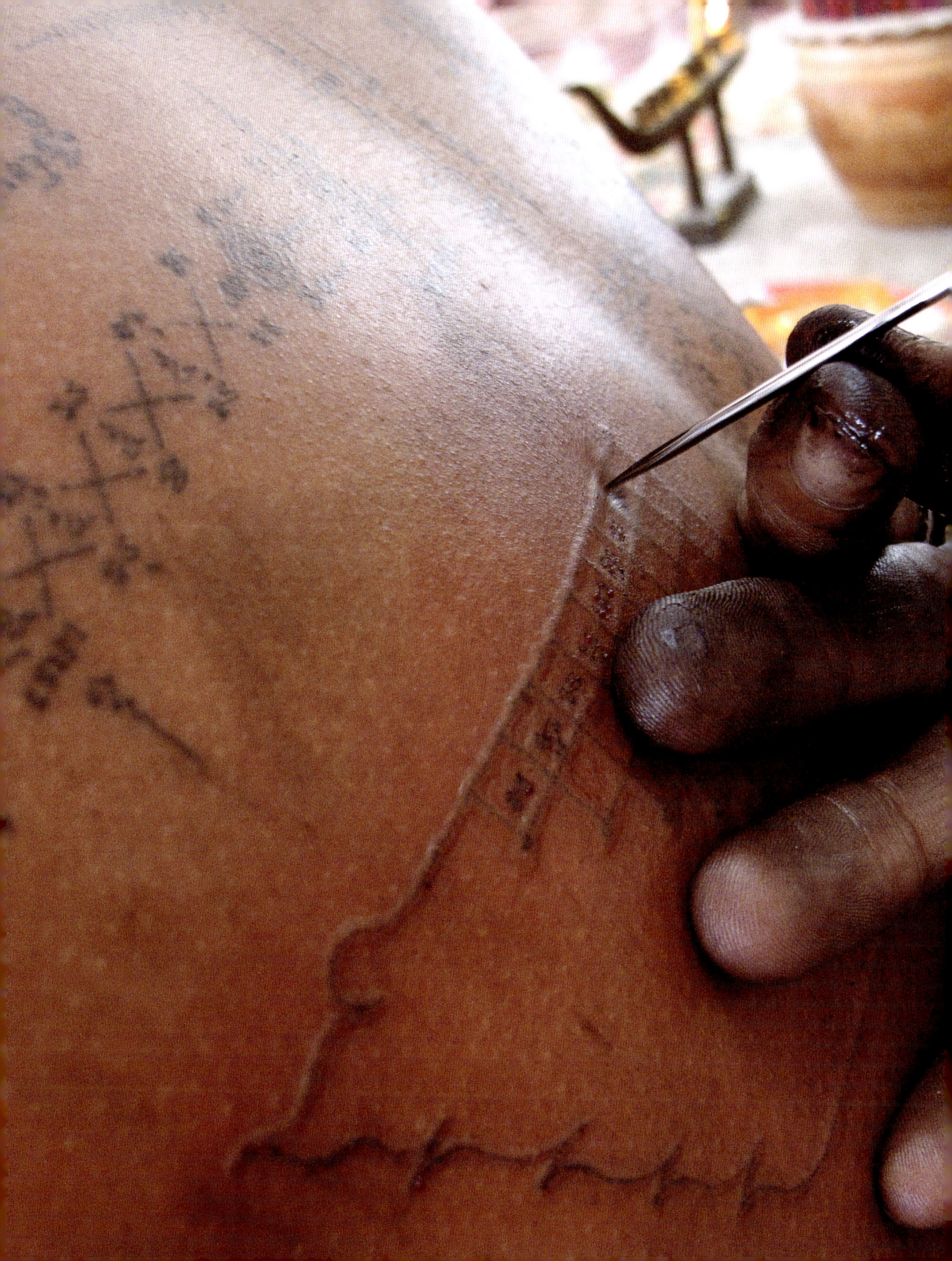

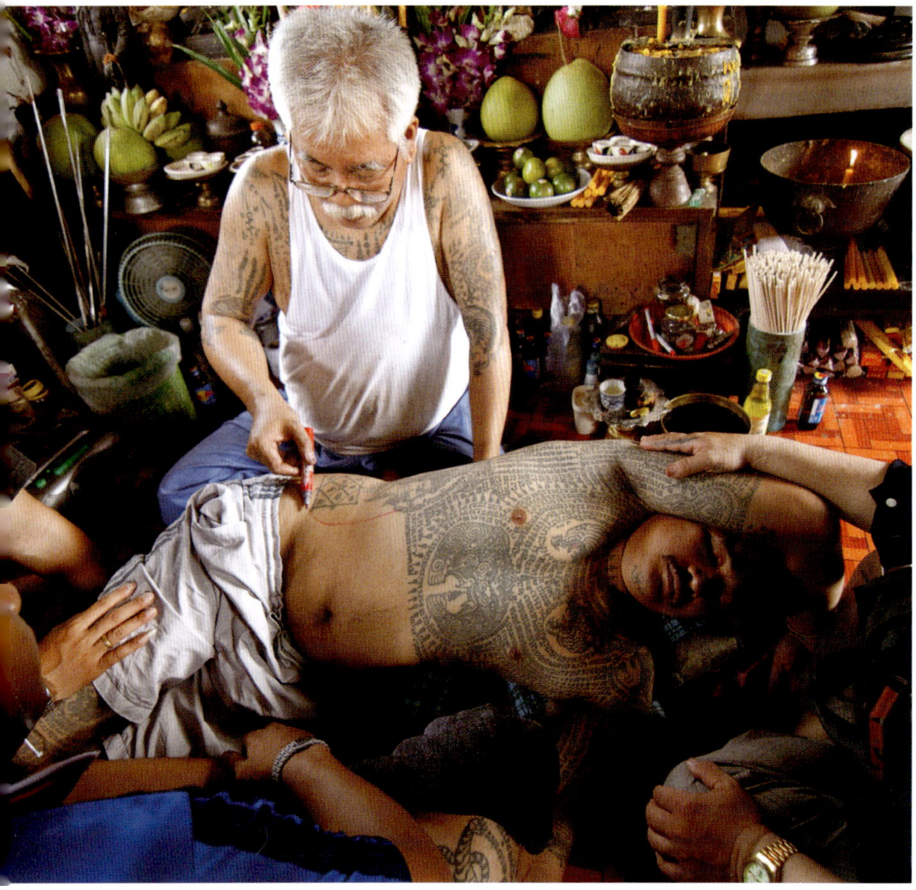

Above: Ajahn Thong, Talat Phlu, Thonburi, uses a Magic Marker to sketch guidelines for his work.

Right: Ajahn Thong, Thonburi, Thailand, tattoos *akkhara* (sacred script).

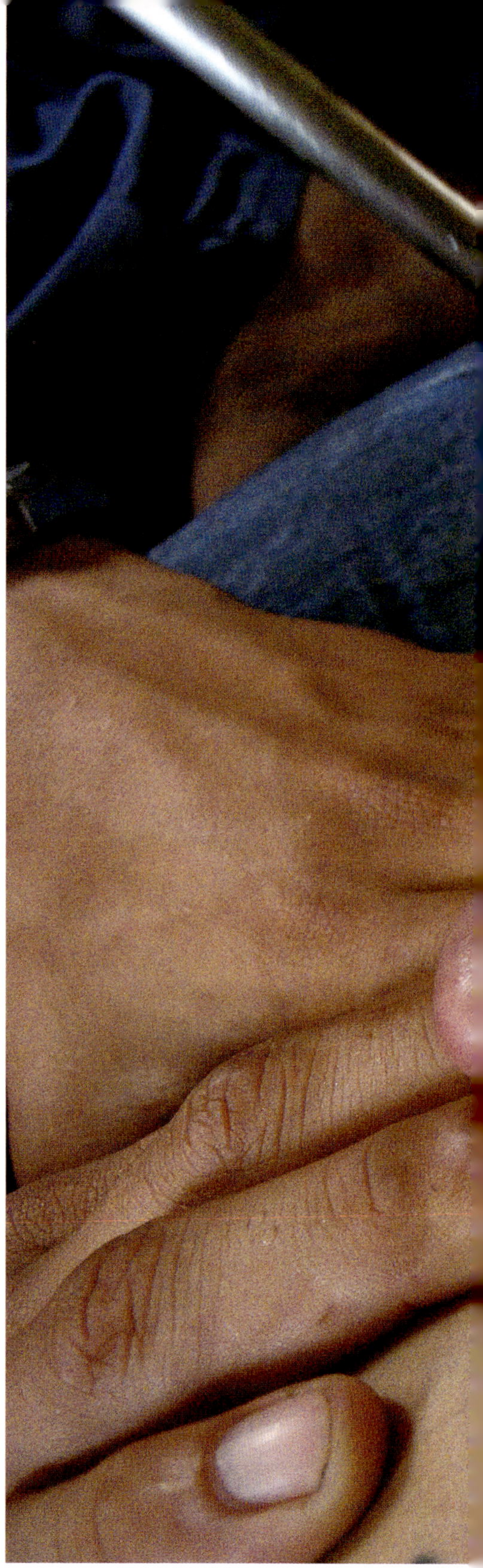

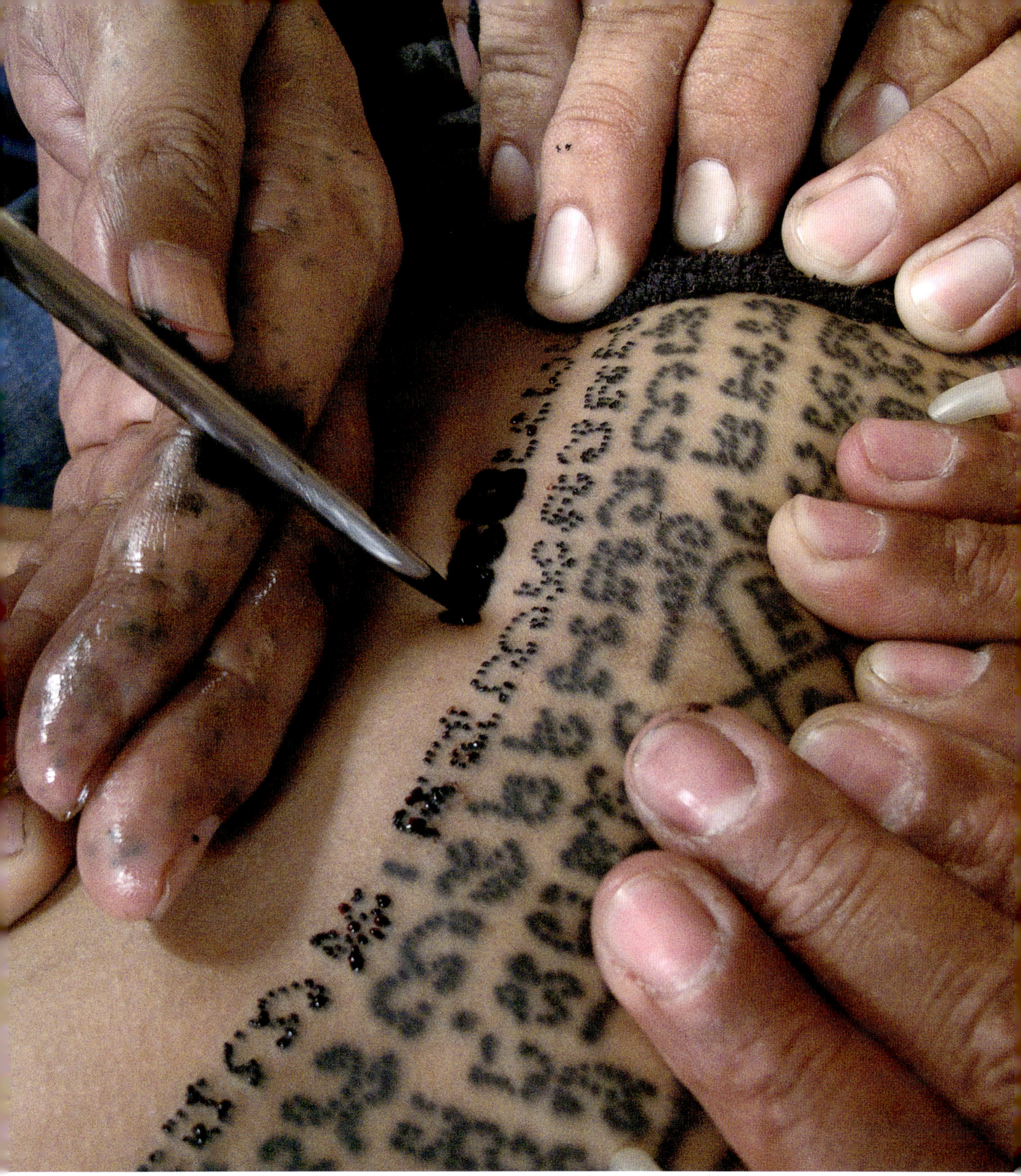

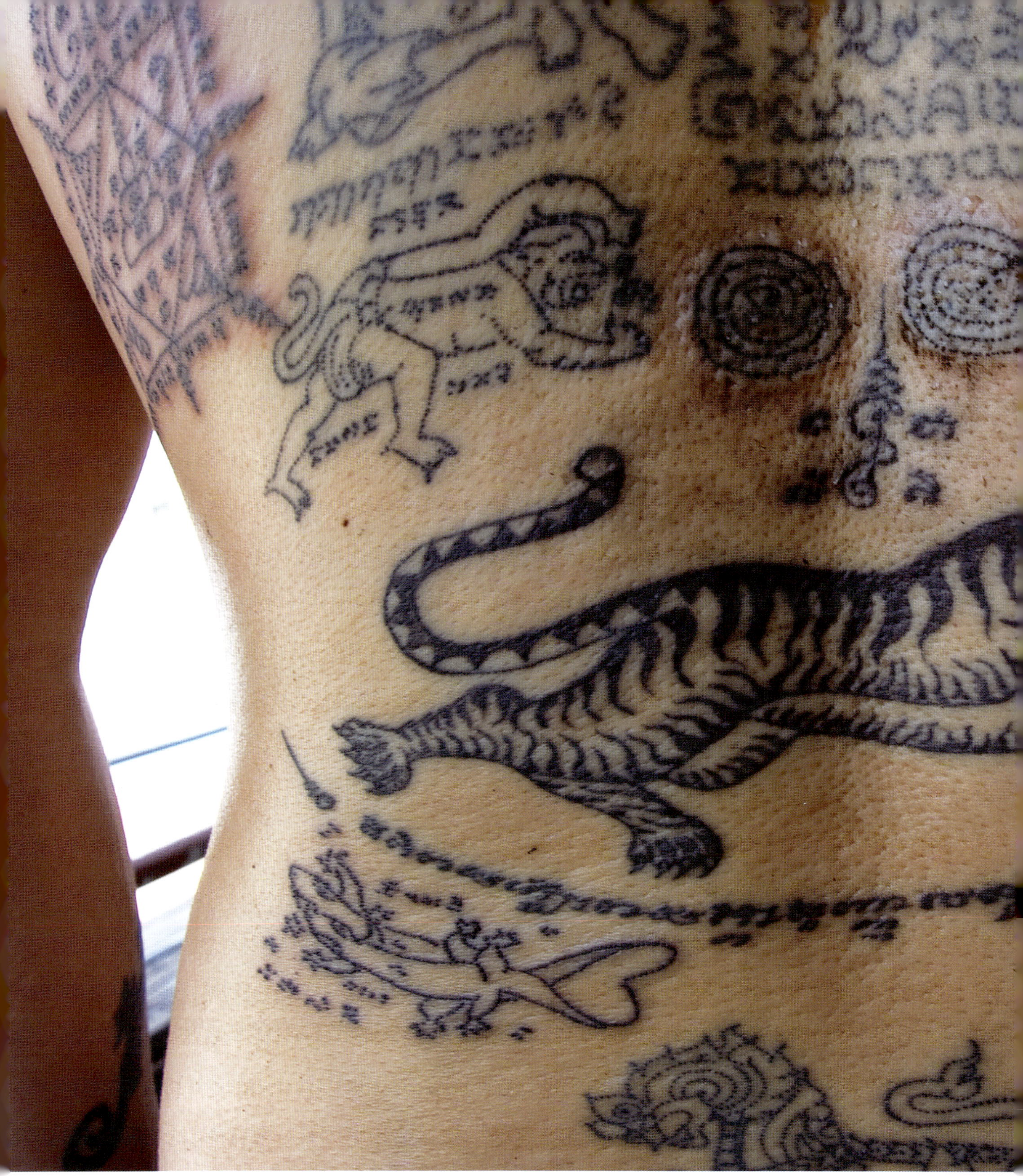

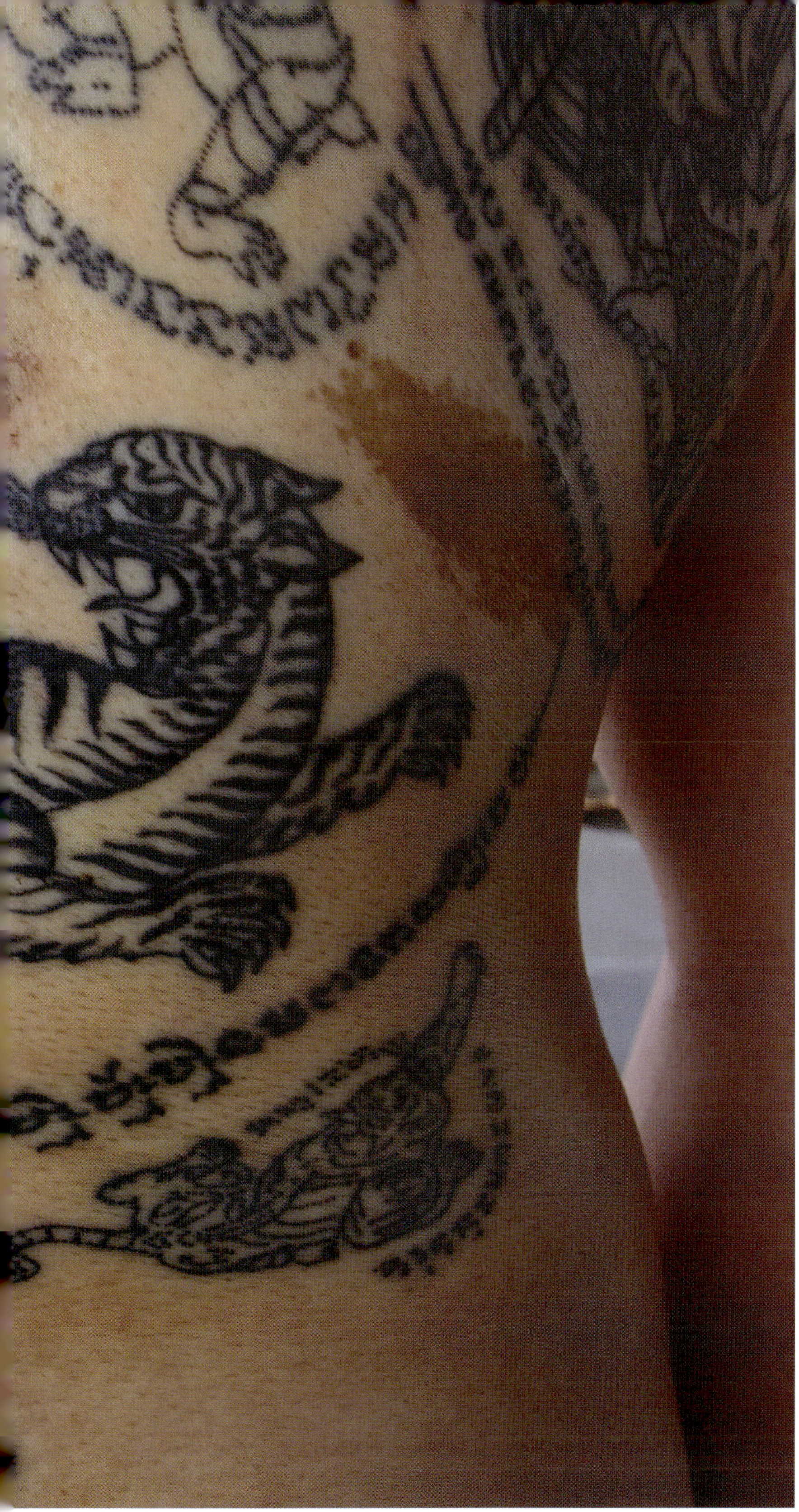

Left: 'Tiger looking back' on a disciple.

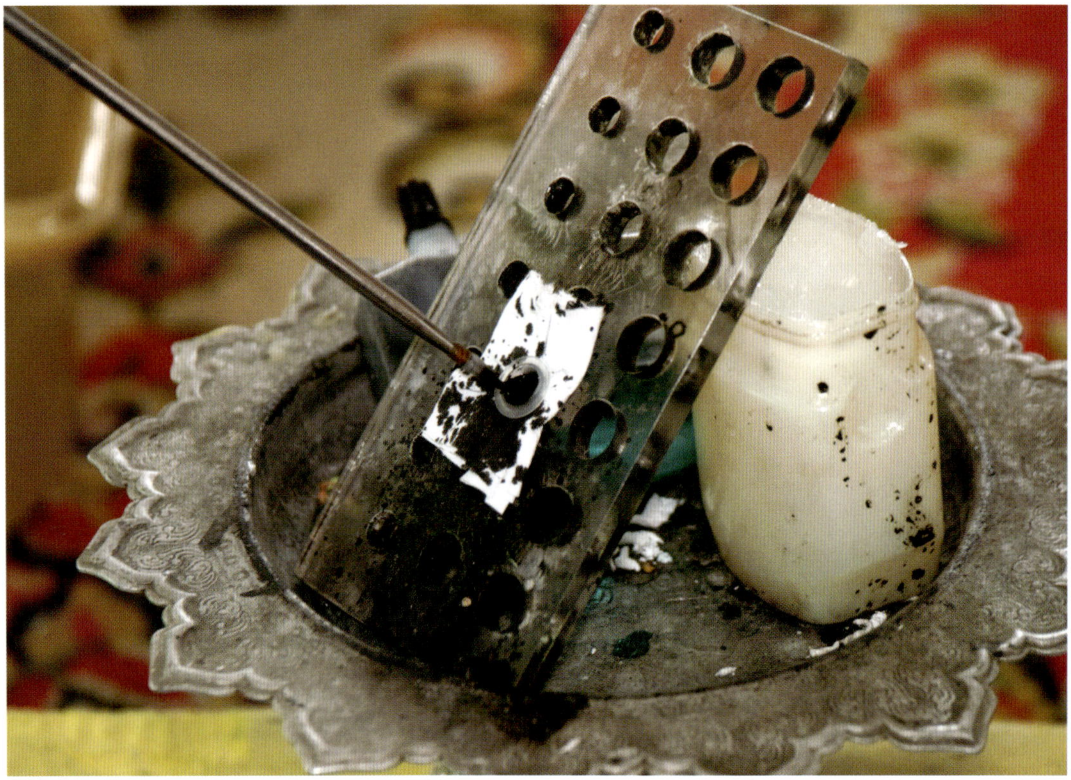

Above: Ink capsules at Ajahn Noo's *samnak*.

Until relatively recently, *khru sak* made their own ink from powdered charcoal, oil, herbs and various secret ingredients known only to those who have mastered the art. In rural areas of northwestern Thailand, some Shan masters still make their own ink by burning benzene, collecting the soot, drying it and pounding it into a fine powder, which is then mixed with sesame oil to create ink.

One of the most common additives is *waan*, a Thai word which may refer to any number of plant materials – typically rhizomes – with medicinal or magical characteristics. The most common *waan* added to tattoo ink is the root of *Curcuma spp*, a wild ginger known for its antiseptic and anti-inflammatory qualities. *Waan* is also a common ingredient for *nam-mon*, the holy water sprinkled liberally onto a fresh tattoo by the master using a reed whisk. Some masters smear a thin layer of *nam-man waan* (sesame oil containing *waan*) over a new tattoo as well.

Nowadays most masters use commercially available inks manufactured in China, Germany or elsewhere. Some add a drop of *meuk sehk* (consecrated ink) given to them by their teachers. Others marinate a variety of roots and herbs in bottled ink, sometimes resulting in ink with a mystic, pleasant fragrance.

Whatever admixture is used, the master expends considerable time and effort to empower the ink through the chanting of Pali Buddhist verses and shamanic Thai incantations, and by placing the ink on the main altar in the *samnak* (room consecrated for *sak yan*).

The most accomplished masters apply *sak yan* freehand, entirely from memory, employing only the occasional bottle cap, jar lid or straightedge for circles and straight lines. Others use tracing paper on which a design has already been drawn. They place the paper onto the client's skin together with a piece of carbon paper, and draw a guide design before tapping the ink into the skin. A modern variation of this involves the use of large rubber stamps which are applied to an ink pad and then stamped onto the skin to serve as a guide.

In comparison with machine tattoo techniques used in most of the world today, a typical *sak yan* can be completed rather quickly – anywhere from five minutes for a small *na* to 45 minutes for a larger *yan*. Blood only appears occasionally, and the process is less painful compared to the average machine tattoo. The typical hand-tattooed *sak yan* is ensconced under the outermost layers of skin, with the needle rarely coming in contact with capillaries. By comparison, a machine tattoo penetrates more deeply into the skin, and hence capillaries are often broken, resulting in bleeding.

LUUK SIT

Anyone tattooed by a *khru sak yan* becomes a disciple *(luuk sit)* of that master. In the world of *sak yan*, responsibility for the efficacy of the tattoos – whether ink or oil – lies with the disciple as much as with the master.

Before, during or after the tattoo application, the master may talk to the disciple about Buddhist principles and about the code of conduct the disciple must follow in order to maintain the power of the sacred tattoos. In general it is accepted by those in the *sak yan* culture that the tattoos only work for people who adhere strictly to Buddhist moral codes. This code typically includes the five precepts of Buddhism: refraining from killing, stealing, lying, sexual misconduct and intoxication. These rules establish *phutthakhun* (Buddhist virtues) for the magic, taking what could be seen as a selfish act to empower oneself and transforming it into the promotion of ethical behaviour.

OIL TATTOOS

Some Thais choose to be tattooed with oil rather than ink. Since oil is absorbed by the body without leaving a visible trace, other than red welts that last a day or two, ***sak nam-man*** (oil tattoo) does its work invisibly. Many women – as well as some men – prefer this type of tattoo because it is inconspicuous in daily life. The base oil is usually sesame, blended with herbs or roots as with ***sak meuk*** (ink tattoos). The main ingredient is ***waan***, and hence the oil is referred to as ***nam-man waan***.

All of the rituals associated with ink tattoos are performed with oil tattoos.

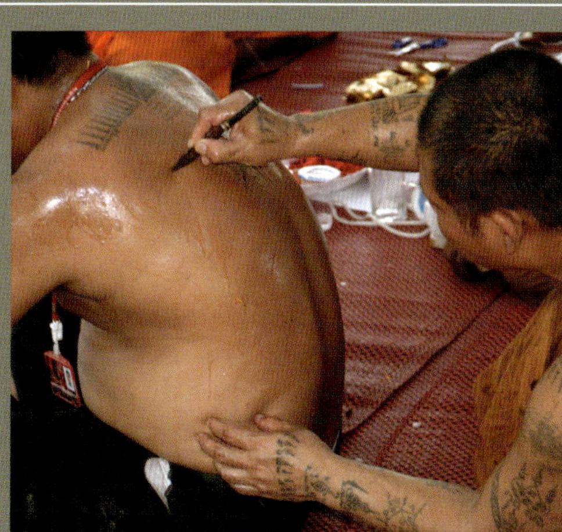

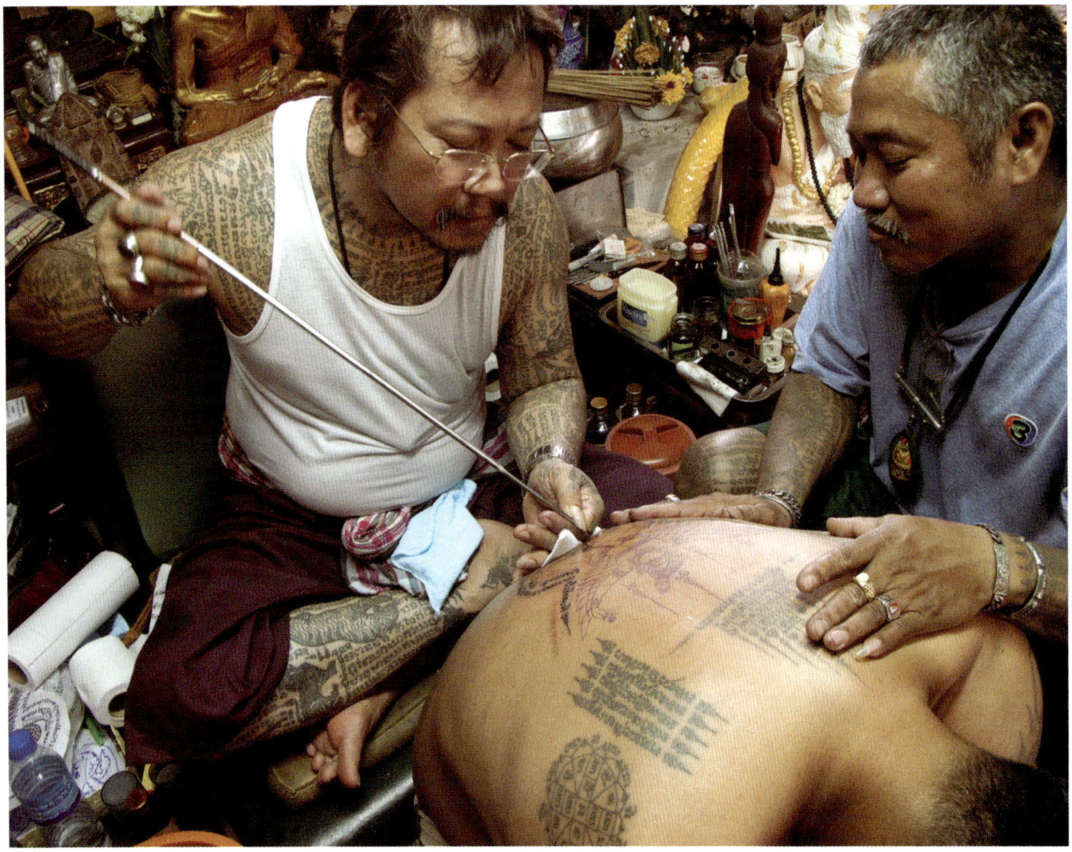

Above: Ajahn Chai, a chief disciple of Ajahn Thong, at work in his *samnak*.
RIght: Work being done on the back of a disciple, following a sketch in ballpoint pen.

To these a master may add a number of seemingly arcane prohibitions on cursing one's parents or master, and refraining from certain foods, such as purple potatoes, gourds, starfruit or raw meat. Some masters specify that the *luuk sit* must don a cap before walking under a bridge, and never drink from anyone's glass but his own. Menstrual blood and vaginal secretions in particular are thought to rob tattoos of their power.

The rules also provide an explanation when tattoos prove ineffective. If someone with a tattoo that protects against bullets and sharp projectiles is killed by a gun or knife, it doesn't mean that his *sak yan* didn't work. It means that he didn't obey the moral code, and thus his tattoos lost their power.

When protection tattoos are complete, the master may "test" the power of the *yantra* as well as the faith of the disciple by passing a sharp blade over the disciple's arms, back or neck in such a way that would seemingly lacerate the skin under normal conditions. In all such demonstrations, of course, the disciple is unharmed.

Every year disciples have the opportunity to "recharge" their tattoos by paying respect to their tattoo masters during an annual *wai khru* (respecting the teacher) ceremony. The dates chosen for

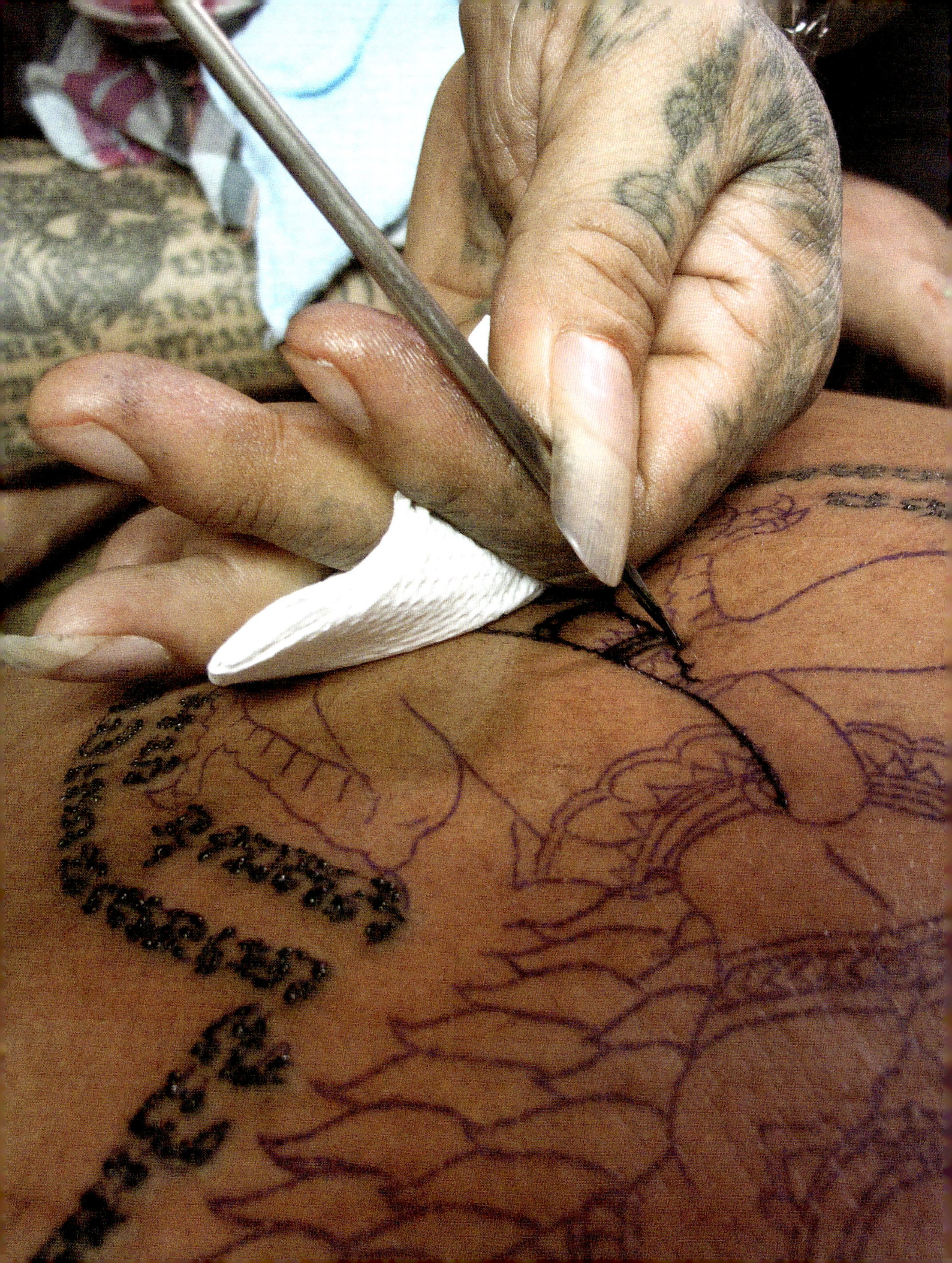

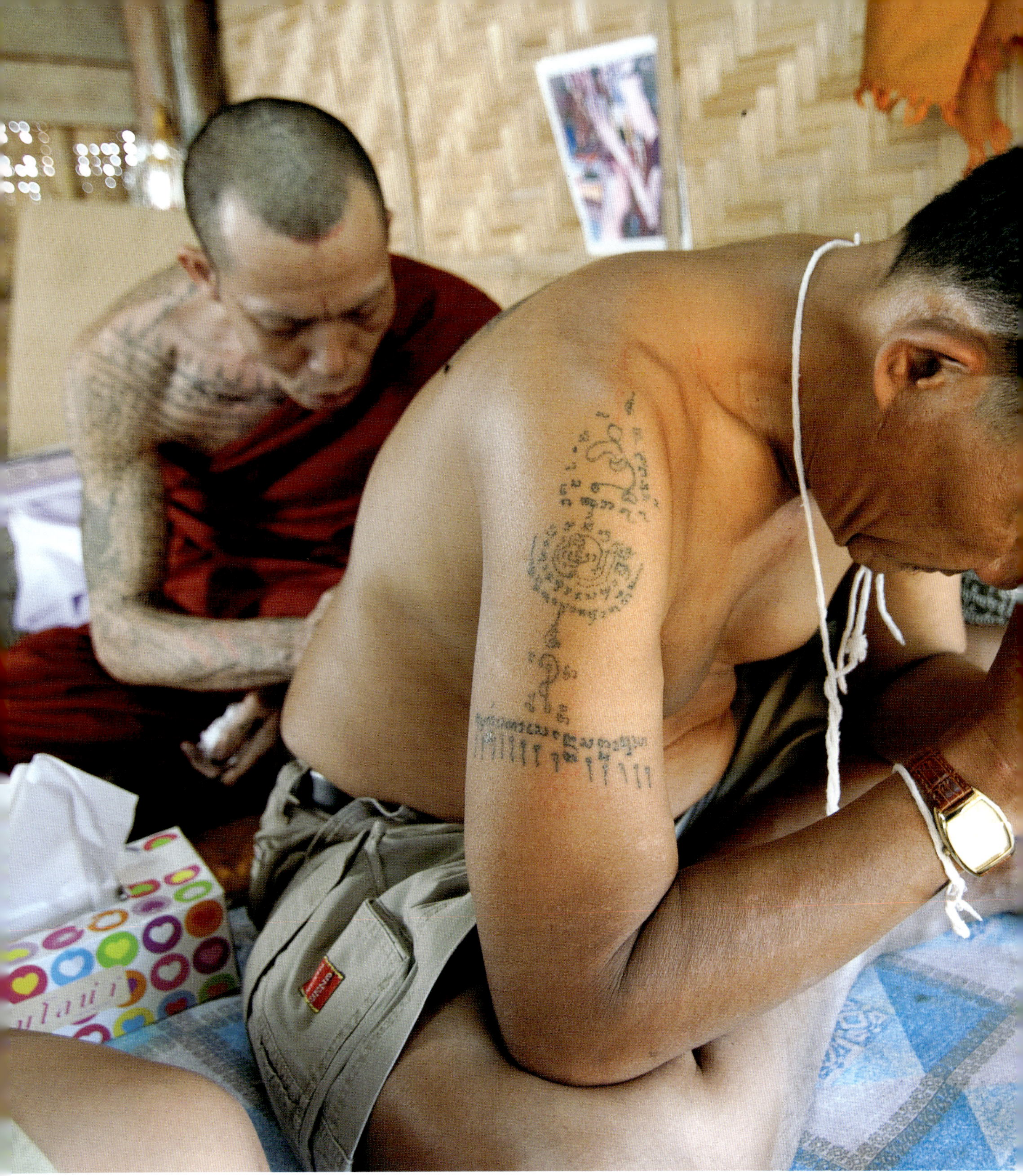

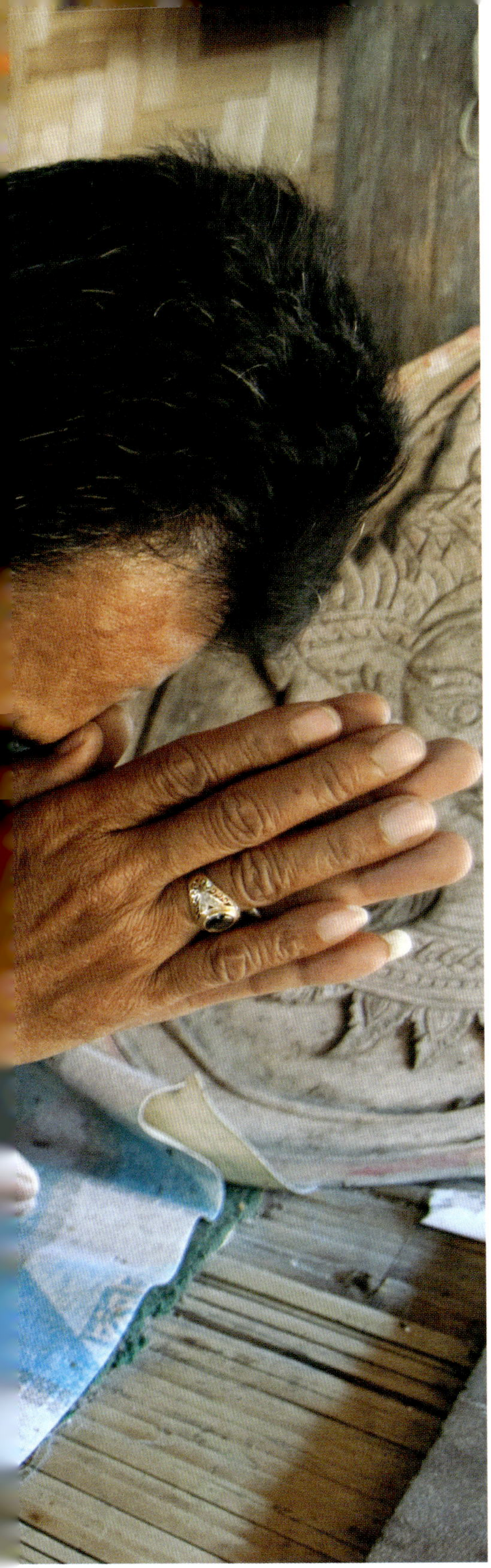

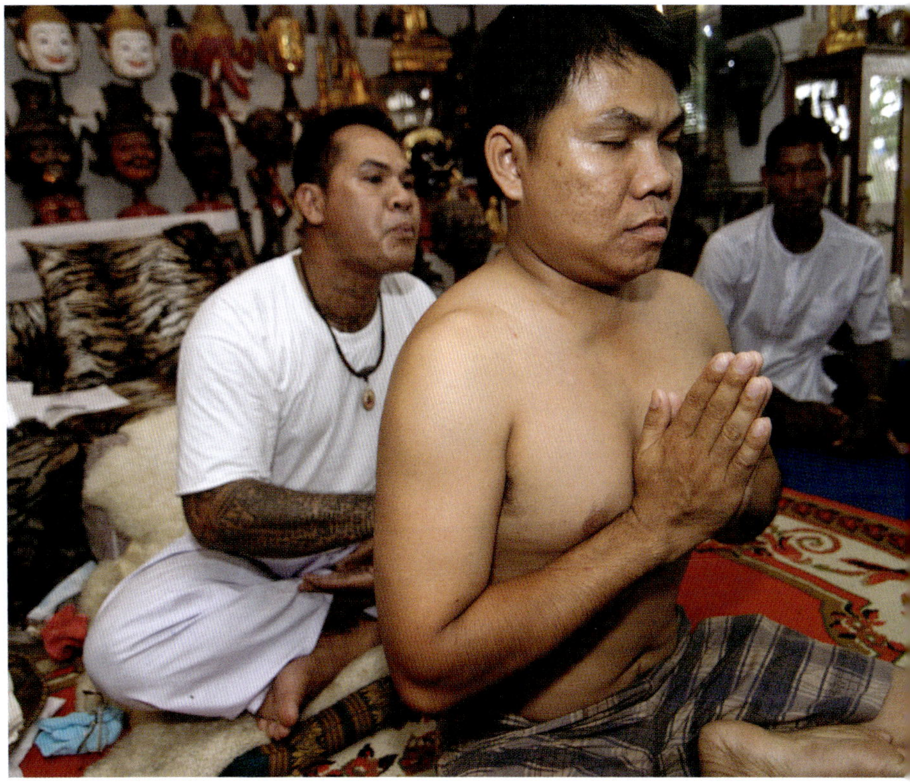

Left: Lanna master Ajahn Pornsit, Sanpatong.

Above: Ajahn Somchat blows on a freshly inked *sak yan* as part of an empowerment ritual.

Next page: Ajahn Noo sprinkles a disciple with sacred water.

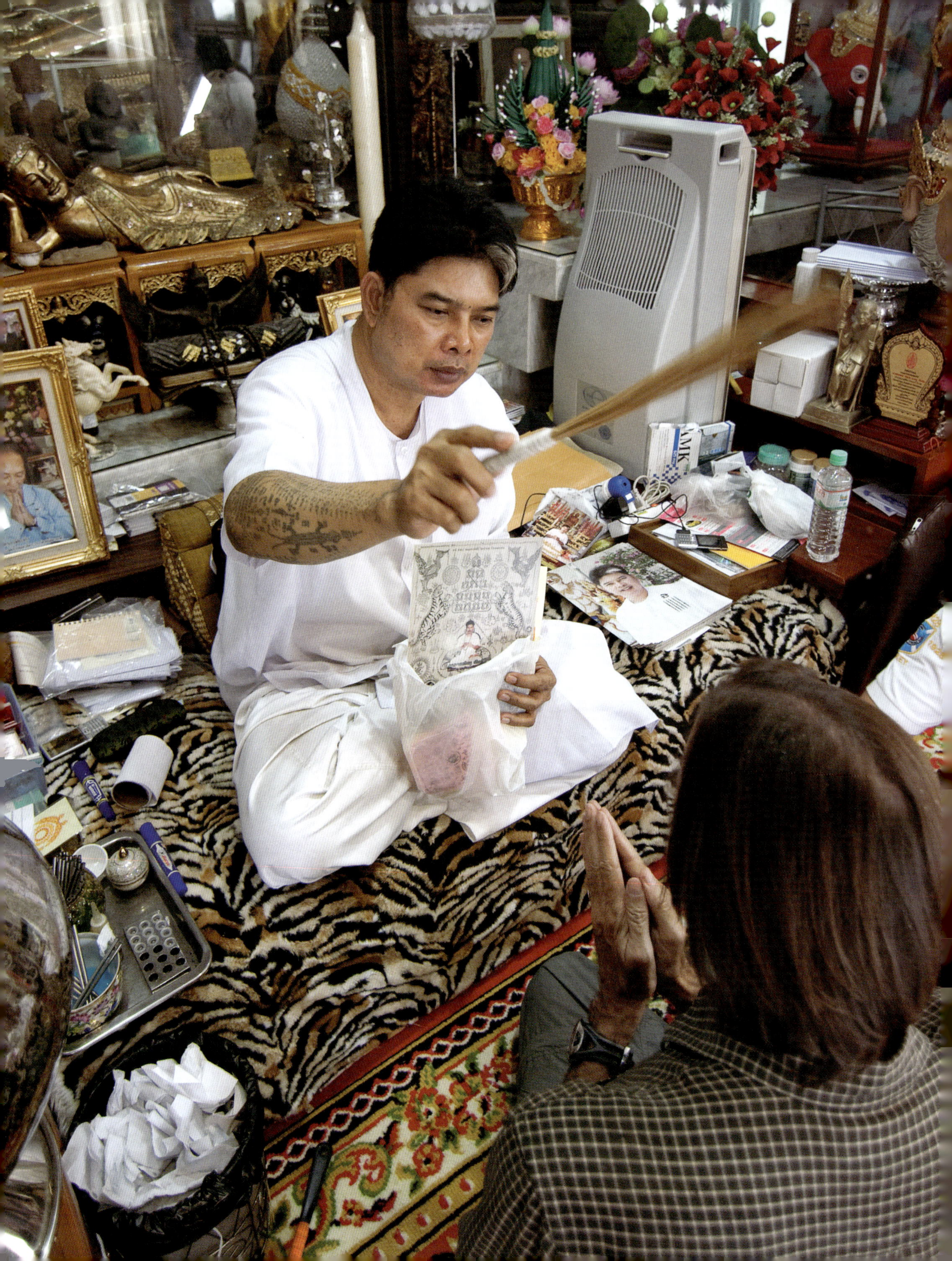

OTHER USES FOR YANTRA

Yan may also be applied to media other than a person's skin. They may be drawn or printed onto squares of cloth called *pha yan* (yantra cloth, to be hung at home or in one's car, or worn as a headband), daubed onto the bonnet or interior of a car, and painted above the entry doors to houses, offices and schoolrooms. Many Buddha amulets *(phra khreuang)* also bear *yantras* on the verso side, while *ta-kroot* (cylindrical amulets) may contain yantra or *akkhara* inscribed on metal.

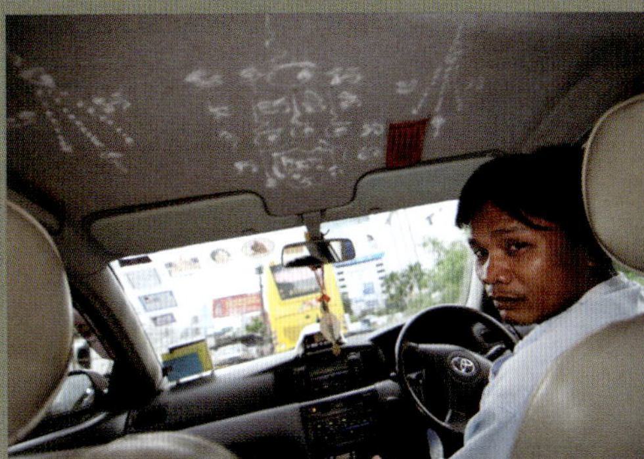

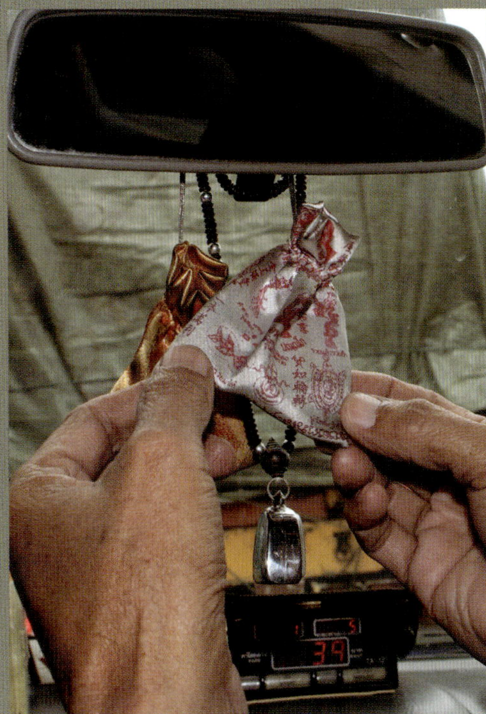

these auspicious occasions vary from master to master. [See the Wai Khru chapter for more detail on these impressive occasions.]

In any case most masters emphasise that the power and magic of *sak yan* come not from the master and designs alone. A proper respect for the tattoos, one's master and one's neighbours, along with an effort to remain mindful of one's conduct in daily life, is considered of uppermost importance. Thus the tattoos are an aid to living a blessed life, but only if the disciple participates in the process.

TRANCE

In the case of aggressive animal tattoos, as well as designs depicting Pho Kae or Chuchok, the disciple may enter into trance during the post-tattoo consecration ritual, and especially on *wai khru* days. In such cases the *khaung* ("stuff," meaning the magic power imparted by the master) will rise *(kheun)* in the disciple, who will began to display the characteristics of his or her principal tattoos. Someone with a tiger tattoo, for example, will start growling and "pawing" the floor with his hands or feet, while a disciple bearing a Hanuman (Hindu monkey god) will start scratching for lice and leaping about. In such cases the master will quietly chant *khaathaa* and eventually the disciples will calm down.

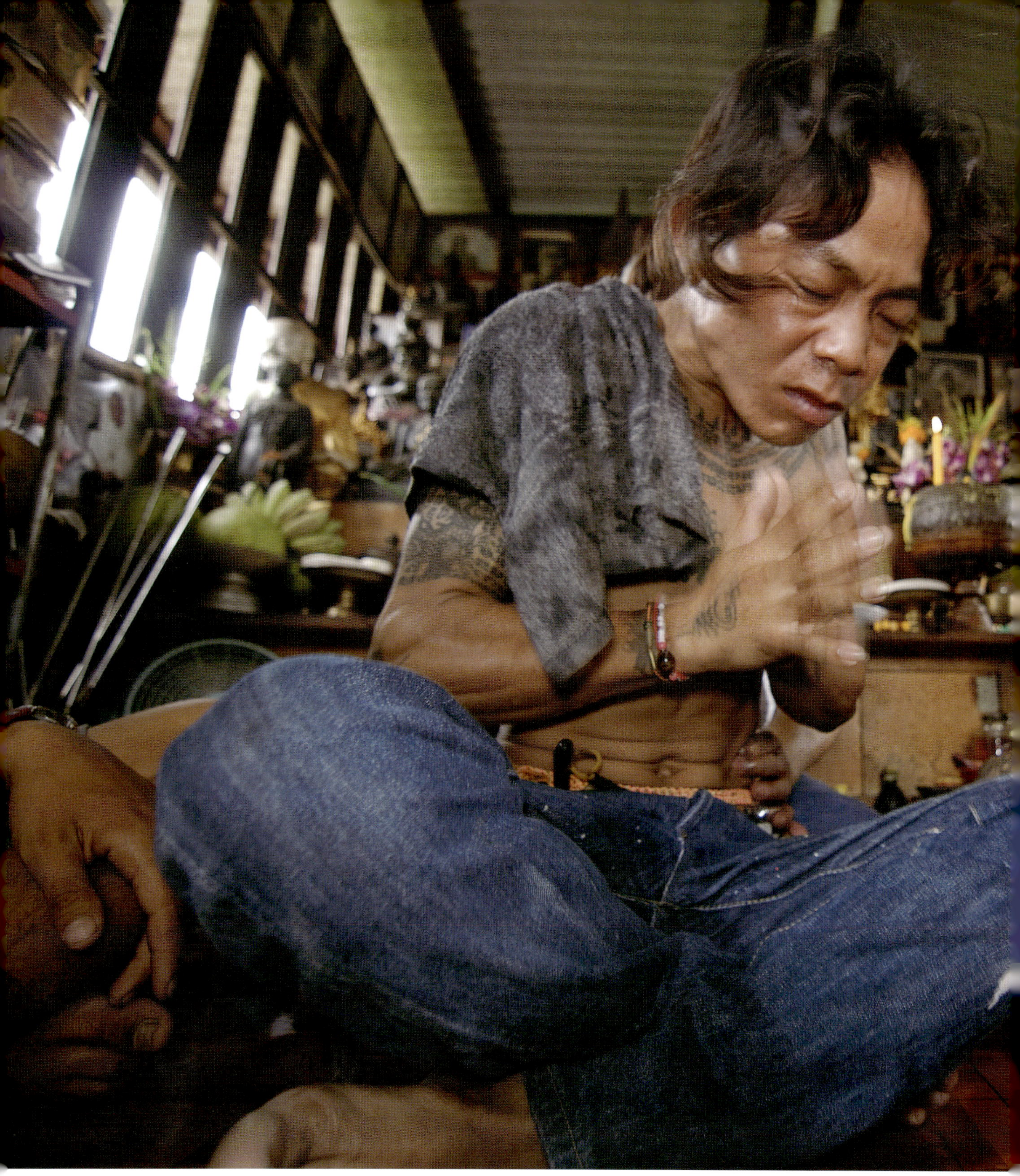

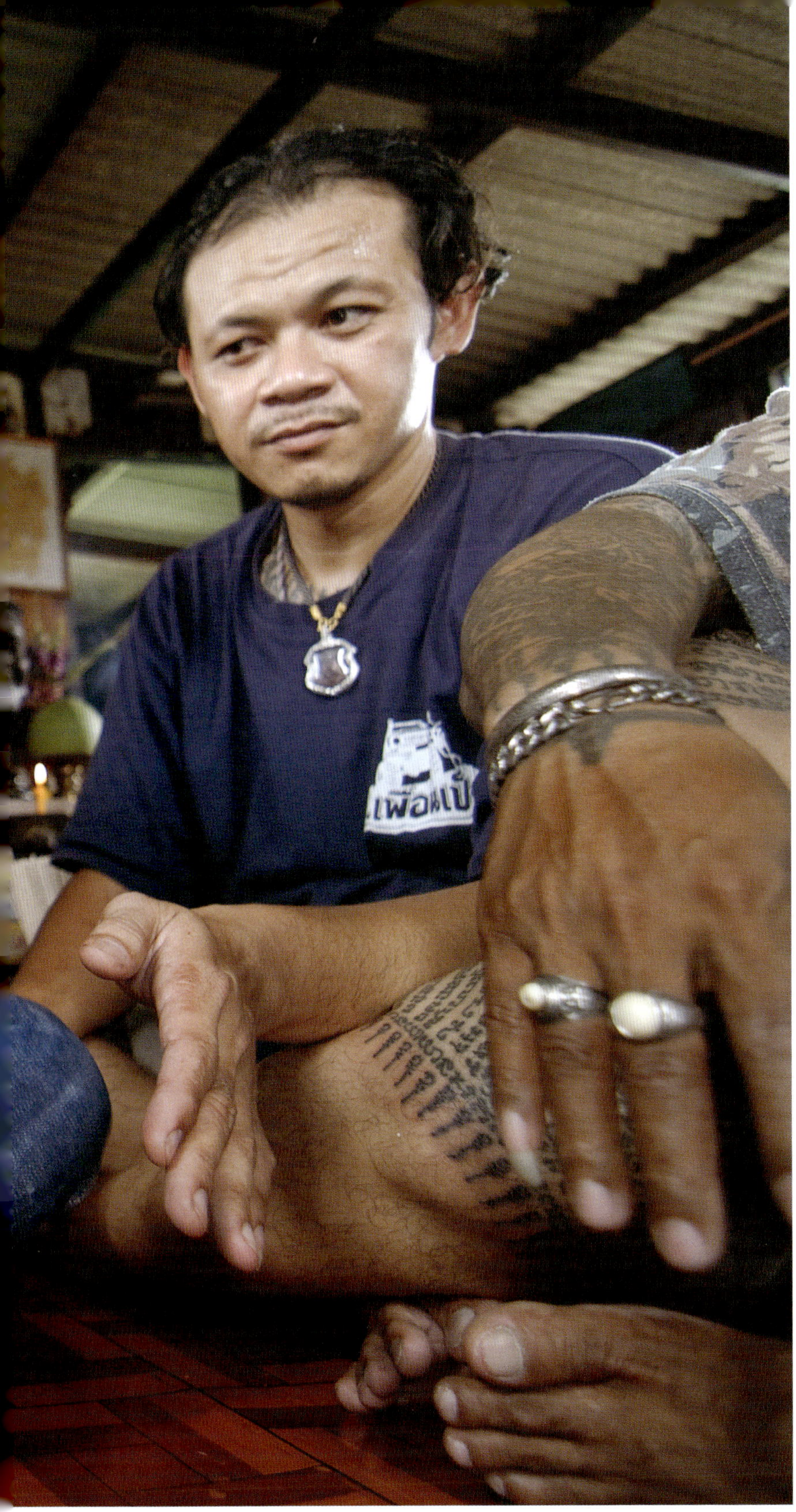

Left: A man who has just received a *sak yan* from Ajahn Tong in Thonburi goes into trance as the master (seated behind the disciple) chants *khaathaa* (verses) of consecration, empowering the tattoo.

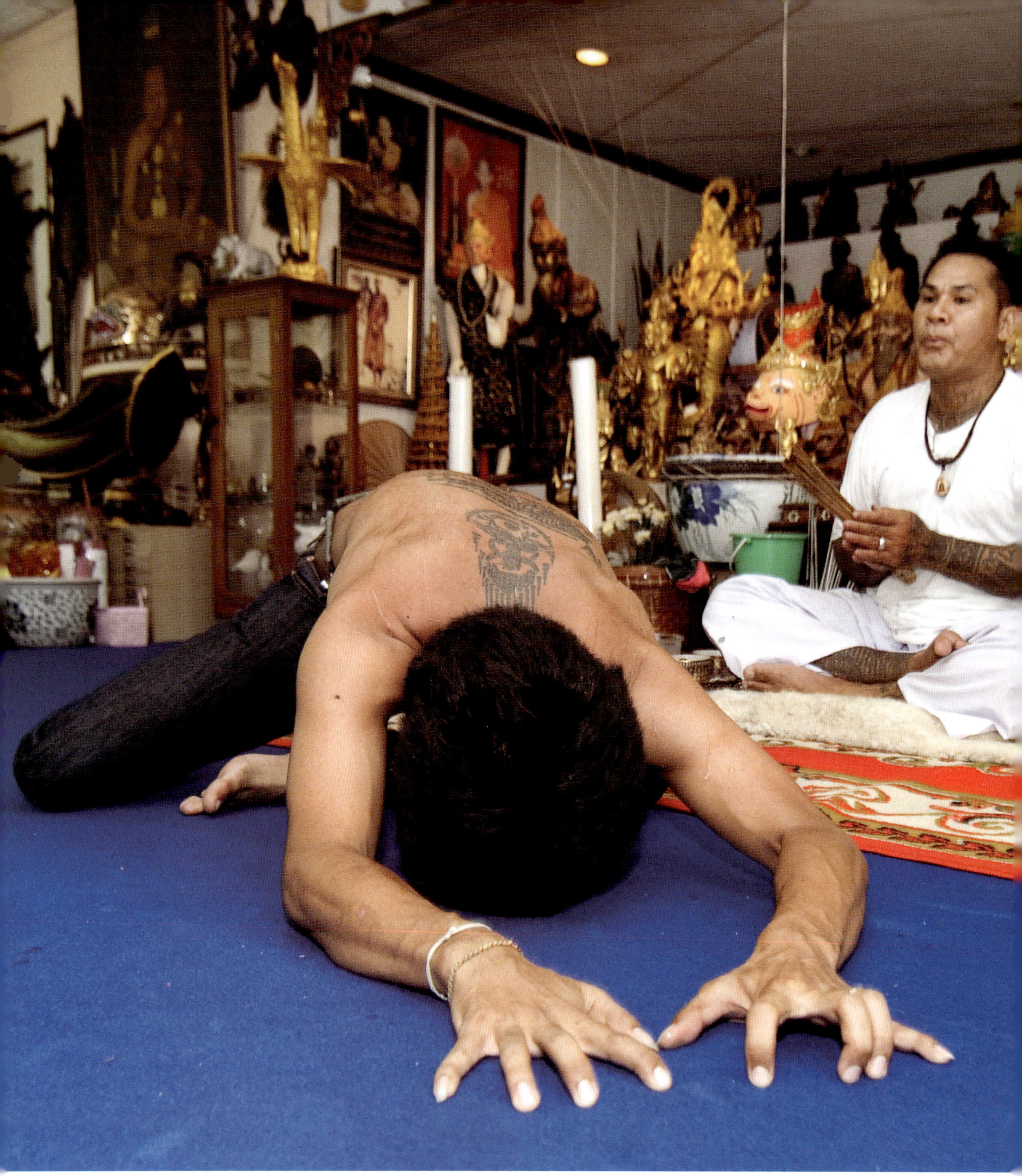

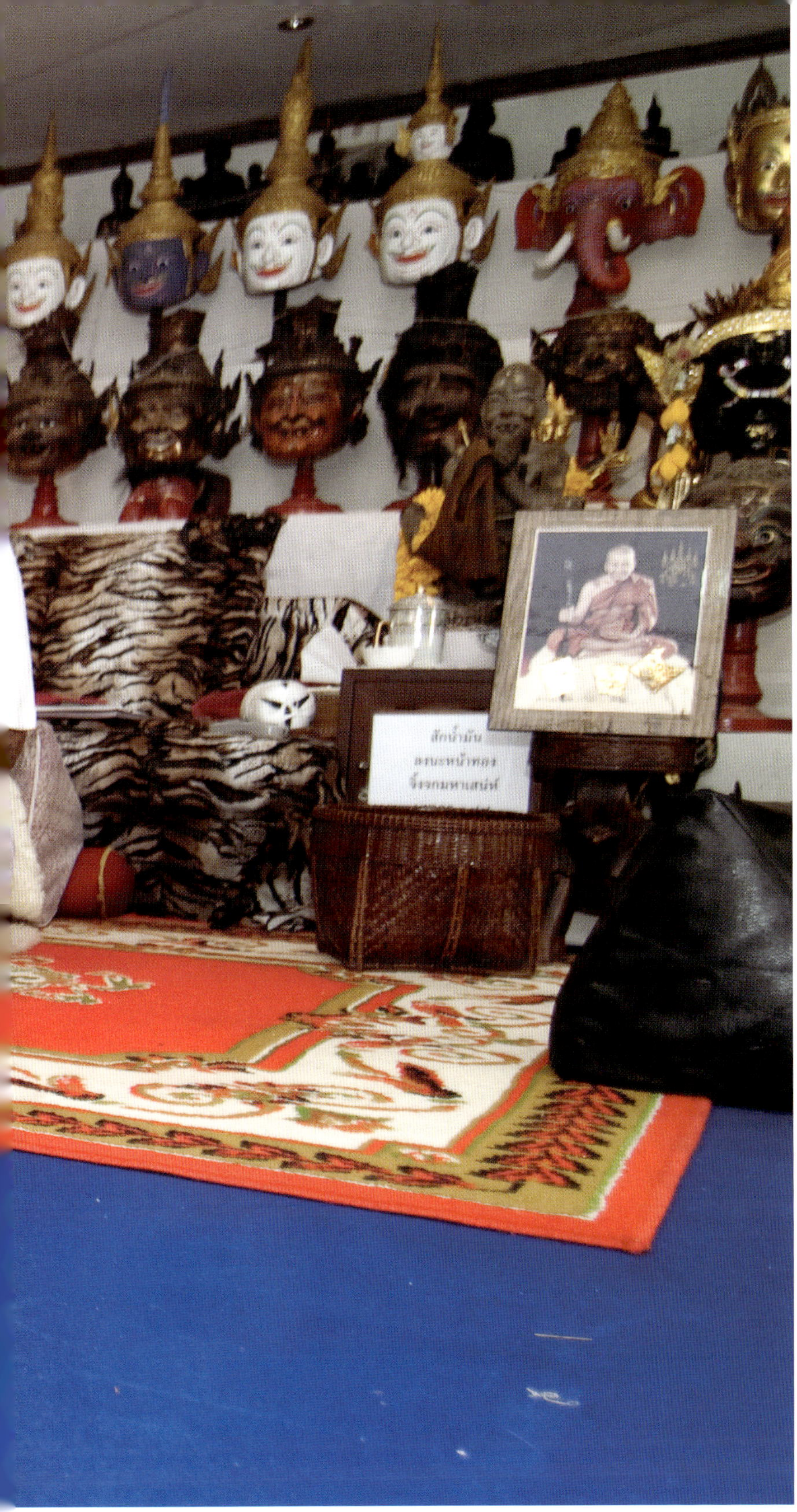

Left: A man inked with a tiger *sak yan* goes into trance while being blessed by Ajahn Somchat.

MAGIC INK: SPELLS & SIGILS

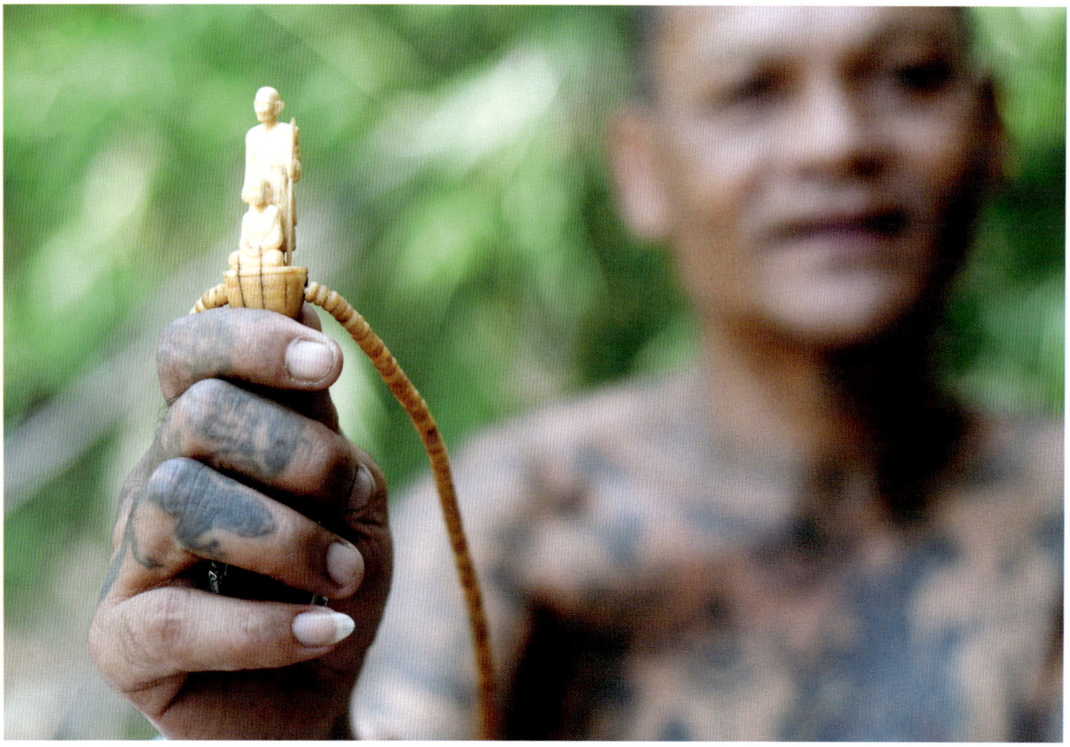

Above: A monk holds up an image of Luang Pu Suk (standing) and Luang Pu Nai (sitting), carved by Ajahn Gop.

Cultures around the world have distinct ways of viewing reality, with corresponding explanations and descriptions outlining their beliefs. In most world religions, including Buddhism, these explanations are written down, first as revered scripture traced to the religion's genesis and later as scriptural commentaries, sermons and so on.

Beliefs regarding *sak yan* have not been neatly canonised and commented upon in the same way. Whether in the different regions of Thailand, in Laos or in Cambodia, sacred tattoo lore tends to be much more esoteric in the way it is learned, archived and passed on. While Thai Buddhist monks, for example, are to some degree monitored and controlled by the Sangha Council and the Department of Religious Affairs, the sacred tattoo master is subject to no corresponding relationship with any public organisation other than within his own tattoo centre (or monastery, in the case of masters who are monks), and within the confines of criminal and civil law.

Knowledge of the lore – usually referred to as *weechaa* in Thai (from the Pali *vijja*, "knowledge") – follows an oral tradition transferred from master to disciple, without any supervision or codification from outside. The oral nature preserves the tradition's esoteric essence, and promotes its seemingly strange, exotic image – and at times, its incomprehensibility – even among most locals.

It also means that every master has his own understanding of *weechaa*, even when it has been largely formed by a particular lineage dating back one or more generations.

Thai, Lao and Khmer cultures are laid upon a substratum of animism in which the existence of spirits *(phee)* and body-souls *(khwan)* is taken as a given. That the socially sanctioned rituals surrounding these beliefs have been completely integrated with Buddhist rituals in general applies equally to the tattoo tradition. Still, the fact that *sak yan* have roots in an ancient animistic tradition that pre-dates Buddhism, yet now exist within a Buddhist context, makes it all the more difficult for outsiders to comprehend.

> *Weechaa* descends from masters who learnt from their masters in the past, and who in turn pass it on to their disciples.

WEECHAA

In the *sak yan* tradition, *weechaa* is the tattoo's main source of power, constituting not only a range of designs and techniques, but more importantly a set of sacred spells and verses to control spirits and supernatural powers. In this sense, the concept of *weechaa* is rather analogous with the concept of "magic" as understood in the West.

In the face of modernisation, urbanisation and empirical science, *weechaa* associated with animism has come under heavy pressure, especially via state-controlled secular education, which competes with traditional, indigenous knowledge. Under these circumstances, the opportunities to acquire *weechaa* from accomplished masters have steadily diminished over the last century.

In Laos and Cambodia, war and the advent of Communist ideology put even more pressure on the practise and transmission of *weechaa*. Many tattoo masters fled these two countries during the 1970s, while many who stayed fell victim to war or state violence. This is one reason why in Thailand, which has largely been spared these added pressures, the *sak yan* tradition still flourishes. In Laos and especially in Cambodia, it has almost completely disappeared.

Weechaa descends from masters who learnt from their masters in the past, and who in turn pass it on to their disciples. When a disciple *(luuk sit)* is accepted for training, his potential to "graduate" *(thaay thaut)* and receive full approval to administer *sak yan*, recite spells and verses, and perform rituals may seem at first to be largely dependent on self-discipline and memory. The master typically begins by teaching his students the alphabet used for *khaathaa* (verses) associated with both tattoo designs and the incantations recited before, during and after the tattoo procedure. This proceeds to basic spells and verses, moving on to more complicated ones and gradually introducing the actual tattooing techniques, starting with basic designs with a minimum of detail. Methods for making *mai khem* (tattoo needle shafts) and mixing ink must also be learnt.

However the learning of the alphabet and *khaathaa* assumes priority. The tattoo designs alone have no power without associated *khaathaa* written alongside them (or integrated into the geometry of the tattoo itself) and chanted by the *khru sak*. The importance of *khaathaa* in empowering sacred tattoos cannot be over-emphasised. It is similar to the importance of Buddhabhiseka, the ritual in which new Buddha images are consecrated and empowered.

Tattoo masters are able to *pluuk sehk* (literally, "plant spiritual power") into tattoos only via ritual and *khaathaa*. The word *sehk* comes from

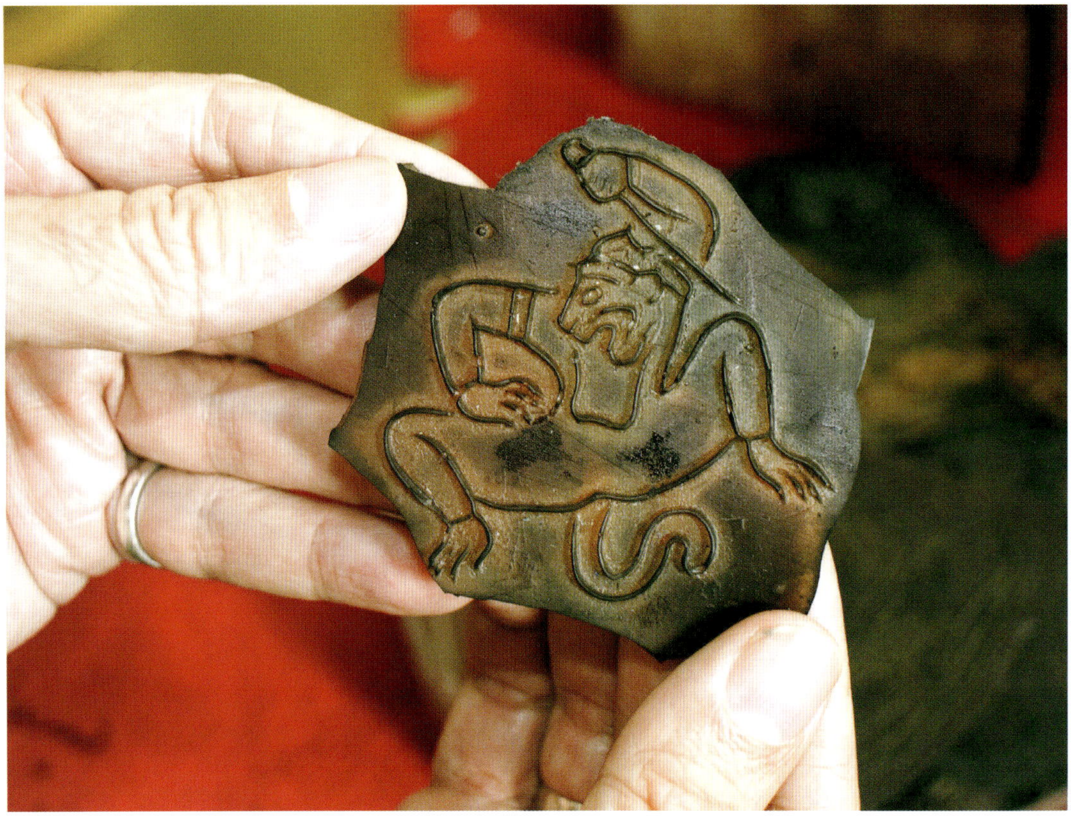

Above: Rubber stamps like this are sometimes used to guide the master with a *yantra*'s basic outline.

abhiseka, a Sanskrit term denoting a ritual or devotional activity associated with religious rites of passage, common to Hinduism and Jainism as well as Buddhism.

Some masters strictly forbid their disciples from writing down the *khaathaa* because it is believed that the spiritual power will be negatively affected. Presumably it also lessens the chance that a disciple will show the *khaathaa* to other masters or disciples, which might dilute the product, especially in cases where a master specialises in a particular design or designs that no one else produces. When the spells are temporarily written down to help with memorisation, the words are often intentionally misspelt in case they fall into the "wrong" hands. Ajahn Noo Ganpai in Pathum Thani, for example, is famous for intentionally introducing errors in the *khaathaa* that appear alongside tattoo designs in the catalogues he provides prospective disciples. Of course, once inked into someone's skin, the tattoos themselves provide a perfect record of the *khaathaa*.

When the transfer of *weechaa* is complete – a process that usually takes a minimum of five years – the disciple in turns becomes a master (although in relation to his master, he will always remain a *luuk sit*) who will be able to produce tattoos that confer all of the benefits claimed for *sak yan*, from *metta mahaniyom* (personal charisma) to *khong kraphan* (protection from bad spirits and harmful spells) and even *nang niaw* (literally "tough/sticky hide", meaning bullet- and knife-proof skin).

SPELLINGS & SCRIPT

The *khaathaa* used in *sak yan* traditions employ scripts and languages which aren't used in everyday practise as the native language of the community. In some cases, a mixture of local and non-local languages may be employed. Central Thai and Khmer tattoo masters, for example, use old Khmer script *(khaum)* for *khaathaa*. Lao masters use Lao *tham* (an early form of the Lao alphabet used in old Buddhist manuscripts), while northern Thai masters use Lanna script (which most northern Thai don't read well, if at all). Only the Tai Lü and Shan use their own scripts, although some Shan masters use Burmese script, which in some quarters is thought to be more powerful.

Whatever script is used, the language spelt out is Pali, the canonical language of Theravada Buddhism, occasionally mixed with local words. The resulting *khaathaa* are unintelligible to the average local in each region. They are made even more so by truncating the Pali terms into single syllables (usually the first syllable of each word), creating a fragmented, telegraphic abbreviation of sorts for each *khaathaa*. The *khaathaa* are so transformed by this process that even Pali specialists cannot translate or decipher the meanings in the majority of cases.

The usual anthropological explanation for the use of non-native languages and scripts for *sak yan* and for the associated spells is belief in "superior out-group magic". The phenomenon is shared by magic and sorcery in all cultures – what might be called the "Abracadabra effect".

The fragmentary nature of the verses adds further esotery to the tradition. Few practitioners today – including the masters themselves – understand exactly what each word means, although each master confidently offers his interpretation or that handed down to him by his preceptors.

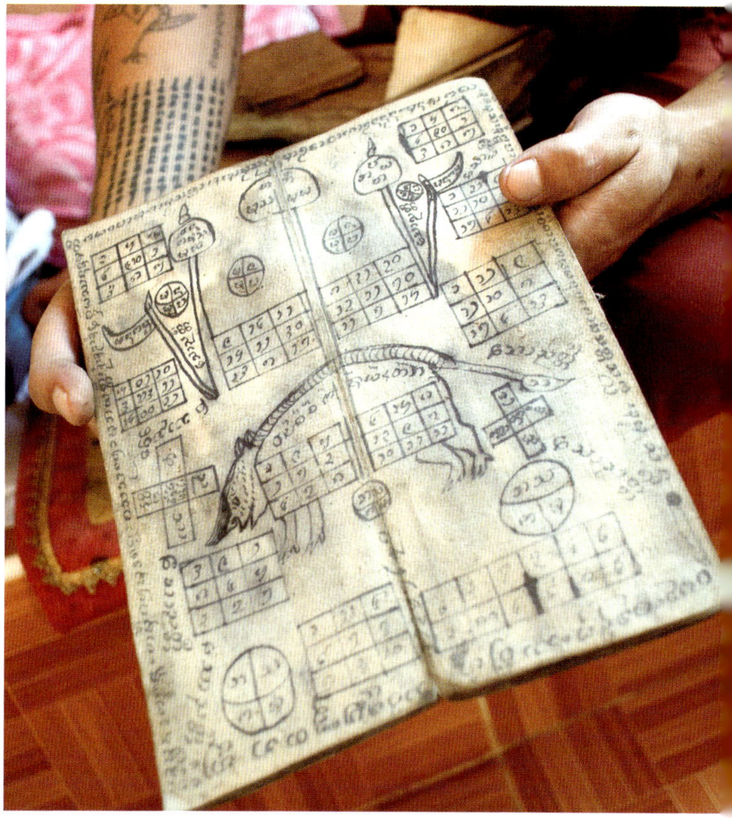

Above: Ajahn Kamthorn opens a mulberry paper manuscript bearing Lanna *sak yan* designs.

The fact that Pali forms the most important *khaathaa* component integrates Buddhism with the *sak yan* belief system. The power of these Pali word fragments is believed to derive from the power of Buddha himself. Fragmented verses are no less effective than the bone relics of the Buddha or an *arahant* (enlightened being), which are thought to bring myriad blessings upon the worshipper.

Verses are also sometimes referred to in Thai as *akhom*, from the Pali-Sanskrit *agama* (body of teaching) or *wetamon*, a compound of Pali-Sanskrit *veda* (textual knowledge) and *mantra* (sacred

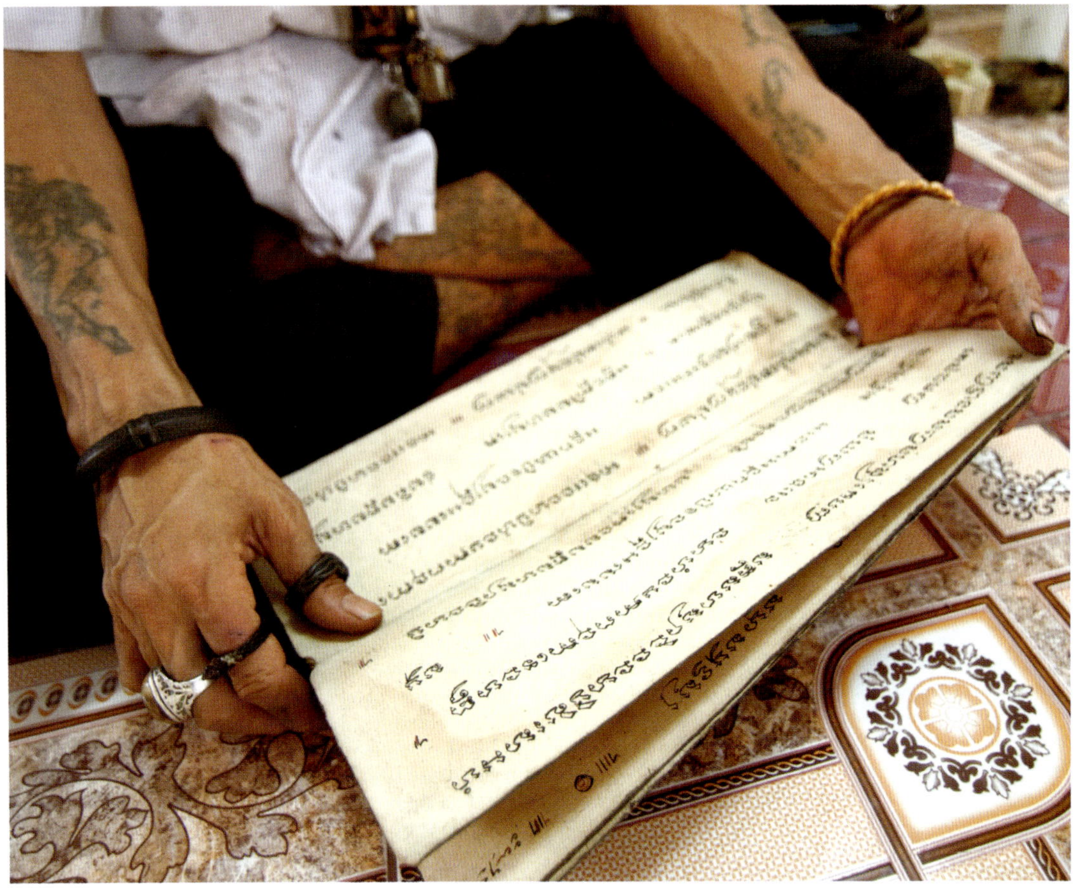

Above: Ajahn Gop peruses a Khmer manuscript. Right: An accordion-like *sak yan* manuscript is unfolded by the late Ajahn Kamthorn.

word). In northern Thai the simple term *kam* (word) is sometimes used. When speaking of the letters involved in *khaathaa*, the term *akkhara* (Pali for "letters") is used.

TRANSFORMATION & DISCIPLINE

The learning of spells and *yantras* goes well beyond memorisation and deft fingers. Ultimately the knowledge is believed to transform the learner's body and become part of it. *Weechaa* is thus perceived as an invisible substance lodged in the body of the disciple and carried with him wherever he goes. A common Thai alternative colloquial term for *weechaa* is *khaung* – literally "stuff". A master or lineage thought to have particularly strong *weechaa* is said to have *khaung dee* (good stuff). When a disciple enters into trance during a tattoo empowerment ritual, it is said that *khaung kheun* – "The stuff is rising".

When a disciple fails in acquiring *weechaa* despite training under a competent master, the fault is typically not ascribed to poor memory or artistic skills. Instead, the explanation is that the body of the trainee was incapable of holding the "good stuff." Explanations such as *khaung mai tit* (the stuff didn't stick) or *khaung mai khao* (the stuff didn't enter) are commonly stated in such cases.

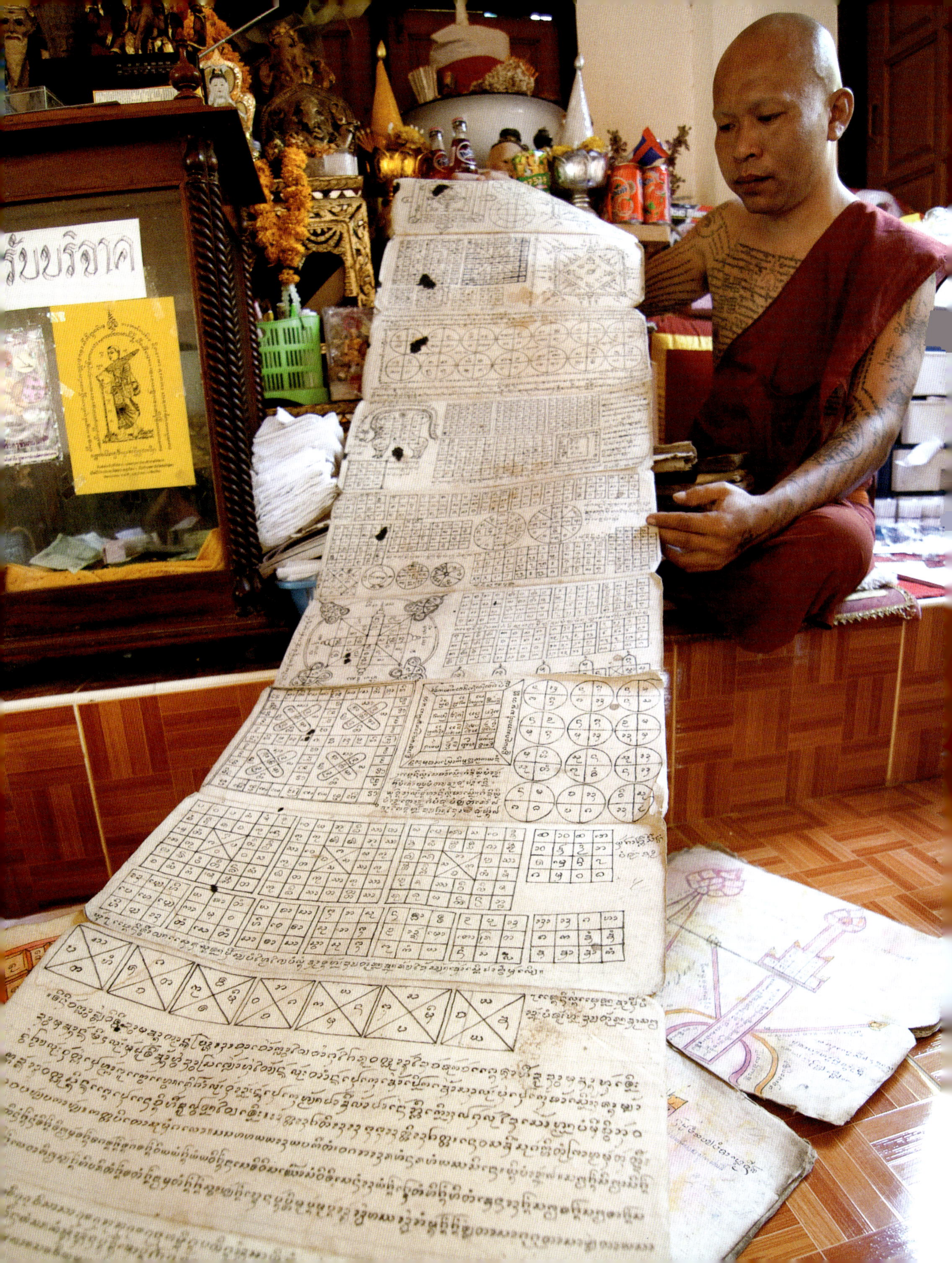
รับบริจาค

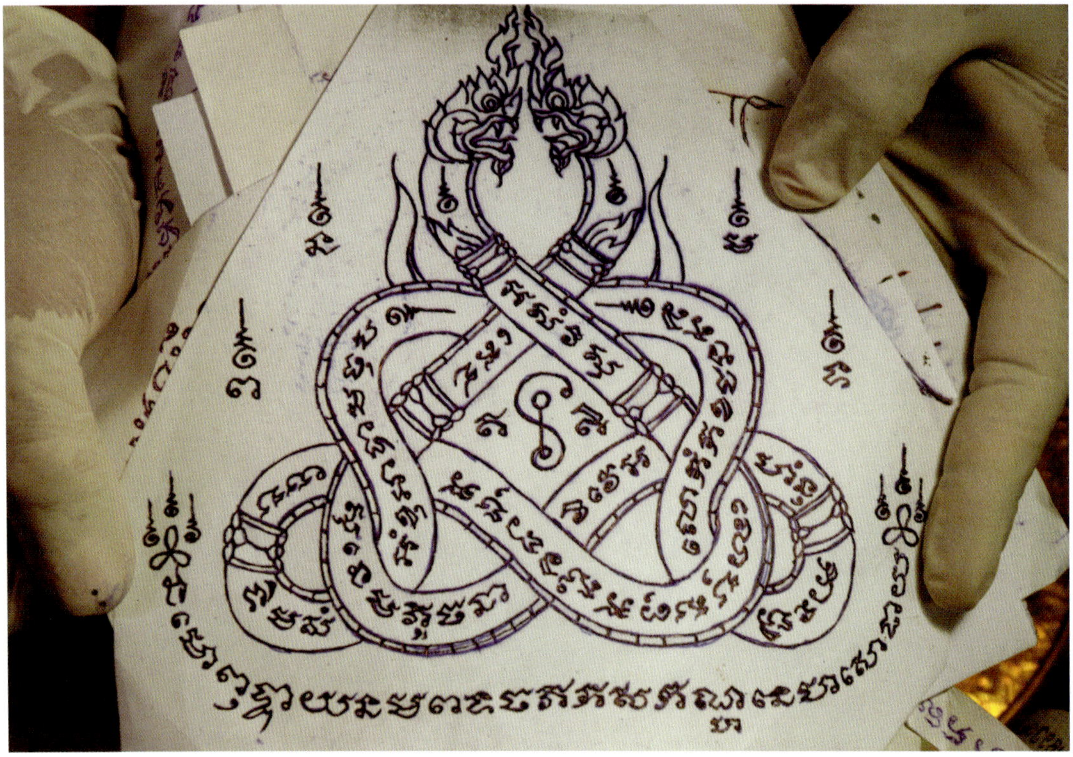

Above: A naga (water dragon) *yantra* with Khmer *akkhara*. Right: A man inked with Burmese anti-snakebite tattoos plays with a pet python.

To maintain *weechaa* in his body, a tattoo master is required to follow a set of rules much like those followed by disciples – but typically stricter. If they are monks, the masters are expected to follow the 227 monastic precepts. Even lay masters must display some degree of withdrawal and restraint from ordinary society in their disciplinary regimen. Many masters will have spent time as monks at some point in their lives.

When tattooing their disciples, lay masters typically dress in white and observe eight precepts. Some choose to wear tiger-print fabrics in the *reusee* (forest sage) tradition. In either case, they may also practise meditation and various rituals alone in forests, graveyards and caves from time to time. All of these renunciatory acts add to the power of their *weechaa*.

The *weechaa* embodied in a tattoo or other talismanic object is dependent on the power of the person who made it. Hence the master is expected to maintain self-discipline and morality not only for his own good and his own power, but for the good of his disciples – even those who may have travelled far away from him.

When a master recites *khaathaa* and inks them into a disciple's skin, the master is lodging some of his *weechaa* into the disciple, where it can ward off what is undesirable and bring about what is desirable. This applies equally to Buddhist amulets, *takroot* (cylindrical vials filled with *yantra* scrolls), *yantra* cloth, betel leaf inscribed with *yantra* (to be eaten) and other magico-religious objects.

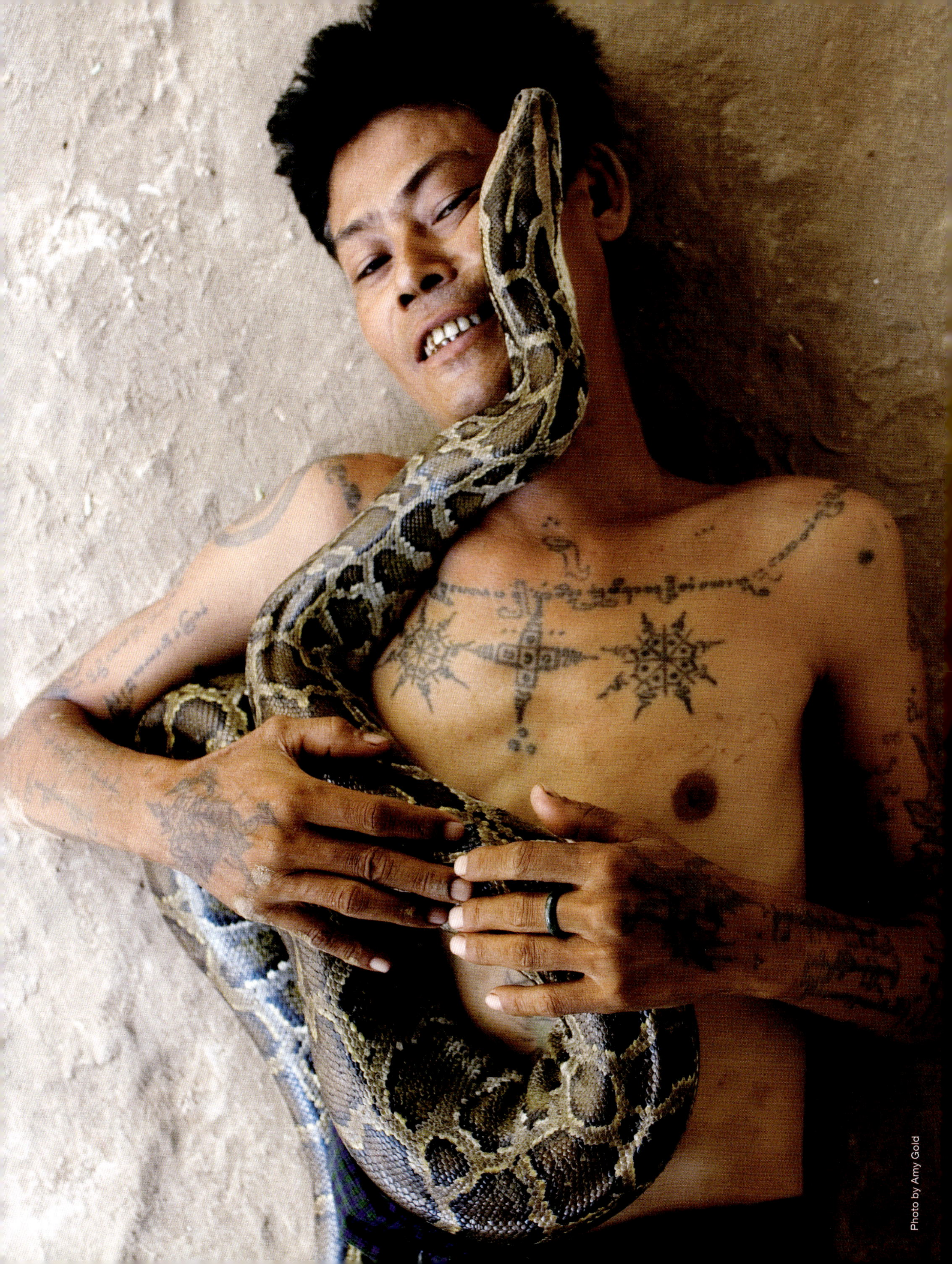

Photo by Amy Gold

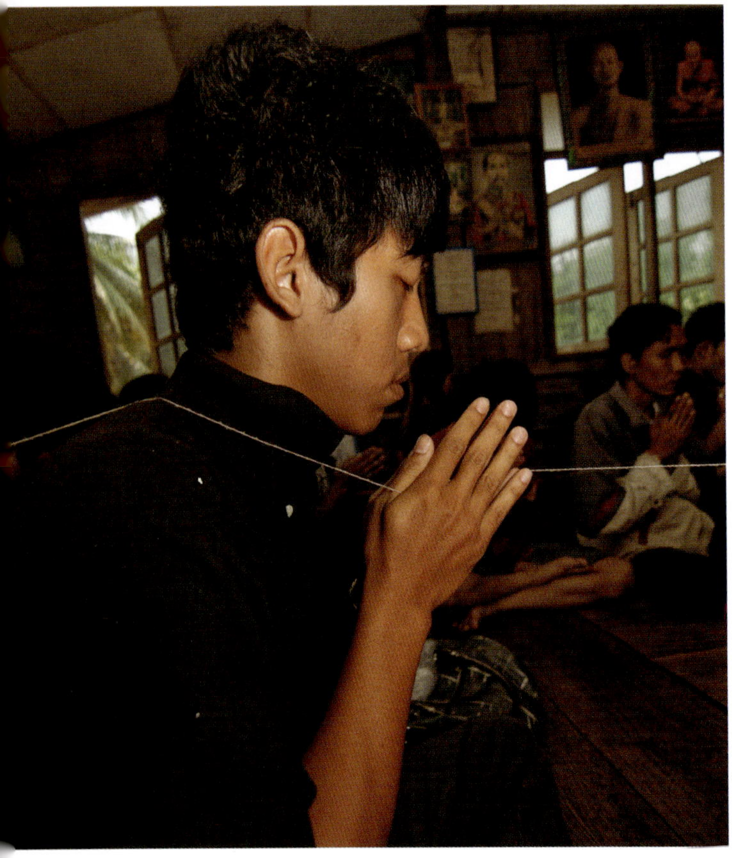

Above: *Wai khru* ceremony at the *samnak* of Ajahn Prawet, Ayuthaya.

SIGILISM

Sak yan design represents the graphic dimension of spells, verses and mantras. More importantly the sacred ink patterns inscribed in a disciple's skin form a portal for the entry of *weechaa* into the body. *Khaathaa* and *sak yan* work together to create the desired results in much the same way that sigils (symbols created for specific magical purposes) in European magic are combined with spells and incantations.

For the cultures of mainland Southeast Asia sacred tattoos have historically served mainly as preventive medicine, protecting the wearer from disease, accidents and violence. These ills were thought to occur primarily during travel, and since men were traditionally more likely to travel than women, they were much more likely to acquire this category of tattoos, a trend that continues to this day. In the Thai language, *yantras* of this sort come under the category of *klaew khlaat* (evading mishaps) and are among the most popular in the tradition.

Another general class of *sak yan* causes others to favour the wearer. These *yantra* are called *metta mahaniyom*, which means "loving kindness and great favour", with the power to influence people to feel compassion for the wearer. Both spirits and people are thought to trust the bearer and treat him with loving kindness. It is a favourite among traders and storekeepers.

A related variant is *mahasaneh*, "great charm/charisma", which attracts lovers. By far the most common tattoo of this nature takes the form of geckos (usually a pair or even a trio).

Yet another *yantra* that influences other people is *maha amnaat*, "great power", believed to be effective in advancing status, career, promotions and so on. This type of tattoo is also said to engender obedience and respect in others and is thus popular among soldiers and police.

Yantras of the *khong kraphan* variety confer invincibility, protecting the wearer from bullets, knives and other weapons. They're also said to help the wearer lead a charmed life in general, and are popular with people who feel they are at risk of being attacked.

Yantras of the *chok laap* kind bring general good luck and prosperity.

Yantras for very specific purposes, such as causing a lover to return home or winning a dispute, are called *taam khwaam*. Because they are so specific, these *yantras* are not very popular as tattoos, and are more likely to be applied to cloth or other objects that can be placed on or near the

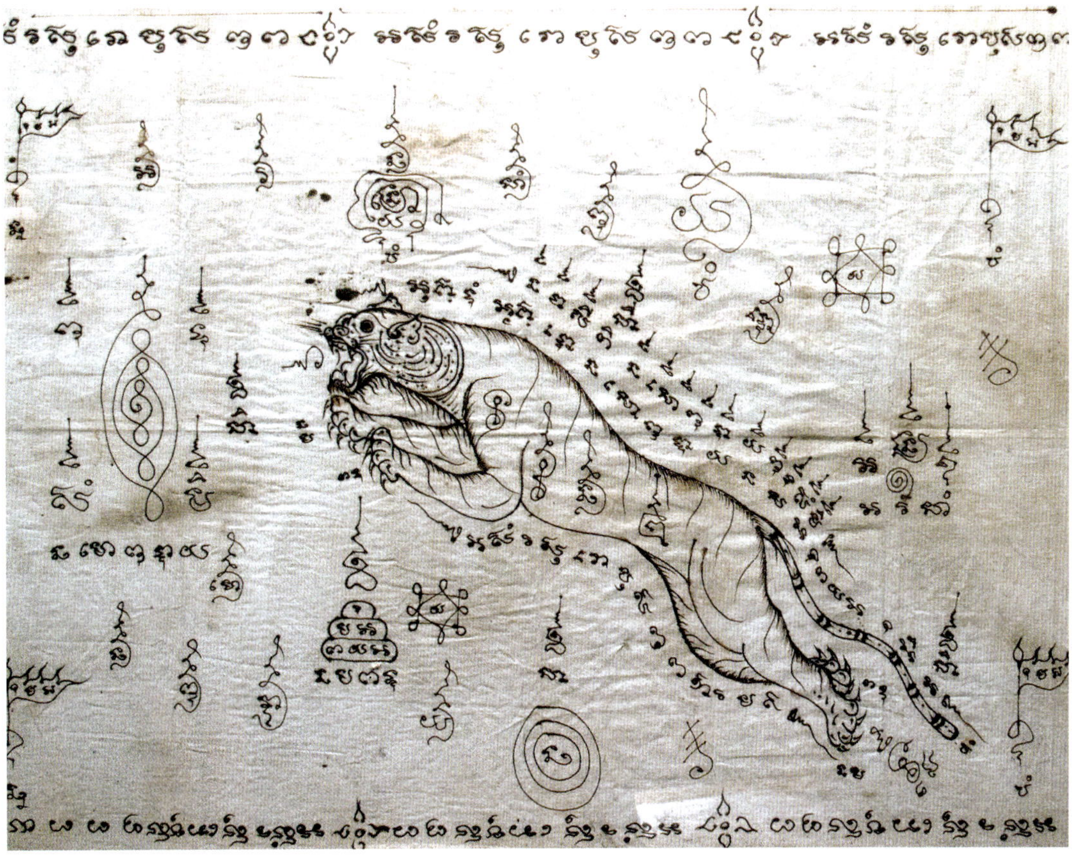

Photo by John LaFortune Collection

Above: The leaping tiger *yantra* on this *phaa yan* is intended to bestow power and tenacity. It is surrounded by smaller *yantras* for good health, wealth and success.

intended recipient of the action. One exception is *yantras* that make the disciple more persuasive, that is, able to talk other people into doing things the disciple wants. One common example of this is a rectangular design that may be tattooed across the throat, on the lower jaw below the tongue or even on the tongue itself. The disciple will usually choose invisible oil tattoos for such locations on the body.

Some masters offer "anti-bite" *yantras* that guard against dog, cat, snake and other animal bites. Other masters have specific tattoos for each. Among the Shan, there is an anti-insect bite tattoo consisting of dots tattooed on the hands and legs. Some masters claim that should an animal bite the wearer of such a tattoo, there will be no pain and no infection, and the animal will die within three days.

There are also anti-poison *yantras*, usually tattooed onto the tip of the tongue with oil rather than ink. Such designs neutralise poisons (especially those created by black magic) and also prevent dangerous objects from entering the mouth.

A completely separate category consists of *sat himaphaan* (Himalayan animals), perhaps the most dramatic-appearing of all *sak yan* designs. Rather than forming geometric shapes, these tattoos

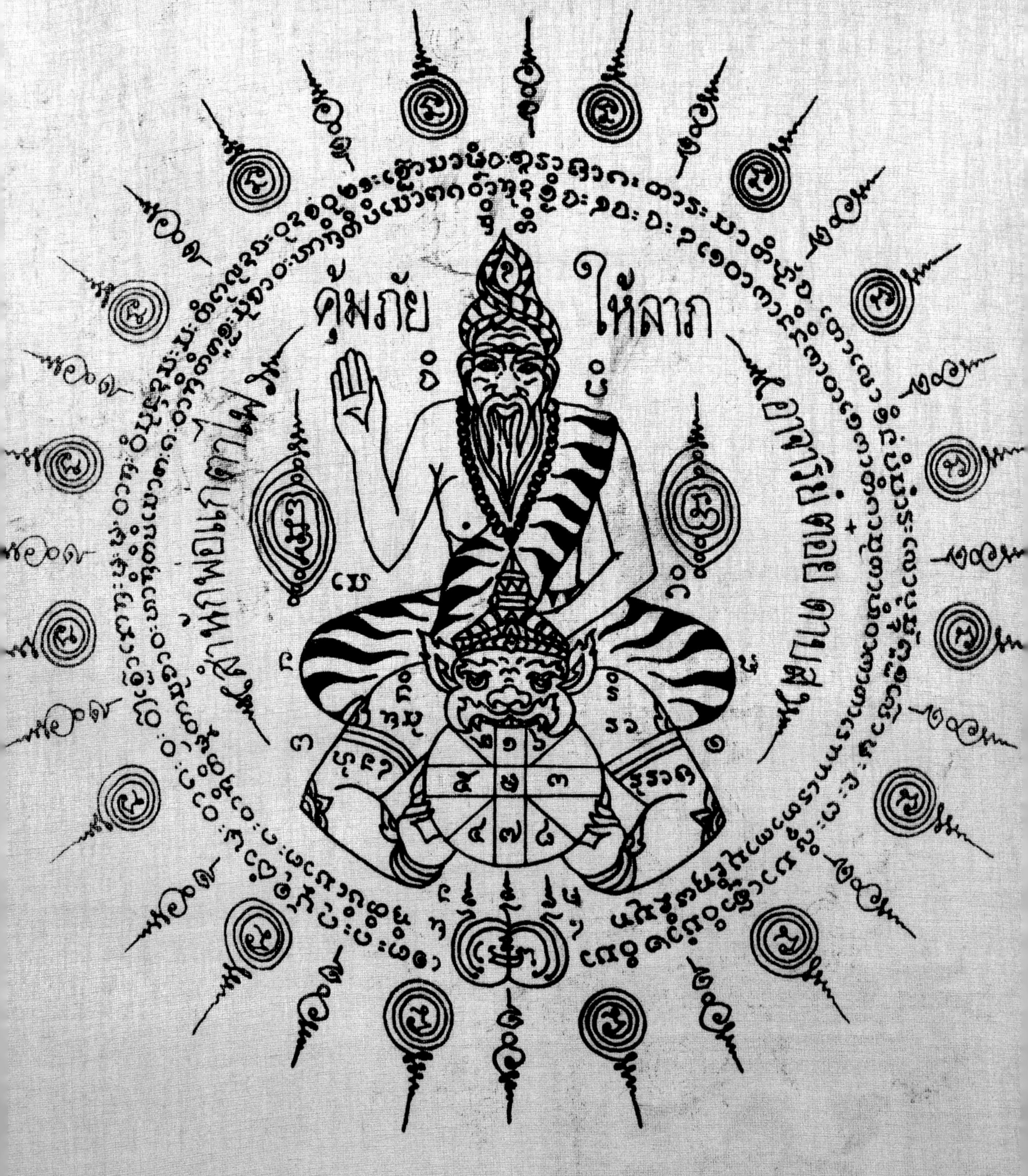
คุ้มภัย
ให้ลาภ

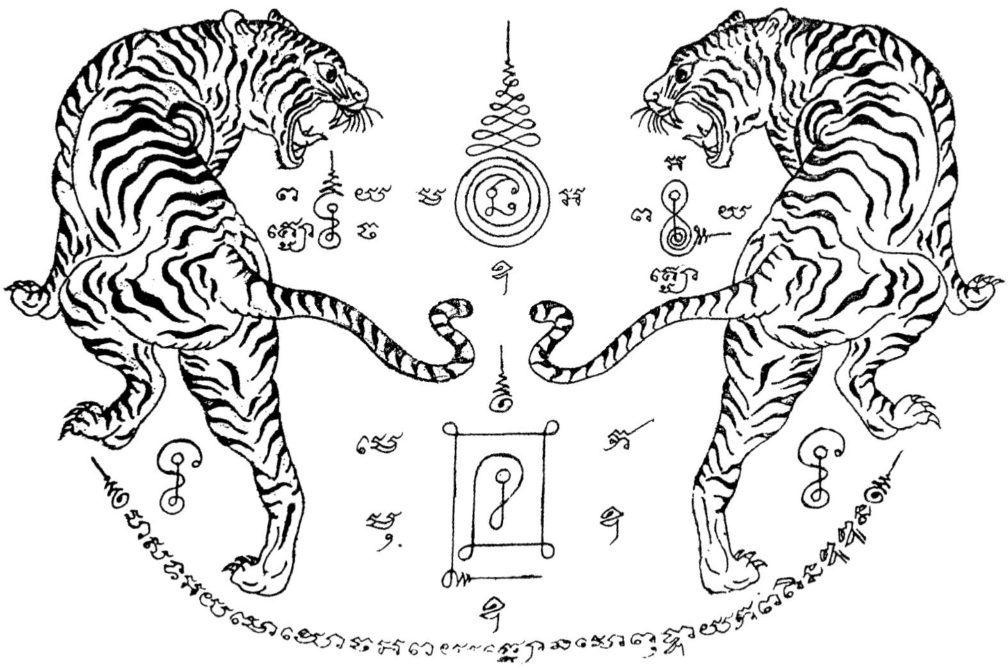

Left: Next page: *Phaa yan* from Ajahn Toy, Bangkok, reads "Control Danger, Bestow Good Fortune". The figure depicted is Pho Kae, the ancient hermit sage believed to have initiated the Tai *sak yan* tradition. Above: A twin tiger *yan*.

depict animals thought to reside in a forest in the Himalaya – not the geographical Himalayas but rather part of a divine realm called Jambudvipa, as described in early Indian literature. Some animals, such as the tiger or crocodile, represent animals known to our world, while others are mythical animals that resemble the lions, rhinos, tigers, deer, horses, elephants, birds, monkeys, but with physiographic twists. An example is the Loto, with looks like a lion except for its bird-like clawed feet. Other fantastical beasts may combine features of several different animals. Some creatures have been taken from the Indian epic Ramayana, while others appear to be solely of Tai provenance.

Other animal-based figures are deities borrowed from the Brahmanist pantheon, including Hanuman (the Hindu-Buddhist monkey deity), Ganesh (elephant-headed son of Shiva) and Indra (king of the deity pantheon).

Typically, the disciple takes on the positive qualities of the animal or deity selected. A tiger tattoo, for example, imparts courage and power. Ganesh enables the disciple to overcome obstacles in his path. Hanuman makes one strong, wily and agile. There are several different postures for each of these deities that emphasise one quality over another in the group.

Many *yantra* combine two or more of the above categories. The *paet thit* (eight directions) tattoo protects, brings good luck and evokes loving kindness. The *haa thaew* (five rows) *yantra* confers good luck, invincibility, power, evasion of mishaps, and loving kindness.

The five-Buddha *yantra (yan phra jao haa phra*

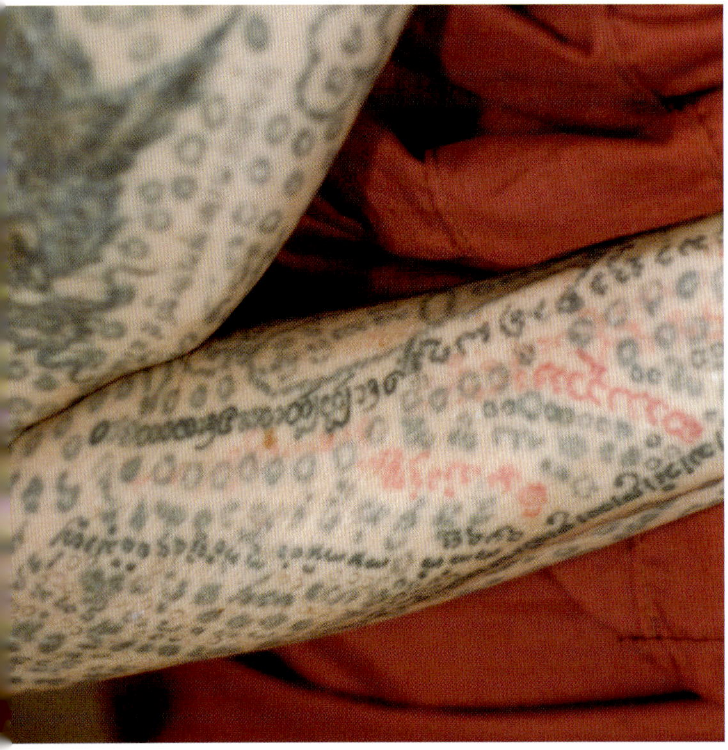

Above: *Akkhara* on the arm of Ajahn Pornsit.

ong) is often said to be the highest and most powerful *yantra* of all, especially for those seeking *metta mahaniyom* and *chok laap*. Only men can receive the tattoo, typically, and the number of rules to follow is usually greater than for other *yantras*. Among the Shan and Lao, the five-Buddha tattoo cannot be inked in a house but instead must be carried out on a special elevated platform built outdoors or in a temple compound.

A limited number of designs represent Pho Kae, the mythical forest sage believed to be the progenitor of the *sak yan* tradition. Pho Kae tattoos bolster intelligence, wisdom, craft and self-reliance. Another human-based figure is Chuchok, a pot-bellied old beggar believed to bring wealth and grant wishes.

A separate category of *yantra* is used to inscribe a blessing on the forehead of the disciple. Called *na naa thaung* (gold-face sigil), this *yantra* is never used for either ink or oil tattoos. Instead the master takes a stylus, rather than a needle, and gently inscribes the sigil on the forehead through a square piece of goldleaf – the same sort adhered to Buddha images for good luck. When the inscription is finished, a few gold flakes remain on the forehead, falling away after a few hours. *Na naa thaung* generally confer *metta mahaniyom* and are favoured by merchants and businesspeople who want to boost sales or gain customers.

TEXT AND NUMBERS

Akkhara (alphabetic letters) form part of every *yantra*, whether geometric, animal or human in shape. Spelt out to form *khaathaa*, they appear alongside, underneath or interwoven with the main lines of the *yantra*. Many *yantra* also contain *lehk* (numbers) that symbolise different qualities embodied in the design. Thus a more formal and complete word for *yan* (*yantra*) is *akkhara lehk yan* (syllables-numbers-design), emphasising the fact that all three aspects are combined together in many tattoo designs.

THE BODY SHIELD

A person tattooed with *sak yan* automatically becomes the disciple of the tattoo master, part of a power chain that functions within disciples wherever they go. Of course, this assumes that the tattoos were correctly applied, the master correctly followed the rituals and the disciple adheres to the restrictions prescribed by the master.

The patterns inked (or oiled) onto the skin thus become a dynamic boundary between the disciple's internal world and the world outside of himself. The *khaung* – the "stuff" – carried forward is not comprised of abstract, symbolic or metaphorical elements but is a sacred, metaphysical object, for which one's body is the container.

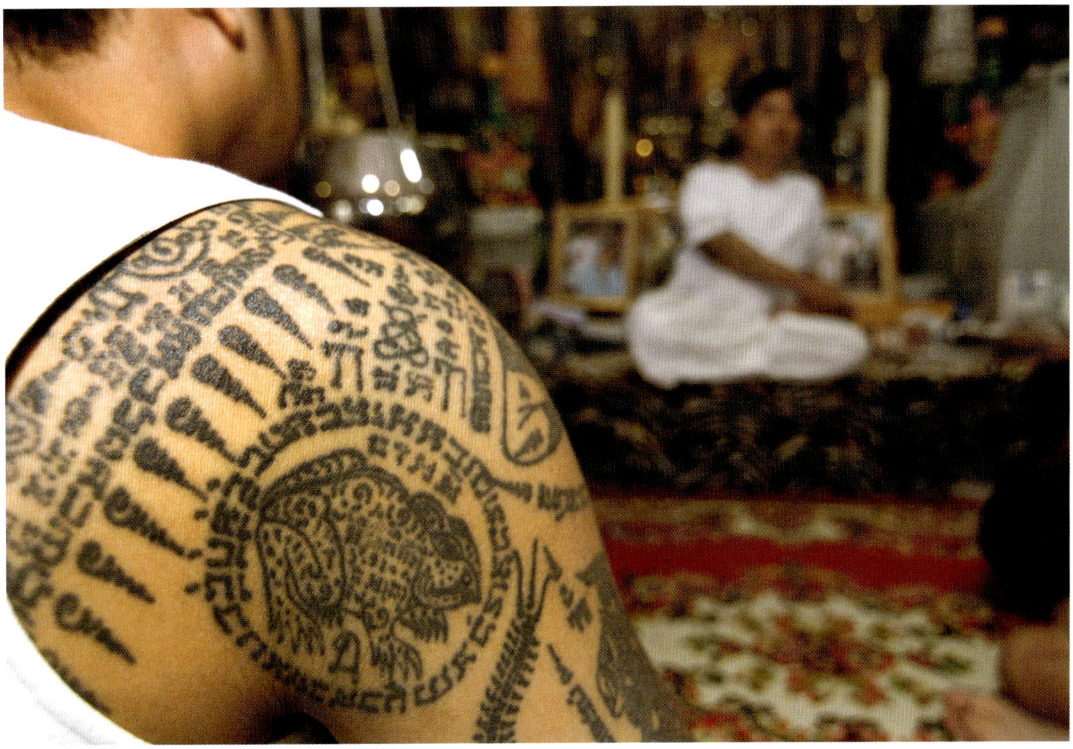

Above: *Samnak* of Ajahn Noo.

The discipline and restraint engendered by following the master's behavioural code – along with Buddhist precepts – forms yet another layer, albeit invisible to the eye, in the body. This layer functions in tandem with the visible *sak yan* layer, strengthening its functions. The better one keeps the precepts, and the more restraint he shows, the greater the disciple's power. With sufficient discipline one can even increase the power of the tattoos beyond the level originally provided by one's tattoo master.

From such a perspective, virtue is not its own reward, and the sacred tattoo is morally neutral. If a disciple uses the tattoos for good, he will receive good in return, and if he uses them for evil, evil will come back to him. Misuse of tattoos may result in accidents, grave illness or untimely death. The tattoos don't make the difference; the wearer does.

Although *sak yan* clearly have animistic origins, the reliance on *phuttthakhun* – Buddhist values – as a significant means to further empower the tattoos is an inescapable part of the tradition. Anyone who keeps the five main Buddhist precepts (refraining from killing, lying, stealing, intoxication and sexual misconduct) is virtually guaranteed to maintain the power transferred through his tattoos from the master. Among the most empowering practices for the *sak yan* disciple beyond the precepts are *vipassana* (insight) and *samathi* (one-pointed concentration) meditation.

Seen in this way, the *sak yan* tradition is not simply animism and Buddhism practised side by side, but rather an integrated system of magic in which neither can exist without the other.

Right: Ajahn Thong inks *akkhara* on the back of a disciple at his *samnak* in Thonburi.

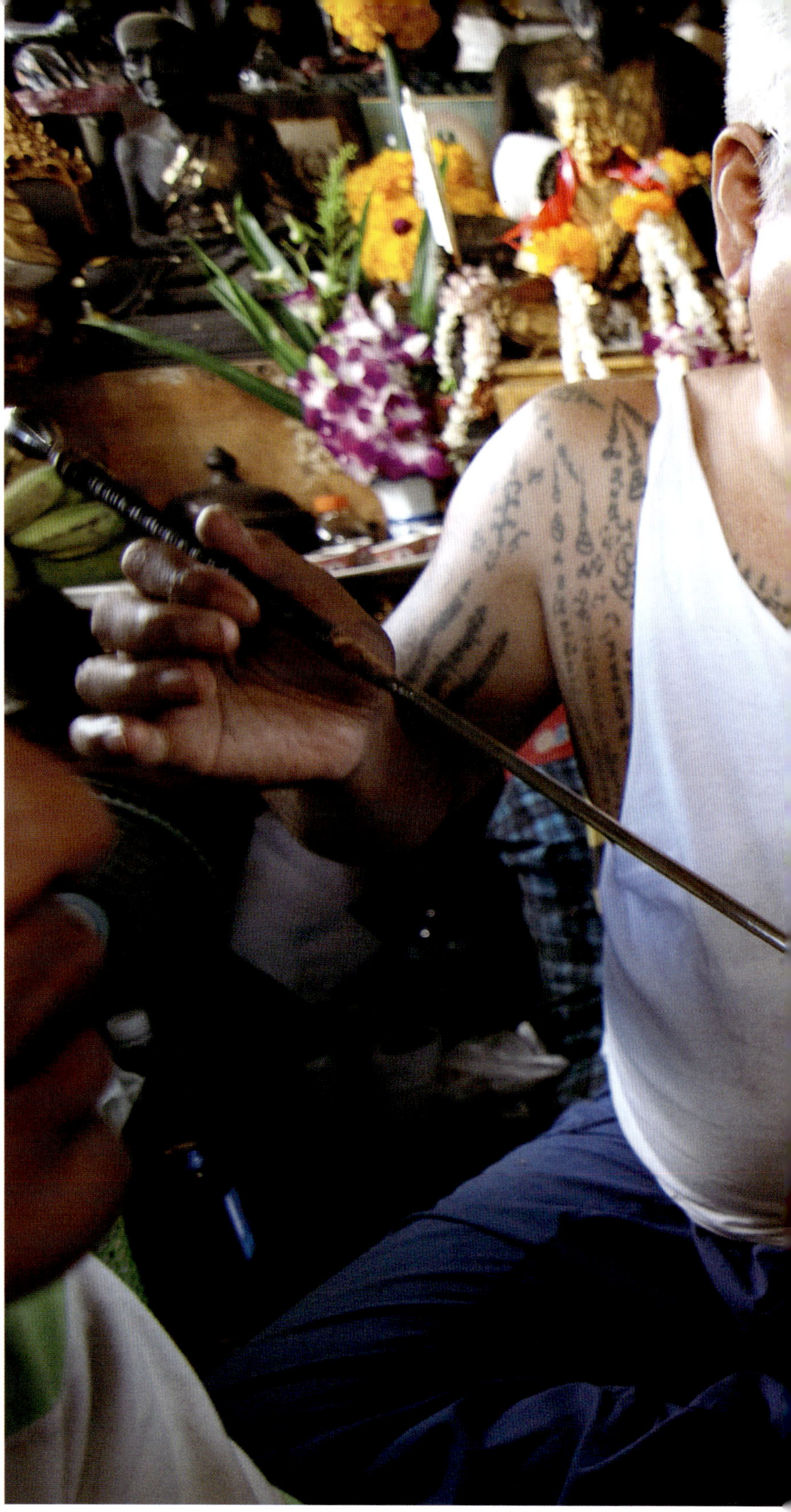

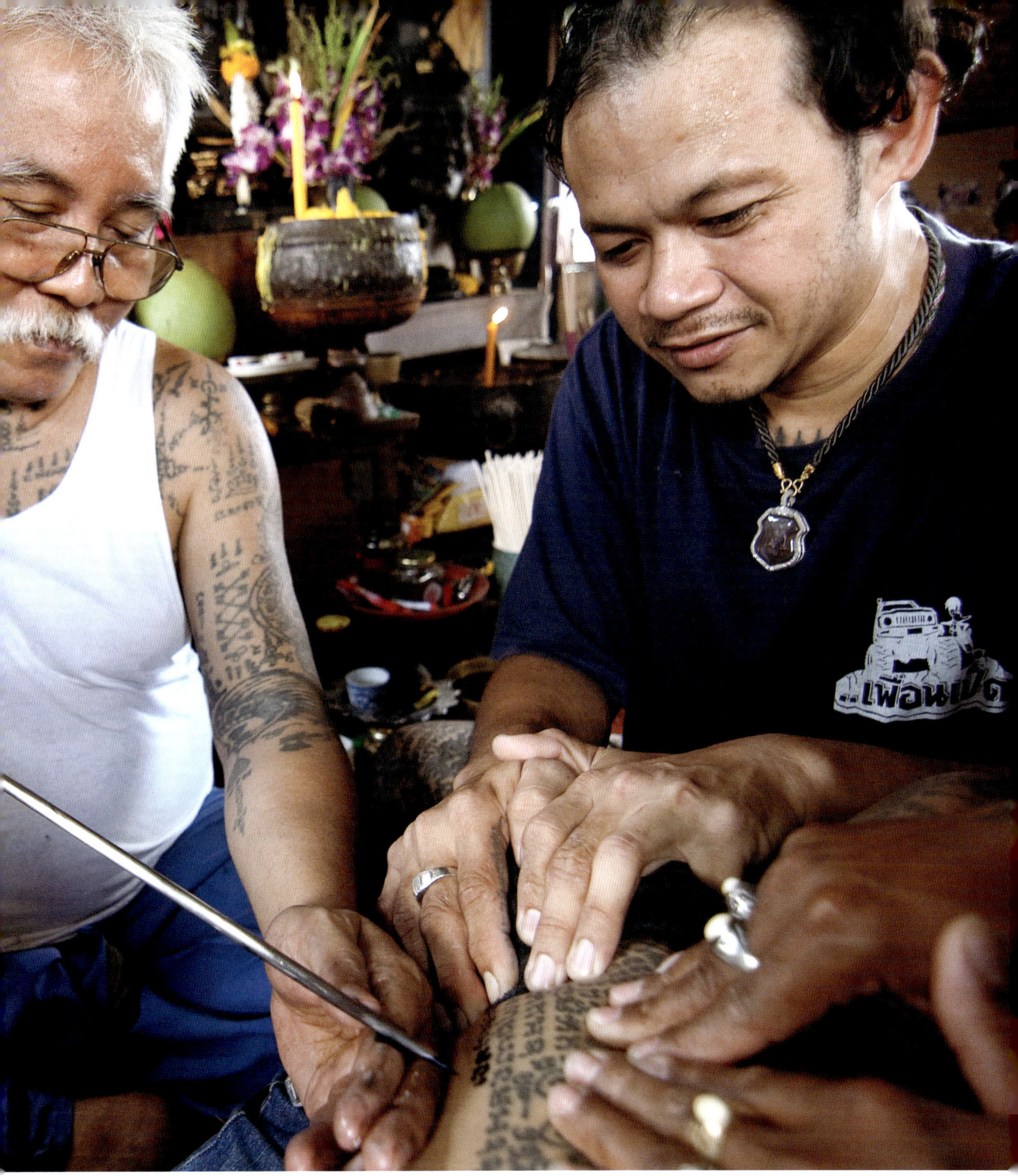

MASTERS OF THE ANCIENT CAPITAL: AYUTHAYA & THE LINEAGE OF LUANG PU NAI

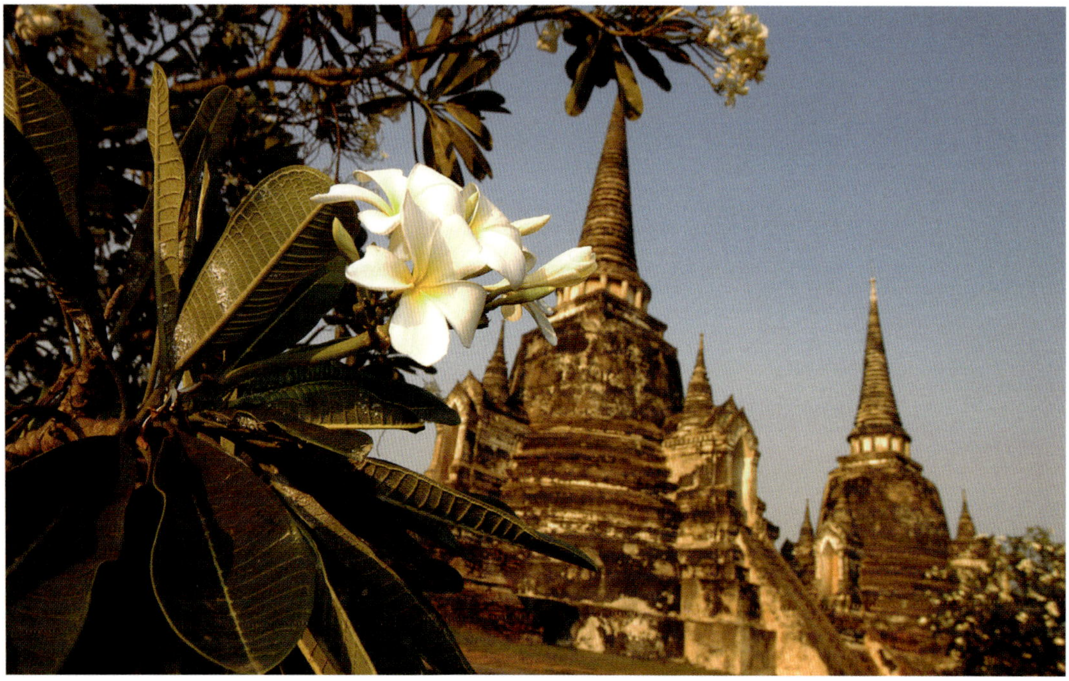

Above: Stupas in Ayuthaya Historical Park.

In 1350 a northwestern outpost of the Angkor Empire in what is today central Thailand (headquartered just 90 km north of present-day Bangkok), was overwhelmed by Thais, who created a new kingdom of their own. They called it Ayuthaya, and less than a century later, in 1431, Thai royal warriors entered and defeated the great capital of Angkor itself. Many Khmer officials, craftsmen and religious advisors from the Khmer royal court, along with Buddhist manuscripts and Buddhist art, were brought back to Ayuthaya. A wide variety of Khmer words became part of the Thai vocabulary, including the Khmer word for the Ayuthaya kingdom itself, 'Siam'. In addition, the Siamese adopted many Khmer customs, including Brahmanist ritual.

We don't know whether the Angkor civilisation had a sacred tattoo tradition (oft-repeated claims about Angkor court tattoos remain unsubstantiated), or if so, whether it influenced the existing Thai *sak yan* tradition at the time. But the once-prominent use of the Khmer alphabet for Buddhist scriptures quite likely influenced the use of that alphabet for *sak yan* in central Thailand.

What we do know is that Ayuthaya flourished

for over 400 years, seeing a line of 33 monarchs and an ever-expanding circle of influence, including trade with Dutch, Portuguese, French, English, Chinese and Japanese merchants. Ayuthaya's population reached one million by the end of the 17th century. Many foreign visitors claimed it to be the most illustrious city they had ever seen. But after the Burmese sacked Ayuthaya in 1782, the kingdom was semi-abandoned and the Siamese royal capital was moved to Bangkok.

Ayuthaya also maintains perhaps the oldest *khru sak yan* lineage, and today boasts the highest proportion of sacred tattoo masters of any city in Thailand.

Dwarfed in size by Bangkok today, Ayuthaya still maintains a reputation for tradition, craftsmanship and independence. The oldest martial arts school in Thailand, for example, is based here, not in Bangkok. Ayuthaya also maintains perhaps the oldest *khru sak yan* lineage, and today boasts the highest proportion of sacred tattoo masters of any city in Thailand.

First and foremost among these is the Luang Pu Suk lineage. Luang Pu Suk, whose official monastic name was Phra Kru Vimolkunakorn, was born in Chainat during the reign of King Rama IV. Ordained at the age of 25, he soon became a wandering *phra thudong* (a monk who takes an additional 13 ascetic vows, including not to sleep under a roof) who developed a special interest in *weechaa* (spiritual power/knowledge). Luang Pu Suk studied *sak yan* and other sacred arts from a variety of powerful teachers, including legendary Luang Pho Ngoen Phutthachot, abbot of Wat Wangtako (now known as Wat Bang Khlan) in Phichit. After he returned to his home town of Chainat, he became the abbot of Wat Pak Khlong Makham Tao. Luang Pu Suk became widely revered throughout Thailand for his spiritual power, including his high attainments in *vipassana* (insight) meditation as well as his skill in making Buddhist amulets, *sak yan* and *yantra* in general. One of his favourite students was Admiral Prince Abhakara Kiartivongse, Prince of Chumphon and founder of the Royal Thai Navy.

Luang Pu Nai was an ardent follower of Luang Pu Suk until the latter's death in 1934 at age 76. He continued his *weechaa* studies with Ajahn Yam Daeng, a close disciple of Luang Pu Suk. Luang Pu Nai eventually served as abbot of Wat Ban Jaeng in Ayuthaya, where he became a renowned expert at making traditional amulets and especially *takroot*, the cylindrical amulets that contain *yantras* inscribed on scrolled metal sheets. He was also adept at *sak yan*, and was especially praised for his *jingjok* (house gecko) designs, which he developed into single, couple and triad versions, effective for good fortune, loving kindness and personal charisma respectively.

Before the abbot of Wat Ban Jaeng passed away in 1987 at the age of 84, he passed his *weechaa* and his *khem sak* (tattoo needles) on to three of his disciples, all of whom assisted him faithfully at Wat Ban Jaeng: Ajahn Prawet, Ajahn Gop and Ajahn Pim. Ajahn Prawet and Ajahn Gop have stayed on in Ayuthaya as renowned *khru sak yan* in their own right, while Ajahn Pim, a monk, moved to Wat Bang Khlan in Phichit.

AJAHN PRAWET & AJAHN BOEM

One of three apprentices to whom Luang Pu Nai passed on the *sak yan* tradition, Ajahn Prawet worked alongside Luang Pu Nai at Wat Ban Jaeng, a countryside monastery in Ban Pahan, Ayuthaya, from 1974 until Luang Pu Nai's death in 1987. After his master's passing, Ajahn Prawet built his own

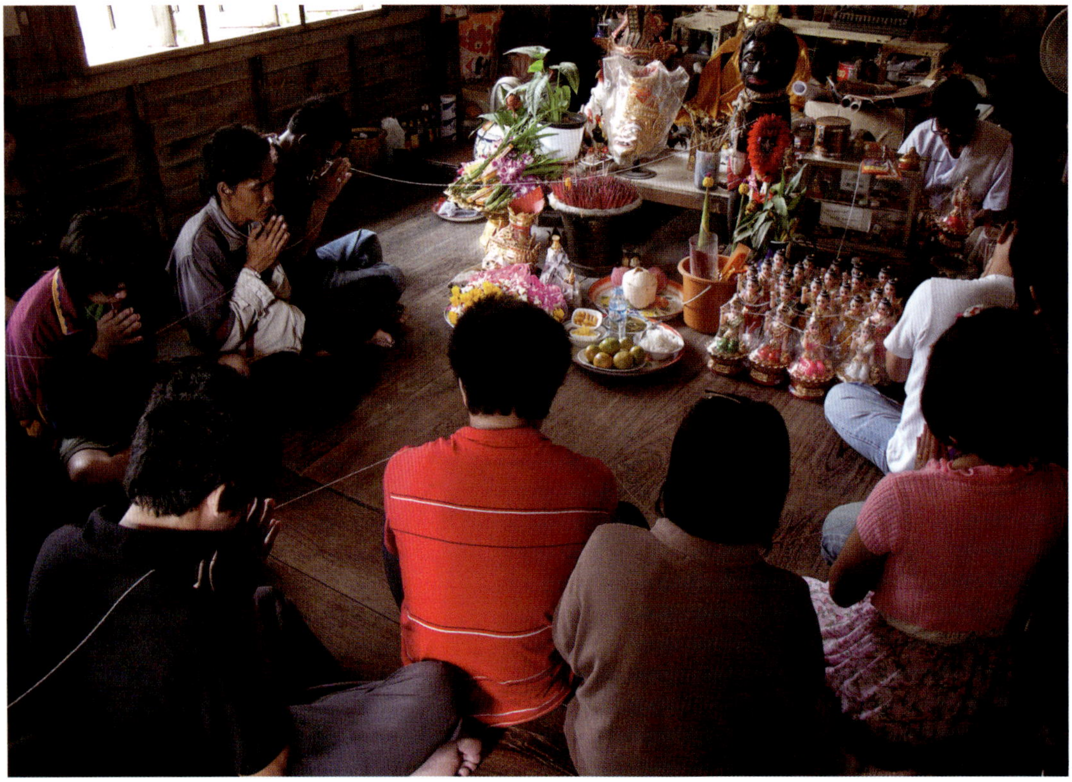

Above: *Wai khru* at the *samnak* of Ajahn Prawet.

samnak opposite one side of the monastery, where it remains today.

Ban Pahan is approximately 50km outside the provincial capital of Ayuthaya. After stopping for directions several times, we finally found Wat Ban Jaeng. It was a hot Thai summer afternoon, and the large monastery grounds appeared to be completely deserted, the resident monks presumably attending to duties elsewhere in the community. A separate shrine hall on the grounds contained a large bronze statue of Luang Pu Nai sitting in meditation pose.

On the opposite side of the two-lane road that ran alongside the monastery, a tiny wooden sign nailed to a fence pointed the way to Ajahn Prawet's *samnak*. The charming teakwood structure was raised high on stilts, with half of the floor sitting higher than the other half to accommodate a sizeable collection of statues depicting Buddha, Luang Pu Nai and Pho Kae, along with offering trays, sand-filled ceramic incense bowls and miscellaneous other ceremonial accoutrements. Slats in the upper walls ventilate the *samnak*, aided by a slowly spinning electric floor fan.

Almost completely filled with disciples seated on the floor, waiting their turn for *sak yan*, the room was charged with reverence and concentration. To one side of the altar, Ajahn Prawet's chief assistant, Ajahn Boem, was applying a Hanuman *sak yan* to the back of a muscled young Thai man. During the course of the day we watched as Ajahn Boem skilfully inked around a dozen disciples,

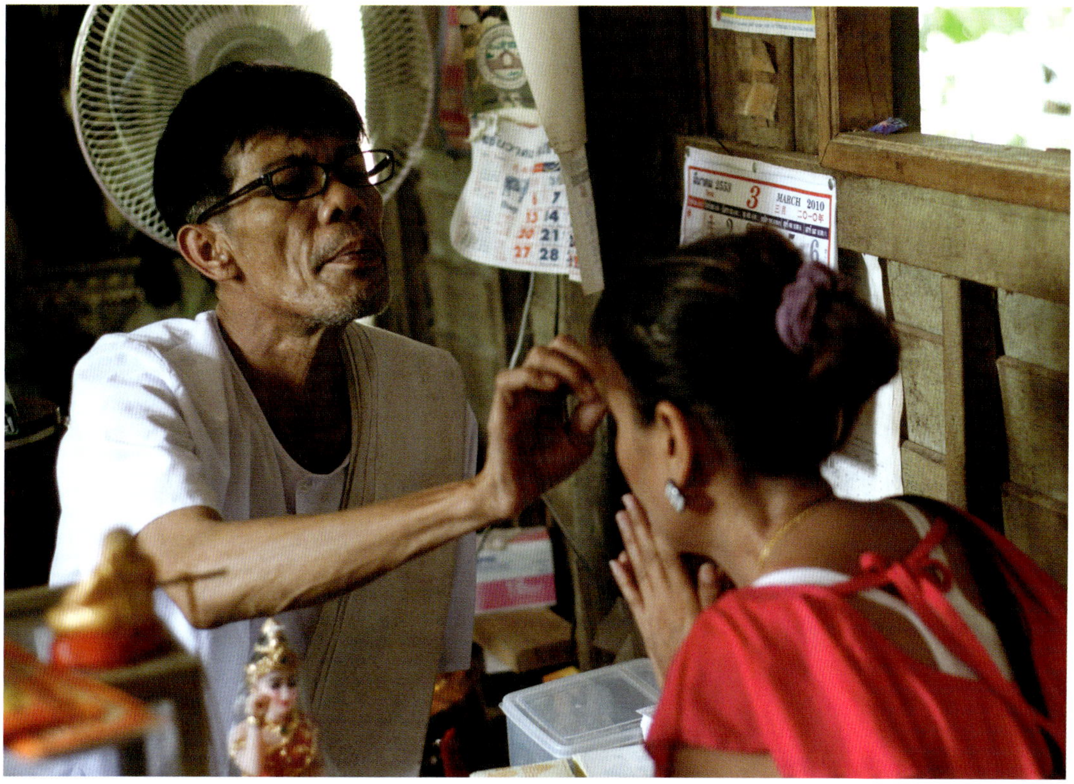

Above: Ajahn Prawet applies *na naa thaung* to the forehead of a disciple.

women as well as men. We paged through a book showing Ajahn Prawet's designs, most of them handed down from Luang Pu Nai. The work was very fine, among the best we'd seen anywhere. Tattoowork of the Luang Pu Nai lineage is characterised by delicate lines, which allows for a great amount of detail without designs coalescing into a dark mass.

As with Luang Pu Nai before them, Ajahn Prawet and Ajahn Boem are especially well known for *jingjok yantras*, of which they can produce myriad variations, for *mahasaneh* (personal charm or charisma). The tiger *yantras*, particularly the popular *seua phen* (leaping tiger) have an appealing vintage look about them.

Ajahn Prawet himself no longer handles the needle-and-ink tasks himself, but will *pluuk sehk* (confer sacred power) on disciples receiving tattoos from Ajahn Boem on request. He also makes himself available for consultations. During the day we spent with him, he received a group of disciples who had come to pay their respects by linking them with sacred white cotton thread, reciting Pali-Thai incantations and sprinkling the assemblage with *nam-mon* (holy water). The pair work every day except *wan phra* (Buddhist holy days fixed by the lunar cycle, occurring once every eight days), starting around 8am and sometimes continuing as late as midnight.

Like many tattoo masters, Ajahn Prawet is cautious when it comes to talking to outsiders about the *sak yan* tradition.

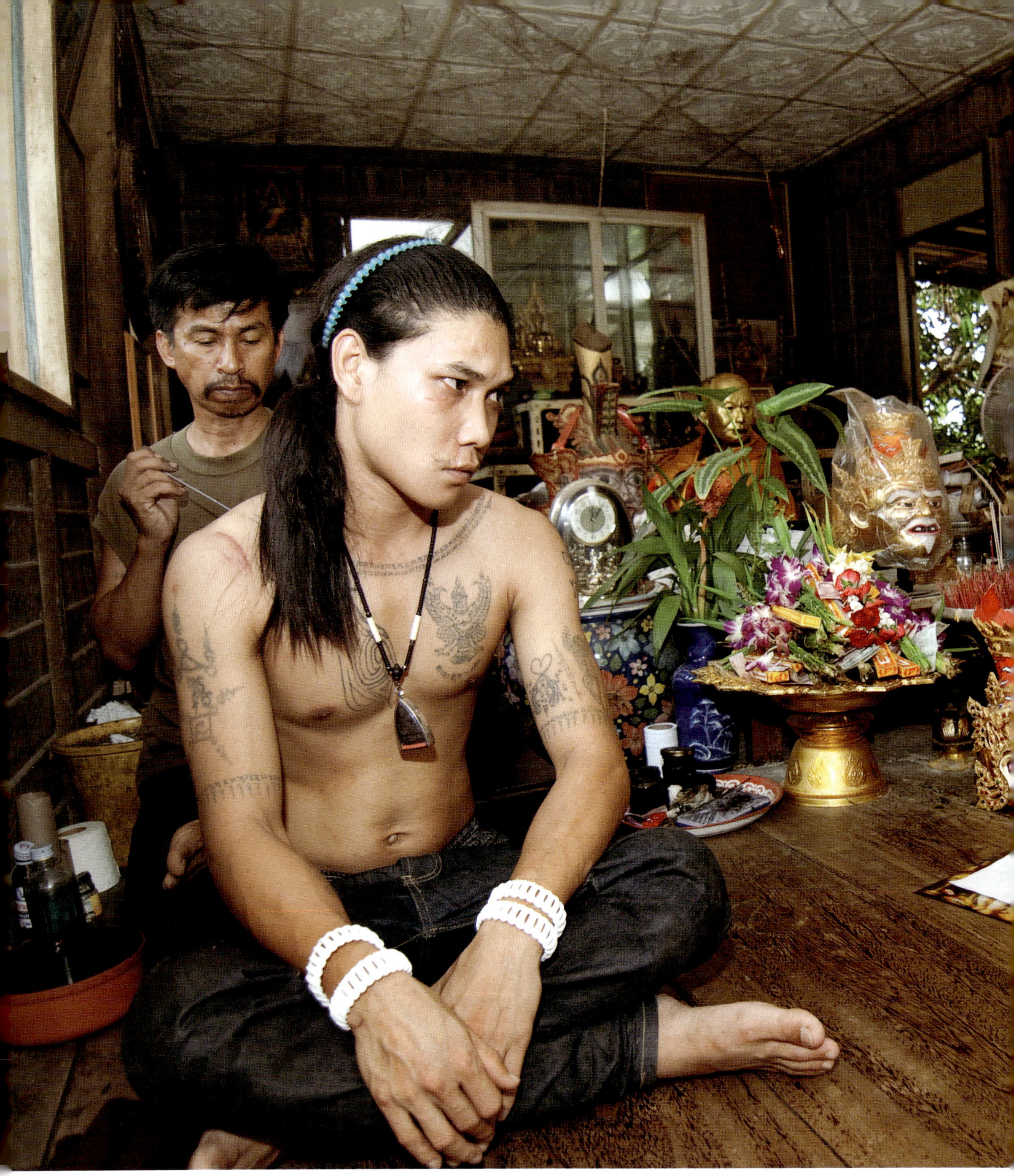

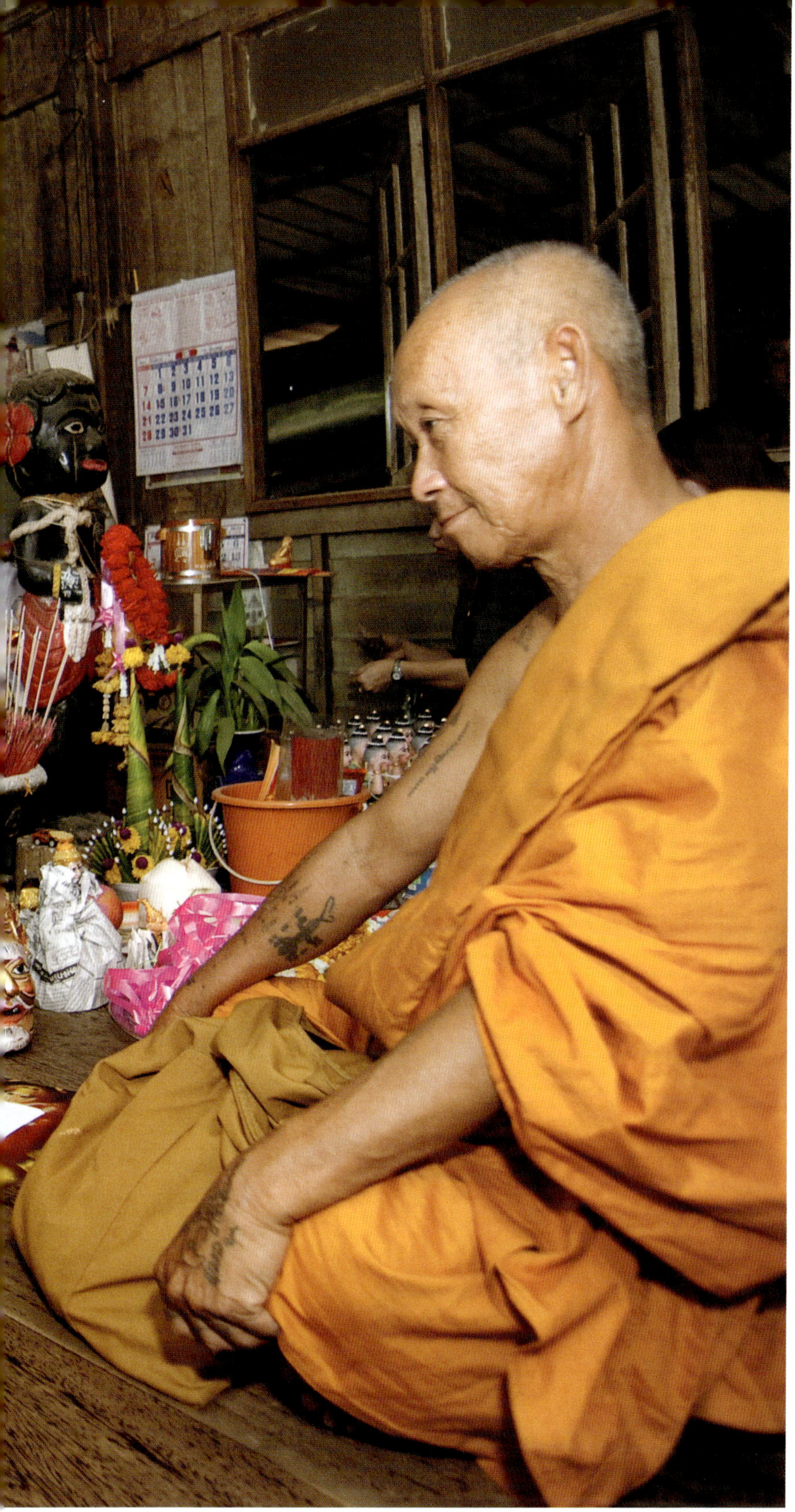

Left: At the *samnak* of Ajahn Prawet.

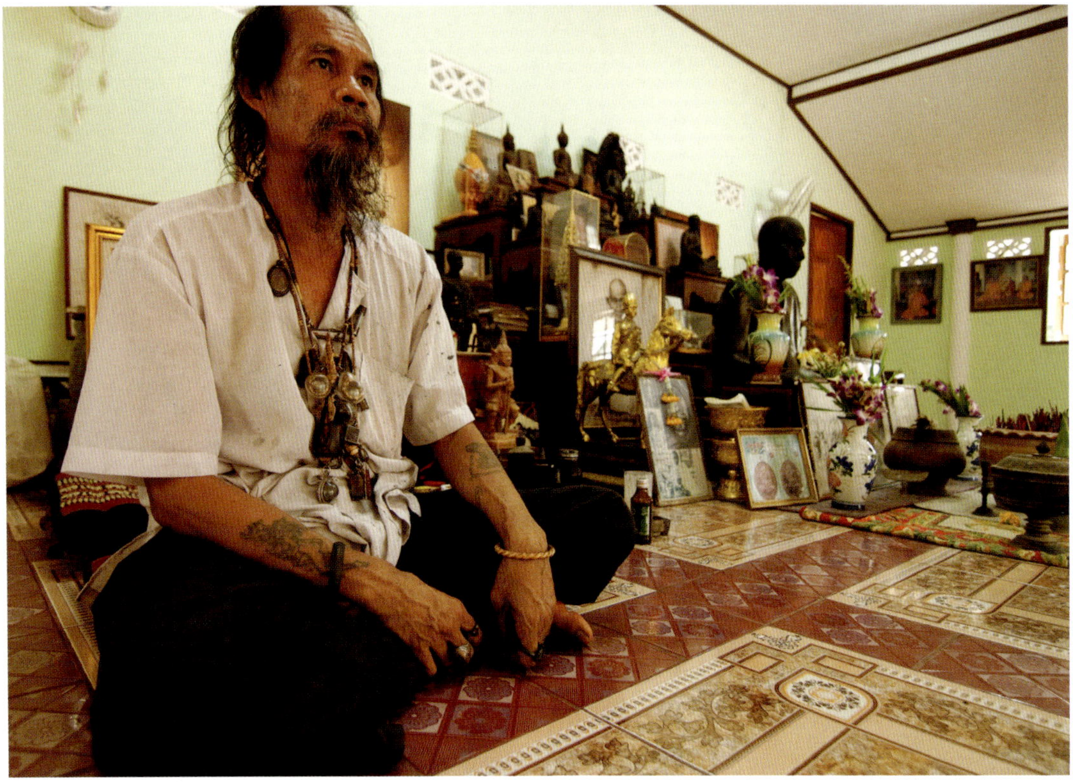

Above: Ajahn Gop. Right: Ajahn Gop uses relatively small needles to create the fine lines he is known for.

"You can't sell this," he told us, referring to the power and magic of *sak yan*. "It's our culture. It operates at the heart level, not the bank level. To get what *sak yan* has to offer, you must have faith, not money."

"People get shot and stabbed all the time. The tattoos protect only those who protect the tattoos. Eventually you're going to die, though. The tattoos don't stop nature. It can stop people and man-made things from hurting you, but not nature."

AJAHN GOP

My first visit to Ajahn Gop's *samnak* in Ayuthaya came about when, after hearing praise from several sources who had received fine-looking *sak yan* from him, I accompanied two American friends who wanted tattoos, and who asked me to translate for them. Situated at the edge of the provincial capital in Khlong Sa Bua, Ajahn Gop's sizeable *samnak* consisted of an open-air, wood-frame pavilion on stilts, with a palm-thatched roof. Ajahn Gop and his son were each busy inking disciples, while a handful of Thais were awaiting their turn. We watched as the son tattooed a rectangular *yantra* on the throat of a young Thai woman, just above her larynx. She lay on her back on the worn teak floor, hanging her head off the edge of the *chan* (raised deck where the altar was located and tattooing takes place) to allow access to her throat. Meanwhile, Ajahn Gop finished inking a form of Hanuman onto the back of a young male disciple. My friends Janette and Hayley thumbed

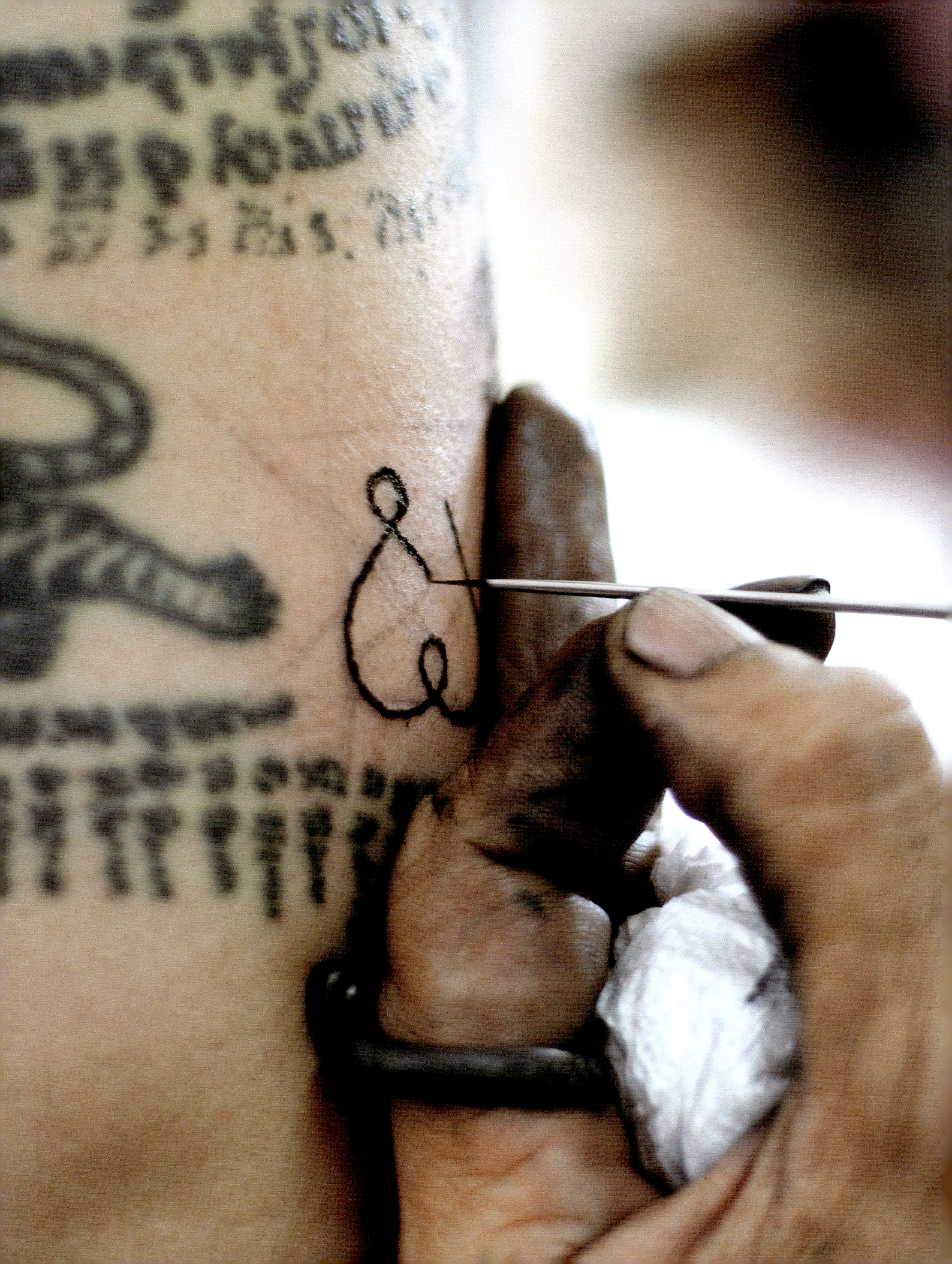

Right: A monk watches as Ajahn Gop applies a tattoo to a foreign visitor.

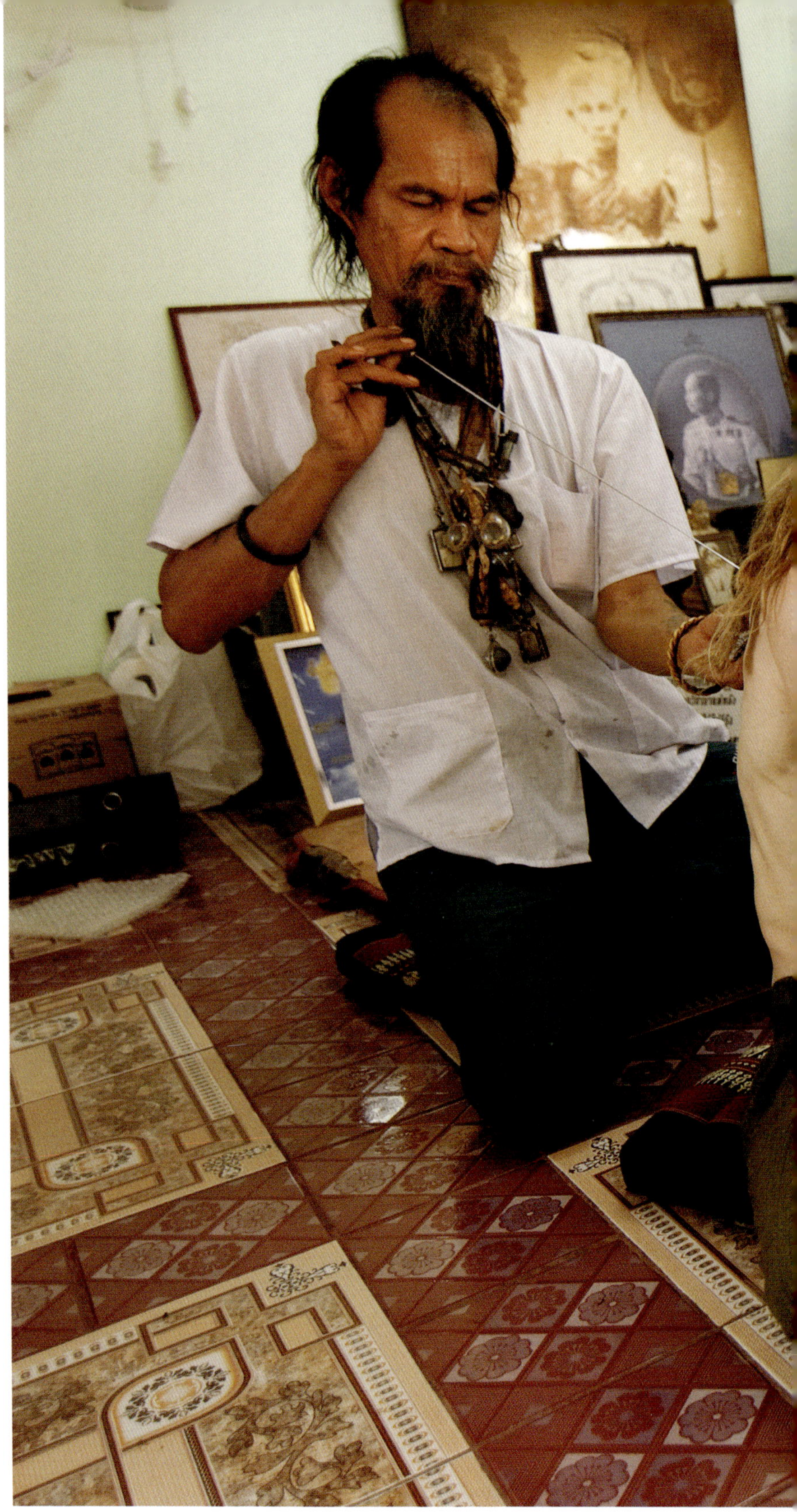

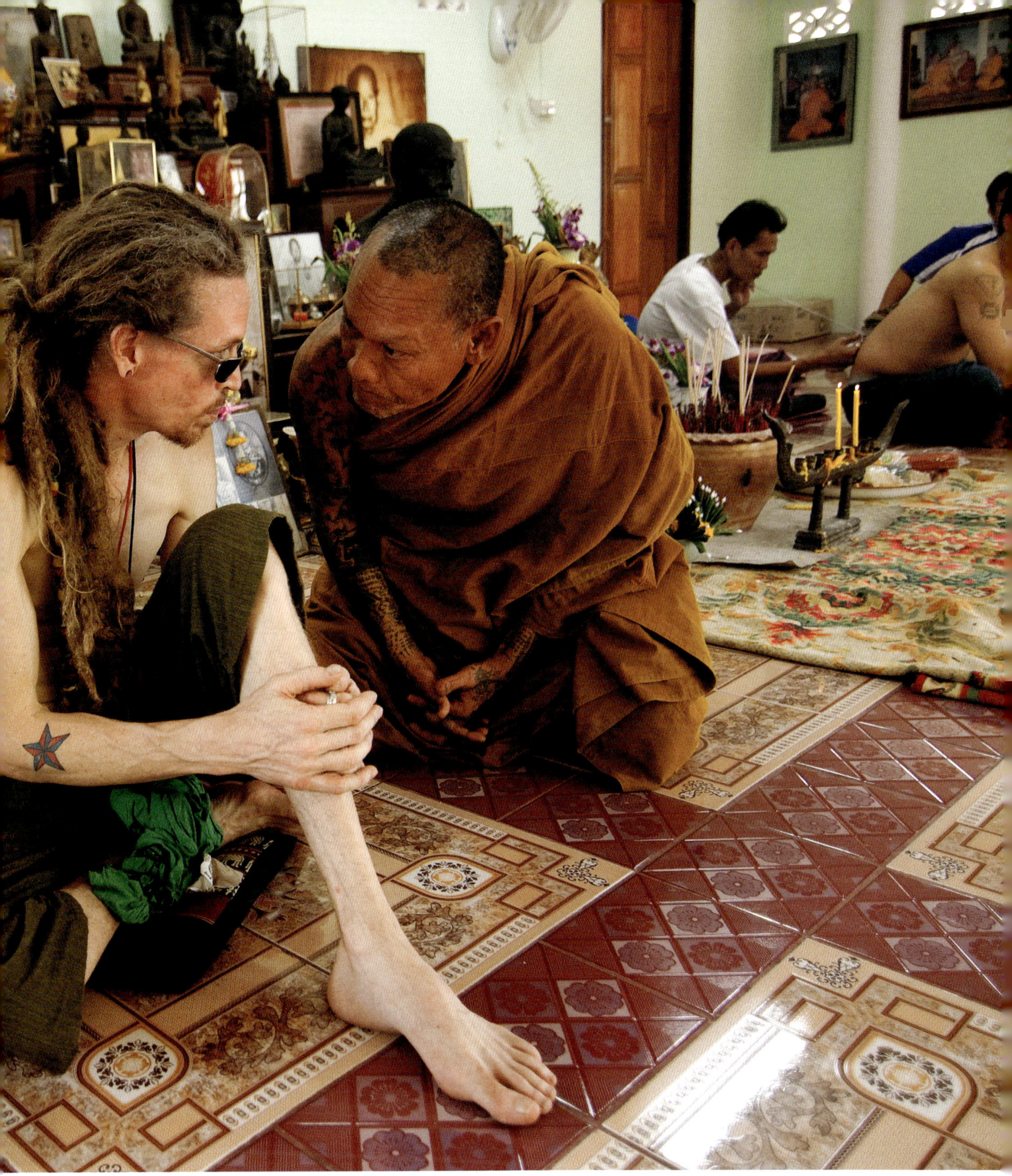

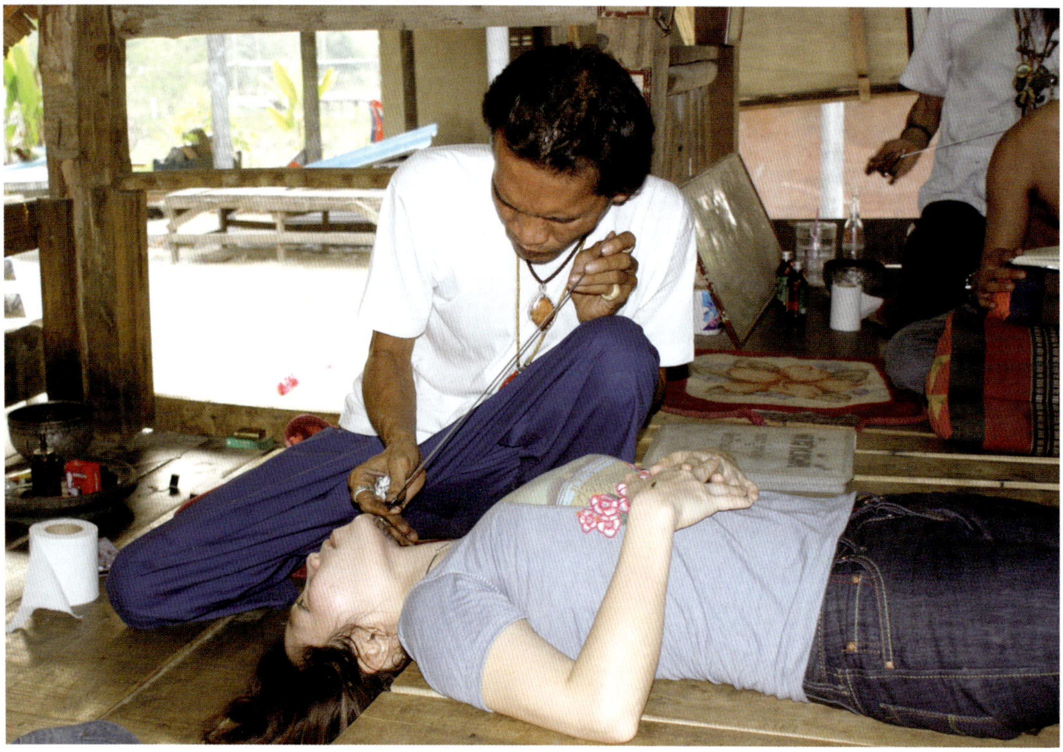

Above: Ajahn Gop's son inks a *yantra* on the underside of a woman's chin. The design chosen is believed to make one's voice more persuasive.

through *sak yan* pattern books, trying to decide what kind of designs they would like to receive. The air hung hot and heavy, and as I could tell it would be at least an hour or two before we'd be seen, I lay down and took a nap on the old teak floor.

When I awoke, the master was sharpening his *khem sak* (tattoo needle) on a whetstone, between inking disciples. He greeted me warmly and asked what my friends needed. I asked about the significance of Hanuman in designs, such as the one he had just finished inking. The smiling, relaxed figure dressed in white, with a wispy beard and tousled, thinning hair answered our questions directly and easily, avoiding any superlative claims.

"We have many Hanuman. Most are for *khong krapan* (warding off attacks), a few are for *amnaat* (power). It varies not only according to posture, but according to the *akkhara* [inscription]."

When asked about tigers, Ajahn Gop smiled. "I don't do tigers. They're too hot. All of the *sat himaphaan* (mythical Himalayan animals) are strong. They require special preparation and special care or they can drive a disciple mad."

For most tattoos, a simple offering of incense, candles and flowers is sufficient, but for Himalayan animal designs Ajahn Gop asks his disciples to prepare a more elaborate offering consisting of a cooked pig's head, boiled egg, boiled chicken, whisky, young coconut, bananas (other fruits may be substituted, except for mangosteen, rambeh and sapodilla, which are forbidden), a slice of *kha-*

nom chan (a nine-layered "good luck" cake for weddings, containing peanuts and candied pomelo peel), *khanom tom khao* (sticky rice and coconut confection), *khanom tom daeng*, (same as *khanom tom khao*, but bathed in raw sugar syrup), all piled onto a large pedestal tray.

"Having to put together this offering requires thought and preparation, which gives the disciple time to think, to take the tattoo seriously. And afterwards, hopefully, they'll protect the power through keeping Buddhaguna (Buddhist virtues)."

His eyes widen, and his smile broadens. "Because if there's one thing more powerful than the tattoos, it's the power of the mind."

By the time of my most recent visit with photographer Dan White, the charming old wood-and-bamboo *samnak* had been torn down and replaced by a larger, two-storey concrete building. Ajahn Gop and his son work on the spacious second floor. With an insulated roof and tile floor, it makes a cooler and more comfortable environment for them and their disciples. It was a slow day in terms of

Admiral & Magician

Among the many lay disciples of legendary Luang Pu Suk was one of royal blood, Abhakara Kiartivongse, Prince of Chumphon and 28th child of King Rama IV. Also known to the Thais as Krom Luang Chumphon Khetudomsak, the Prince studied naval warfare in England, and when he returned to Siam he reorganised and modernised the fledgling Royal Siamese Navy to the point that today he is referred to as "Father of the Royal Thai Navy". He was also well known for his interest in *saiyasaat* (magic sciences), and spent much of his spare time visiting and learning from monks and lay masters around Siam.

Sak yan were said to cover virtually every part of the Prince's body save for his face and hands. Legend says he personally tested the avowed properties of *sak yan* using both blades and bullets. The Prince was particularly impressed with Luang Pu Suk, who taught both *weechaa* and *dhamma* (Buddhist philosophy) at great depth to the young man, and tattooed him several times. The prince also mastered Thai herbal medicine, and became known as "Doctor Phon" among the many patients he treated. He died in 1923 at the age of 44. Statues and frescoes of the prince can be found today at Wat Pak Khlong Makham Tao, the Chainat temple where Luang Pu Suk was abbot. Many Thais, particularly those in the armed forces, pay homage to the prince's spirit. There is an array of amulets bearing his likeness on one side and clusters of *yantras* on the other.

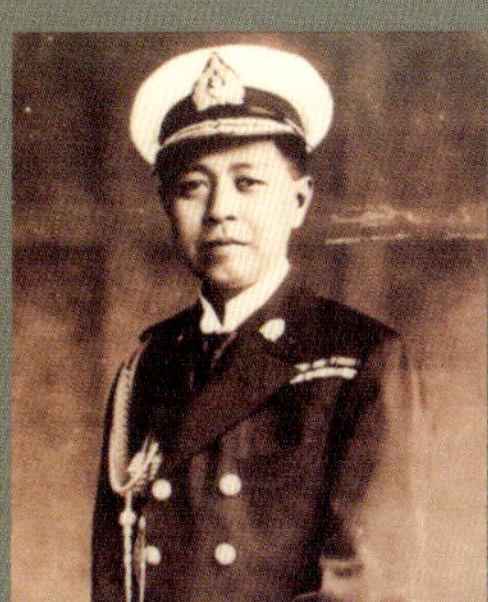

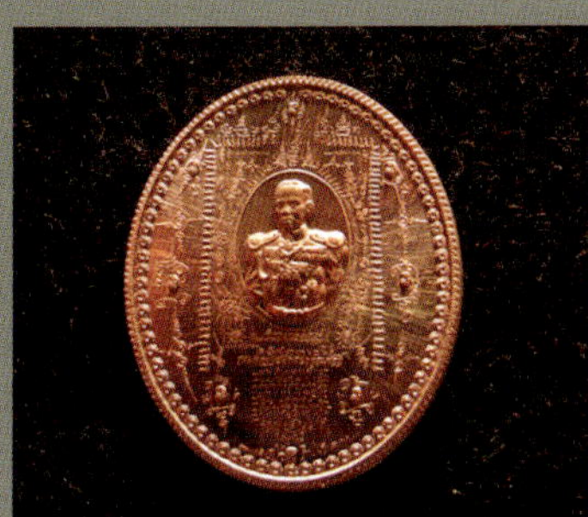

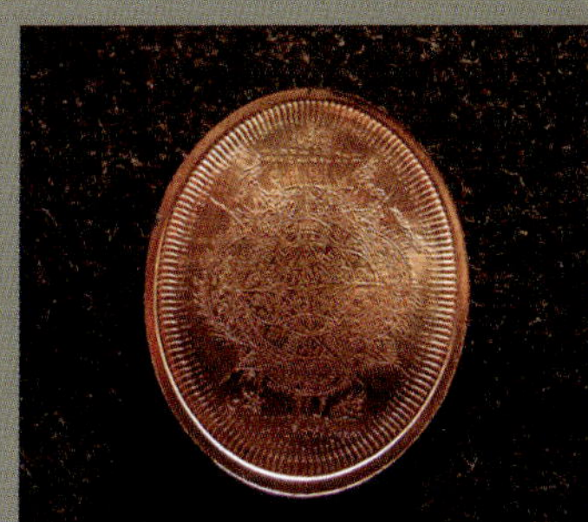

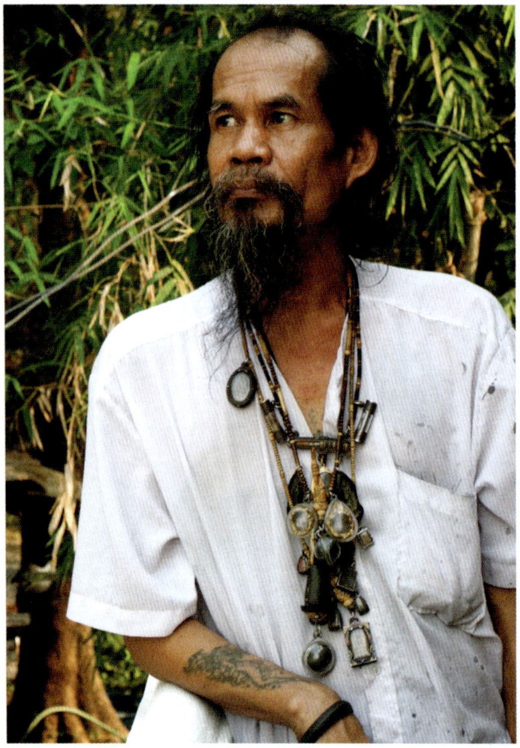

Above: Ajahn Gop.

visiting disciples, so Ajahn Gop generously and patiently sat for a long conversation about *sak yan*.

"I've been doing this work for 36 years now. I was Luang Pu Nai's nephew, born here in Ayuthaya. I didn't much care for *weechaa* and *sak yan* when I was a teenager. I knew you had to study *khaum* (Khmer script) first, and it looked so difficult. By the time I was 20 years old, though, I could see the value, and Luang Pu Nai invited me to train with him at Wat Ban Jaeng. At first it was like being in school, lots of study. I learnt *weechaa* as a layperson, but after a while I went away to ordain as a monk for three months in Sadao [on the Thai-Malaysian border] because it was a quiet place to practise meditation.

"You not only have to study the *khaathaa* and learn the *yantras*, you have to learn to meditate to develop concentration and power. You have to be steady in this business. You can't drink liquor either, ever, or your hands may shake.

"I worked alongside Luang Pu Nai at Wat Ban Jaeng until he died in 1988. After that, I left the temple and opened a *samnak* here. Most Thais coming here want the same *sak yan* that Luang Pu Nai made famous: the *kao yaut* (nine peaks) and *jingjok* (house gecko), which Luang Pu Nai himself learnt from his teacher Luang Pu Suk. Luang Pho Poen [see The Tiger Lineage chapter] is famous for tigers; we're famous for house geckos," he chuckled gently. "I don't specify what their first *sak yan* should be. A *kao yaut* takes 40 to 50 minutes and some people can't take it. So maybe they'll ask for something small like a *jingjok* their first time."

He admitted to adding one of his own to the repertoire: *jingjok song khreuang* (complex/fancy house lizard), a highly stylised gecko so bristling with energy lines that it almost resembles a caterpillar. I asked what it meant, and with a glint in his eyes, he replied, "Extra special personal charisma."

Like the work of Luang Pu Nai's more senior disciple, Ajahn Prawet, the work of Ajahn Gop emphasises fine, delicate lines – perhaps even finer than those of Ajahn Prawet. Ajahn Gop's *mai sak* (needle shafts) are among the smallest and lightest we've handled, and he wields them with a light touch. This means less pain for the disciples, some of whom claim that tattoo ticks from Ajahn Gop feel like "falling raindrops." We never saw a single drop of blood on any of the disciples receiving tattoos from Ajahn Gop while we were there.

Ajahn Gop uses plain black ink, usually German-made Rotring Drawing Ink, which is designed for isograph pens, drafting and detailed graphics. According to Ajahn Gop, the older generation of *khru sak* would add the sap, leaves, root or bark of *waan* (an all-purpose term for plants with medicinal/magical properties, especially wild ginger). to their ink.

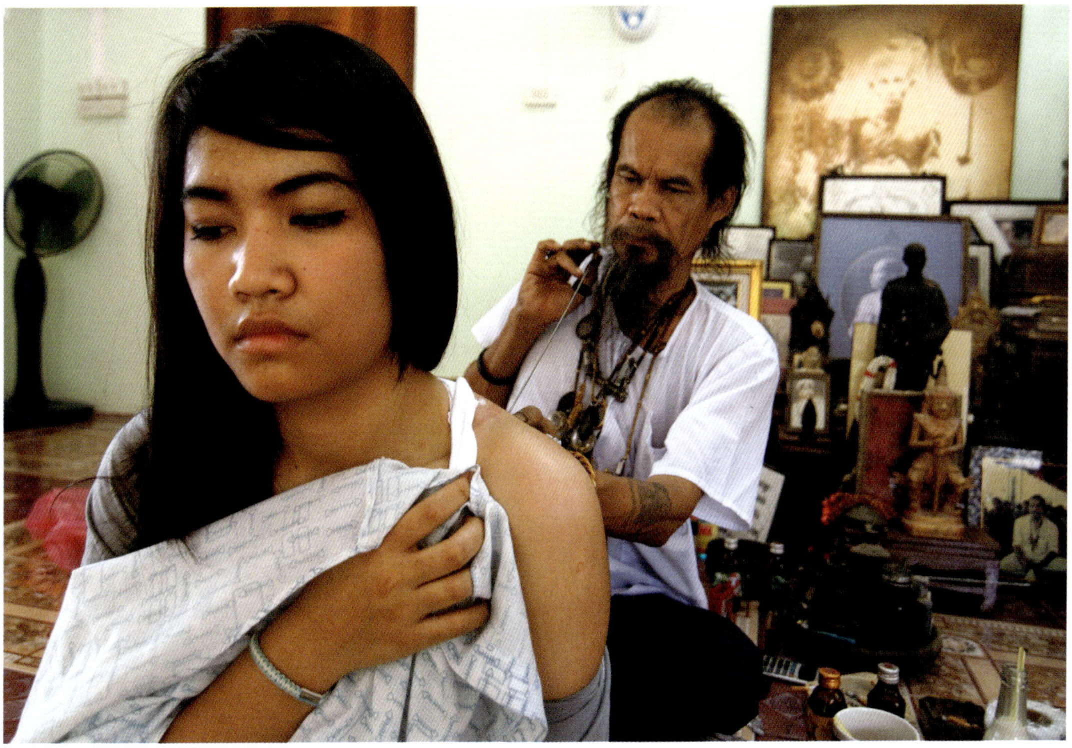

Above: Ajahn Gop and a female disciple.

"Luang Pu Nai gave me two bottles of *meuk sehk* [consecrated ink, presumably containing *waan*], and I mix one drop together with about 40 bottles of commercial ink." Asked whether the supply will run out, Ajahn Gop replied, "I've tattooed an average of five people a day since he passed away in 1988, and there's still plenty left."

On his days off (Wednesdays and Buddhist holy days), he carves beautiful three-dimensional miniatures of Pho Kae, Luang Pu Nai and Luang Pu Suk from ivory or water buffalo horn, to sell to disciples and visitors. They are meant to be worn with mantra beads around the neck.

Most of his disciples come from other provinces outside Ayuthaya. The previous week 10 Thais had driven all the way from Mae Hong Son to receive tattoos. "I won't tattoo anyone under 20 years old, or anyone who drinks to excess. Most of my disciples are in their 30s, 40s and 50s. Keeping the five Buddhist precepts is the minimum basis for maintaining power, and not cursing your parents or your master is also required. Some disciples follow the correct way, but it's impossible for them all to do so.

"Practically every *khru sak* nowadays copies designs from Luang Pu Nai. You meet 30-year-olds who claim they are direct Luang Pu Nai disciples, which is impossible since they were born after he died. They can't decipher the Khmer *akkhara*, they don't know what they mean. They just have the pattern, but not the *khaung* ("stuff" – the consecrated power), so their followers go through the pain of the needle, and get no result."

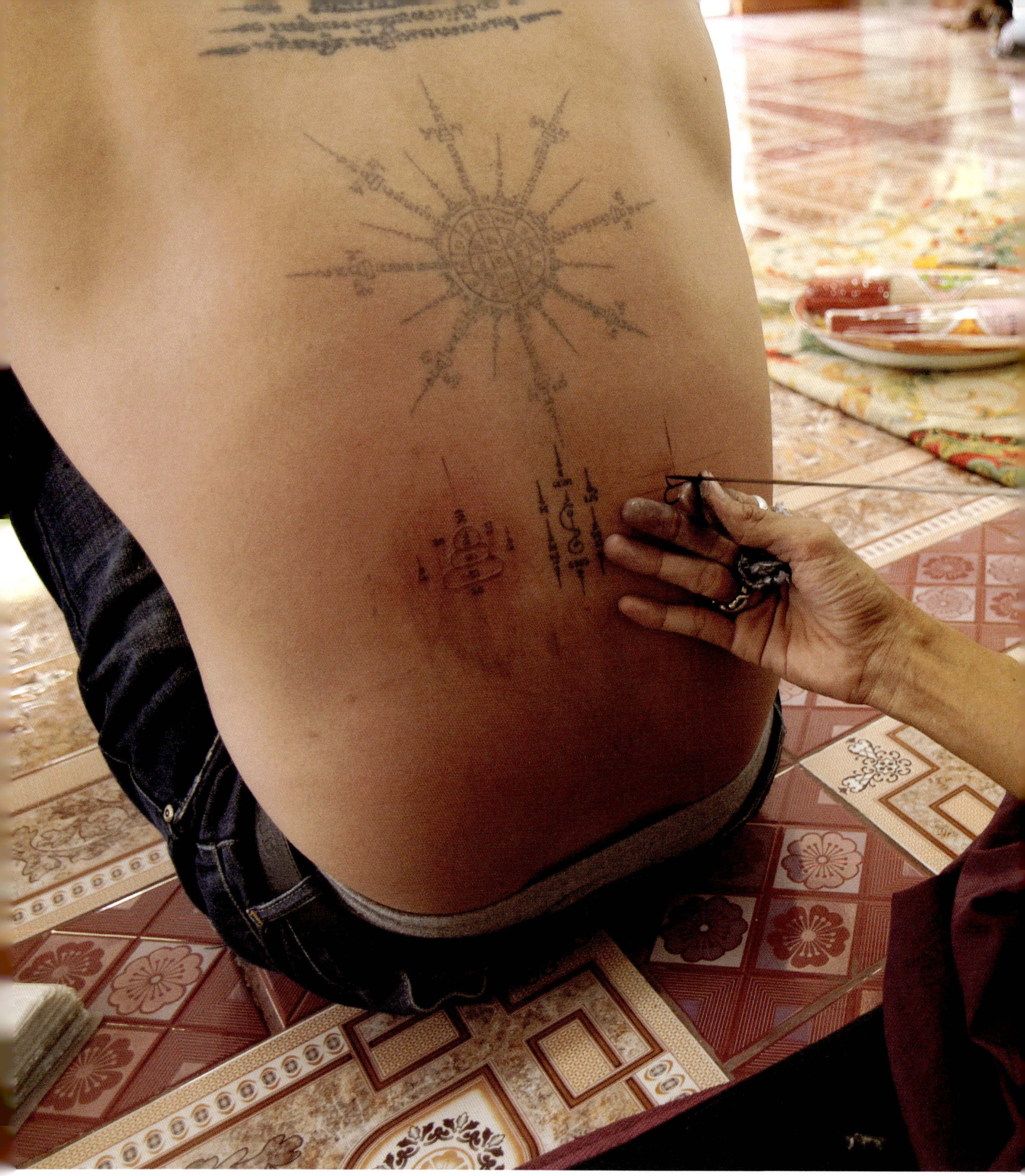

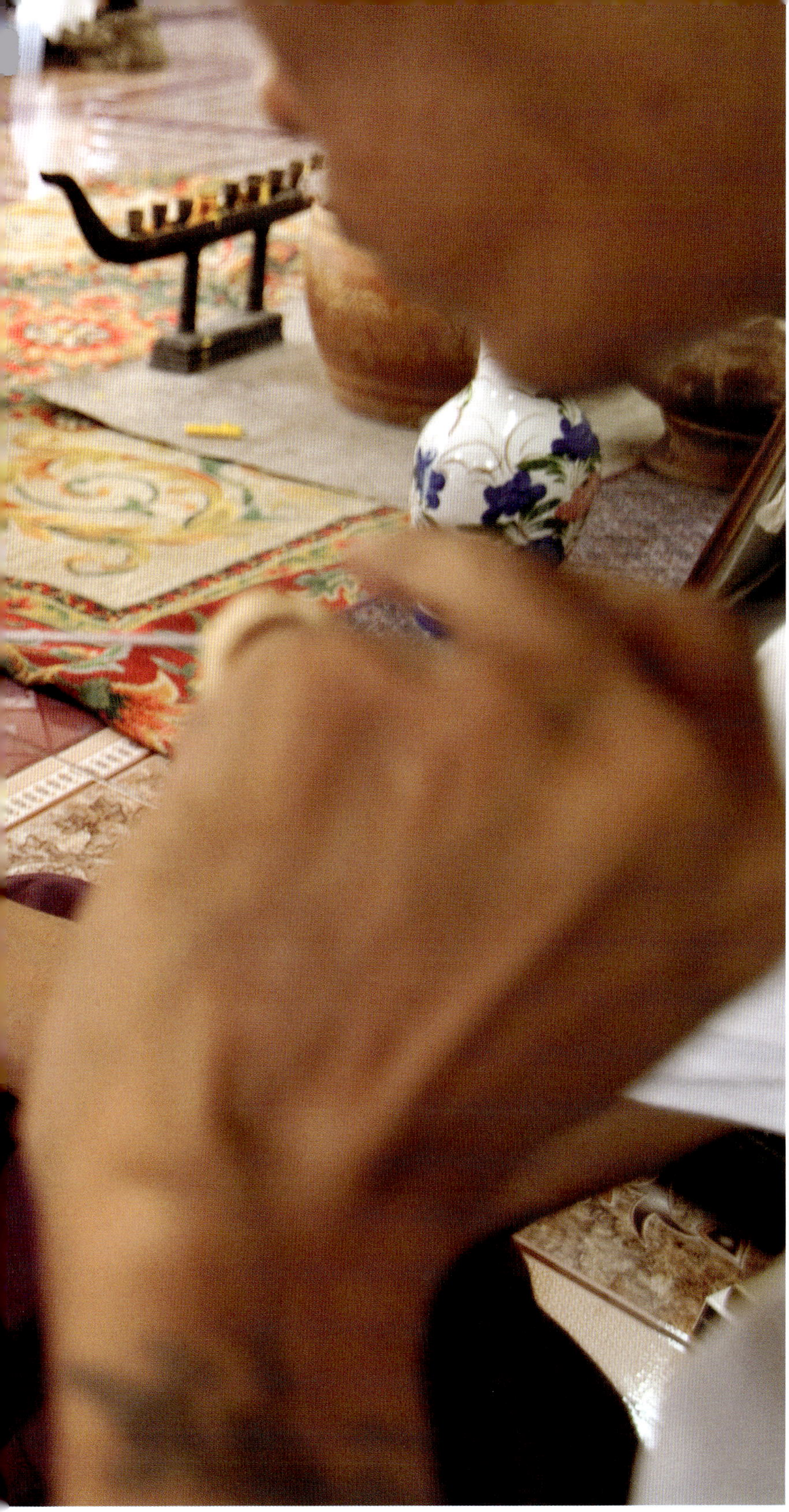

Left: Adding a trio of *yantra* selected for protection (left and right) and compassion (middle).

RIDING THE TIGER: THE LINEAGE OF LUANG PHO POEN

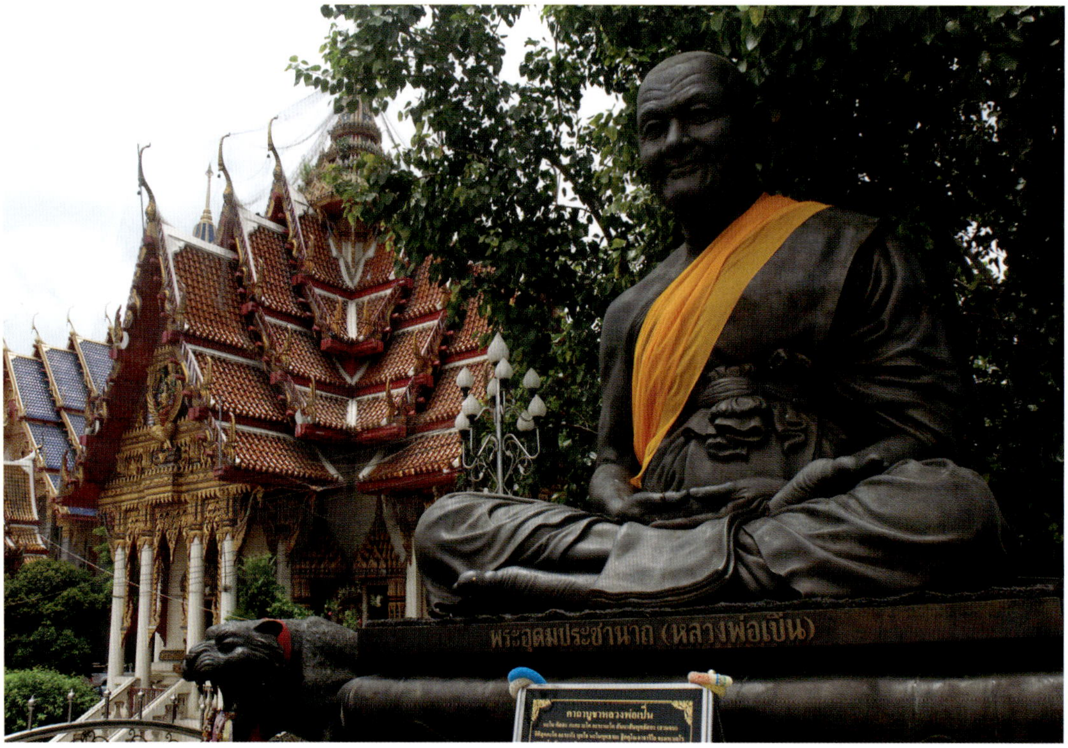

Above: A huge black statue of Luang Pho Poen stands in front of Wat Bang Phra, Nakhon Chaisi.

On the banks of the Nakhon Chaisi River in Nakhon Pathom Province stands a Buddhist monastery that dates to the late 18th century, just before the second fall of Ayuthaya. Inside a small, elegant ordination chapel, the only significant remains of the original wat, sit two Buddha images, Luang Pho Sit Chaiyamongkon and Luang Pho Kai Sitmongkhon. According to legend, they were being transported downriver from Ayuthaya to save them from plundering Burmese troops when the boat carrying them capsized. When the images were later pulled from the river, they were kept in the monastery that came to be known as Wat Bang Phra (Monastery of the Buddha Riverbank Settlement).

The monastery might have been just another country wat with a fading history were it not for the later fame of abbot Phra Udom Prachanart, more commonly known as Luang Pho Poen, the most widely respected *khru sak yan* of the 20th century. Born in Ban Kaew Fa adjacent to Wat Bang Phra in 1923, Poen showed a keen interest in *weechaa* and *khaathaa* from a young age. When his family moved to nearby Suphanburi, the young man seized the chance to further his studies in these subjects, along with meditation and Pali, under Luang Pho Daeng at Wat Thung Kok. Luang Pho Daeng was considered one of the most accomplished *weechaa* masters Thailand had ever known, and any amulets, *phaa yan* or other sacred objects infused with his magic are highly collectable today.

After serving two years in the Royal Thai Army, Poen ordained as a monk at Wat Bang Phra at the age of 25 and continued his studies with abbot Luang Pu Him Inthasoto. Luang Pu Him was an accomplished *sak yan* master, and even though Poen had never been tattooed himself (and never would be), he took up the sacred art at Luang Pu Him's feet. When Luang Pu Him died four years later, Poen – by this time known as Luang Pho Poen – carried on the *sak yan* tradition.

In 1953, feeling he needed further withdrawal, renunciation and solitary meditation, Luang Pho Poen undertook *thudong* (*dhutanga* in Pali), a set of extra ascetic vows beyond the normal 227 monastic precepts. These include sleeping in the forest, eating only one meal a day and forgoing all vehicular transport. His travels on foot took him west to a remote area of Kanchanaburi Province on the Myanmar-Thailand border.

At the time, villagers in the area were beleaguered by wild tigers that had mauled or killed several locals. After Luang Pho Poen arrived in their midst and learned of the villagers' predicament, he offered *khaathaa* and *sak yan* to protect them. From that point forward, no one who received the monk's protection was ever attacked by a tiger or other wild animal, earning Luang Pho Poen a powerful reputation as a master of incantations and tattoos.

After many years away from home, during which he helped villagers renovate abandoned monasteries in Kanchanaburi and Nakhon Pathom, Luang Pho Poen returned to Wat Bang Phra. He was made abbot in 1974 and, aside from passing *weechaa* on to younger resident monks, the abbot busied himself with improving the welfare of local residents. He used temple donations to build a bridge over the adjacent river so that farmers could more easily bring their crops to market in Nakhon Chaisi or beyond, and constructed the local public hospital that today bears his name.

From that point forward, no one who received the monk's protection was ever attacked by a tiger or other wild animal, earning Luang Pho Poen a powerful reputation as a master of incantations and tattoos.

As his reputation for wisdom and loving kindness grew, thousands of Thais travelled to Wat Bang Phra to receive the blessings of the great monk and to become his lifelong disciples. Many received *sak yan* from the abbot and the monks he assiduously trained. By the time Luang Pho Poen passed away in 2002 at the age of 79, he had become one of Thailand's most well-known and beloved monastics. Because of Luang Pho Poen's association with the border tiger legend, devotional images of the late monk today often depict him meditating on the back of a tiger.

Today Wat Bang Phra maintains a pre-eminent position in Thailand for its long *sak yan* tradition. Not every monk living at the monastery is trained in the ancient art, including the current abbot, Luang Pho Sam Ang, who is skilled in *khaathaa* only. Currently five resident monks, along with the occasional assistance of visiting white-clothed lay masters, work tirelessly to ink increasing numbers of disciples.

On weekends it's not unusual for a hundred or more visitors to receive tattoos. During the monas-

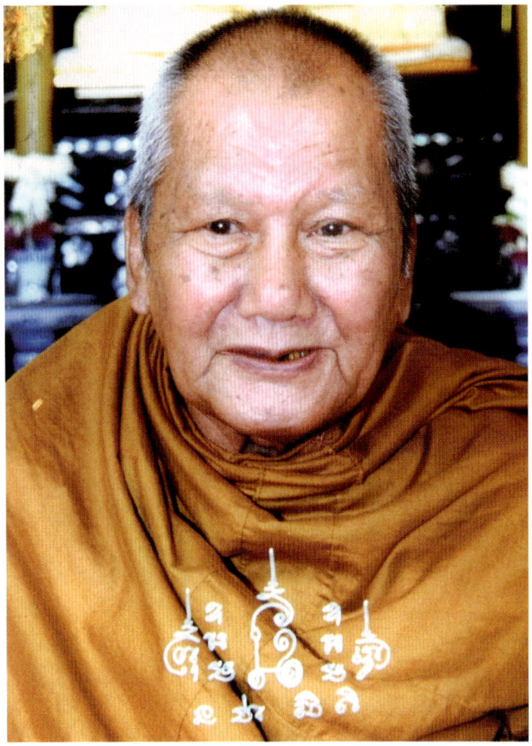

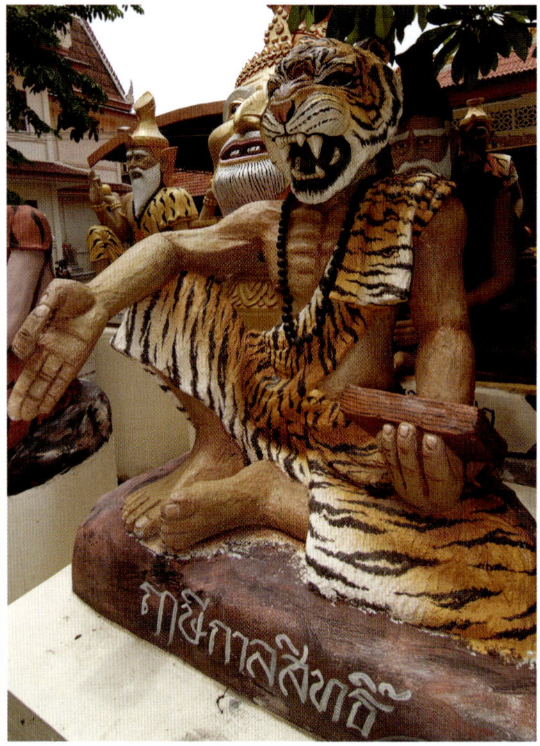

Above: The late Luang Pho Poen. Above right: Statue of a tiger-headed *reusee* at Wat Bang Phra.

tery's annual *wai khru*, when disciples return to pay respect to their masters, re-new the spiritual power of their *sak yan*, and receive additional tattoos, the number of supplicants approaches a thousand.

Not surprisingly, considering Luang Pho Poen's history, one of the most favoured *sak yan* at Wat Bang Phra is the *seua phen* (leaping tiger) tattoo. The design and its accompanying *khaathaa* are believed to impart great power, and to protect the wearer from black magic and from physical attack by one's enemies.

Before a disciple can receive any other *yantra*, an initiatory *yan khru* (master *yantra*) is required in the form of *kao yaut* (nine peaks), inscribed at the nape of the neck or high up between the shoulder blades. The design and accompanying *akkhara* confer a broad spectrum of blessings on the disciple, including good fortune, loving kindness, success in one's career and affinity for Buddhist virtue. For some Wat Bang Phra disciples, this will be the only tattoo they ever receive or ever desire.

For those who continue with additional *sak yan*, the recommended follow-up is *paet thit* (eight directions), a large compass-shaped design placed below the *kao yaut* and believed to offer protection from evil forces coming from any direction. After the master-disciple relationship has sufficiently deepened, different *sak yan* may be added as needed, after a short discussion about one's life circumstances. The monastery has no *yantra* catalogues for disciples to pick from.

Most of the *khru sak yan* at Wat Bang Phra rely on rubber stamps for complex designs such as Hanuman, tigers and Pho Kae. The master stamps the

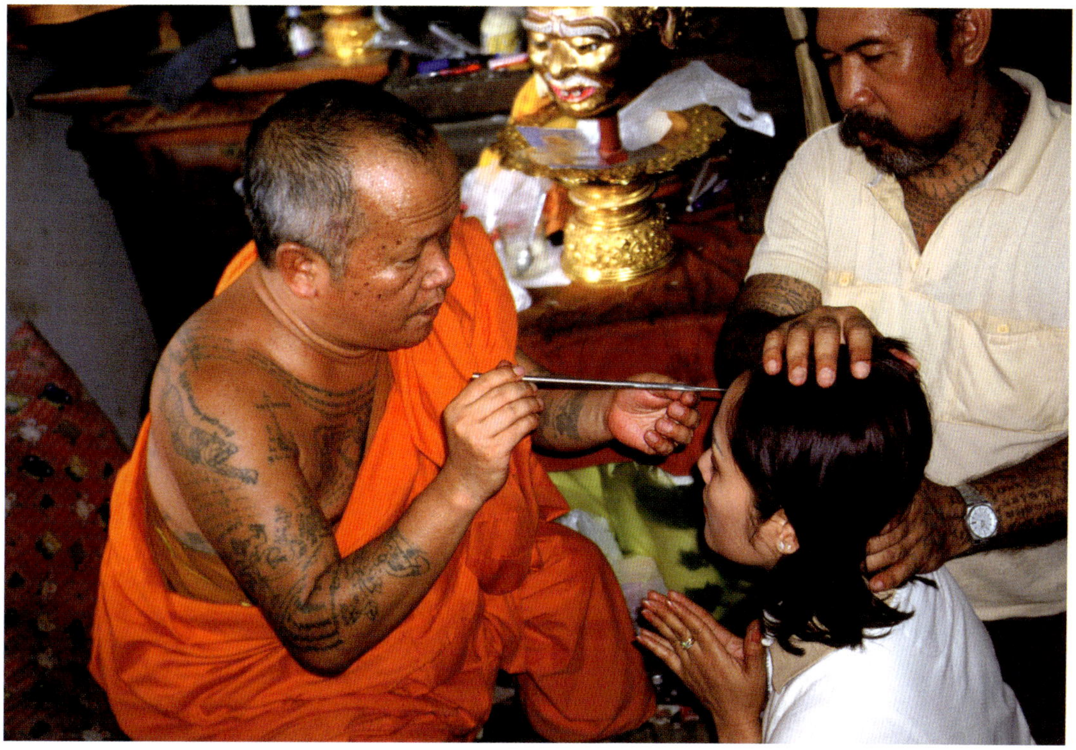

Photo by Joe Cummings

Above: Ajahn Ting applies *na naa thaung* to the forehead of a female disciple.

rubber form into an ink pad and then stamps the disciple's body with the outline. The master then needles the design into the skin, tracing the stamped outline. *Akkhara* are added freehand after the main design is inked. *Sak yan* at Wat Bang Phra tend to be rather bold, with relatively thick, heavy lines.

MASTERS AT WAT BANG PHRA

Luang Pho Poen passed on his *weechaa* to three primary heirs at the monastery: Phra Ajahn Ting, Phra Ajahn Tauy and Phra Ajahn Aphinya. Two other resident monks, Phra Ajahn Nun and Phra Ajahn Paew, also practise Wat Bang Phra-style *sak yan* tradition.

Phra Ajahn Ting, Luang Pho Poen's most senior disciple, studied with him from 1981 until the abbot's passing in 2002. He works in his own sizeable *kuti*, seated alongside a huge altar stacked with Buddha images, images of Luang Pho Poen, Pho Kae and various Hindu-Buddhist deities. Nowadays Luang Phi Ting focuses almost exclusively on two *sak yan* made famous by Luang Pho Poen. One is the *saarikaa lin thong* (golden-tongued sarika), a design in the shape of the sarika (Indian mynah), which enhances one's power of verbal persuasion. The second is *kwaang liaw lang* (deer turning to look back), which boosts personal charisma. Any disciple coming for one of the aforementioned tattoos will usually also receive *na naa thong* (goldleaf blessing on the forehead). In fact many Thais visit Luang Phi Ting only for *na naa thong*, which is particularly popular with women visitors.

Quiet, bespectacled Phra Ajahn Tauy, also known as Luang Phi Tauy, is the next senior-most disciple of Luang Pho Poen. He usually works in a larger hall

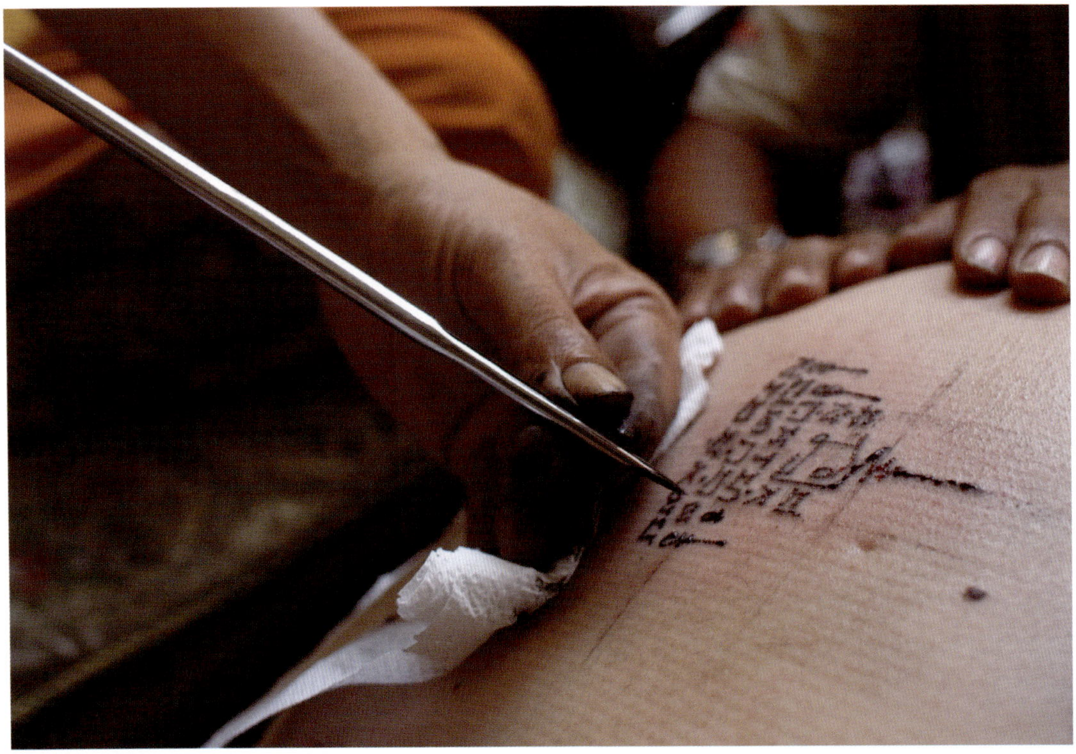

Above: Ajahn Paew inks a *yantra* for luck and prosperity. Right: Ajahn Tauy adds a *yantra* to the lower back of a disciple.

together with lay master Ajahn Nuad, his principal student. Here he sits beneath a large portrait of his late master, Luang Pho Poen. His knowledge of *sak yan* designs is quite broad but he is especially well known for *yan hom siang* (a grid of 108 small squares containing Buddha-like figures, a powerful protective *yantra*) and *phra jao haa phra ong* (five Buddha figures conferring Buddhist virtues, prosperity and protection).

Phra Ajahn Aphinya – Luang Phi Ya in everyday parlance – can usually be found at the main building that contains a large shop where amulets, *phaa yan*, and other sacred materials are sold to visitors.

Two more monks who are active in *sak yan* at Wat Bang Phra are Phra Ajahn Nun and Phra Ajahn Paew. Phra Ajahn Nun works quietly in the monastery's main building, usually in the same hall as Luang Phi Ya. He is known for his exacting work, although he is one of the newer hands at Wat Bang Phra.

Jolly and engaging Phra Ajahn Paew meets disciples on an outdoor veranda of one of the ancillary halls. Phra Ajahn Paew is a favourite of younger disciples, and the queue waiting to see him is often rather long on weekends and holidays. He is also one of the most photographed monks at Wat Bang Phra, no doubt because he tattoos outdoors in natural light, remains easily accessible and is the most heavily tattooed of the five resident *khru sak yan*. He jokes with disciples and visitors alike, often enjoining photographers to sit down for an inking. Phra Ajahn Paew has been at Wat Bang Phra around 12 years, and his lines tend to be slightly finer than what is typical here.

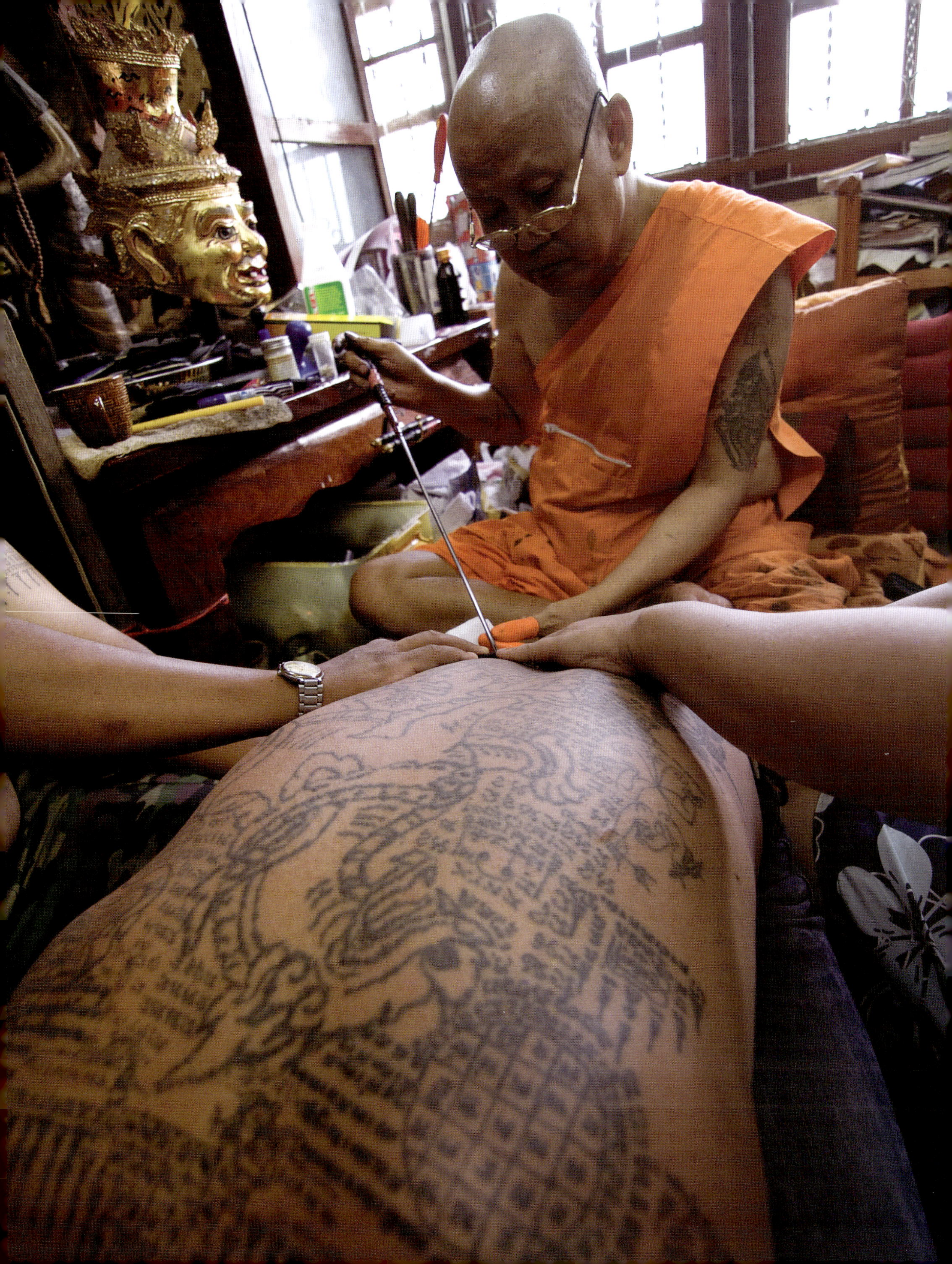

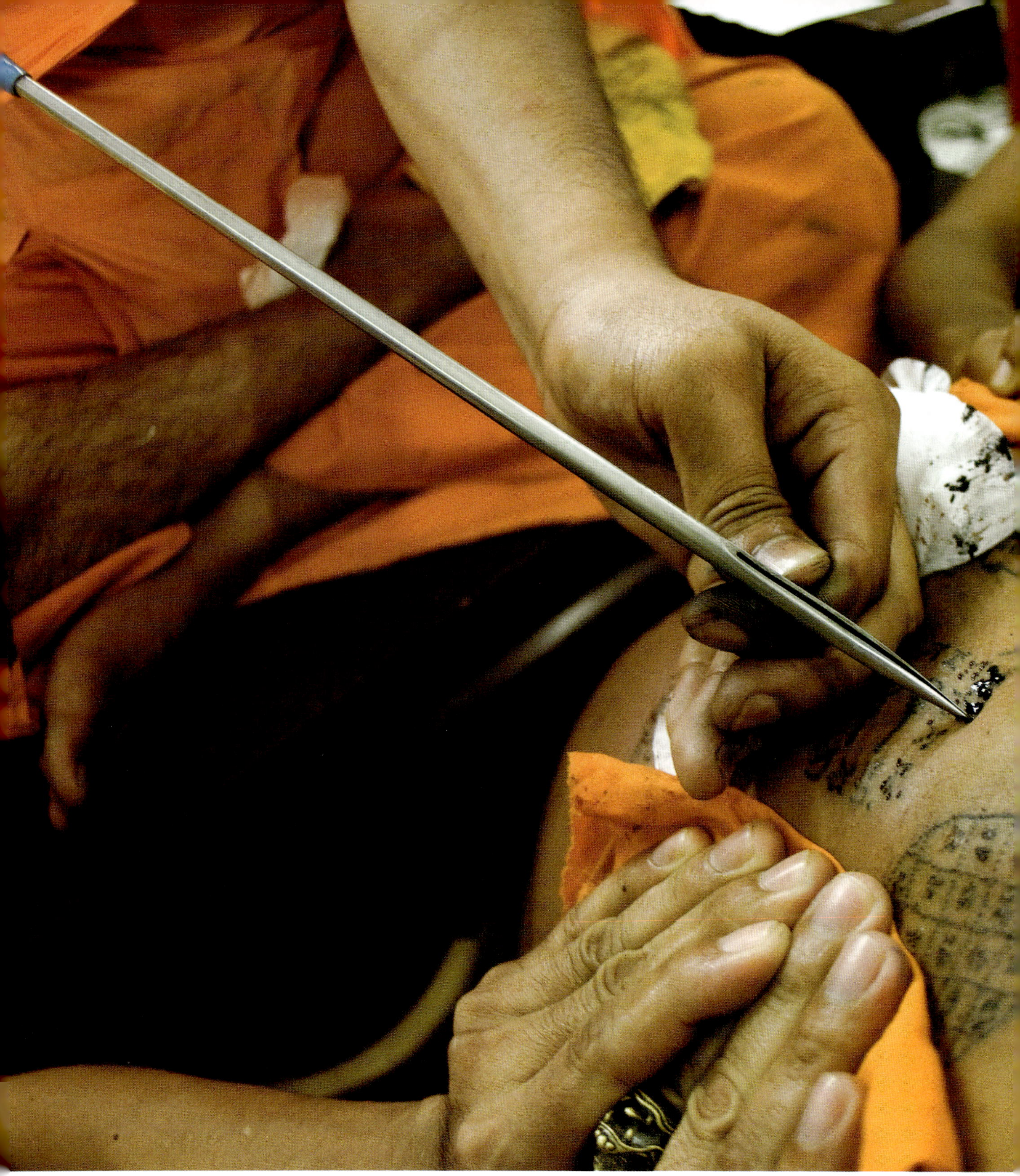

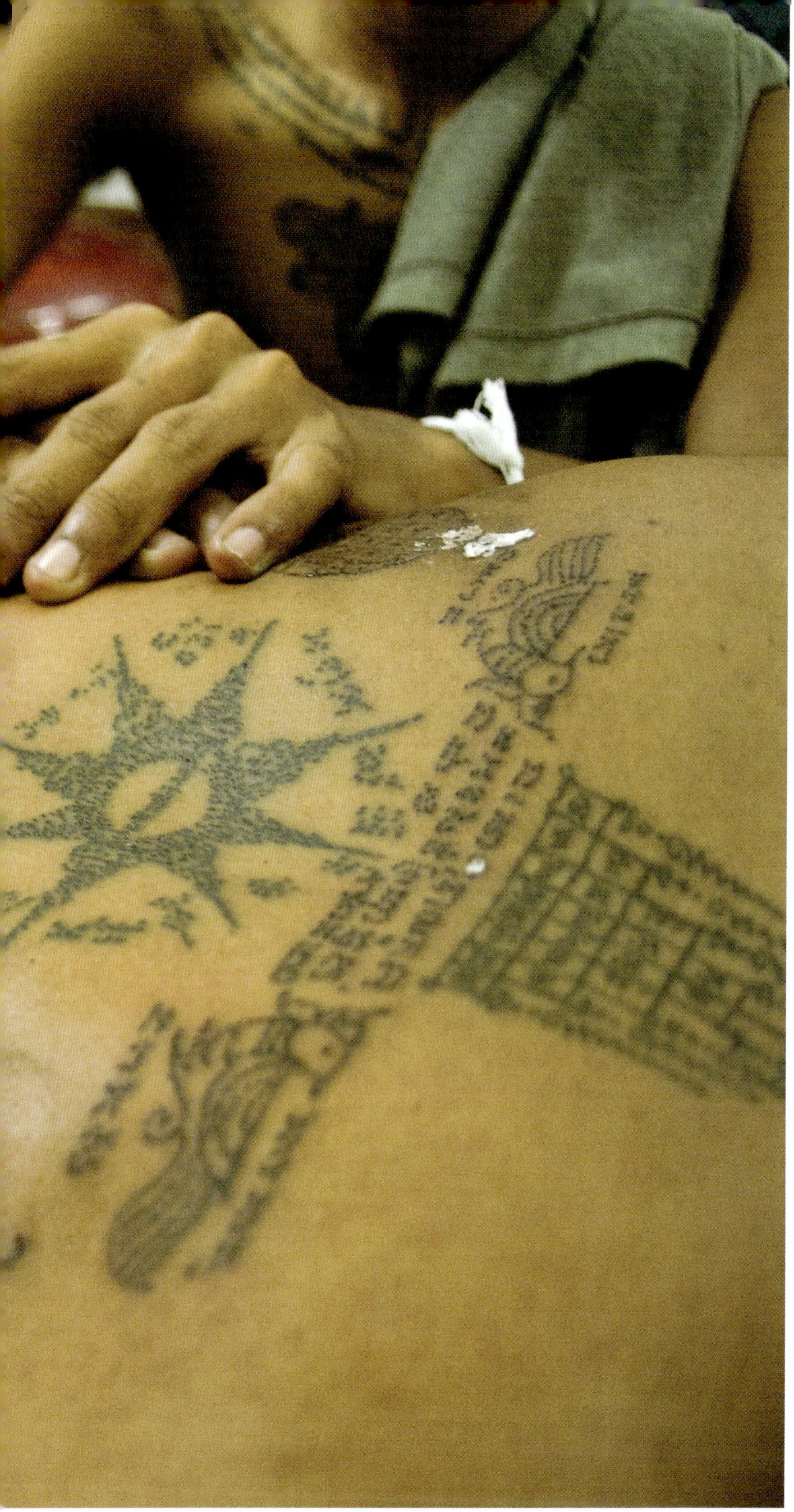

Left: The larger needle used here by a visiting monk at Wat Bang Phra is more typical of what was used in the past than the smaller needles favoured today.

A sixth monk who used to offer *sak yan* at Wat Bang Phra, Phra Ajahn Phan, moved to Wat Kho Poon in Chaiyo, Ang Thong Province, a few years ago. Along with Phra Ajahn Aphinya and Phra Ajahn Tauy, he was one of Luang Pho Poen's original disciples, and his work remains in much demand.

Ajahn Nuad is a *phraam* – white-clothed tattoo master – who travels from his *samnak* in Kanchanaburi every Saturday and Sunday to help the resident monks meet the high demand for *sak yan* at Wat Bang Phra.

He cuts a striking figure with his namesake beard (Nuad means "beard" in Thai) and long hair tightly bound up in a bun at the back of his head. He originally comes from Samut Prakan, east of Bangkok. Ajahn Nuad became a student of Luang Phi Tauy when he was 30 years old. He has been working in the Luang Pho Poen tradition for 10 years.

Although he is still relatively young, Ajahn Nuad's work is highly detailed, with a forte for heavily geometric *yantras* such as the *yan plaa lai* (eel *yantra*, for loving kindness) and *yan krau phet* (diamond armour *yantra*, for protection). Many disciples also come to him for tigers and Hanuman, especially *hanuman auk seuk* (Hanuman goes out to fight) and *hanuman om meuang* (Hanuman swallows the city), designs that confer courage and power.

Ajahn Nuad Speaks

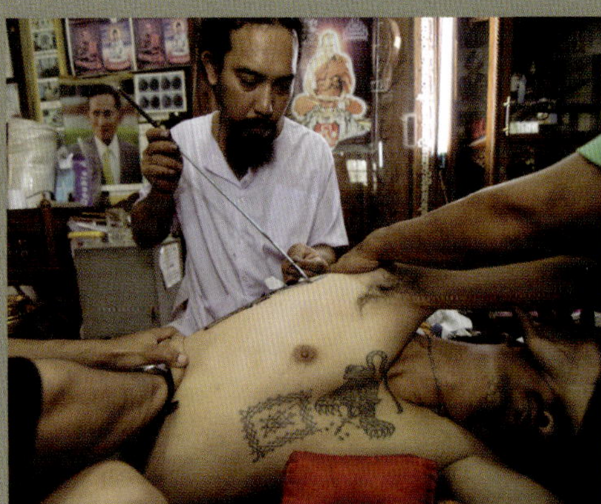

Perhaps because he is neither a monk nor a permanent resident at the monastery, Ajahn Nuad seems less constrained when talking about the Luang Pho Poen tradition. In addition to showing us his needles, rubber stamps, ink and other tools of the trade, he shared his thoughts about the state of the *sak yan* tradition in Thailand.

"We don't sell *sak yan* here, we make merit. Real *sak yan* can't be bought or sold. We take donations, whatever they put on the offering tray. Most disciples give just 25 baht. All the money goes to the monastery, not to me or the monks."

Asked about some of the famous lay masters who charge up to 100,000 baht or more per tattoo, he shrugged. "Sure, some of the ajahns have big houses. For them it's a business. That's not the real thing though.

"It's not entirely their fault. So many Thais these days want *sak yan* because it has become fashionable; they think the tattoos are beautiful. Here at Wat Bang Phra, we're not into beautiful tattoos. If you get a tattoo for the look, you get nothing. For us this is spiritual practice."

On weekends Ajahn Nuad can be found at Wat Bang Phra. The rest of the week he practises at his *samnak* in Kanchanaburi. He occasionally travels to meet disciples in Hong Kong, Malaysia or Singapore.

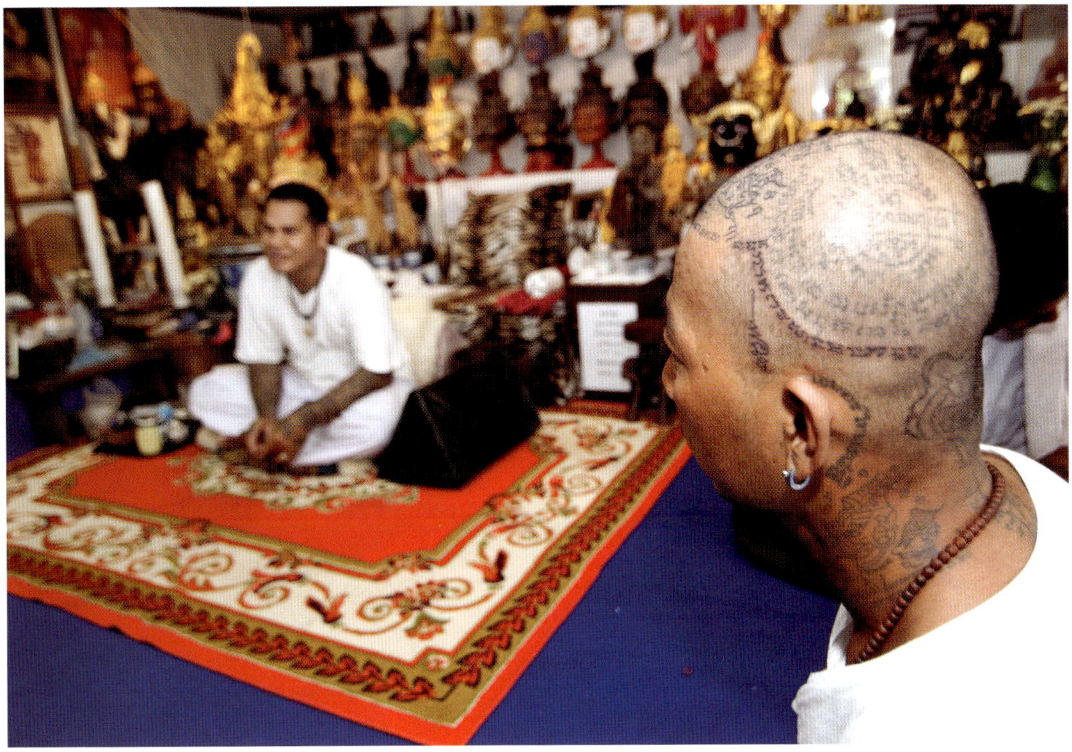

Above: A disciple's head bears fresh *akkhara* at the *samnak* of Ajahn Somchat.

GANGSTER TO GURU

A meticulously arranged altar extends across the entire length of one wall, filled with images of Buddha and Pho Kae, as well as a series of *khon* (classical dance-drama) masks representing characters from the Ramakien, Thailand's version of the Indian epic Ramayana.

In front of the altar, dressed in white and backed by cushions covered with tiger-print fabrics, the powerful figure of Ajahn Somchat Nakajan sits in half lotus. Meaty forearms coated in thick-lined *sak yan* rest easily atop his thighs as he listens to a shaven-headed disciple describe a conflict in his current life, for which he is seeking a remedy.

After a short discussion, the master instructs the disciple to sit sideways. As he takes out a long stylus and dips it into an inkwell, two other disciples move in to steady the man's head and body. Holding the stylus nearly parallel with the floor, Ajahn Somchat takes a deep breath, and without further hesitation begins jabbing the needle rapidly into the side of the disciple's head, just above the ear.

As the stylus gradually works its way around to the back of the man's head, then around to the other side, the disciple's stoic demeanour slowly erodes. Tight-shut eyes are joined by gnashing teeth, heavy breathing and grunts of pain. The master does not stop or slow down in response. Instead he keeps up a steady, determined rhythm, knowing that the best way to relieve the sting of skin-on-bone punctures is to finish as quickly as possible. The master's eyes shine with both compassion and the professional equanimity of a surgeon.

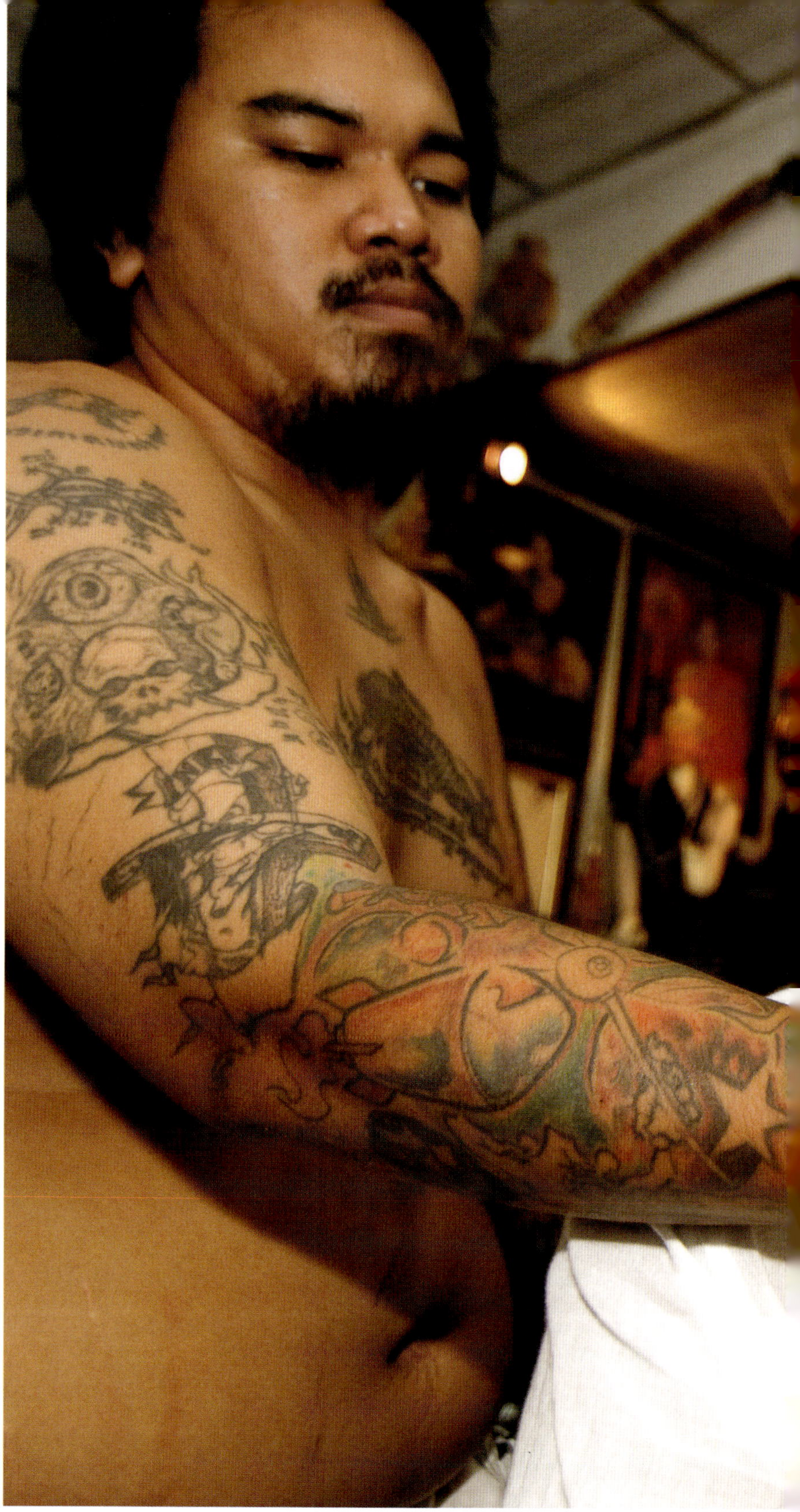

Right: The head is the most painful part of the body to tattoo.

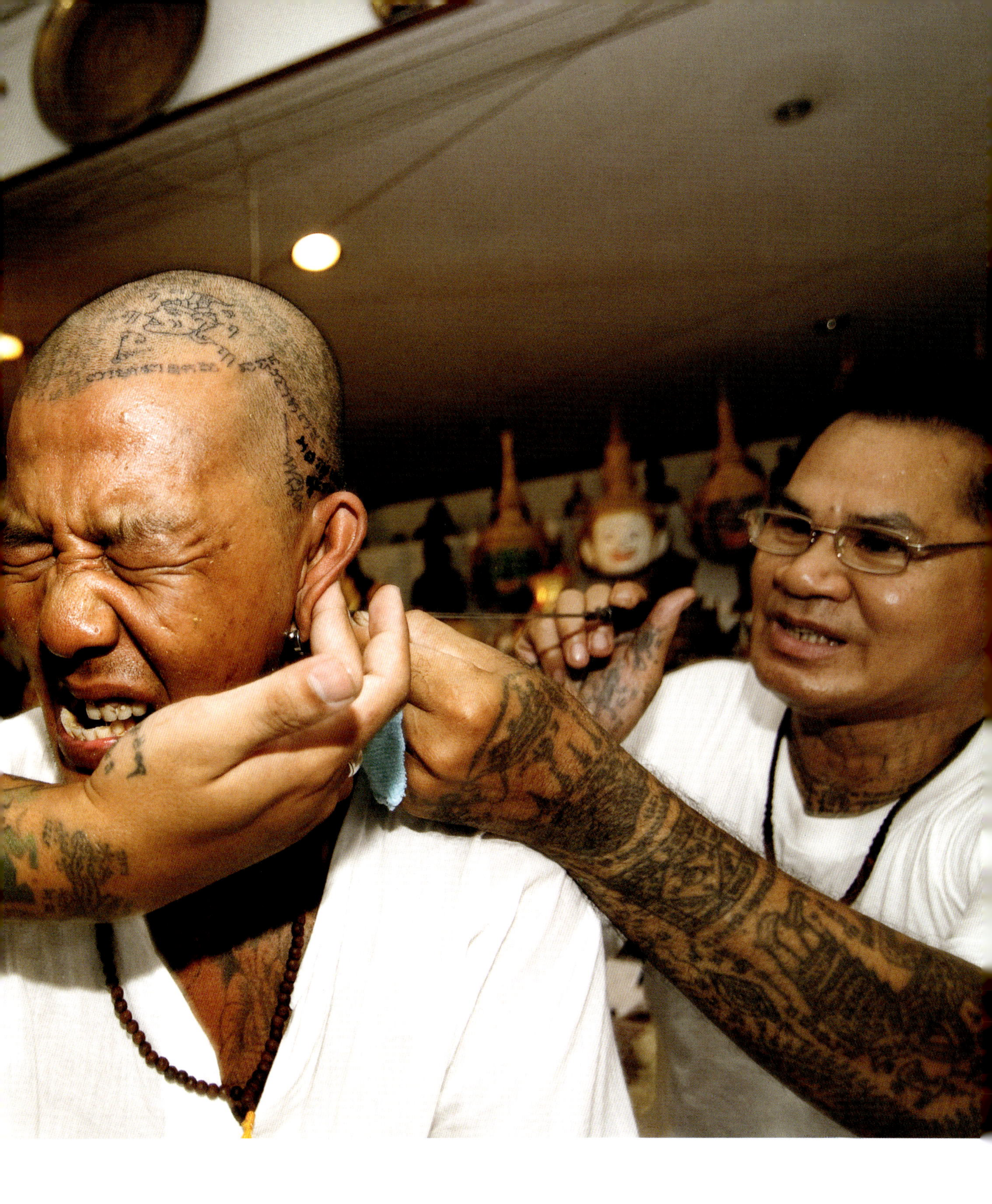

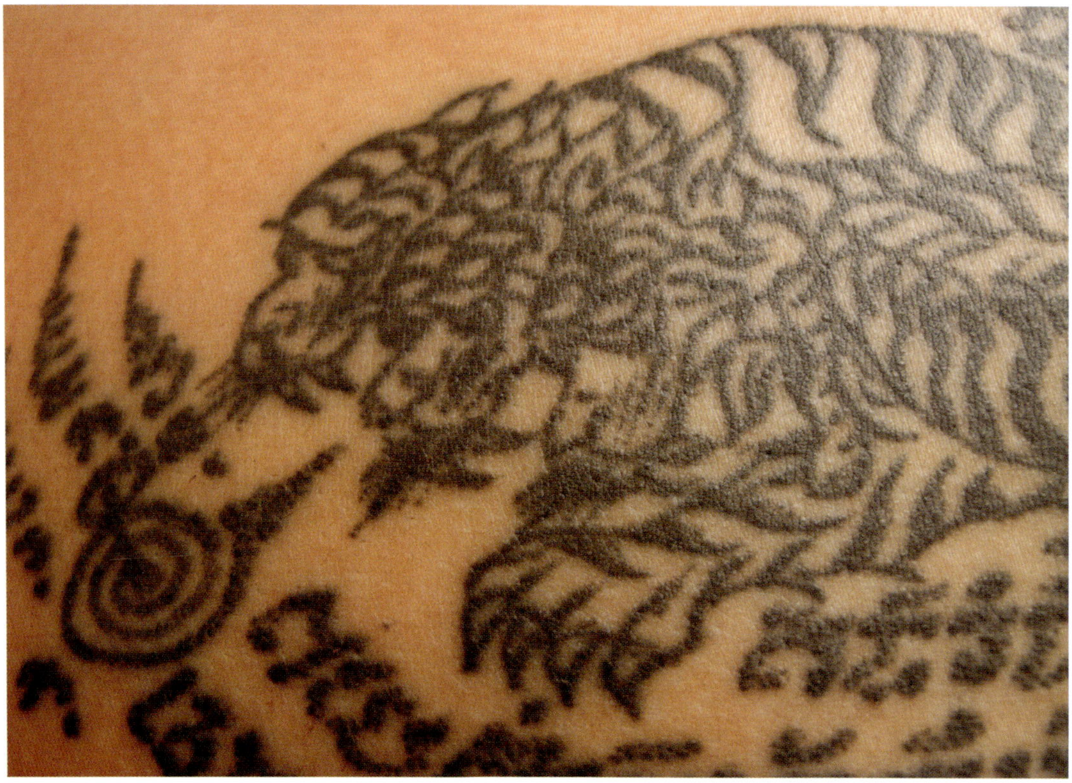

Above & Right: Ajahn Somchat's three-headed tiger. The master inks only one per year.

Somchat was born in Nonthaburi in 1961, and from an early age was known to be an unruly child. By the time he was a teenager he was working for a local gang as a hard-headed bouncer in illegal gambling dens.

Constantly harassed by local police, the young man sought out steady work as an undertaker at Wat Saphan Sung Bang Seu, moving and preparing corpses for cremation. Most men fear and avoid such work due to widespread Thai belief in ghosts and evil forces. Somchat, however, didn't believe in the supernatural at all, and he feared nothing.

One night he had a vivid dream in which the forest hermit Pho Kae, in statue form, introduced himself and invited Somchat to pay respects to the sage under the holy banyan tree on the monastery grounds, where the spirit claimed to have resided for a long time. He told Somchat that if he paid homage, his life would improve tremendously.

When Somchat awoke he dismissed the dream and went about his daily work as usual. However at the end of the day he decided he would have a look at the banyan tree, even though he had been there many times before and never seen any representation of Pho Kae there.

At the base of the tree stood a statue of Pho Kae, where previously there had been none. When no one in the temple could explain how it came to be placed there that day, Somchat decided that there was more to the world than what he could see and think. He began reading about the oc-

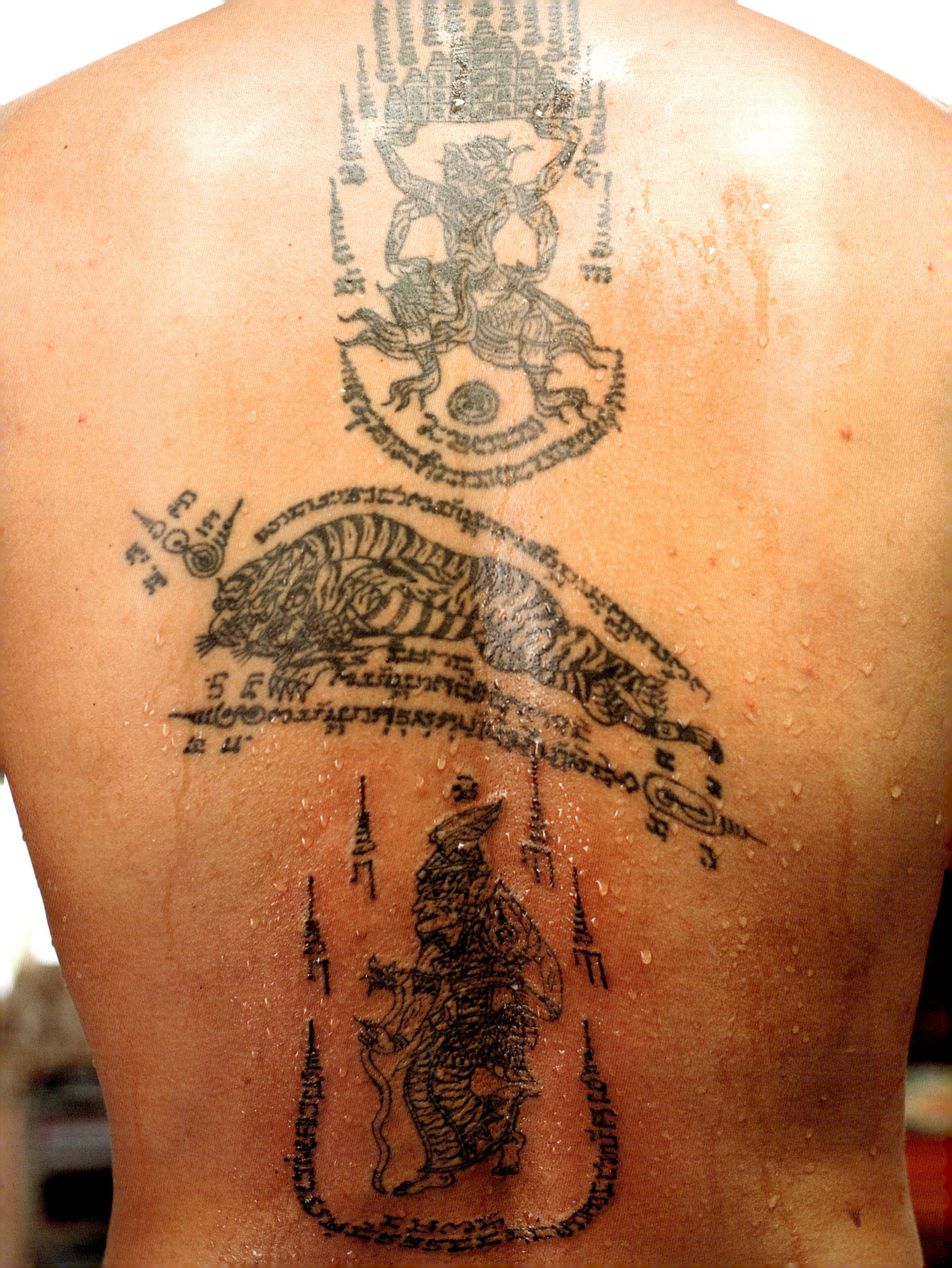

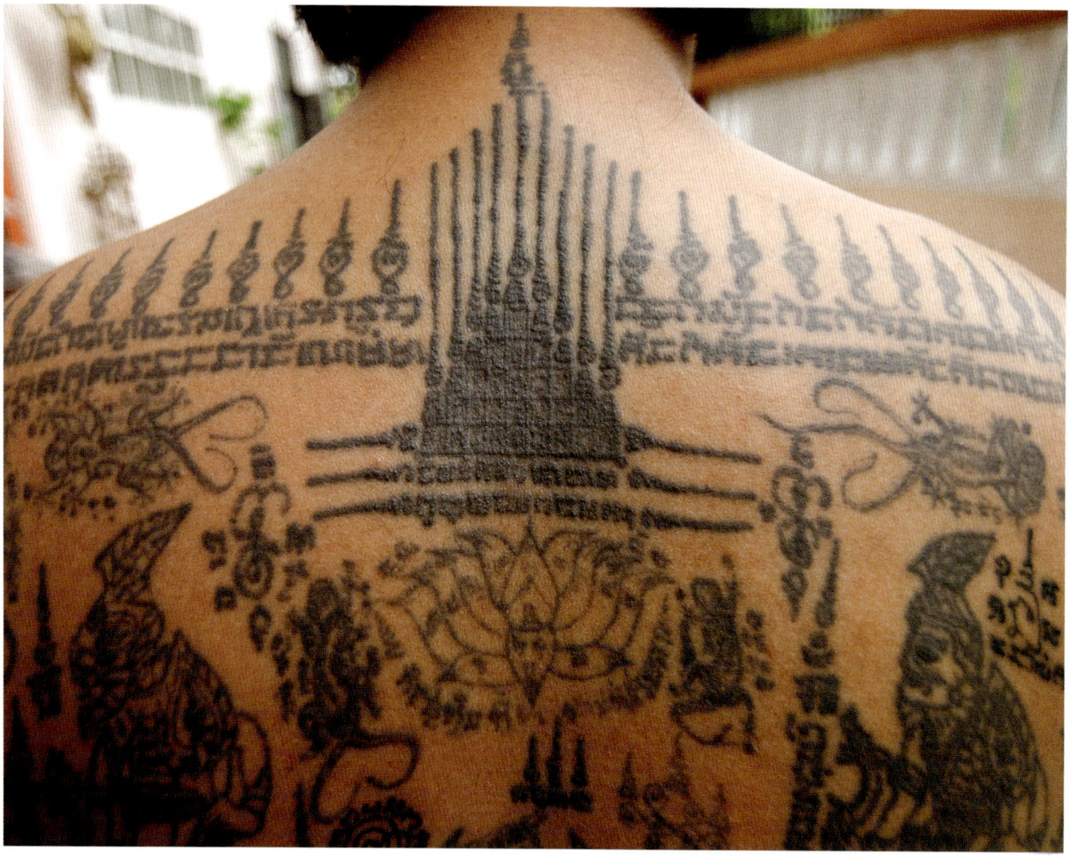

Above: The work of Ajahn Somchat shows the unmistakable influence of the late Luang Pho Poen.

cult, and his interest eventually led him to Wat Bang Phra, where he became one of the last direct disciples of Luang Pho Poen.

Along with *sak yan* Somchat studied the arts of *na naa thaung* (applying goldleaf to the forehead), *lin thaung* (applying goldleaf to the tongue) and fortunetelling. Once he finished his studies he moved back to Nonthaburi to open his own *samnak* and start a family, completing his complete transformation from gangster to guru in the space of a decade.

As Ajahn Somchat's disciples increased in number, his first *samnak* in Nonthaburi proved to be too small, so he moved to a larger two-storey house and *samnak* near Wat Saseng Siritham in Tha It subdistrict, Nonthaburi, where it remains today. He still returns to Wat Bang Phra from time to time to help the monks with *sak yan*.

Ajahn Somchat welcomes disciples on Thursdays, which he considers the most auspicious day of the week for creating *sak yan*. If Thursday happens to be a *wan phra* (holy full moon day), however, he closes.

Ajahn Somchat offers a wide range of *yantras*. In the *yantra* catalogues available for perusal, we saw more crocodiles and spiders than we had seen elsewhere, including one design depicting a naked woman riding on the back of a crocodile, said to evoke strong *saneh* (personal charisma).

Perhaps the most unique and intriguing *yantra* on offer at his *samnak* is a three-headed leaping tiger *(seua sam sian)*. The three heads reportedly guard one's karma in the past, present and future simultaneously. The master inks only one three-faced tiger per year; one must book the tattoo a year in advance.

While we are visiting the *samnak*, we see ample evidence of the power of his animal tattoos, with strong trance performances from freshly tattooed disciples. A man inked with a tiger begins growling fiercely and pawing the floor as Ajahn Somchat completes the *pluuk sehk* ceremony. Later another disciple leaps about like a monkey as his Hanuman *yantra* is empowered. A third, emblazoned with a figure of Pho Kae, laughs maniacally, sending a dog on the veranda into a barking fit.

On close examination of Ajahn Somchat's work, one can discern the Luang Pho Poen influence in the bold, flowing black lines and squared-off Khmer *akkhara*. We ask Ajahn Somchat which of his *yantras* is most well known.

"My disciples tell me that the *yan hua jai sethee* [wealth heart *yantra*] helps increase their business and make money. I get a lot of businesspeople and merchants coming in for that one.

"Our *yan kao yaut* (nine peaks *yantra*) is also popular, because it can be done quickly, in just 10 minutes if it's an oil tattoo, not more than 20 minutes if it's ink."

He shows us the oil he uses. It's called *namman kao klin*, which means "nine-fragrance oil", presumably because one can count nine auspicious aromas in the exotic bouquet. We sniff; it has a very pleasant and compelling fragrance.

He pulls out a canister filled with wood chips, leaves and other dried organic matter.

"This is *waan* 108. I mix it up myself, taking a blend of dried herbs, *waan* (wild ginger and other roots), dried centipedes and other materials and soaking them in sesame oil. I blend in just a little olive oil too."

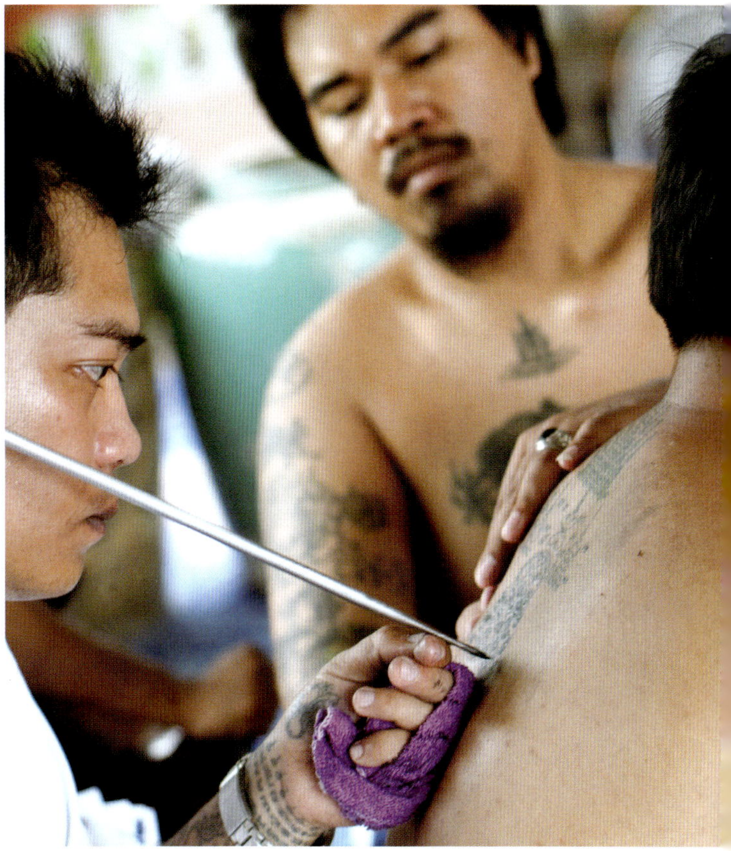

Above: Ajahn Somchat's assistant at work.

We leave the *samnak* impressed with the master's work, with the tidy environment and most of all with Ajahn Somchat's openness to outsiders and disciples alike.

AJAHN MONTREE PHUMTHIP

In 1967, Luang Pho Poen's *thudong* travels in northeastern Thailand brought him to Kalasin, where he met Bunmee Phumthip. Bunmee and his wife, who had moved from Ang Thong to Kalasin six years earlier, after the birth of their son Montree, helped support Luang Pho Poen's *thudong* in Kalasin. In

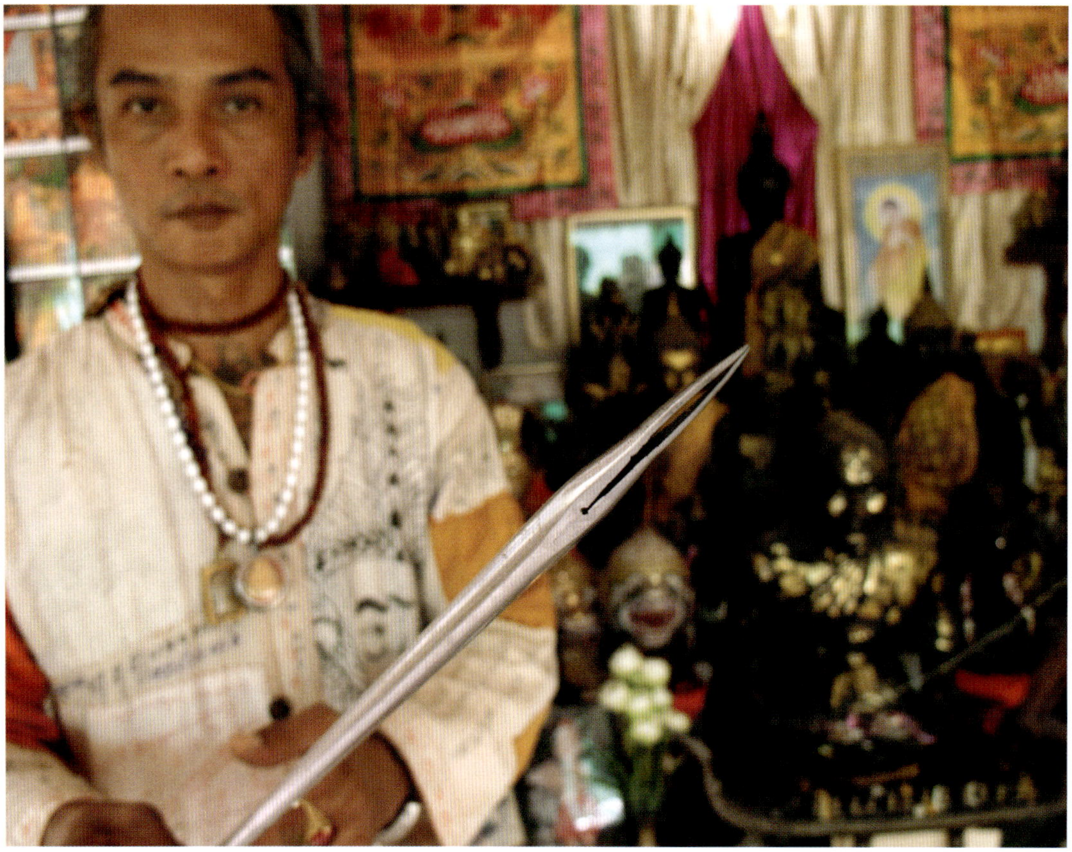

Above: Ajahn Montree, Kalasin, holds a giant *mai sak* given to him by his master, the late Luang Pho Poen.
Right: Ajahn Montree displays one of the *yantra* jackets he has made himself.

return the monk began teaching Bunmee the ways of *weechaa, sak yan* and herbal medicine.

Luang Pho Poen returned to Kalasin yearly, each time staying at Bunmee's house and passing on his knowledge while accruing many local disciples. In 1981 Luang Pho Poen declared that Bunmee had fully mastered the arts and could conduct *wai khru* on his own. That year marked the beginning of the one and only northeastern Thai branch of the Luang Pho Poen lineage.

Meanwhile, Bunmee's son Montree Phumthip, at the age of 15, began travelling frequently to Wat Bang Phra to study *weechaa, aakhom* (Pali in Khmer script) and *horasaat* (Thai astrology) with Luang Pho Poen. Back home in Kalasin, he took up the *khem sak* and learned the sacred tattoo arts from his father. Together they opened separate *samnak sak yan* in town.

When we met Ajahn Montree at his *samnak* behind Wat Klang in Kalasin, his father Ajahn Bunmee had retired and was in deteriorating health. Also known as Ajahn Ott Phakhao ("Ott" being his nickname, and *phaa khao* a reference to his white clothing), Montree is well known throughout Thailand as the only direct pupil of Luang Pho Poen practising in the northeast. His name cards read "If you have a faithful and pure heart you can make an appointment behind Wat Klang."

Ajahn Montree wears his hair long, tied in a neat chignon at the back of his head, and his smooth, handsome features belied his age of 50 years. He was generous with his time, showing us *yantra* shirts he had sewn together using aging squares of *phaa yan* made by the late Luang Pho Poen. Each shirt was made of bleached local cotton, the hems hung with tiny votive bells that tinkled when the garments were moved.

We watched as Ajahn Montree applied *kao yaut*, in *nam-man waan* (blessed oil mixed with herbs), to a female devotee using a very long *khem sak*. Afterwards he talked with us about the acquisition and application of *weechaa*.

"When someone comes to me with a problem, I have to figure out what the best medicine is. If you have a headache, it's not enough just to stop the pain. You need to ask, 'What's the cause?'. Tattoos are like this. You need to know the cause of a problem, not just the symptoms. If you ink the wrong *yantra* it won't help.

"The best masters rely on four spheres: science, including both Thai herbal treatments and Western medicine; magic, for spells and *yantras*; Buddhism, for morality; and astrology, to understand one's tentative destiny. These four cover the universe. One alone is not enough."

Ajahn Montree's always disciples start with *kao yaut* and *paet thit*.

"After that, I check with each person to see what they need. Together we figure out what design and *khaathaa* are best. You can't come and complain that you need this or you need that. I won't tattoo people just because they want a tattoo. A person should wear just enough *sak yan* to do the job, and no more.

"Some masters just keep filling up the space on a disciple's skin, on demand. That's not correct prac-

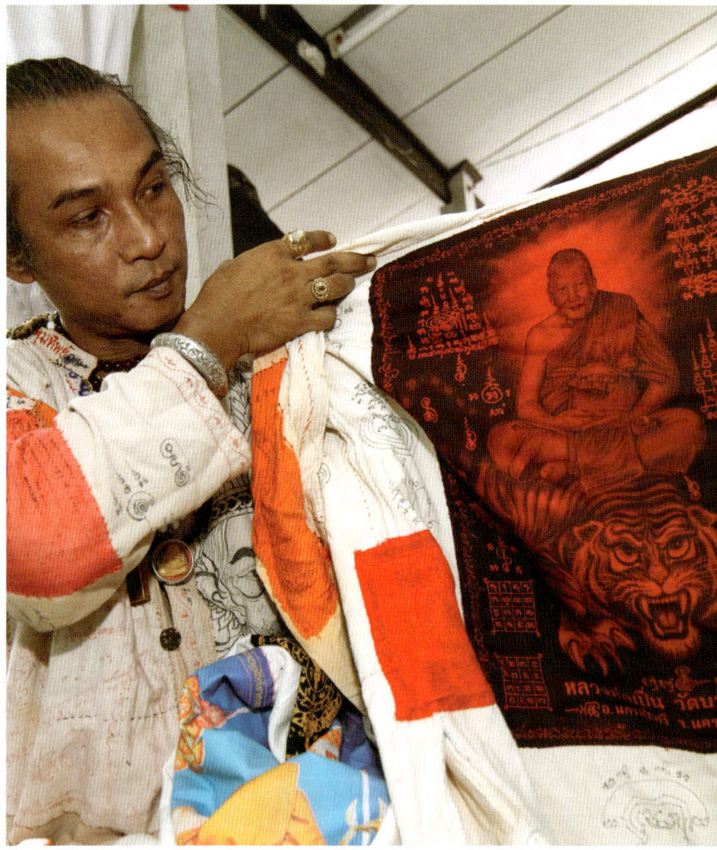

tice. I won't tattoo people who come here with lots of tattoos from all over the place."

Asked whether he tattoos monks, Ajahn Montree replied, "I believe it's bad karma to tattoo someone who keeps more precepts than you do, so I won't tattoo monks. Only monks should tattoo monks."

Not long after our visit, Ajahn Montree's father, Ajahn Bunmee, died after several years under constant medical care. He was 80 years old.

Ajahn Montree has been passing on what he learned from his father and from Luang Pho Poen to two young disciples from nearby towns. One, a young woman, has already finished a course in astrology with Ajahn Montree, while the second, a young man, is currently learning *sak yan* in the Luang Pho Poen style.

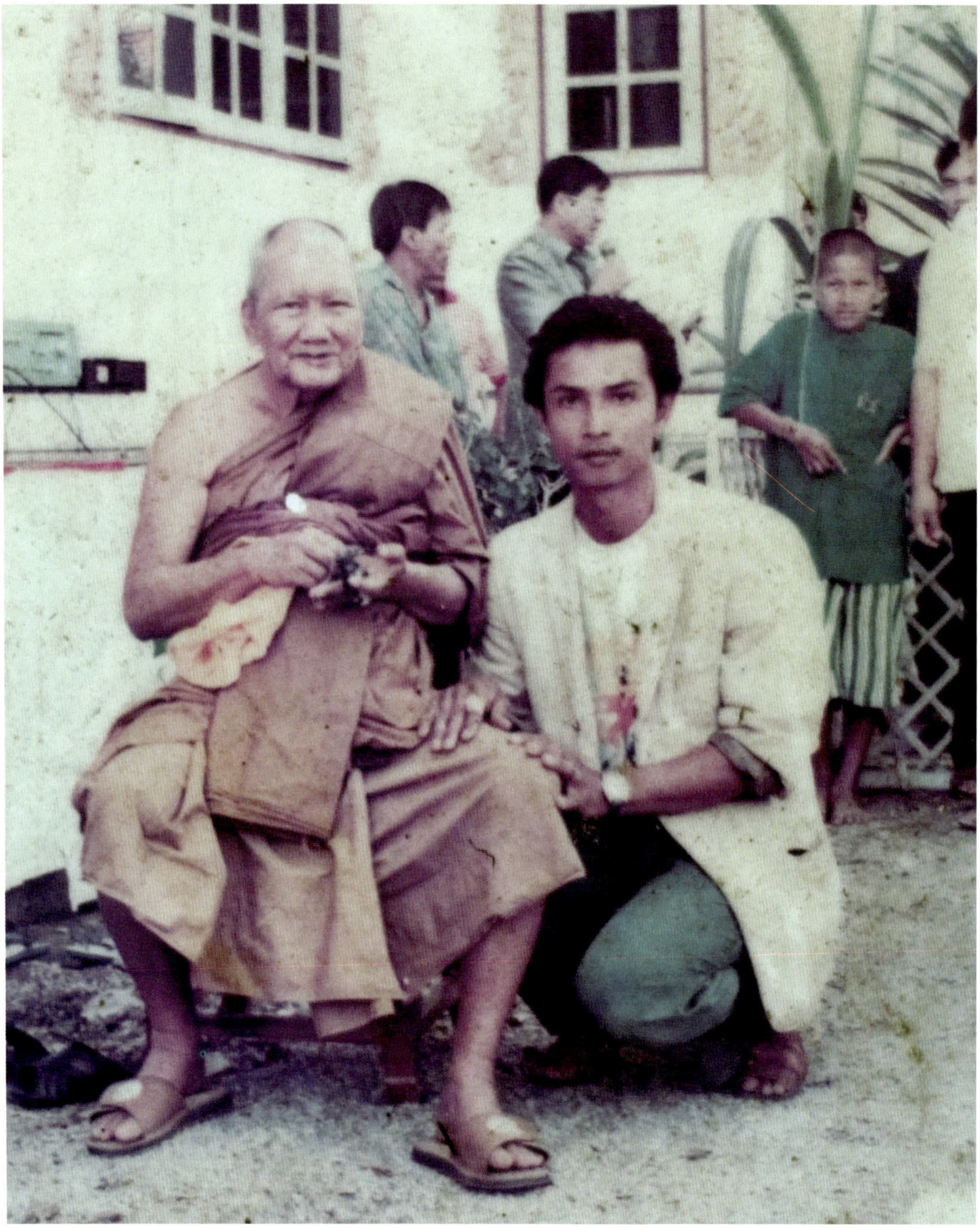

Above: A young Montree squats beside his master, Luang Pho Poen.
RIght: All of Ajahn Montree's many *sak yan* were inked either by his late father, Ajahn Bunmee or by Luang Pho Poen.

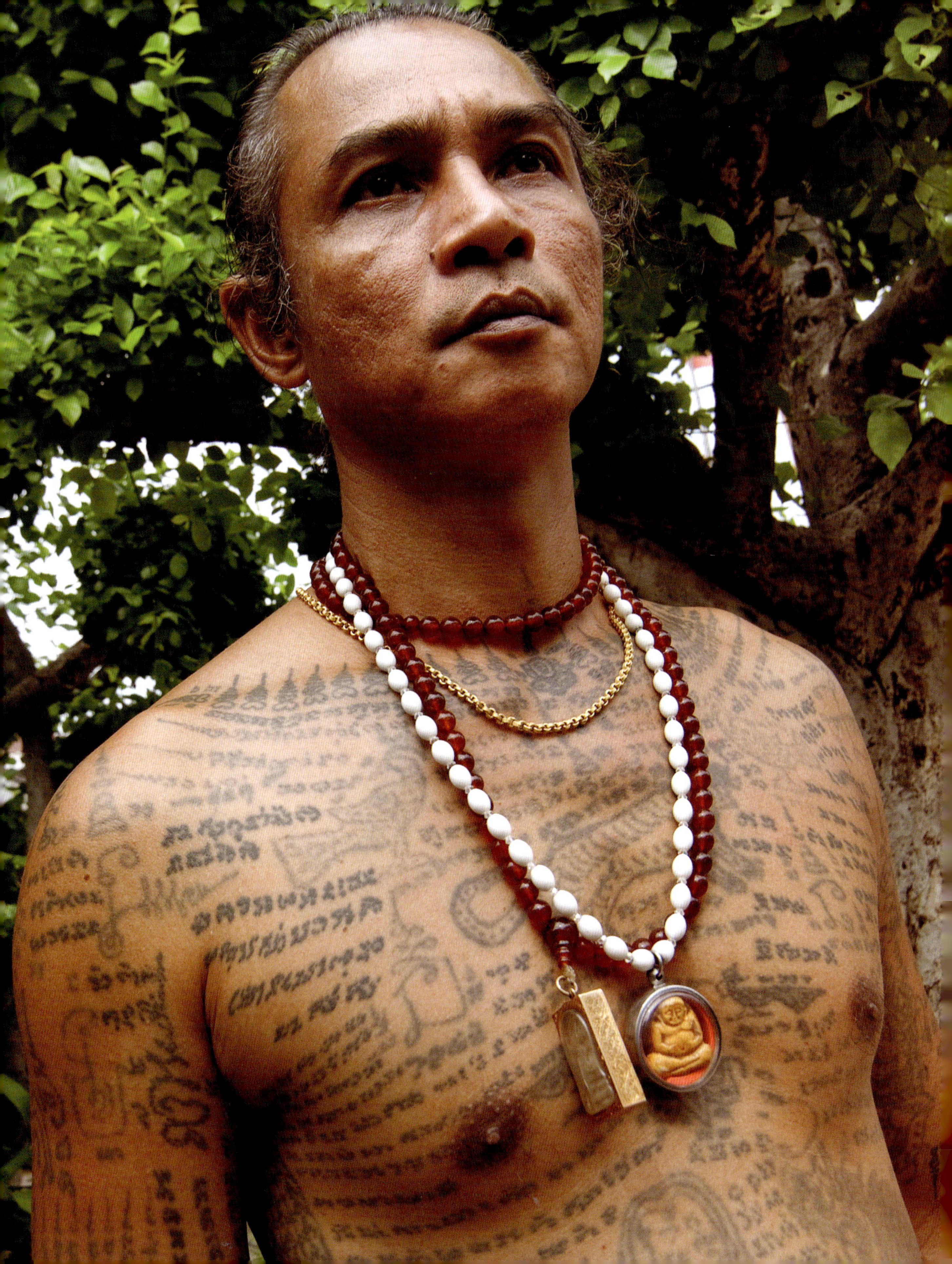

THE LINEAGE OF THE HERMIT SAGE

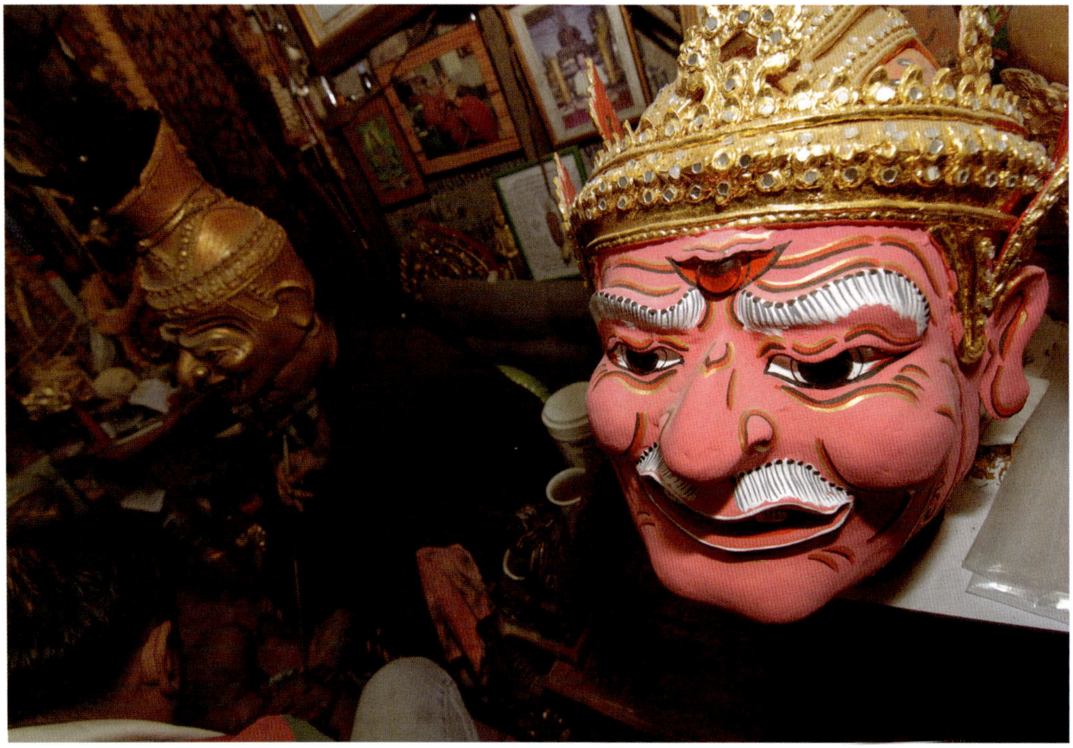

Above: A pink-faced mask of Pho Kae Ta Fai at the *samnak* of Ajahn Toy.

Sak yan devotees usually claim that the sacred tattoo tradition originated among wise hermit sages who lived in wild forests, in deep caves or on high mountains. The Thais call these men *reusee*, taken from the Sanskrit term *rishi*, which in the Vedic literature of India refers to hermit sages with special powers to transform themselves and others, garnered through years of study and apprenticeship. In Western thinking, the concept corresponds closely with that of seers or wizards.

Reusee develop their psychic powers through renunciation, meditation, ritual and the recitation of *khaathaa* (sacred verse). They also cultivate a rich knowledge of herbs, minerals and other substances which have the power to heal or to cast spells.

Because of their habit of living in the forest, accomplished *reusee* are thought to have a special affinity for wild animals, including tigers. One of the most feared animals in nature, the tiger represents the king of the jungle, and thus mastery over nature. Whenever *reusee* appear in Hindu-Buddhist art and iconography, this connection is illustrated by the tiger skin tunics they wear. Thais also refer to the hermit sage as *nak buat laay phayak* – tiger-pattern monastics.

Khru sak yan who come from the *reusee* tradition are few in number in Thailand compared to those who are Buddhist monks or who wear the white robes of the layman. Unlike the *reusee* of the past, they tend to live in villages and towns rather than in the forest, although they will often retire to the forest for a few days or weeks at a time to meditate and practise *khaathaa*. Like the white-robed *khru*, they may have families.

Reusee in modern-day Thailand no longer wear actual tiger skins. Instead they wear either maroon-coloured robes or tiger-print cloth. They seldom shave their beards or cut their hair, which may be worn in a topknot in a manner reminiscent of the way Shaiva sadhus in India wear their hair.

Like their counterparts in the Buddhist monkhood and among the white-clothed *khru*, the *reusee* offers a variety of magico-religious services to the community, including astrology, fortune-telling, herbal cures, spells and sacred tattoos.

Reusee develop their psychic powers through renunciation, meditation, ritual and the recitation of *khaathaa*.

The Indian connection with the *reusee* is almost entirely lost in Thailand, where it seems more linked to animism than Vedic thought. Despite claims to the contrary, there is no standard *reusee* pantheon in Thailand. Devotees debate the different classes of *reusee*; some say there are four types of hermit sages, others eight or nine.

Thai *sak yan* devotees generally agree that the lineage began with Pho Kae (Old Father), a wizened old sage with white hair and white beard.

One of the more persistent legends says Pho Kae lived in the kingdom of Si Thep, a Hindu-Buddhist state that flourished in what is today Phetchabun province in northern Thailand from the 7th to 11th centuries. To make matters more confusing, the mythic figure of Pho Kae is sometimes referred to as Phra Isuan (Lord Isvara), an epithet for the Brahmanist deity Shiva. An aesthetic link is clear. Shiva wears his long hair in a topknot, dons a leopard-skin tunic; he is a master of herbs and lord of beasts, the primordial shaman in touch with nature's mysteries.

Pho Kae is sometimes depicted with a third eye, similar to Shiva's third eye. Such figures are referred to as Pho Kae Ta Fai (Fire-Eye Old Father), and devotees believe that when the sage opens this third eye, all that falls within its gaze will burst into fire.

Another permutation of Pho Kae includes Pho Kae Chiwok, identified with Jivaka, the Buddha's chief physician and a master of herbal medicine and massage. Yet another, Pho Kae Ta Wua (Cow Eye Old Father), bears the head of a cow on a human body, and is believed to be a master alchemist.

AJAHN TOY DABOT

One of Thailand's most well-known *khru sak yan* in the *reusee* lineage works in a ramshackle *samnak* behind Wat Thong Nai in Bangkok. When Ajahn Toy Dabot (also spelt Thoy Dabos) is present, long-time disciples typically gather beneath the striped awning out front while newer aspirants sit on the raised wooden floor inside waiting for consultations and *sak yan*. A hand-lettered sign over the inside doorway reads "This place isn't excellent, but excellent people like to come here".

An elaborate altar to one side sags under the weight of dozens of statues of Buddha and Pho Kae Ta Fai. The larger Buddha images on the altar are adorned with delicate white jasmine garlands, while the Pho Kae figures have heavy yellow marigold garlands, contrasting Thai versus Indic connections. A large wooden Garuda figure sits beneath the principle Buddha, a nod to the master's many disciples from the ranks of army and police. Just under the corrugated gypsum roof, a grid of sacred cotton string creates diamond patterns above the room.

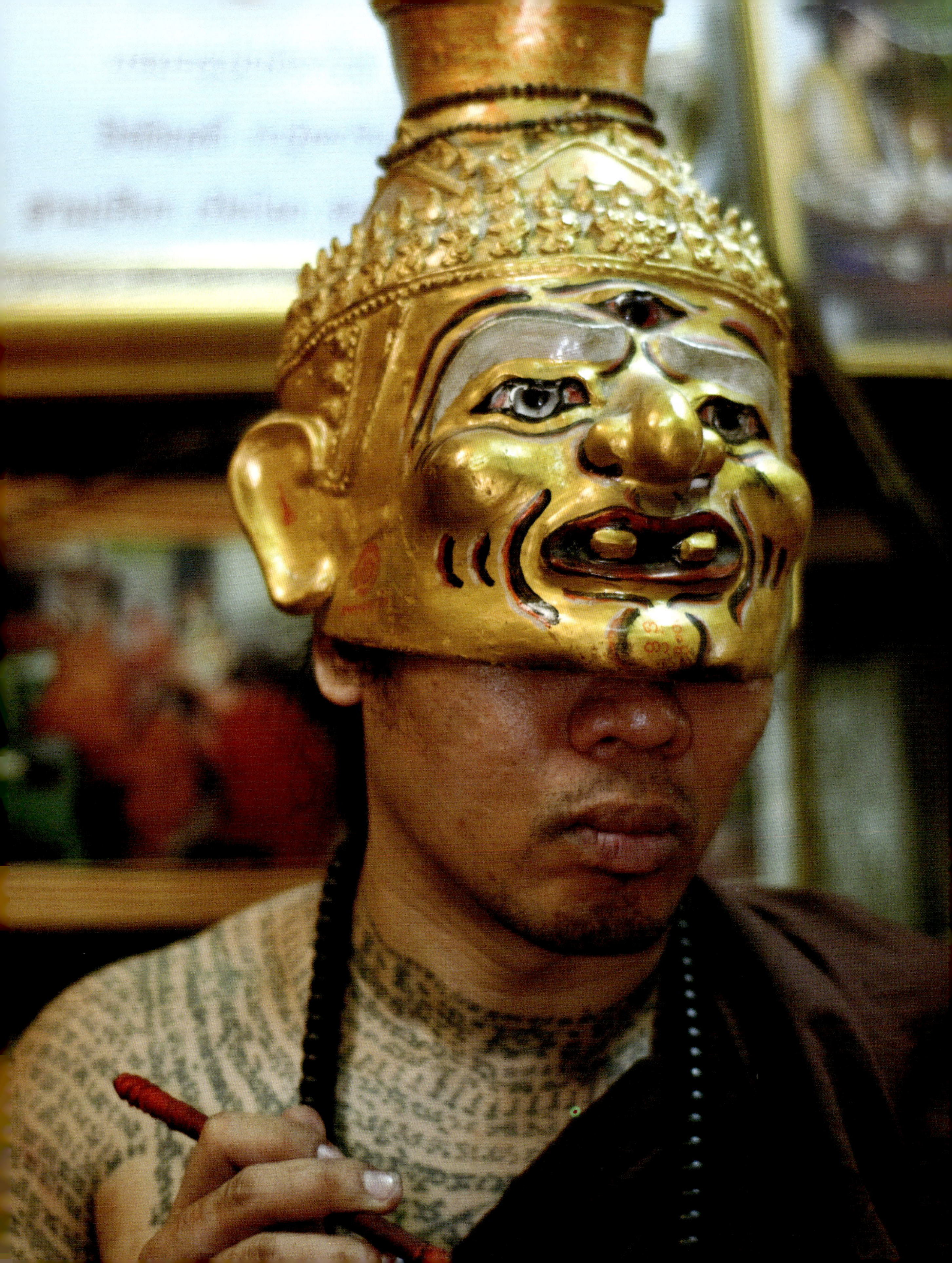

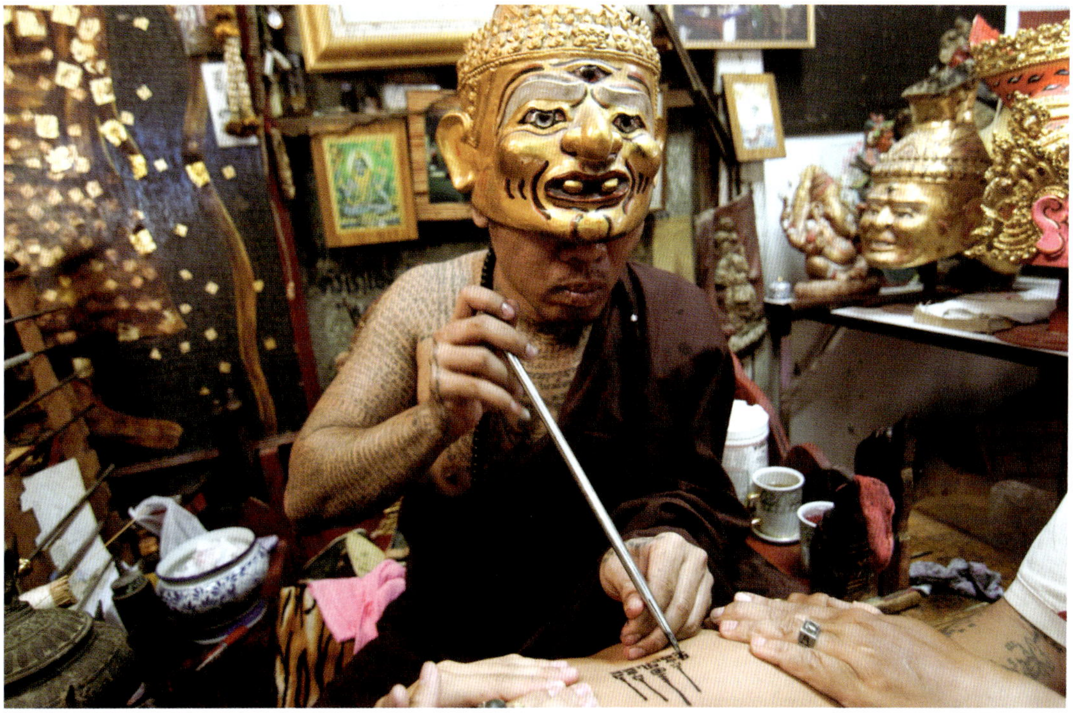

Left & above: Ajahn Toy dons the Pho Kae mask to invite Pho Kae's spirit to inhabit his body.

When Ajahn Toy enters the room on our first visit, he is wearing maroon robes, his long dreadlocks gathered into a loose knot atop his head. He sits down next to the altar and lifts an elaborate gilded mask from its stand, wedging it tightly onto his head and stuffing his topknot into the crown of the mask until a few strands sprout from the hole in the top. Called *sian reusee* (*rishi* head), the mask is thought to harbour the ancient spirit of Pho Kae Ta Fai himself.

With the mask covering the crown of his head and the top half of his face, Ajahn Toy utters *khaathaa* to "awaken" Pho Kae. After a few minutes of incantation, the robust 43-year-old begins to age before our eyes as his mind and body are taken over by Pho Kae. His spine slackens from the upright posture of an athlete until he is bent over nearly double, shaky hands grasping the edges of his seat for support. He coughs loudly, spitting into a container next to the seat, and the ongoing incantations take on the voice of a much older man. Without question, watching Ajahn Toy transform into Pho Kae is one of the most impressive sights in the *sak yan* world.

Ajahn Toy remains in trance for most of the day, letting "Pho Kae" apply *sak yan* and counsel his disciples. With the mask over his eyes, it appears to casual observers that Pho Kae is working blind.

When every disciple who has been waiting to see him has been inked or counselled, Pho Kae removes the *sian reusee* with some difficulty and recites *khaathaa* inviting the spirit to leave Ajahn Toy's body and return to the mask on its stand. In a reverse of the earlier transformation, Ajahn Toy's vitality returns, his spine straightens and soon he is talking normally again.

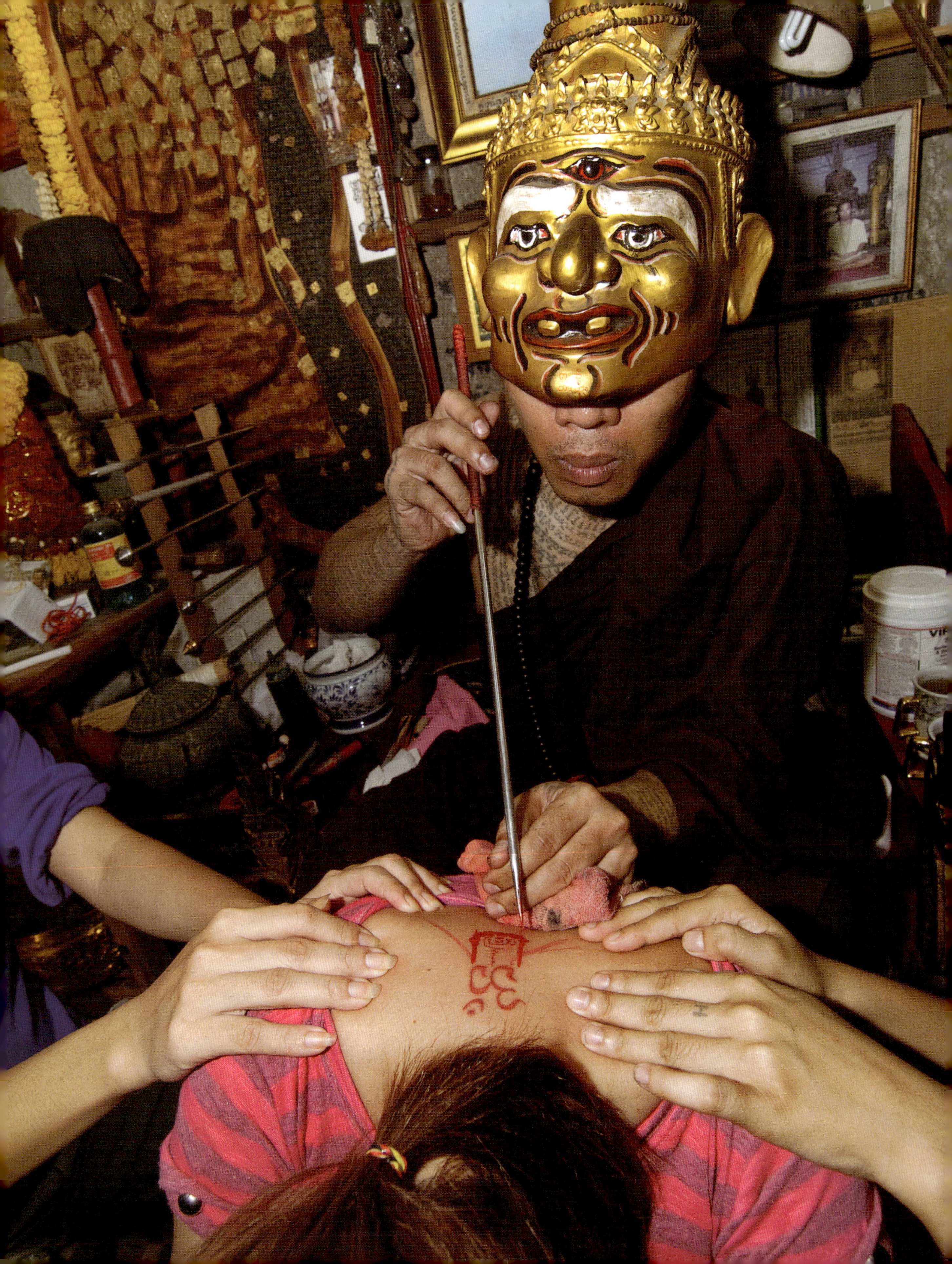

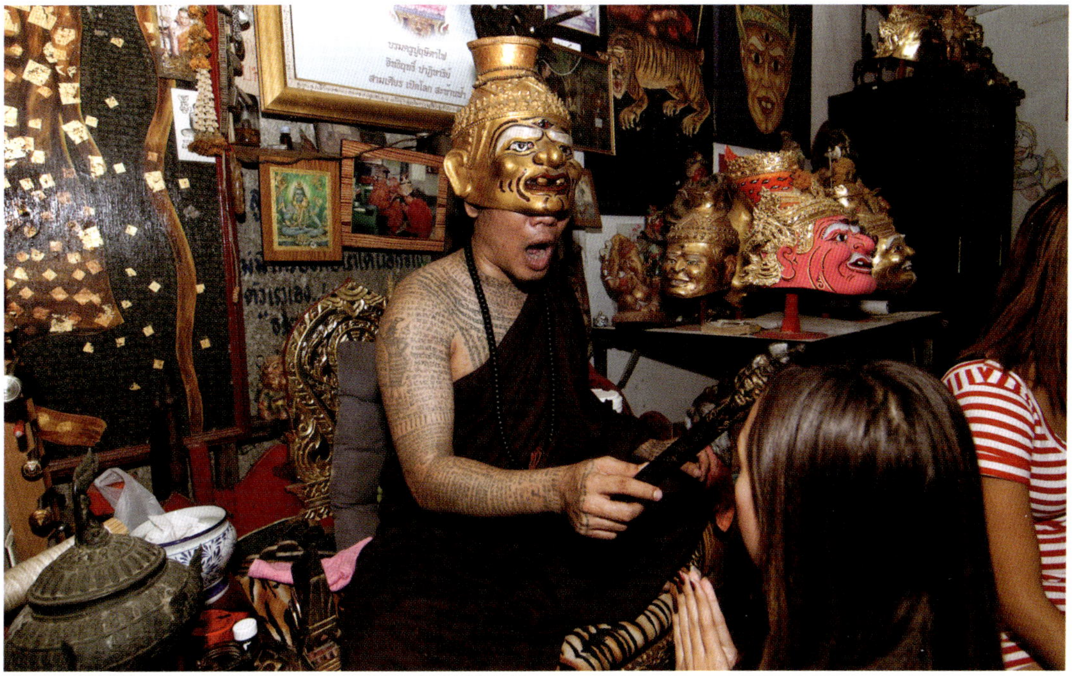

Left: Tattooing in red ink. At one time, some masters used their own blood for ink. Above: Ajahn Toy blesses a female disciple.

"All you need is Pho Kae, that's the best overall *yan*," Ajahn Toy tells us in the darkening room at the end of the work day when we ask about designs he recommends most.

"You'll get what you need, and perform your duties with alacrity. Luang Pho Kae can control everything. Then get a different *yan* if you want."

On request, Ajahn Toy will apply tattoos himself rather than as Pho Kae, and the resulting work is noticeably different, stylistically speaking. The master explains, "I tattoo both ways, *saay kharawaat* [layman lineage] and *saay pho kae* [Pho Kae lineage]. If you see *khai plaa* ["fish eggs," lines of dots whose discontinuity is easily distinguished from a short distance away], then Pho Kae made the tattoo. When I do it myself it's a solid line. Foreigners usually want lines, not *khai plaa*. But *khai plaa* is the original style, and it's what most Thais will choose."

When Ajahn Toy handles the needle, the resulting lines are solid and strong. Pho Kae's work, on the other hand, has a lighter overall feel.

Asked about his background, Ajahn Toy recounts, "I was born in Bangkok, and started studying *weechaa* when I was 20 years old. I studied under more than 10 teachers. The ones who taught me the most were Ajahn Phan To Thong, Pho Tai Phan Kam, Luang Pho Thong Dam, Pho Yeua and Ajahn Chuan Sai See."

Ajahn Toy's arms and torso are covered in *sak yan*. Most of the work, he says, was applied by Luang Pho Thong Dam and Ajahn Chuan Sai See.

"I was ready to work independently by the time I was 27. At that point I decided to become a *thudong* monk so that I could travel in the forest. After a while I left the monkhood and meditated in the forest as a *reusee*, first in Si Saket and later in Nong Bualamphu.

"In the old days going deep into the forest was the best way to gather the power you need to

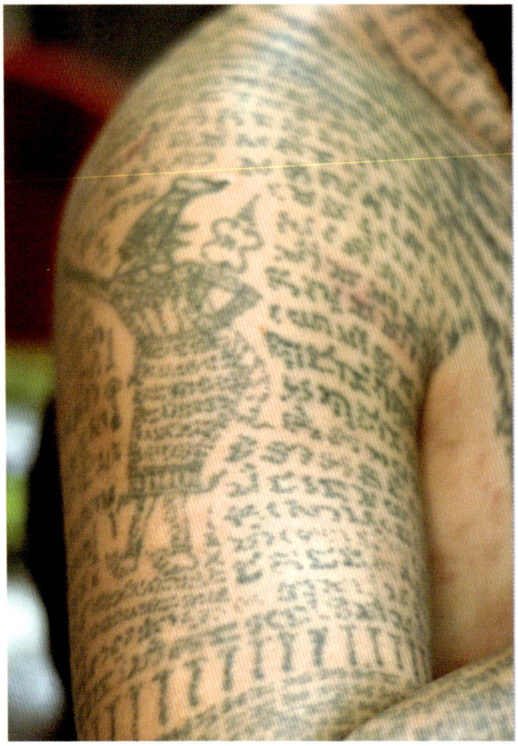

Above: Ajahn Toy's right shoulder bears a Pho Kae *yantra* surrounded by akkhara.

make powerful *sak yan*. A lot of the younger *khru sak yan* don't do that anymore. The way I see it, they don't have the real stuff if they don't renounce the world first."

Showing us a set of dusty volumes of palmleaf *sak yan* manuscripts, Ajahn Toy explained, "We learned the old way, putting in a lot of study with old manuscripts like these. A lot of the younger guys just buy *yantra* books with copied designs. They don't know the meaning of the *khaum* [old Khmer]. Tattoos made from designs in books, without understanding the script and using the correct *khaathaa*, have no power."

Ajahn Toy is mentoring a young man who studies with him daily. "He's not making *sak yan* yet, only studying the *khaathaa*. That's the first step, and you can't skip over it or you have nothing. Next he'll practise meditation.

"The most important thing is a strong, concentrated mind, and for that you need to practise meditation daily. Tattoos are only as powerful as the nature of the person making them. You won't have the energy to do this kind of work if you don't meditate a lot.

"Anyone who practises will eventually make pretty tattoos. But not correct tattoos. It's not about beauty, it's about the sacred. There are lots of masters who make prettier *sak yan* than I do! They're richer too!"

The master is vocal about *khru* who get rich from the art of *sak yan*.

"At first they charge the same as we do, but then they get famous and ask for 10 times, 20 times as much. When happens to poor people who can't afford it anymore? If you don't have *metta* for your disciples, you're not a real *ajahn*."

The master brings out his collection of *mai sak*. All of them are solid metal from handle to tip, which is bifurcated into the traditional *paak pet* (duck mouth) needle.

"A lot of people nowadays just buy a book in the market and use machines or ordinary tattoo needles. For the real thing you have to use needles like this, no machines and no bound sewing needles. You have to bless the needles before inking too."

The master shows us how he sterilises his needles in alcohol after every use. He then brings down a pair of large *khem boraan* (traditional needles) kept on the altar purely for worship. He knocks them together, producing a loud clanking to show how heavy they are.

"These are nearly a hundred years old. You don't have to worry about whether it hurts when you make tattoos with one of these – because it hurts for sure!"

Ajahn Toy offers an extensive variety of *yantras*,

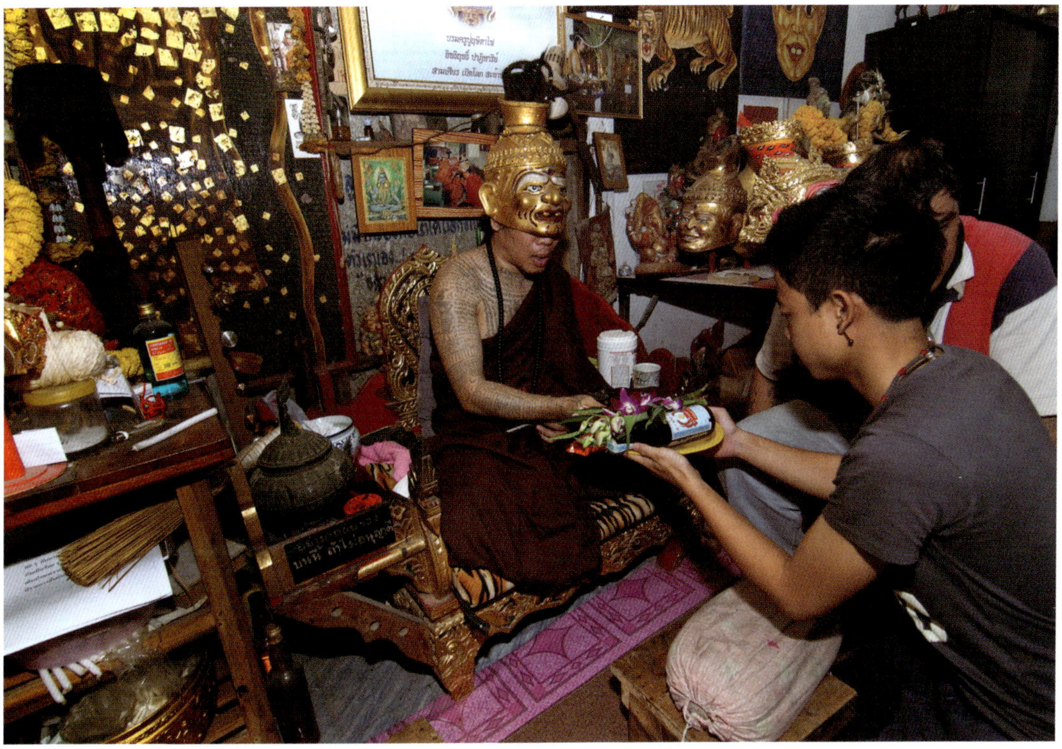

Above: A disciple hands an offering to Aahn Toy.

including a few not often seen elsewhere, such as the *phayaa khwai thanu* (Lord Bow-Horned Buffalo). The snorting buffalo, with sharp horns and a severe hump on its back, protects the wearer from black magic and evil spirits, and, more uniquely, protects any land he may own from encroachment.

Among Ajahn Toy's most popular *sak yan* are *kao yaut* (nine peaks), *haa thaew* (five rows) and *phayaa tao reuan* (Lord House-Turtle) *yantra*. The latter confers good fortune in business, long life and protection from physical danger.

His repertoire of designs also includes several types of crocodiles (evoking loving kindness from others), *hong* (mythical swan; loving kindness and charisma), wild boar (ferocity and courage), Nai Khanom Thom (legendary Thai kickboxing hero; courage and strength) and mermaids (charisma).

Most of Ajahn Toy's *sak yan* cost between 199 baht and 399 baht. Pho Kae, with the potential to confer wealth, wisdom and power, costs 299 baht. His most expensive design is *hanuman sip kaun tem lang* (10-armed Hanuman, covering the full back) at 1500 baht.

"We don't charge much for our tattoos, but we expect disciples to behave themselves. If you have *yantra* for protection from guns and knives, will you use it to bully people? If so, your tattoos can't help you. You have to decide what you're going to follow, the law of the gang or the law of karma.

"You must believe in goodness and practise good deeds. If you do that, the power of the Buddhas and Bodhisattvas will protect you. And if you don't, nothing will protect you."

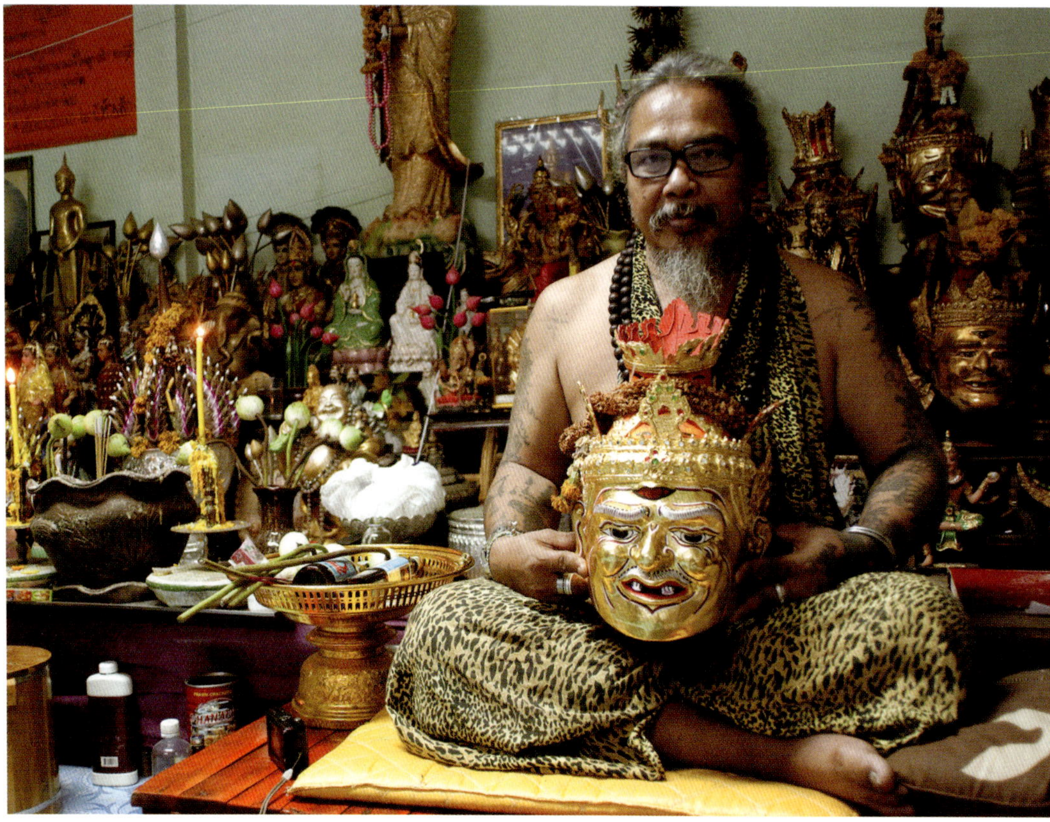

Above: Ajahn Anek, Chonburi, poses with a *reusee* mask. Right: This disciple of Ajahn Anek bears a pair of swans (charisma and romance) over his shoulder blades, an Eight Directions *yantra* (protection from danger) in the middle of his back and a fighting Hanuman (power, courage) on his lower back.

AJAHN ANEK

Alongside a country road in Chonburi Province, a sign bearing white Thai letters thickly hand-brushed onto a blue background reads "Road to the Palace of Reusee Ta Fai, Luang Pu Dam, Ajahn Anek". The "palace" would be a nondescript modern home were it not for a shrine in front occupied by a brightly painted, two-metre sculpture of Pho Kae.

When we arrive, Ajahn Anek is waiting inside a large room set aside as his *samnak sak yan*. An ample figure dressed in street clothes, he looks as if he would be comfortable commanding a successful chicken rice shop. He beckons us to sit on the floor, then hands us a thick, tattered photo album. Snapshots of the master inking both Thai and foreign disciples fill the pages.

Asked how the foreigners know about him, Ajahn Anek explains that someone set up a website (www.poodumtattoo.com) for him, and that many people contacted him online. He showed us a couple of albums containing line drawings of the *yantras* he offers.

"To some extent, I let people choose what *yan* they want, especially if they're looking for *metta*

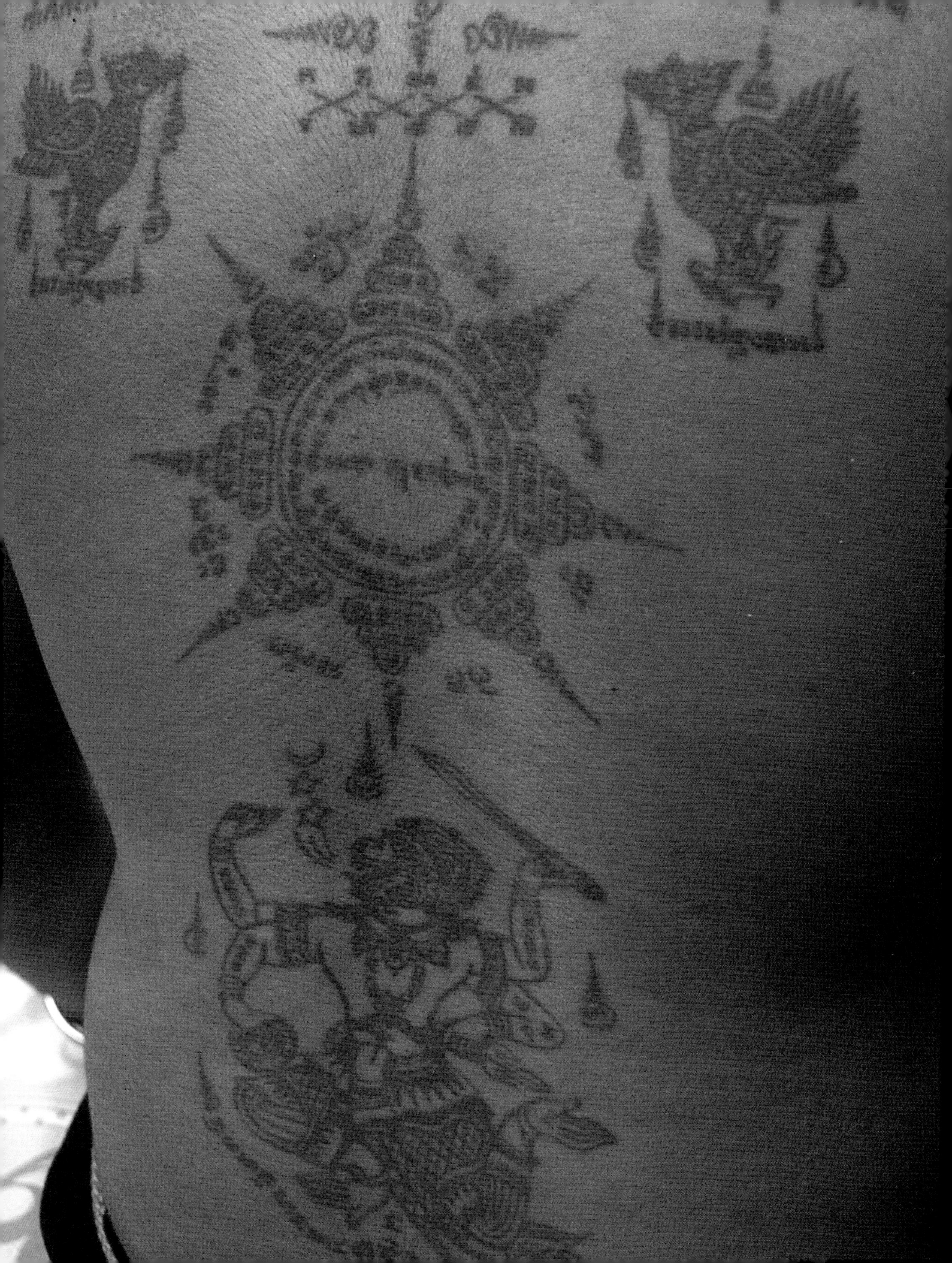

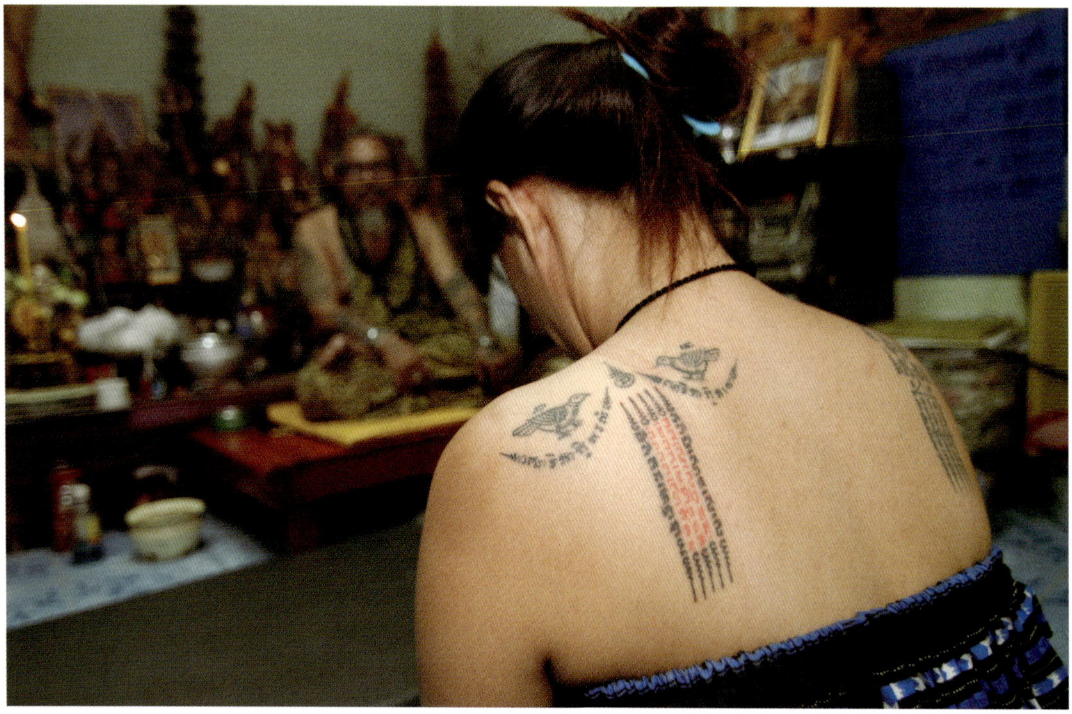

Above: A pair of sarika (mynah birds, for personal charisma) surmount a *haa thaew* (Five Rows) *yantra* on Ajahn Anek's disciple. The inside of the latter tattoo has been rendered in red ink for added *metta* (loving kindness).

mahaniyom (loving kindness, charisma), which are good for just about everybody. But I won't do other kinds of tattoos if I think they are inappropriate for the person. I like to talk with them awhile first.

"I don't do tigers, too powerful. Lions are okay. Hanuman I'll do only for some people."

One of Ajahn Anek's specialities is a large three-headed elephant (*chaang saam sian*, also known as *chaang phra in* – Indra's elephant), which covers nearly the entire back and takes up to seven days to apply. The elaborate design evokes *mahaniyom* (charisma) and *amnaat* (power).

A placard on the *samnak* wall lists fees of 1500 to 3000 baht. The master confessed that he usually charges foreigners double that because, "They can afford it, and the language barrier makes them a lot harder to deal with."

Ajahn Anek's tattoo styluses are of traditional length, longer than what most *khru sak yan* use nowadays. However the actual needle array at the end of the styluses is more modern, binding together sewing needle points in groups of four, five or six.

When we inquire about his lineage as a *khru sak yan*, Ajahn Anek points to an old photo on one wall showing two monks in a cave. The thin, old man seated in the background, he says, was Luang Phu Dam. The robust young man standing in the foreground is Anek himself.

"That cave is in Saraburi. Luang Pu Dam was my uncle, and he taught me everything I know. He learned from one of our greatest *sak yan* masters, Luang Pu Thong (abbot of Wat Ratchayotha, also known as Wat Lat Bua Khao, in Bang-

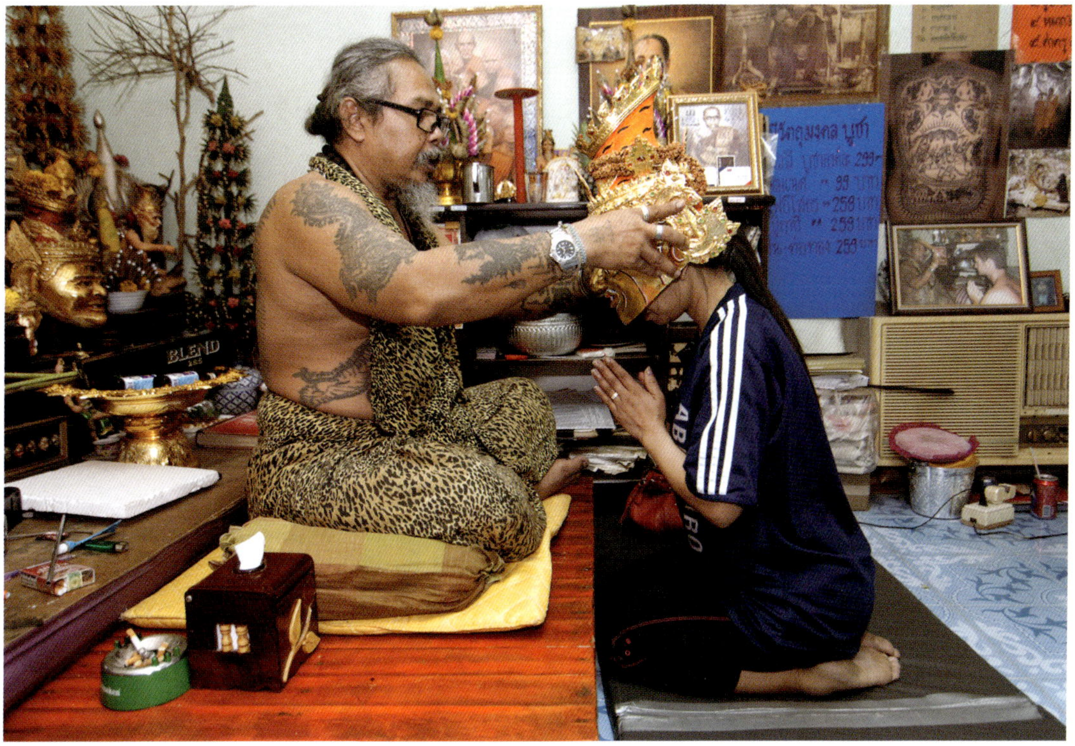

Above: During an empowerment ritual, Ajahn Anek places a *reusee* mask over a disciple's head.

kok). I studied with my uncle for 12 years, and was a novice monk most of that time. After that I went off to practise on my own. He died around 30 years ago."

All of the designs on Ajahn Anek's heavily inked skin came from Luang Pu Thong and were inked by Luang Pu Dam. Ajahn Anek firmly believes that the *weechaa* of both masters thus invested in his body guides his hand while he is applying *sak yan* to his own disciples.

The following day we have a chance to observe the lineage at work as Ajahn Anek tattoos a handful of Thai disciples, along with one foreigner. He is dressed in a tiger-print tunic and wearing large beads around his neck.

When their turn to consult the master arrives, each disciple offers a platter on which are laid lotus buds, a packet of cigarettes, a bottle of Red Bull, a bottle of rice liquor, candles and incense.

To guide the accuracy of his designs, Ajahn Anek takes a piece of tracing paper bearing the chosen template, slips a sheet of carbon paper beneath, and traces over the design to leave a carbon impression on the disciple's skin.

Noting that Ajahn Anek himself apprenticed to two monks, we ask how it came to be that he dons *reusee* garb when administering to his disciples.

"Although he was a monk, my *khru* was devoted to Pho Kae. So was his *khru*, Luang Pu Thong. Everything they taught me comes from Pho Kae. After I left the monkhood, I wandered in the forest, and I practised on my own. Eventually I came into direct contact with the spirit of Pho Kae and I knew: I'm not a monk; I'm not a layman. I'm *reusee*."

Right: After a disciple passes a tray of offerings to Ajahn Anek, the master in turn dedicates the offerings to the deities on his altar.

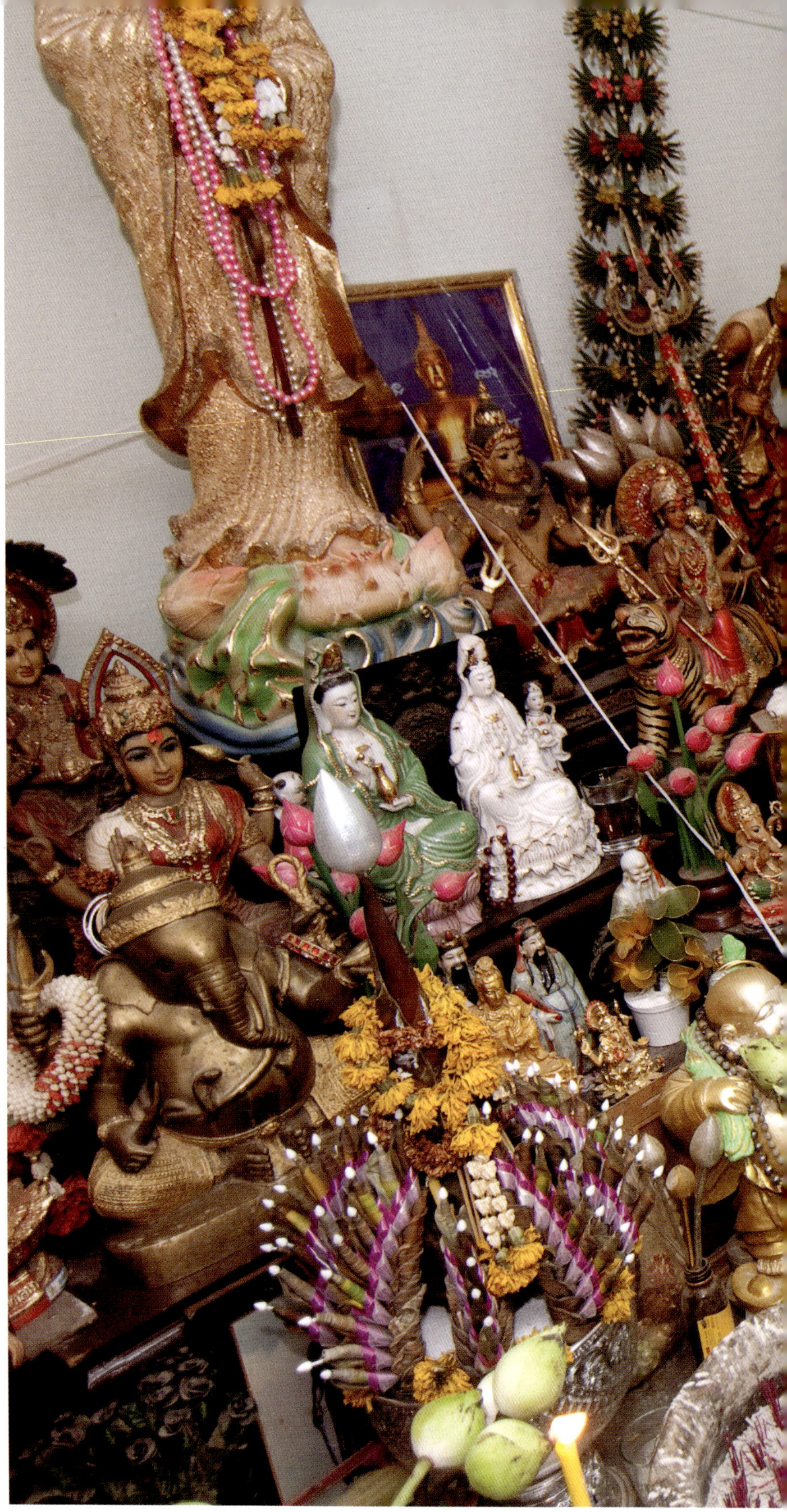

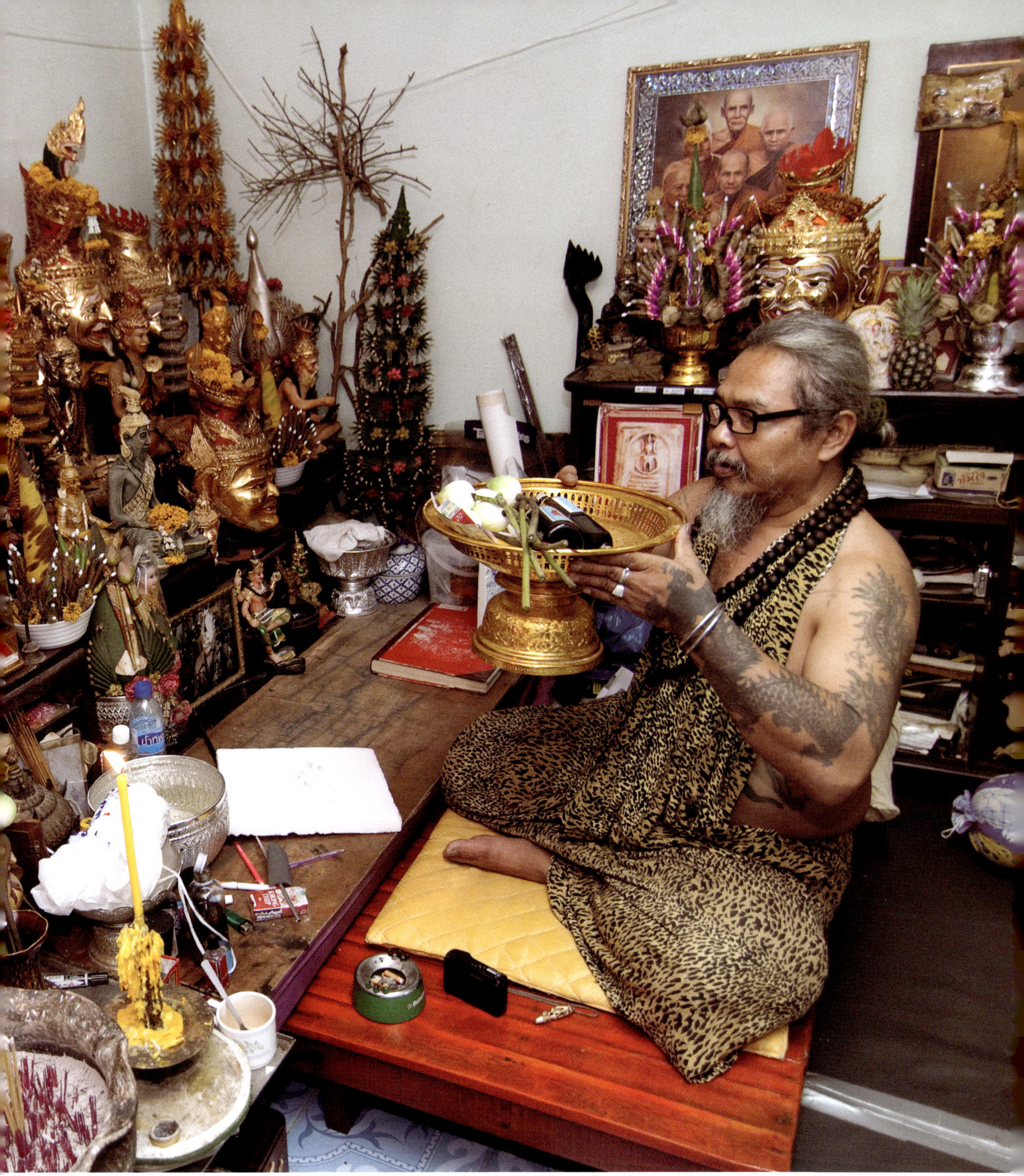

MASTER TO THE STARS: AJAHN NOO GANPAI

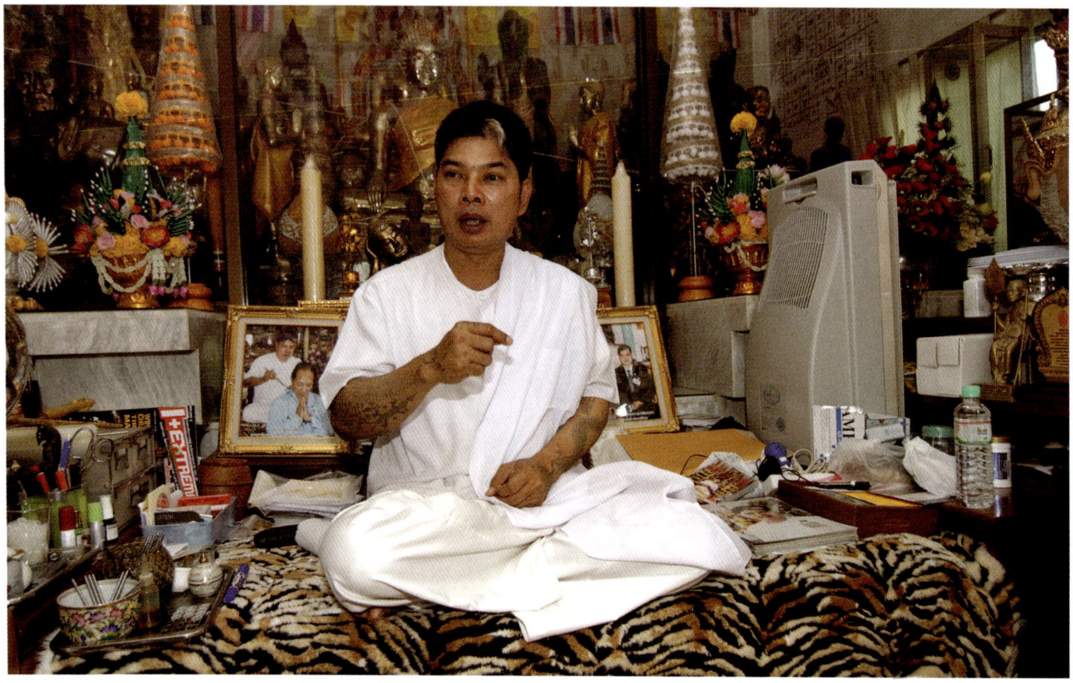

Above: Ajahn Noo Ganpai.

Commanding a legion of loyal followers, Ajahn Sompong "Noo" Ganpai has attained near-iconic status in Thai society and has been credited with bringing Thai *sak yan* onto the international stage. Although his disciples have long included a coterie of high-ranking police and military men, along with several TV and film personalities, it wasn't until after 23 April 2003, when Ajahn Noo applied his signature *haa thaew* (five rows) design to the left shoulder blade of American actress Angelina Jolie, that the moustached, white-clad *khru sak* became the most sought-after traditional Thai tattoo master in the land.

Ajahn Noo's path from a humble birth in Nonthaburi to the two-storey, marble-floored *samnak* in Pathum Thani where he and his four assistants carry out their work is paved in legend. I first visited Ajahn Noo in 2005, a year after he had inked Jolie a second time. I was accompanying Anne Chebanier, a Parisian acquaintance who wanted a tattoo like Jolie's. She was the first of several foreigners who have since asked me to help them find Jolie's tattoo master. I translated for Anne as she negotiated a price on Ajahn Noo's legendary *haa thaew*. By this time Ajahn Noo was already so famous that he rarely did the work himself, and so one of the master's assistants applied the design. It looked identical to the one Ajahn Noo himself had given to Jolie, and Chebanier was pleased with the results. Ajahn Noo then empowered the *yantra*, chanting *khaathaa*, stroking the tattoo and blowing forcefully through his lips to *pluuk sehk* – "plant" the magic.

On a subsequent visit, I travelled with drummer Ming Roth and actor Erich Fleshman. Erich, who drove us to Pathum Thani from Bangkok in his wife's car, had a long-time interest in everything Thai, and was curious to see what the tattoo subculture was about. Ming was already a Thai tattoo veteran who had been inked by three lesser known *khru sak* in Bangkok and in northern Thailand. As usual I acted as interpreter while Ming chose a couple of designs from Ajahn Noo's thick catalogues.

A gentle haggling over the fee was necessary and expected. Each time I visited Ajahn Noo, the prices seemed to be a little higher than the time before. One of Ajahn Noo's disciples quoted a price of 25,000 baht for the design Ming said he wanted. He was able to bargain down to 10,000 baht. I never encountered this approach among other *khru sak* in Thailand, Cambodia or Laos. Then again, no one else in the three countries commanded such high fees.

Once Ming's *sak yan* was finished, and Ajahn Noo had performed the empowerment ritual, the three of us gathered our things to leave the *samnak*. While Erich was walking towards the door, Ajahn Noo asked him whether he wanted to receive *sak yan*. Erich, who had never been in a *samnak sak yan* before, said *mai ao* (don't want), laughed nervously and walked out.

An hour later as we drove down a major street in the centre of Bangkok, a car coming in the opposite direction spun out of control, crossed the centre yellow line and broadsided our vehicle. No one in either car was injured, but we were all shaken and the damage to Erich's wife's car was relatively severe. Ming, who unreservedly believes in the power and efficacy of *sak yan* culture, felt that the accident was somehow linked to the fact that Erich had been disrespectful of Ajahn Noo. Erich later did receive *sak yan*, but from another master.

By the time photographer Dan White and I visited Ajahn Noo to photograph him and his disciples, and to interview him in depth, the master knew me by sight. We had not made an appointment, and we found the *samnak* filled with dozens of monks and laypeople who were participating in an elaborate set of blessing ceremonies. The compound was strung with *bai see* (blessed cotton string) and *phaa yan* (*yantra* cloth) banners. The ceremonies were led not by Ajahn Noo but by the monks, who had come from Wat Mae Takrai in Mae On District, Chiang Mai Province. Wat Mae Takrai's rotund, heavily tattooed abbot, Phra Thianchai Suphathutho, was also on hand.

Ajahn Noo then empowered the yantra, chanting *khaathaa*, stroking the tattoo and blowing forcefully through his lips to *pluuk sehk* – "plant" the magic.

As it turned out, by coincidence the date we chose to visit was an auspicious date for the blessing of a large number of Buddhist amulets, *phaa yan* and other *watthu mongkhon* (blessed materials) dedicated to the late Luang Pu Thuad, a monk who was known for powerful *weechaa*. All of the *yantra* appearing on these objects were designed and consecrated by Ajahn Noo. Among the most popular objects was a rectangular metal medallion, similar in shape to G.I. dogtags, which bore an image of Luang Pu Thuad on one side and Ajahn Noo's *yan krau phet* (diamond armour *yantra*) on the reverse side.

Eventually we made it to the *samnak* on a non-ceremony day, and on a day when the usual throng

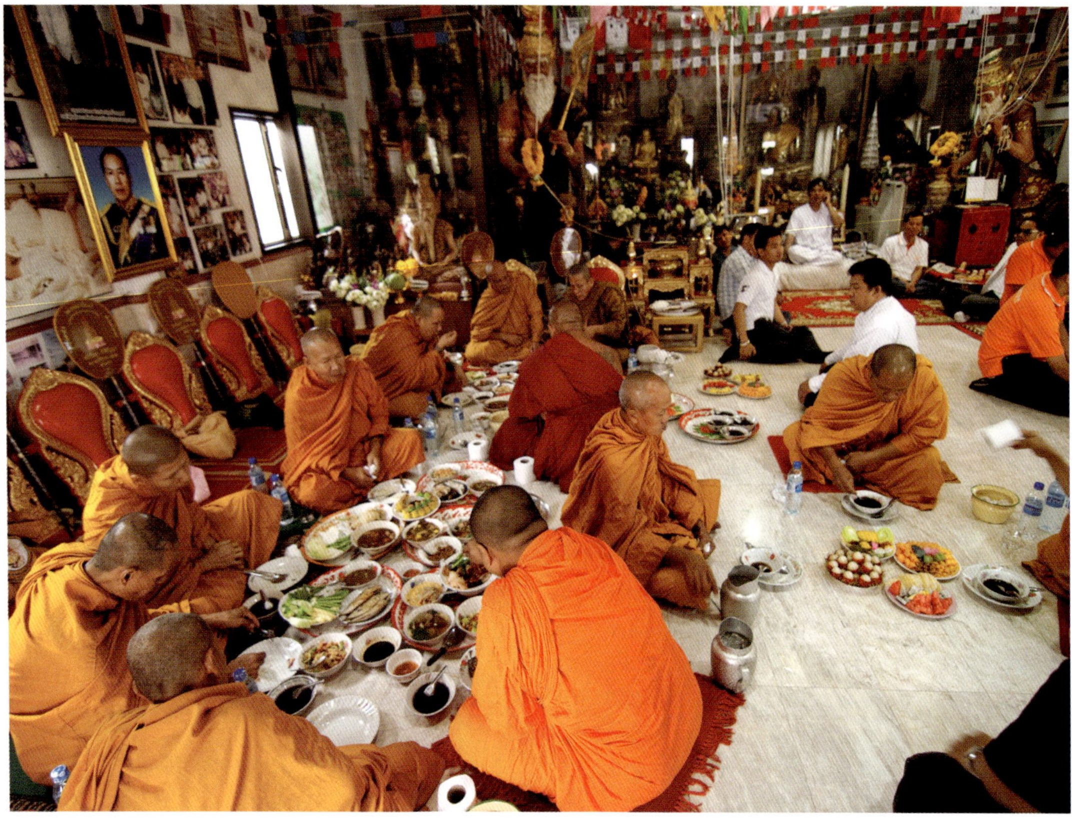

Above: Monks from Wat Mae Takrai share mid-morning almsfood at Ajahn Noo's *samnak*.

of disciples had thinned to just a handful. When I finally had a chance to chat with Ajahn Noo about his training and background, I understood why existing books and articles describing his history tended to conflict.

To begin with, while many other *sak yan* practitioners claim a single line of succession, when I asked Ajahn Noo where his designs came from, the master responded, "They all come from Buddhism." Yes, but which teacher, I persisted. "From the Buddha."

Most third-person accounts of Ajahn Noo's childhood and apprenticeship trace the roots of his early mastery of *akkhara* (sacred script used for amulets, *sak yan* and so on) to a book of spells belonging to his father and said to be written entirely in *khaum* (old Khmer). The book was said to contain *khaathaa* (verbal spells) used by generations of Thai bandits for protection.

Ajahn Noo, however, told us the book belonged to his grandfather, and that there was actually more than one. "My mother's father was a monk and he studied *weechaa aakhom* (mastery of spells)," Ajahn Noo said when I asked about the legendary text. "He taught me some of what his books contained, and some of it I learned from studying the books on my own."

Asked what lineage these books followed, Ajahn Noo answered, "It's the lineage of dhamma, of white magic."

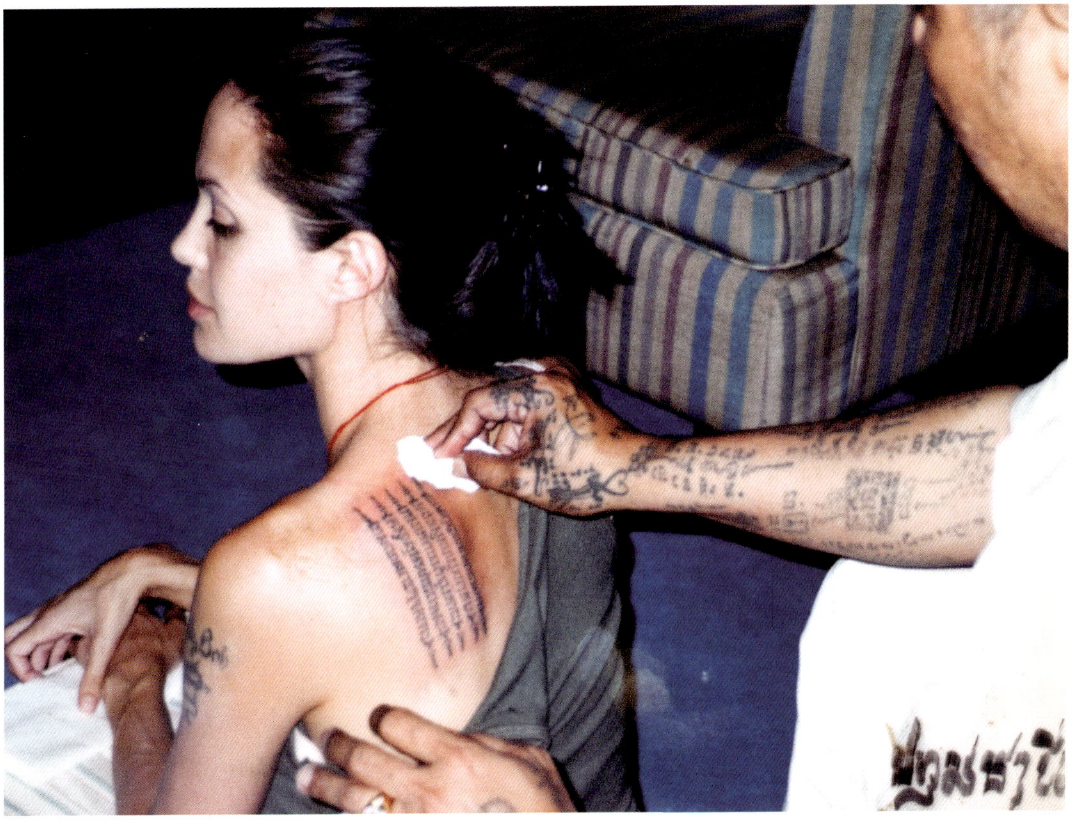

Above: Ajahn Noo puts the finishing touches on a *haa thaew* for actress and philanthropist Angelina Jolie.

According to most sources, Noo began spending nights chanting at an early age with the elder monks at Wat Laharn in Bang Bua Thong, Nonthaburi. By the time he finished fourth grade, his family noted Noo's obsession with learning and reciting verses from his grandfather's book. By the time he was 13, the confident young man was already proficient in the *khaum*, and could recite many *khaathaa* from memory.

A reckless, experimental phase followed, during which the boy would initiate fights on a daily basis, and even invite friends to stab and shoot him in order to test the power of *khong kraphan* (invincibility) magic. Among the local community he became known as Noo Johm Saep (Noo The Hooligan).

According to a much-repeated tale, after the young tough finished his daily work as a ticket seller on a local bus, he noticed some merchants in a nearby market being bullied by local mobsters. Deciding to intervene on the merchants' behalf, he confronted the gangsters, one of whom was seen by several onlookers (including the police, it is said) to stab Noo repeatedly in the torso. By the time the police had halted the scuffle and taken the ticket seller away, they were surprised to find Noo unharmed, although his shirt was in tatters from knife slashes.

Bang Bua Thong residents say that Noo's reputation for *weechaa* began with his seemingly miraculous survival. The very next day, so the story goes, a *sinsae* (Chinese soothsayer) visited Noo's mother to warn her that her son would either be killed within three days or live to become a powerful and famous figure. The police, meanwhile, issued a shoot-to-kill order for all members of the gang, as well as Noo. To allay the fears of his mother, Noo ordained as a novice monk at Wat Laharn immediately after the *sinsae* left.

One day a man who felt he needed supernatural protection came to see the young novice at Wat Laiharn. Assuming Noo harboured sacred objects that gave him supernatural powers, he begged him to share some *khaung dee* ("good stuff", that is, anything charged with magic power). Having no such objects on hand, the novice Noo instead offered to apply protective *khaathaa* as *sak yan*. Noo created the first tattoo of his career by binding a sewing needle to the stem of a coconut leaf, dipping it into Chinese ink, and tapping *akkhara* onto the man's skin. Shortly after, the man was attacked by someone wielding a knife and stabbed repeatedly. Again the blade failed to penetrate the skin, and Noo's reputation grew further, bringing him a number of disciples.

Yan Haa Thaew - Five Rows Yantra

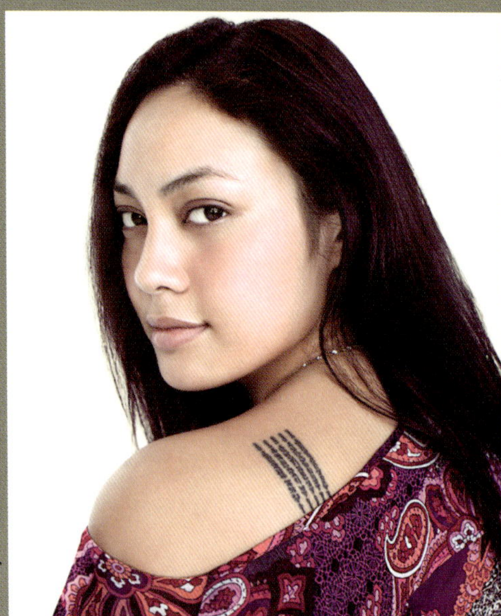
Photo by Pratch Siridhara

In terms of popularity, one yantra stands far above all the rest at the house of Ajahn Noo. Usually applied to back of the left shoulder, over the shoulder blade, the design consists of five rows of neatly inked Khmer script. According to Ajan Noo, "It is an ancient belief that this yantra represents a different spell in each row. The first row provides protection from danger, the second brings good fortune, the third provides good business and a successful career. the fourth encodes the astrological status [of the bearer] and the fifth is for personal charisma."

Each line of script is tagged at either end with *unalom*, a squiggly line extending from a simple spiral motif, an elaboration of the Thai numeral '1' and believed to invoke the Buddha and all his virtues.

The *yan haa thaew*, like many other *yantras* used in *sak yan*, also makes an appearance on amulets, stickers, yantra cloth and other materials infused with the power of *weechaa*.

Before Angelina Jolie received the *yan haa thaew* from Ajahn Noo, it was a favourite among Thai businessmen. Post-Jolie, the design has become a perennial choice for many Thai actresses and models, who perhaps hope to emulate Jolie's success in the film industry. Female Thai celebrities who bear the yantra include Odette Henriette Jacqmin, Florence Vanida Faivre, Phenphak Serikul, Yotsawadee Hatsadiwijit, Chomphoo Araya Hargate and, pictured here, Bongkoj Kongmalai.

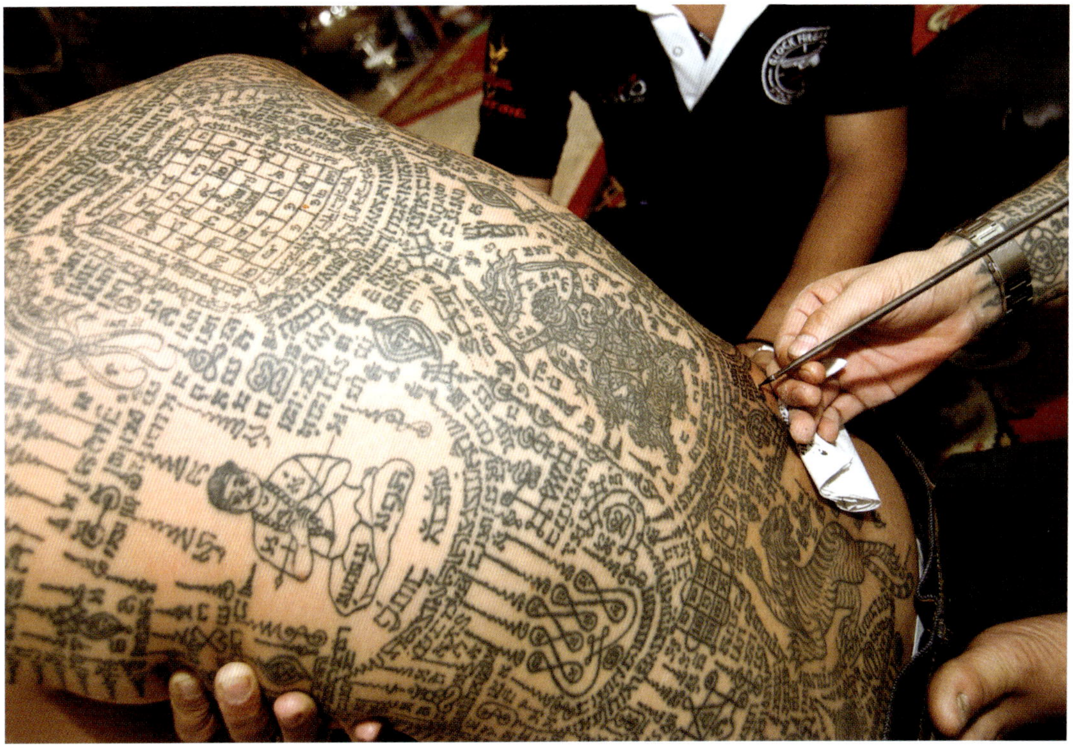

Above: The heavily inked back of a disciple has another corner filled by Ajahn Kai, one of Ajahn Noo's chief assistants.

After disrobing as a monk in order to earn money for his family – by which time the police left him alone, convinced he had reformed his behaviour – Noo continued to practise *sak yan*. When he reached 20, the age at which one can become a fully ordained monk, he took up robes and bowl again at Wat Laharn. As his interest in *weechaa* continued to grow, he took leave of the monastery to go on pilgrimage to Rayong in eastern Thailand to find monks who possessed powerful *weechaa*.

Ajahn Noo told us very little of his pilgrimage except to say that he came into contact with renowned masters and texts, and that it was during this phase that he received the bulk of his education in *saiyasaat* and *aakhom*.

The most important of these masters was Luang Pu Tim (1879–1975), creator of the original Luang Pu Thuad amulets, considered to offer very powerful protection. Another teacher in Rayong was Luang Ta Put, also known as Luang Ta Khamen (Venerable Uncle Khmer), who was Thai but thought to be Cambodian possibly because of his dark complexion. The latter had been a disciple of Luang Pu Suk (see Chapter 5), one of the most highly revered monks in Thai history with respect to *weechaa* and *aakhom*. Initially put off by the old monk's loud voice and what seemed to be strangely erratic behaviour for a monk who had practised meditation for years, Noo said he was stunned by Luang Ta Put's ability to read his mind and evaluate his quest for *weechaa*. Ajahn Noo stayed with Luang Ta Put for a year, learning how to meditate properly and to control his body, while continuing to study *khaathaa* in Pali and Khmer.

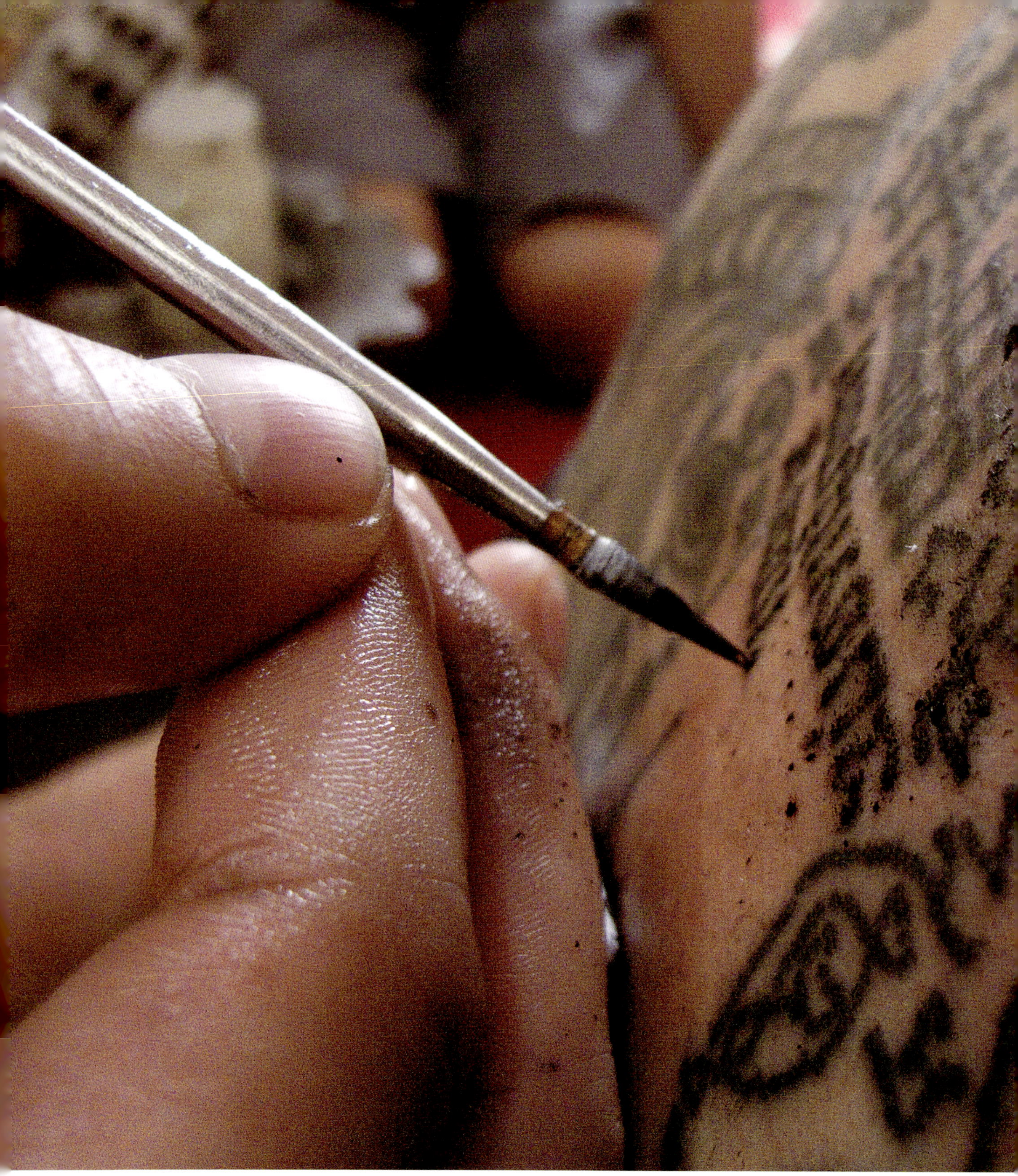

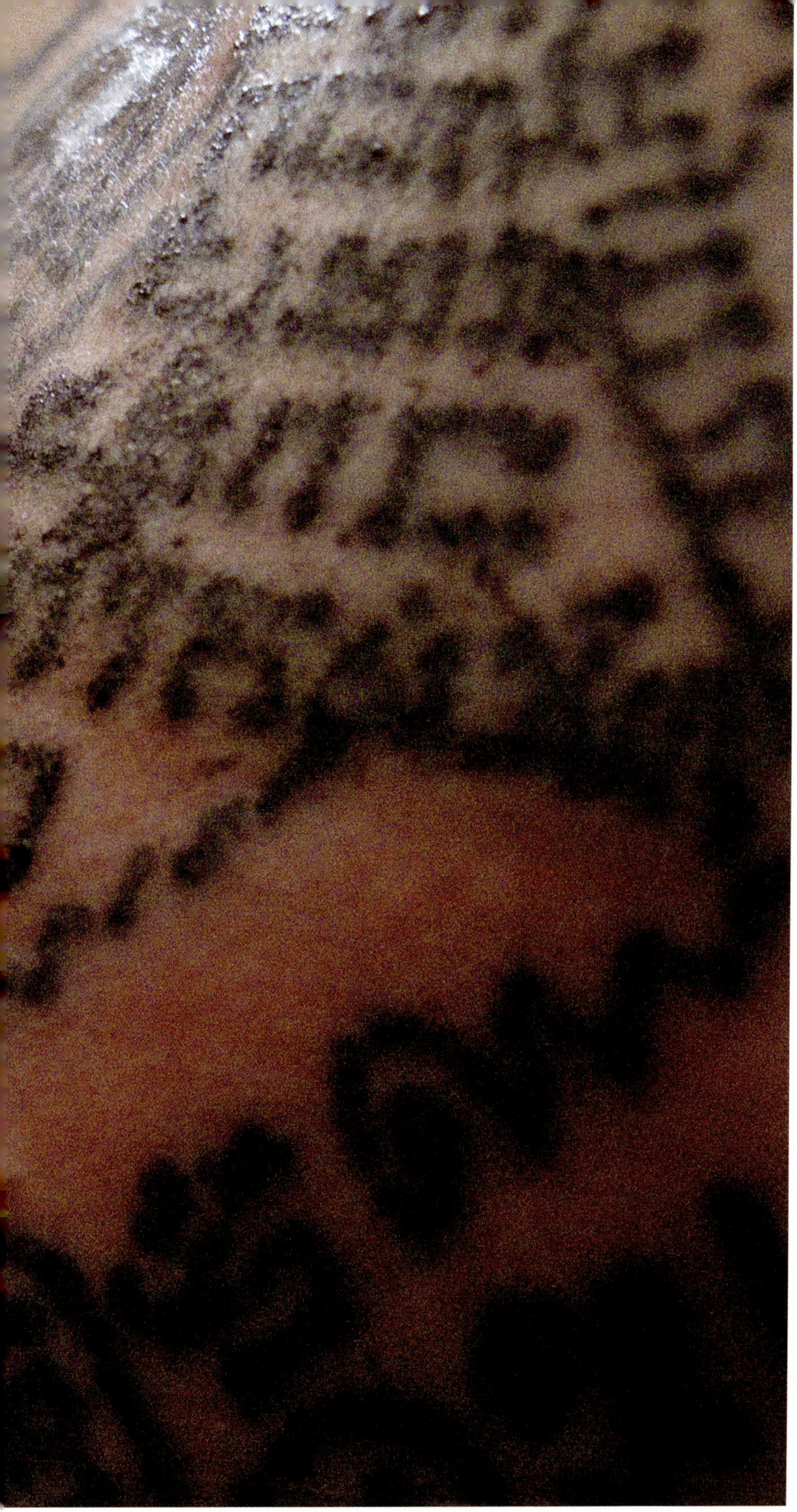

Left: One of Ajahn Noo's disciples adds *akkhara*.

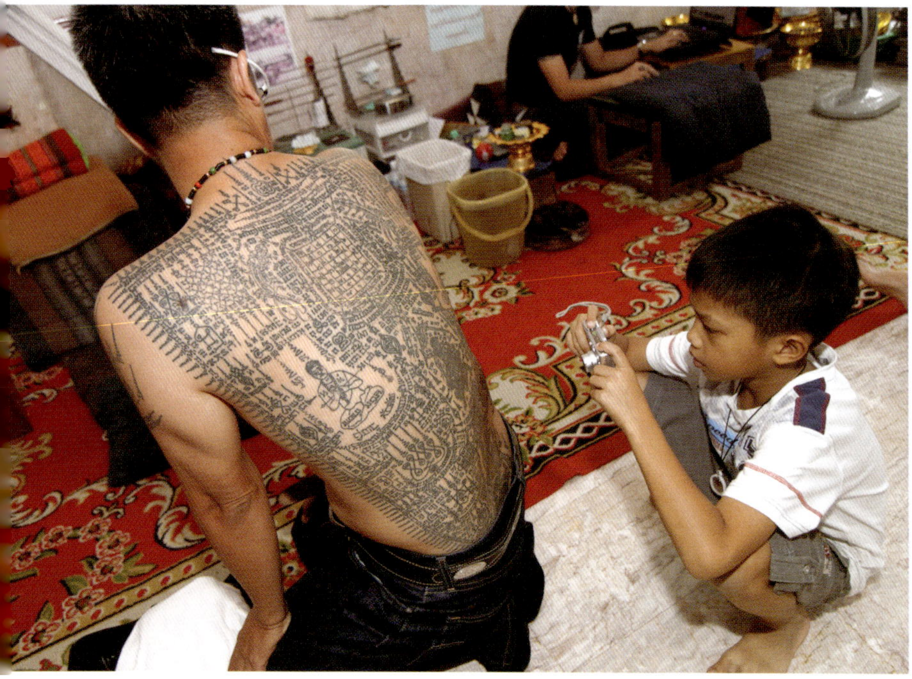

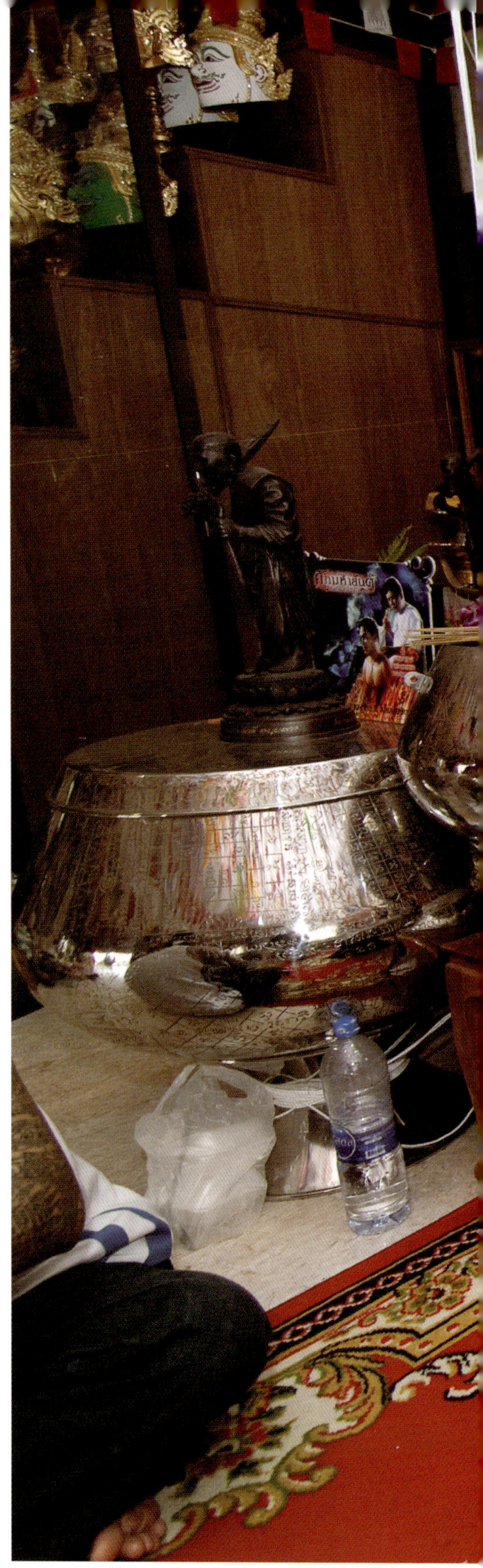

Above: A man's son snaps a photo of his father's latest *sak yan* acquisition.

Right: Ajahn Noo blesses a disciple.

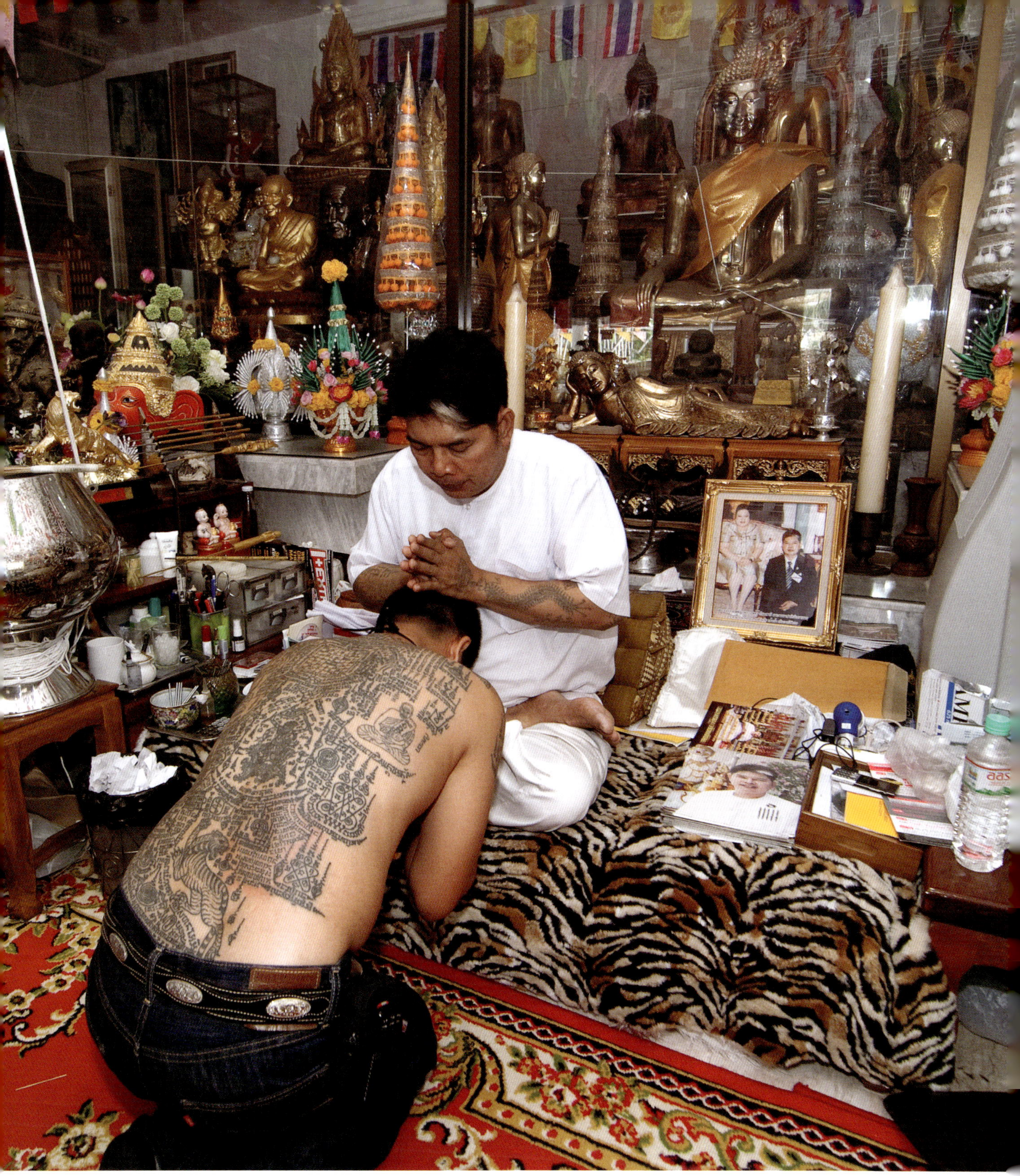

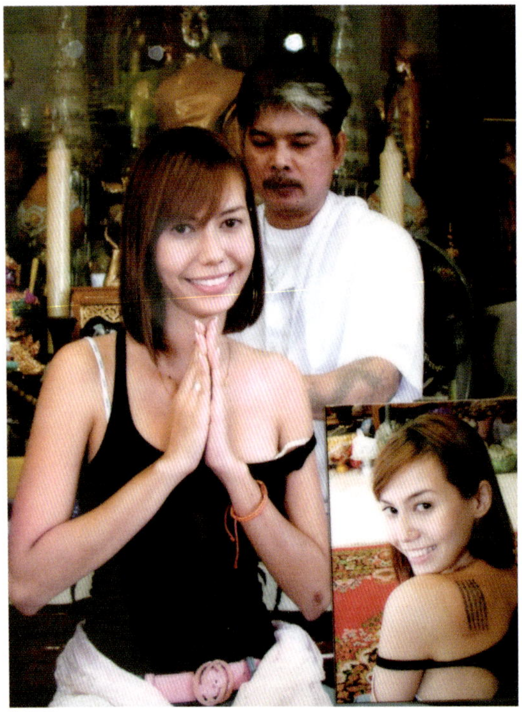

Above: French-Thai celebrity Odette Henriette Jacqmin.

Ajahn Noo extended his pilgrimage to all corners of Thailand, investigating additional *khaathaa* in Mon, Lanna and Burmese. Among the renowned masters he studied with, he credits Luang Pho Ngoen (Wat Bang Khlan, Phichit), Luang Pho Klan (Wat Phrayaht, Ayuthaya) and Luang Pho Phring (Wat Kao Yaut, Bangkok) as the most important.

In his early 30s, Ajahn Noo returned to Pathum Thani, where he took up residency at Wat Talat Nua. During this period he was praised for helping end violent feuding between workers at two different soft-drink plants, Pepsi and Coca Cola, by tattooing the workers and teaching them the ethical principles behind *sak yan*.

When Wat Talat Nua's abbot resigned, Ajahn Noo was invited to take his place.

"I had had second thoughts about practising *sak yan* as a monk already, and knew that as an abbot I probably wouldn't have time to keep up the practice or to carry out my responsibilities towards my disciples," Ajahn Noo explained.

"So rather than decline the invitation, I decided to leave the monkhood altogether, and to devote myself to *sak yan*."

He opened a small *samnak sak yan* behind the monastery. The one-storey structure had wooden floors and a low tin roof.

"Very few disciples visited me at first. Sometimes three or four people a day, sometimes just one. As my disciples saw that my *weechaa aakhom* worked, and they spread the word, I started getting more and more new disciples. "By around 1995 I was seeing over a hundred people a day. I started screening disciples more carefully, since it was difficult to get to know each one well. I stopped tattooing anyone under the age of 20, and I wouldn't take drunks."

Ajahn Noo acknowledges that Jolie's visit in 2003 shot him into the major leagues, bringing a steady stream of international disciples.

"I didn't know who she was when she showed up at my old *samnak* with three large bodyguards, only that she was an actress from America. I'm not sure how she found me but I think she heard about my work from high police. She wanted *sak yan* and asked if I could do the work at her room in the Mandarin Oriental.

"I agreed. I told her beforehand, 'I don't care what religion you are, but you must be a good person. You must respect your parents and cultivate the four *brahmavihara* (loving kindness, generosity, forgiveness and equanimity), practise an honest livelihood, and have mindfulness.' I told her to read about the history of Thailand, and I explained how the ancient *akkhara wetmon* (written mantras) and *akkhara lehk* (written numbers) work."

Ajahn Noo told us that he didn't charge Jolie for the *haa thaew* he applied to the back of her left shoulder, but that he asked that Thai reporters be

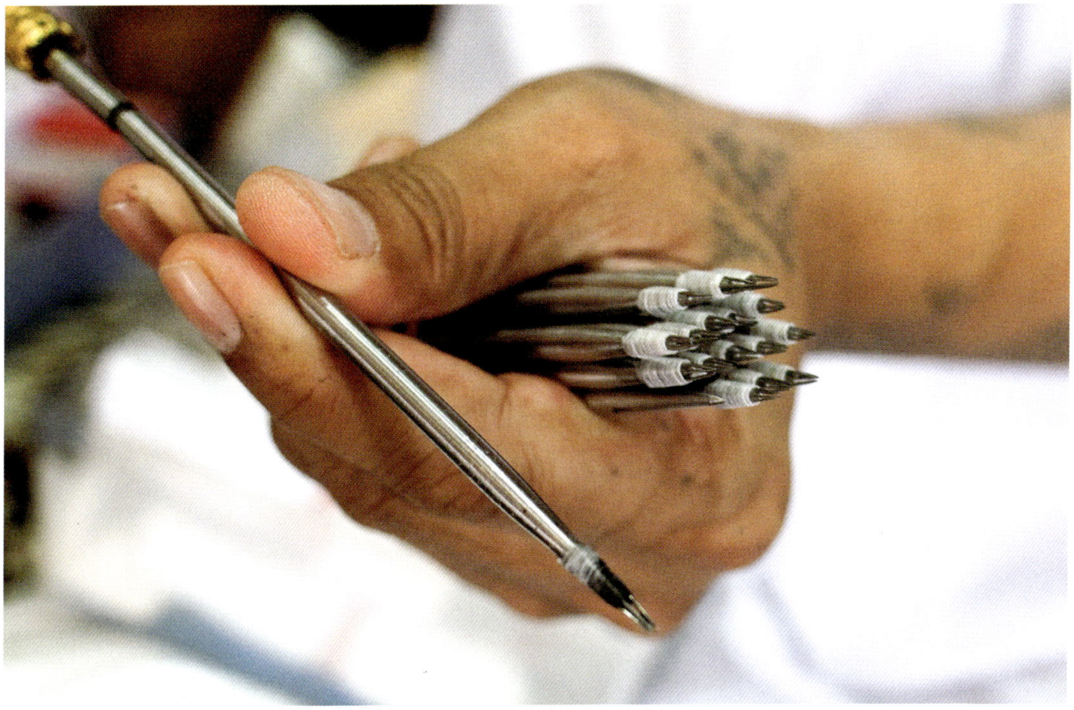

Above: Ajahn Noo shows how his removable needles can be screwed onto the *mai sak*.

allowed to take a few photos and write about the event. The design took 15 minutes to apply.

As Ajahn Noo's reputation soared to hitherto unseen heights, for a *khru sak yan*, he was compelled to build a larger *samnak* to accommodate the triple-digit numbers of disciples that began seeking him out. His two main assistants – his younger brother Ajahn Nid and his most senior disciple Kai, who have been with him for more than 10 years – were joined by three younger assistants.

Obviously impressed with the master's work, Jolie returned to Thailand for a second *sak yan* on 8 July, 2004. This time she received a much larger and more powerful *yantra*, the *yan phayaa seua khrong liaw lang* (royal tiger looking back), on her lower back. Ajahn Noo finished the work in around two hours. Unlike in the previous encounter, Jolie requested that no press be informed until after she left Thailand. And this time, Jolie paid for the tiger.

Aside from providing *sak yan* for a growing mass of disciples in Thailand and around the world, Ajahn Noo has served as a consultant to Thai film productions which involve *sak yan*. These have included *Suriyothai, Maha-Ud. Jaum Khamang Wet (Necromancer)* and *Haa Thaew*. The more dramatic events in Noo's life have been dramatised in an action-packed feature film entitled *Noo Kanpai: Seuk Mahayan (Great Yantra Warrior)*, released in 2010. Ajahn Noo readily admits that the script was pumped up for entertainment value.

Asked whether he thought Jolie would return for further *sak yan*, Ajahn Noo admitted that he is not in contact with the star but that he expected she would come back for more.

"Her career has been doing very well since 2003 and 2004," he added with a smile.

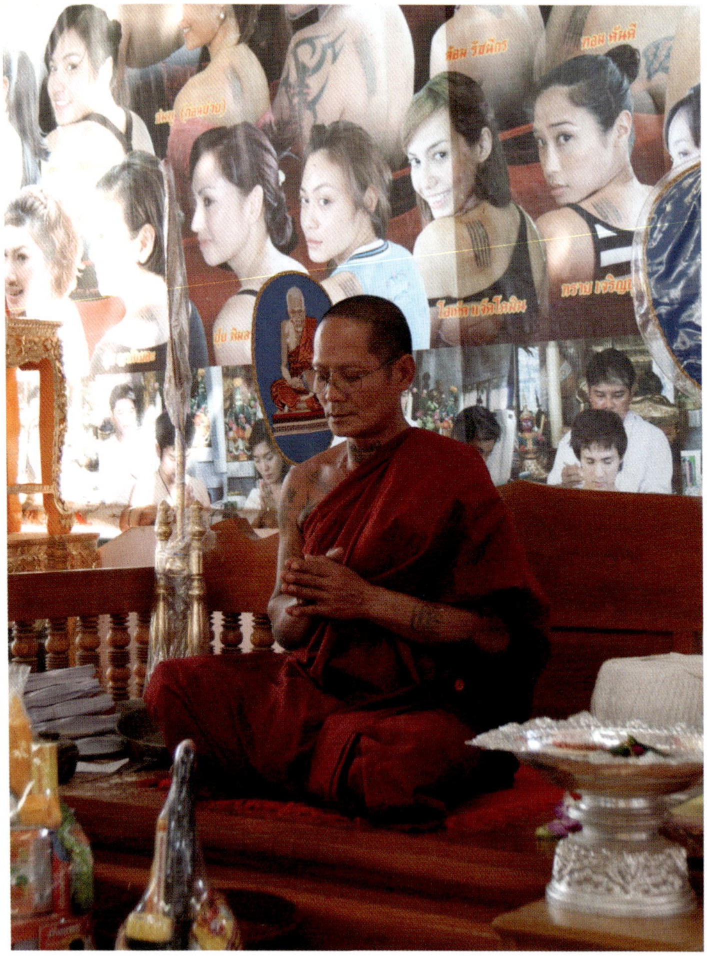

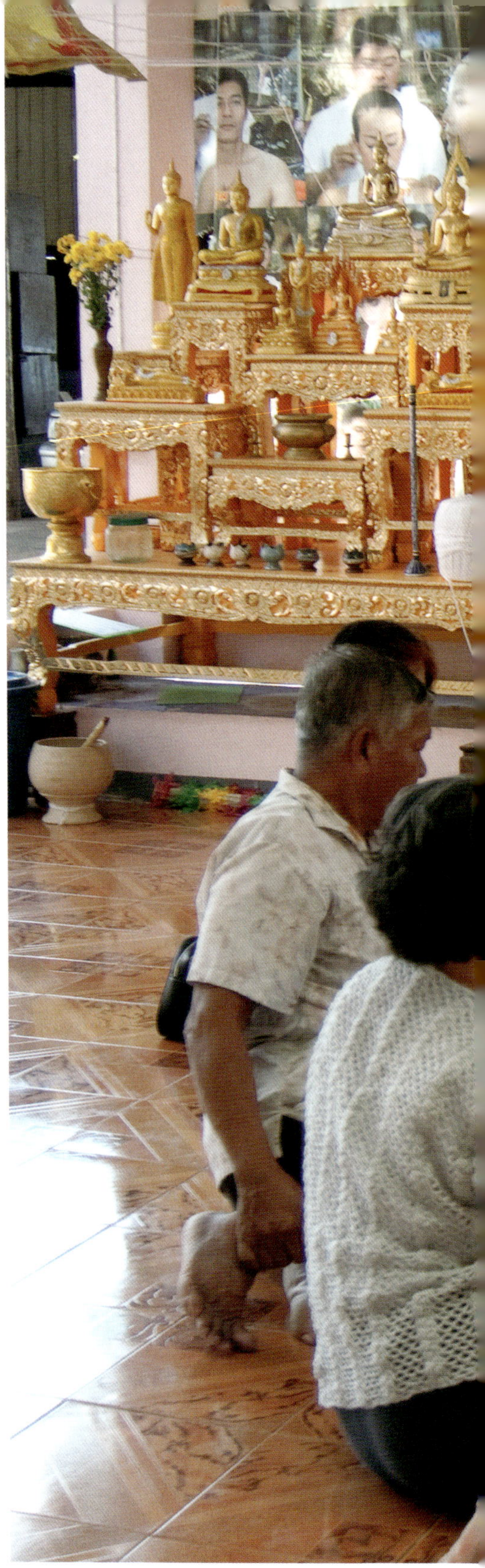

Above & Right: A high monk at Wat Mae Takrai, Mae On District, Chiang Mai Province, receives visitors. The wall behind him is plastered with photos of Thai celebrities who have been inked by Ajahn Noo.

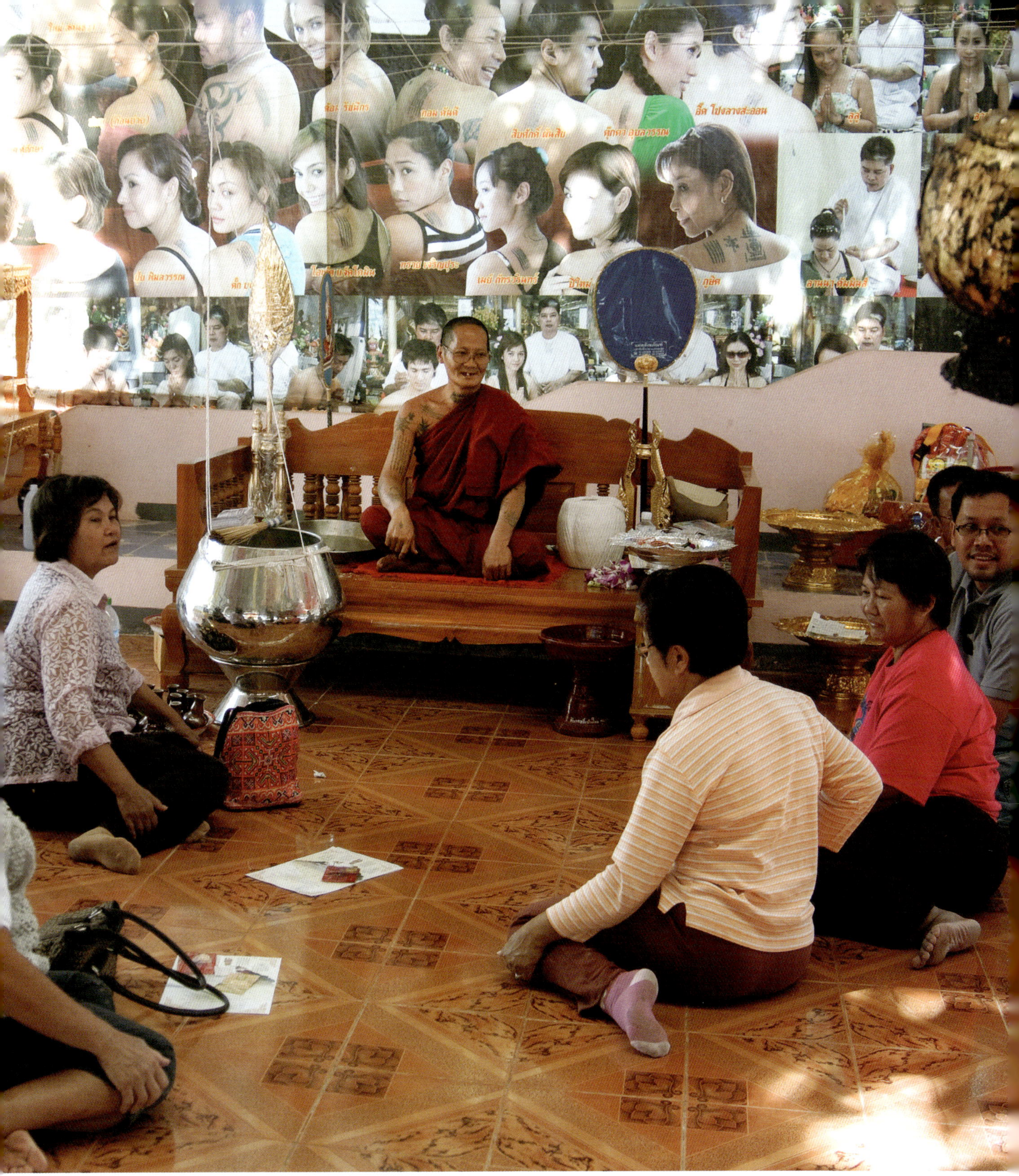

THE NORTHERN TRADITION: LANNA & LAOS

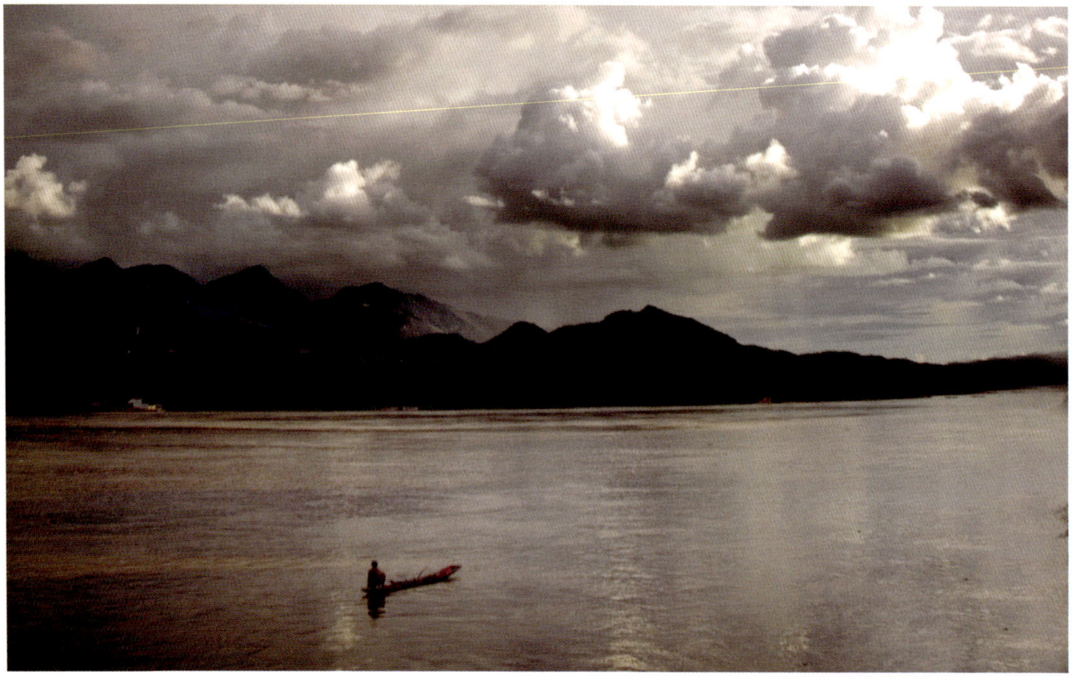

Above: The Mekong River at dawn.

The *sak yan* arts originally developed among the early Tai Diaspora extending west from northern Vietnam, across Laos, southern Yunnan and northern Thailand and into the Shan territories of today's Myanmar. By the 14th century, Chinese chronicles were reporting that the tradition was so entrenched that it was uncommon to come across Tai males who were not tattooed.

These chronicles describe the use of geometric and animal-design tattoos to protect the bearer against malevolent forces and to boost power and charisma. Buddhist content in the form of abbreviated Pali verses were no doubt introduced to the magic arts as Buddhism became institutionalised in the area. The earliest alphabet used for this purpose was based on Mon script, and used with only subtle variation right across the region. Since writing at the time was used mostly for archiving and teaching Buddhist thought, the script was simply referred to as Dhamma, pronounced *tham* or *tam* in southwestern Tai languages. Many old palm-leaf manuscripts preserved in northern Thailand and Laos – as well as in neighbouring Yunnan and northeastern Myanmar – contain writings in this alphabet.

While Tham script in Thailand and Laos is mainly reserved for historical and magico-religious purposes, it is still the chief alphabet for three living languages: Kam Muang (also known as Lanna, numbering six million speakers) in northern Thailand, Tai Lü (670,000 speakers) in northern Thailand, Laos and Yunnan, and Khün (around 120,000) in Chiang Mai and Kyaingtong, Myanmar. In northern Thailand there has been a revival in the study of the script – called Lanna by most Thais – in public schools and Buddhist monasteries.

Although syllables tattooed in Tham may be pronounced differently according to which ethnic group one hails from, in fact the same alphabet is used with only slight regional variation.

Unlike most masters, Ajahn Pornsit does not use rubber stamps or paper templates of any kind, preferring to create *sak yan* entirely freehand.

LANNA MASTERS

While the days of complete body tattoos are long gone, due mainly to Christian missionary influence, many males continue to acquire Lanna-text tattoos from monks and laymen in northern Thailand. Some may be familiar with Khmer *akkhara* but because they and their disciples identify with northern Thailand, they will ink in Khmer only on special request.

One monk considered an expert in Lanna *akkhara*, Ajahn Kamthorn (Phra Khru Baipika Kamthorn Kittisopanno), granted us an interview at his *samnak* at Wat Nong Khaem in Sanpatong district, Chiang Mai province. Two months after our visit, in September 2010, he sadly passed away.

Wat Nong Khaem's compact compound is located far off the main roads, near Wiang Tha Khan, a little-known, ancient Mon Buddhist site dating to the 11th century. The centrepiece of Wat Nong Khaem itself is a stucco-encrusted Lanna/Shan-style stupa which dates to 1897. We found Ajahn Kamthorn in his *samnak* to one side of the compound.

"When I was young just about anyone who lived in monasteries around here learned how to read and write Lanna," explained the heavily tattooed Lanna monk. "If you were a *dek wat* (child who lives at a monastery and helps with daily chores in return for Buddhist training and a basic education), you had to learn it.

"Nowadays government schools teach Lanna as an elective, and it's out of the monks' hands. So the kids don't take it as seriously.

"I was interested in *sak yan* and *weechaa*, so I travelled all over the north to find masters who could teach me. Wherever I found an excellent teacher, I stayed for awhile."

The monk opened the doors of a wooden cabinet nearby and pulled out several rectangular bundles given to him by his masters. He opened one and pulled the pages out so that they unfolded, accordion-like, into one long page. Sketched onto the rough, rustic-looking *saa* (mulberry paper) was a long series of *yantras*. In contrast to the designs we had seen in central Thailand, most of the *yantras* were geometric rather than related to animals or deities, and they featured copious amounts of text, both alphabetic and numeric. The attractive, curlicued text was Lanna.

Asked about the use of mulberry paper, Ajahn Kamthorn said, "You can use *bai lan* (palm leaves) for general Buddhist texts, and for *khaathaa*, but for drawing out *sak yan* you have to use mulberry paper. Otherwise the pen gets stuck in the palm fibre."

One animal that turned up frequently in his *saa* books was the pig.

"We don't go for animals so much here. I do a few tiger *yantras*, but pigs are more popular. They're

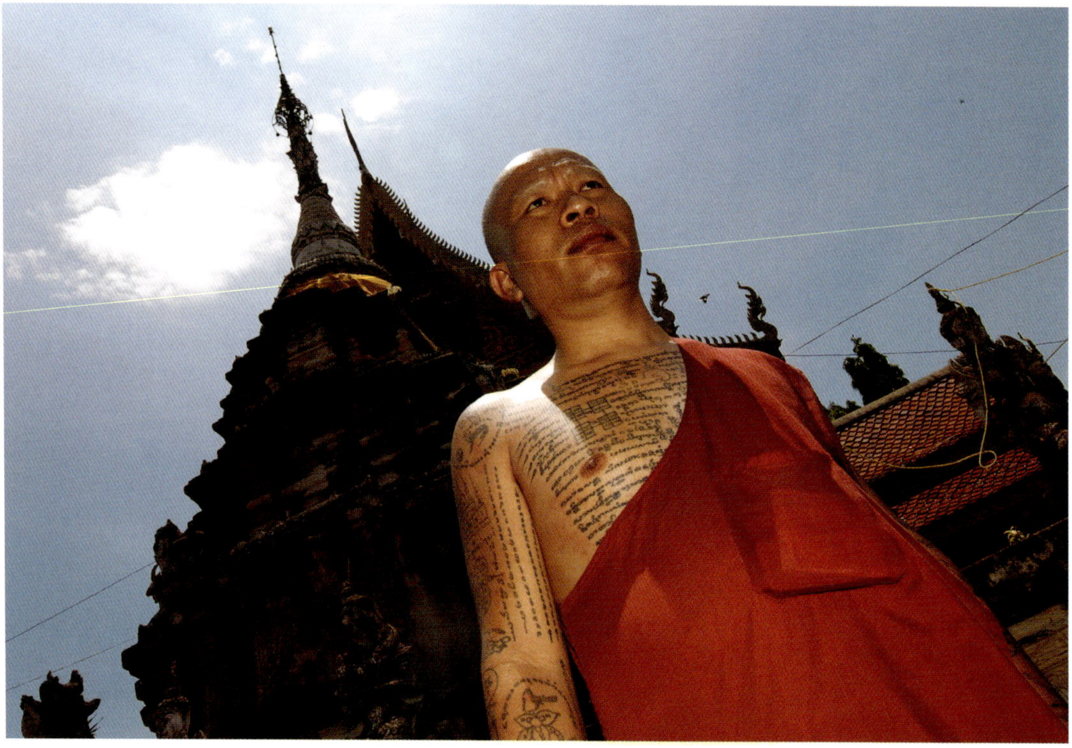

Above: The late Ajahn Kamthorn stands in front of an ancient Shan-Lanna stupa at Wat Nong Khaem.

different from the *moo thong daeng* (copper pig, for prosperity) you see down south. The *moo lang hak* (broken-back pig) is more popular because that's the kind of pigs you see around these parts. And it's more for *khong krapan* (protection from danger) than for making money."

Ajahn Kamthorn's *mai sak* were of standard modern length, with the traditional *paak pet* (duckbill) tip. One difference we noted was the bulbous metal grip added to the ends of his needle shafts. Aside from making the shaft more comfortable to handle, they add mass and weight, meaning less effort is needed to puncture the skin. This might signify an influence from neighbouring Myanmar, where tattoo artists use carved weights akin to the famous opium weights (except they are cast to represent deities rather than animals).

Sanpatong district is home to a second *khru sak yan* who specialises in Lanna *akkhara*, Ajahn Pornsit Thammatharo at Wat Sawang Arom in Thung Satok subdistrict. Again we travelled down dusty roads off Route 108 to find the *wat*, stopping frequently for directions along the way.

The first time we arrived, Ajahn Pornsit was away on business, so we admired the *wat*'s century-old Shan-style stupa, its teak-and-brick Tipitaka library and the little country school adjacent. On a wall of one of the school buildings, a series of weathered black-and-white photos showed the temple's gradual evolution since its founding in 1898.

In fact it took several visits before we found the master on the premises. Despite the temple's backwater appearance and paucity of resident monks, Ajahn Pornsit is a very busy person. He has served as abbot since 1996, assuming not only his spiritual leadership duties in the area, but taking on Lanna language education in the adjacent primary school.

When we finally found Ajahn Pornsit in residence, he was seated in an open-air, bamboo-thatched cubicle alongside the old Tipitaka library. A newer and much larger building containing a refectory for the abbot had almost completed construction, and when finished, the abbot told us, he might still do most of his *sak yan* and consulting outdoors.

"I'm getting old, and the light is better here," he explained with a chuckle.

Asked where he had learned the sacred tattoo arts, the abbot told us how Khruba Booncheun Upaseno, the abbot from 1944 to 1978, had been a master of *weechaa*. Khruba Cheun, as he was more commonly known, trained Phra Anan Worapanyo as his resident successor. Phra Anan remained at Wat Sarang Arom for only 10 years, serving as abbot half that time, before leaving the monkhood in 1984.

As a layman, Anan continued to practise *sak yan*, taking Pornsit on as a disciple while the latter was also a layman. The Lanna tattoos covering Ajahn Pornsit's chest, arms, back and legs were inked by Anan.

After Pornsit had acquired *weechaa* and *tamraa* (formulae) from Anan, he took up robes and bowl, and went on *thudong* (ascetic wandering on foot) to find other teachers and acquire more knowledge and technique. When word reached him that Wat Sawang Arom needed an abbot, Pornsit volunteered to take the helm.

At the time of our visit, Ajahn Pornsit had already been practising *sak yan* for over 20 years. He can create *yan* using Lanna, Shan or Khmer script, having studied all three.

"It's all Pali, and it all translates the same, so it's not really important which script you use. I mostly do Lanna *akkhara* because I'm Lanna so it means more to me.

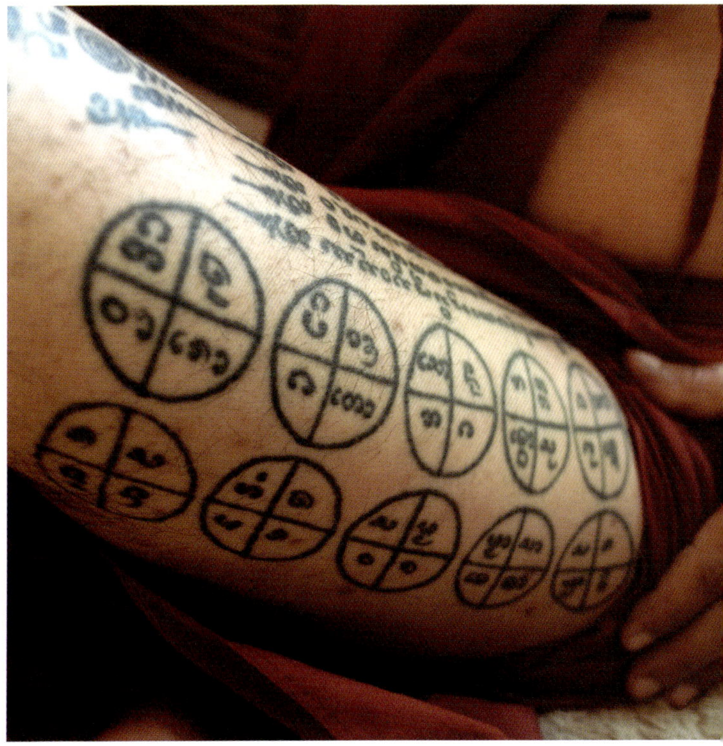

Above: Lanna tattoos on Ajahn Kamthorn's thigh.

"Whichever script you use, you had better do it correctly, or it won't have any power. Whether it's Lanna or Khmer, you had better study till you know it backwards and forwards, and not just copy if from books.

"The most popular tattoo here is *kao yaut* (nine peaks). For us it's the highest of the high, it offers just about all the benefits any *yan* can offer. I do tigers, Hanuman and a few other Himalayan animals too."

Unlike most masters, Ajahn Pornsit does not use rubber stamps or paper templates of any kind, preferring to create *sak yan* entirely freehand.

His needles are traditional metal shafts with *paak pet* tips, which he sterilises by wrapping them in a cotton ball and lighting it afire.

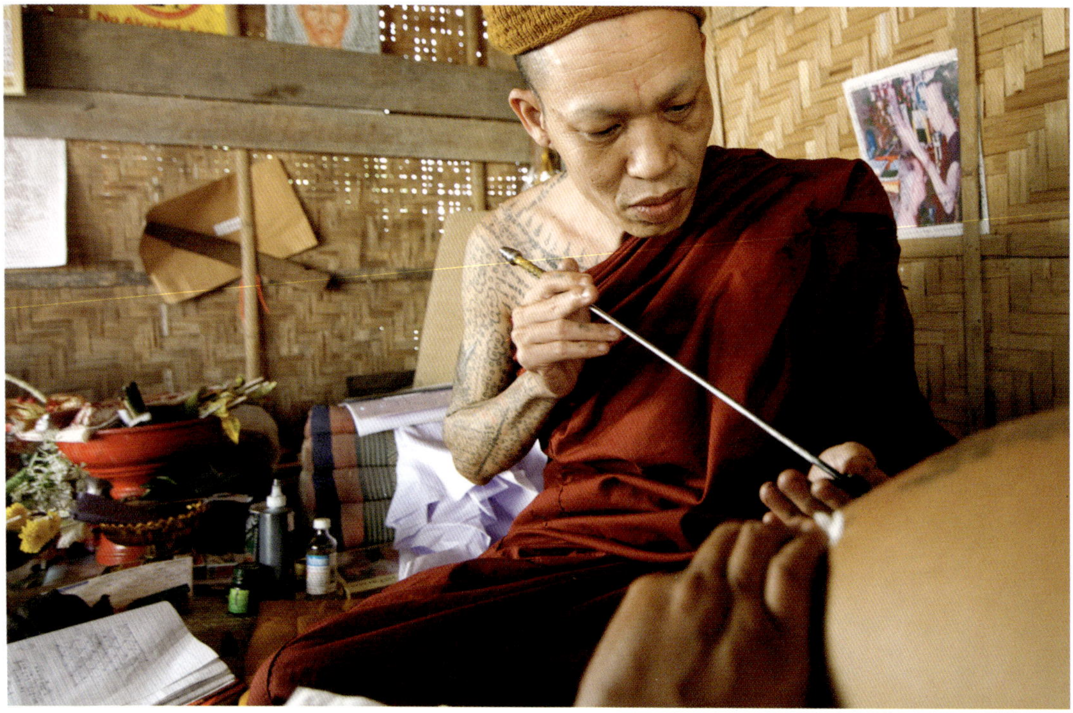

Above: Ajahn Pornsit at work in his bamboo-thatch *samnak*. Right: A crocodile *yantra* with Lanna *akkhara* evokes power and *metta* (loving kindness). As is traditional in the north, animal designs are inked on the thighs.

He keeps two kinds of ink on hand, using either depending on the preferences of his disciples.

Handing us a plastic bucket filled with a black, toul-smelling sludge, he explained "This is *meuk boraan* (traditional ink), made by hand from burnt coconut husk mixed with coconut oil, along with a lot of other organic ingredients." The strong aroma suggests that some of the organic ingredients have decayed or composted.

"It doesn't make for a very lively coloured tattoo, but it's powerful.

"For people who can't stand the smell, I have regular Chinese ink, which makes a much darker, longer-lasting colour. I mix in a dab of the *meuk boraan* for power."

Disciples offer a uniform 359 baht, along with eight sticks of incense, four lotus buds and eight candles, for any design they like, and as many designs as they can tolerate in one sitting.

"I don't do as much *sak yan* as I used to. I'm very busy in the community now, and I teach school, so if people really want to get a tattoo, they usually have to come three or four times until they find me here, or until I have time to pick up the needle.

"I could ink from dawn to dusk but it's too much. Having three tattoos is just as good as filling your whole body with them. I don't want disciples that look like that. Sometimes having a lot of tattoos makes it harder to find a regular job.

"I won't tattoo women or anyone under the age of 20. I also don't work at night. You don't want to see *khaung kheun* ("stuff rise", referring to *sak yan*-related trance states) after dark. That's a time for calm and contemplation."

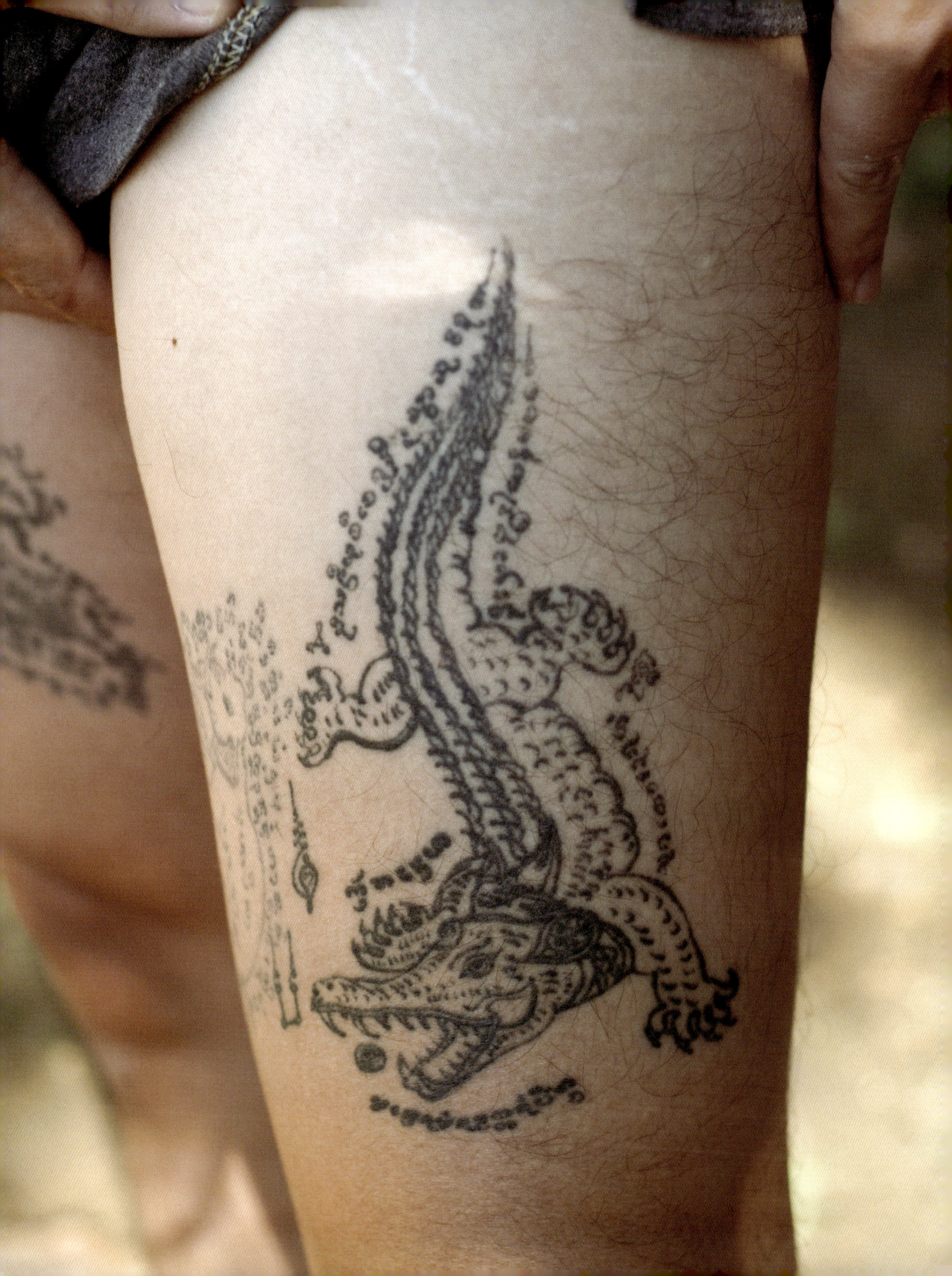

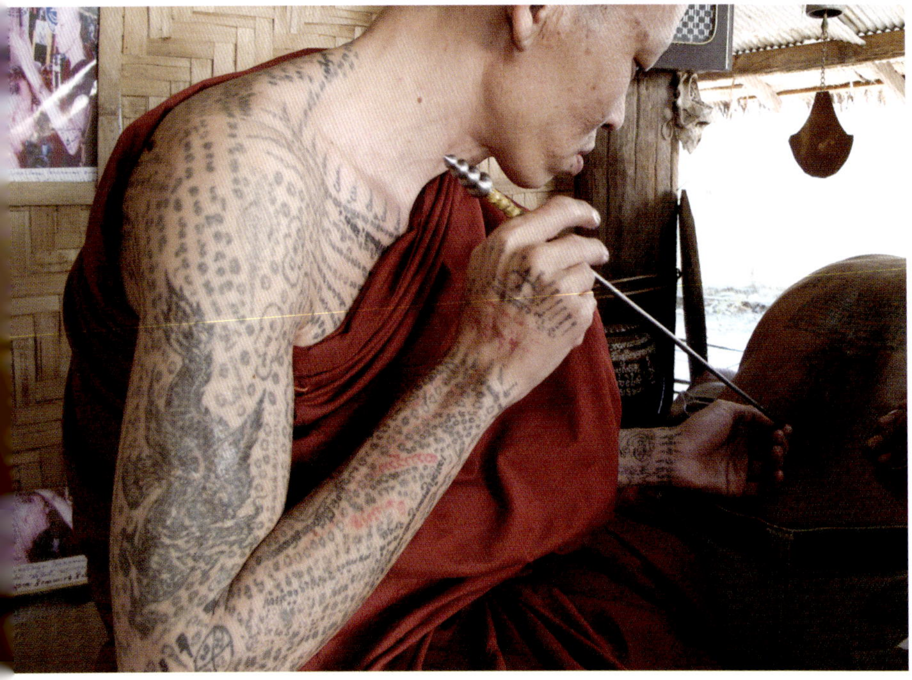

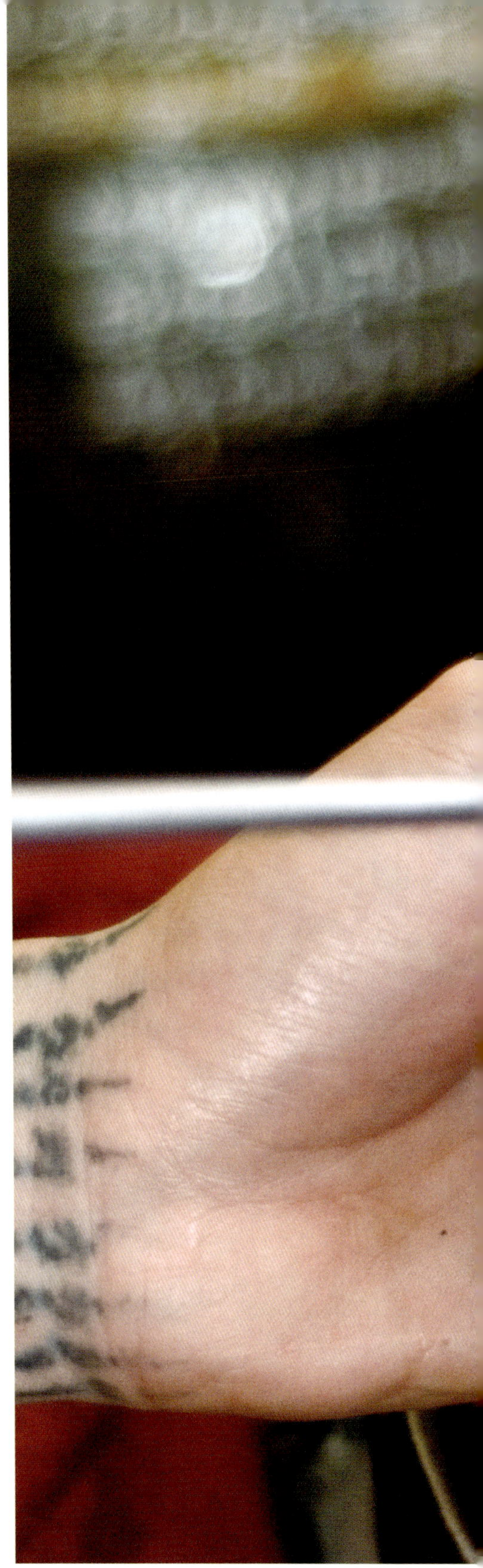

Above & Right: Ajahn Pornsit creates *sak yan* freehand.

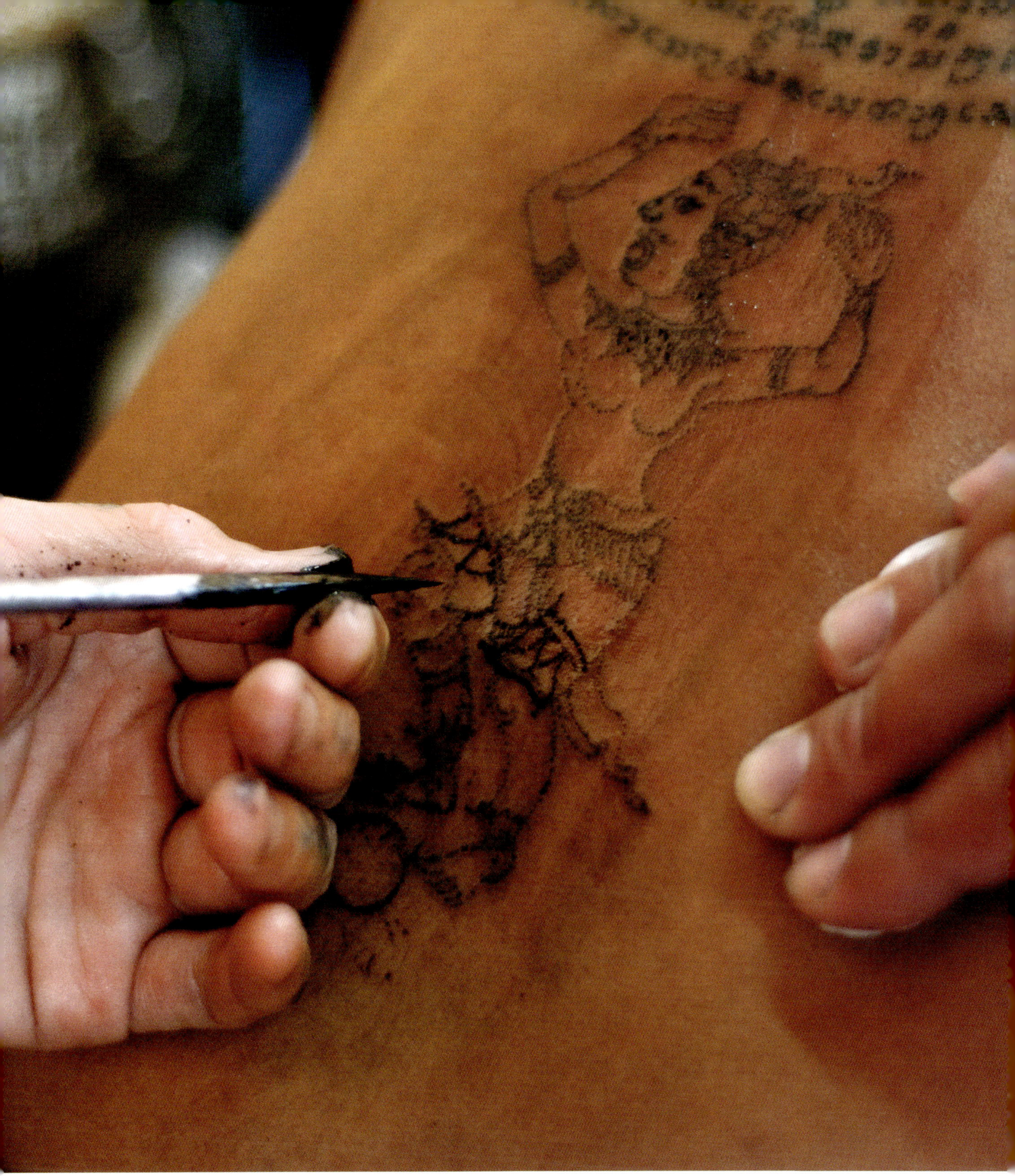

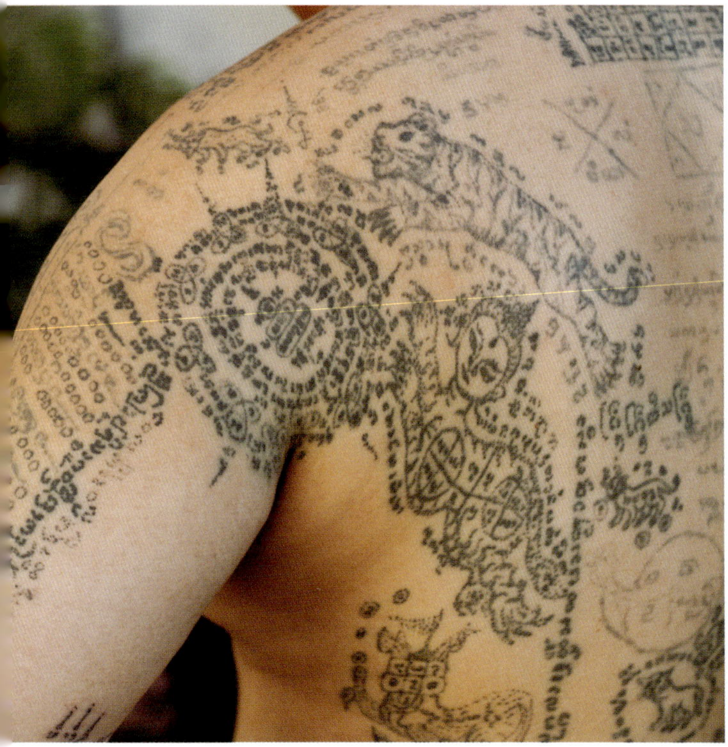

Above: One of Ajahn Pornsit's disciples displays an unusual *yantra* in which a tiger bears a Buddha's head.

When we asked whether he was training any successors, Ajahn Pornsit replied, "I have disciples who can work the needle, but the *sak yan* they make isn't *khlang* (magically potent). In fact sometimes the tattoos they make just disappear after awhile. So far I haven't been able to find a disciple with the proper concentration."

LAO MASTERS

Luang Prabang, in northern Laos, served as the last royal capital of the former Lao kingdom before the communist Pathet Lao took over the country in 1975 and abolished the monarchy. It has also been a historic centre for Lao Buddhism, and today its charming monasteries, protected by Unesco World Heritage status since 1995, are a prime tourist attraction.

The city once boasted a rich *sak yan* heritage. Sadly the 11-year war preceding the 1975 creation of the communist-inspired Lao People's Democratic Republic forced many *sak yan* masters to flee the country. Following the communist takeover, yet more masters left Laos, often settling in Europe and America. The lack of masters led to a steep decline in tattoo arts after 1975, a situation later compounded when the government announced a prohibition on the inking of tattoos of all kinds, which was seen to run counter to communist principles.

Among other policies that altered the course of Lao Buddhism, the government curtailed donations of food to monks, and replaced them with a government rice ration. The number of monastic ordinations in Laos declined during the late 1970s, while the exodus of monks either fleeing to neighbouring Thailand or returning to lay life increased. In 1979, the country's Supreme Patriarch, Sangharaja Thammayano, floated across the Mekong on a raft of inflated car inner tubes to seek refuge in Thailand.

In pre-1975 Luang Prabang the most important monastery for *sak yan* was Vat Manoram, where abbot Sathu Ong Ta presided over the practice. The master died in 2003, leaving behind no trained disciples in Laos to carry on the tradition.

The current abbot, Sathu Boonloet, showed us some of the tattoos he himself had received from Sathu Ong Ta, and explained the situation to us in diplomatic terms.

"During the war people were still keenly interested in *sak yan*. Now that people aren't shooting at each other, people don't need that kind of protection anymore here in Laos," said the elderly monk.

While quite a few older Lao men bear beautiful *sak yan* received under the old royal regime, one rarely sees newer work. Nonetheless we found a few Lao masters still practising *sak yan*, to a greater or lesser degree, under semi-clandestine condi-

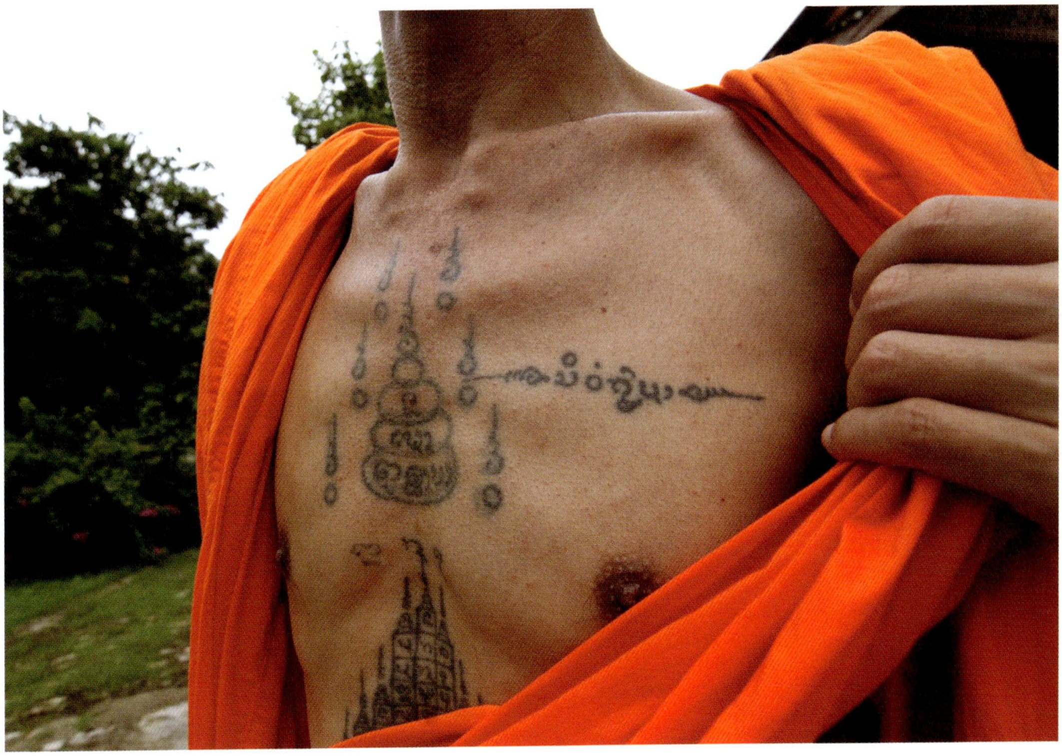

Above: Ajahn Sai at Vat Kok Bap displays the *yan metta* tattooed in Lao Tham script over his heart. In the centre of his chest is a Five Buddhas *yantra – pha phutthajao haa pha ong*.

tions. Given the legal status of tattoos in Laos, only one of these masters agreed to go on record with interviews, photographs and mention of his name and whereabouts.

Ajahn Sai, abbot at 170-year-old Vat Kok Bap, on the wooded west bank of the Mekong River opposite Luang Prabang's historic temple district, is the last monastic to practise *sak yan* in Luang Prabang, albeit sparingly.

"Soon after I ordained, I spent a lot of time in the forests, caves and ruined temples of the north. By nature I was a very timid, even frightened person. I decided to confront my fears so that I could learn to be more daring.

"While wandering, I met a lay master of *sak yan*, and asked for *yantra* to keep me safe while travelling. Afterwards I became interested in the art, and trained with him. This was during the old democratic regime."

Ajahn Sai remained a monk throughout the war, and spent several years at Vat Manoram, where he no doubt learned more about *sak yan*.

He eventually settled in at Luang Prabang's Vat Chum Khong Surintharam, now beautifully restored. When funds became available for the renovation of three abandoned royal temples on the right bank of the Mekong opposite Luang Prabang, he volunteered to take responsibility for Vat Kok Pap, the most badly preserved of the three.

Today, five years after the 50-something monk took over Vat Kok Pap, the simple forest monastery has developed a small but viable monastic com-

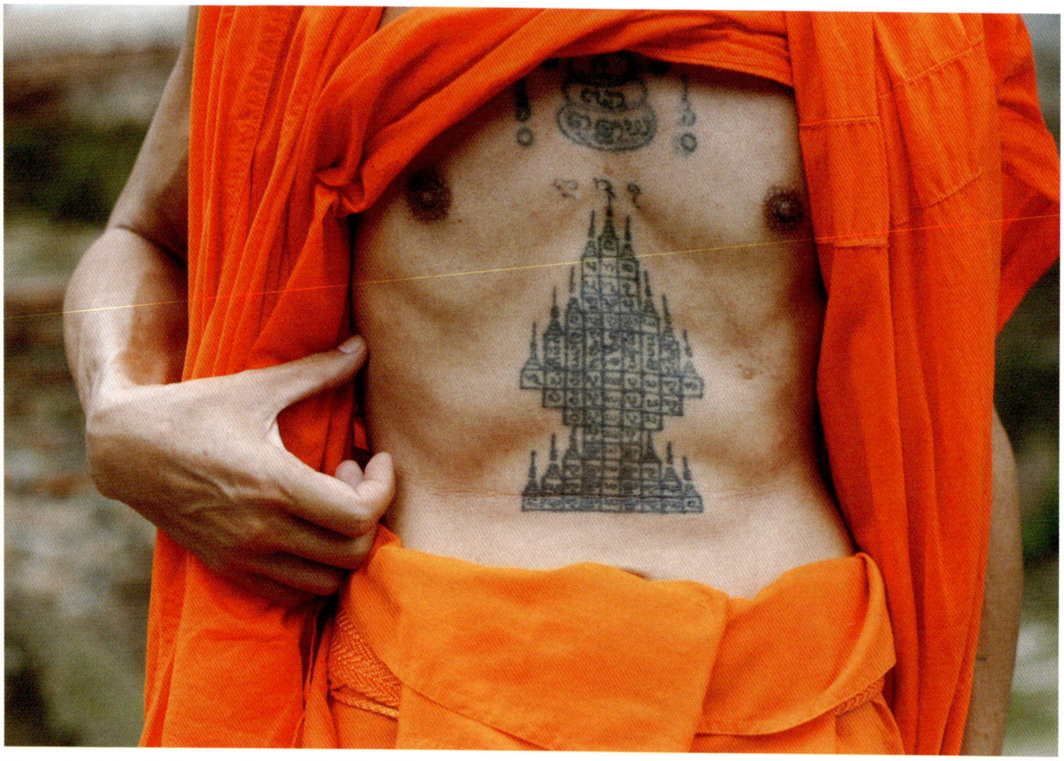

Above: An elaborate stupa *yantra* on Ajahn Sai's abdomen.
Right: A monk at Vat Kok Bap receives his monthly headshaving in the shallows of the Mekong.

munity. Like its two neighbouring temples Vat Hat Siaw and Vat Long Kun, Vat Kok Pap boasts a venerable brick-and-stucco hall devoted to walking meditation. Renovation at the monastery is not yet complete, and the hall is crumbling and overgrown. The *sim* (ordination chapel) is also in need of a thorough renovation.

When we first arrived in a small boat piloted by one of the novice monks, Ajahn Sai was away in Europe, but his monastic charges were kind enough to show us around the grounds and to reveal the *sak yan* he had applied to their chests, arms and backs. It was strong, rustic work, with all *akkhara* appearing in Tham script. Two of the five monks we met had trained with Ajahn Sai and told us they were planning to carry on the tradition.

When we finally met the abbot after his return from Europe, we asked about the fragile *sak yan* tradition he maintained despite official prohibition.

"In the beginning it was difficult to find any monks who would come and stay at this monastery. Young monks in particular were worried that since the site had been abandoned for over 150 years, that it would be haunted by evil spirits and visited by dangerous wild animals.

"I decided to offer tattoos to the prospective residents to ward off evil and protect them from animal attacks. It was one of the only ways to attract novices and monks.

"I didn't really want my disciples to have *sak yan*, or to teach them the tradition, not at first anyway. I would rather they practised dhamma and then later

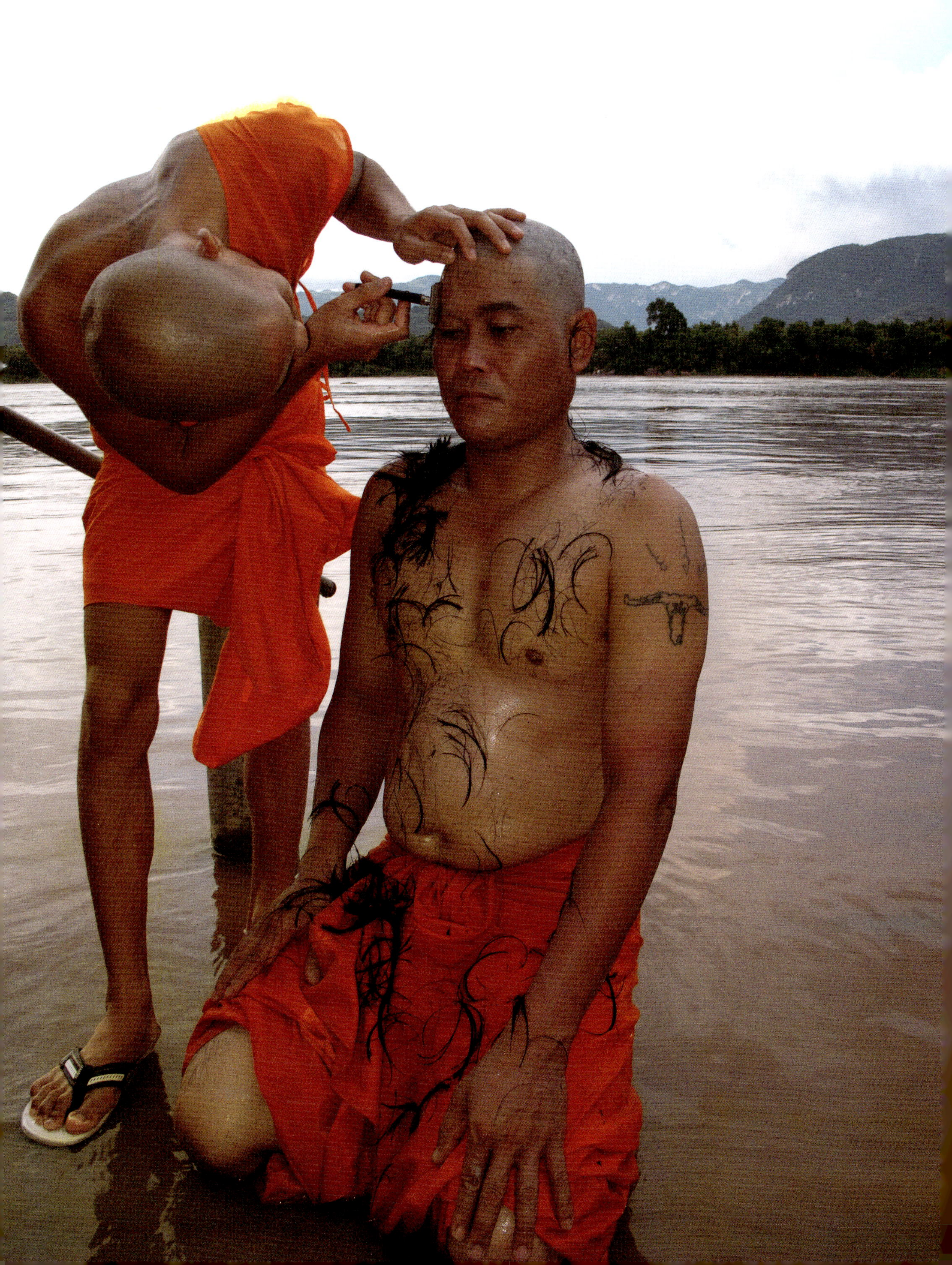

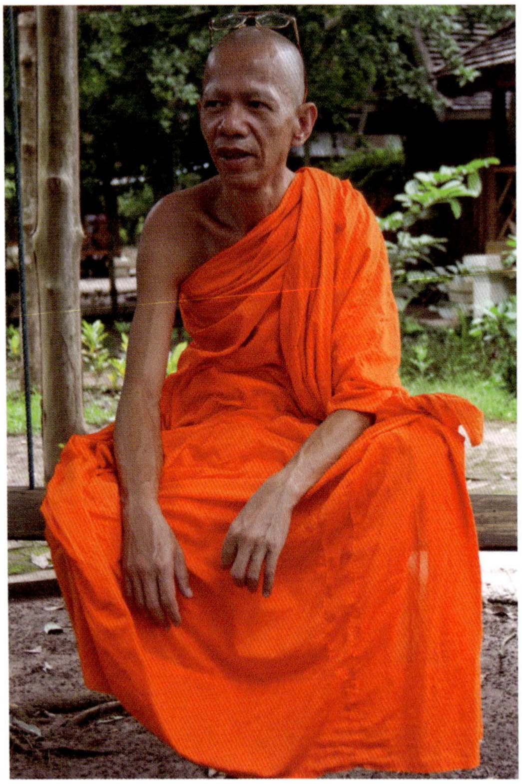

Above: Ajahn Sai talks about dhamma and *sak yan*.

learn about *sak yan*. In fact I only get out the needle when they are afraid of being here.

"Once they're protected, I try to teach them that while the *yantras* can be helpful, it's much better to train the mind. A trained mind protects against everything. What matters is learning meditation and dhamma. The tattoos are only supplementary to those things. And that's where *sak yan* power comes from."

We were fortunate to meet one of Ajahn Sai's older lay disciples, a local silversmith named Tan Saub, whose family used to work for the Lao royal family. The artist had come to make offerings at the table, meditate and seek counsel from his master.

"I'm very careful who I give *sak yan* to," he explained when we asked about his lay disciples.

"Intention is key. Sometimes people just want a tattoo but they don't know why. Others seek power to feel bold enough to commit crimes, so that they can be gangsters. That's wrong. It's not the road to nirvana, it's the road to hell."

"Even when you just want to protect yourself, you must think about the consequences of your actions, what you really want from *sak yan*. If you say you want your skin to be impervious to sharp instruments, be careful. You don't want to protect your skin too much, because otherwise how will a doctor perform surgery with a scalpel if needed?

"Lord Buddha taught people to wake up, not to sleep. *Sak yan* has its place, but it can also make you lose yourself, make you go to sleep rather than wake up to dhamma."

Asked about *wai khru*, Ajahn Sai said he tells his disciples they don't need to set aside a special date to pay respect to their teacher.

"Having a special day just for the master suggests that he is the owner of the tattoos, when clearly he is not. If they want to honour me or any other teachers, they can do it anytime. No need to wait for a specific date.

"You shouldn't depend on masters or their *sak yan* too much, but develop those good qualities you seek on your own, through mental or physical training.

"Good people naturally get *metta mahaniyom* (loving kindness and the favour of others) without *sak yan*, just by following the five precepts. That's the real test, because anyone who can do that faithfully will have *metta mahaniyom* on their own!"

When Ajahn Sai does consent to create *sak yan*, he uses a very simple *khem sak* made from two sewing needles bound tightly together with string, without a shaft of any kind. Gripping the bound needles in his bare hand, he dips the sharp tips into ink and taps the design into the disciple's skin.

"If you want *sak yan* from me, you need to buy

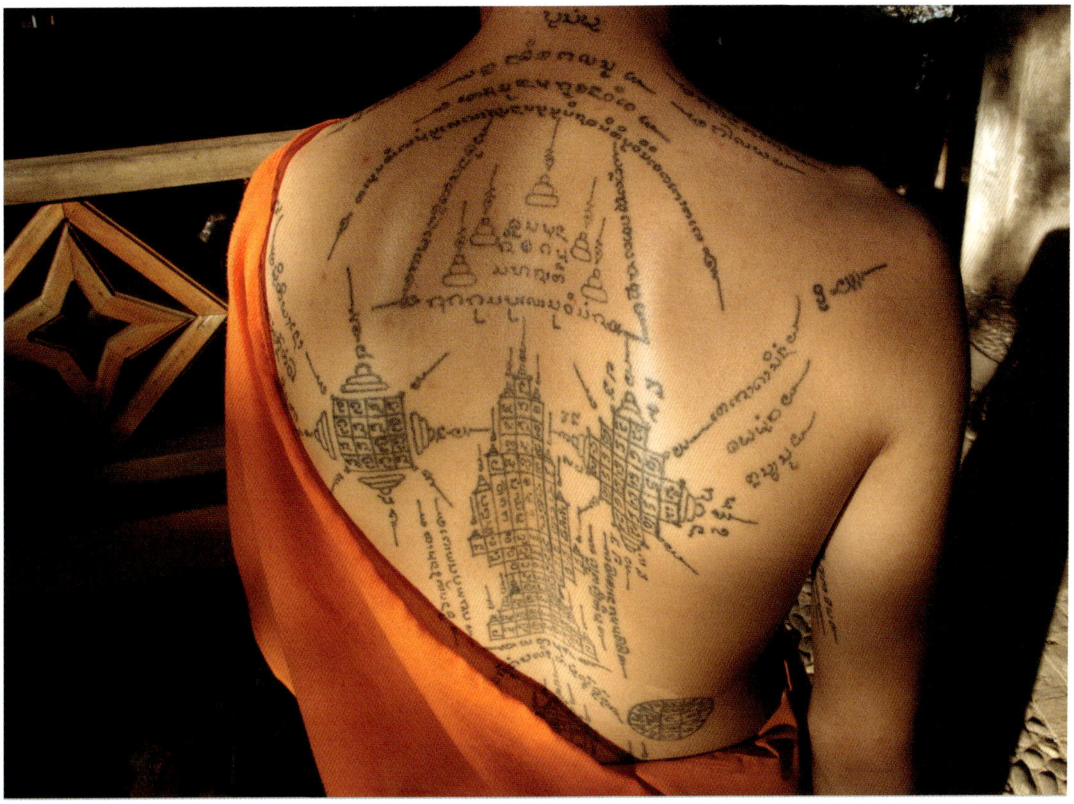

Above: A young monk at Vat Kok Bap displays Lao *sak yan* received from the abbot.

a pair of sewing needles yourself and bring them to me. I don't keep them around here, so that the monks won't be tempted to use them when I'm not here. If they fool around with them, they might do something incorrectly. I haven't passed on all my *weesaa* (occult knowledge) yet."

After he has finished inking a design, Ajahn Sai performs a simple empowerment by firmly placing his right index finger into the centre of the *yantra* and transferring energy directly into the disciple while reciting *khaathaa*.

Ajahn Sai's first prescribed *yantra* is usually the Five Buddhas – *pha phutthajao haa pha ong* – a design whose origins may refer to the five Buddhas of Tantric Buddhism. The design takes half an hour or less, and can be placed on the back or the chest.

Another *yantra* most of his disciples have is *yan metta*, a flowing geometric design inked on one's chest, over the heart. It is meant to invoke loving kindness, both in one's self and from others.

"After those, it depends on what you need, what you think you're missing in your life. Mostly I tattoo designs for *metta mahaniyom, khong krapan* and *amnaat*. This *yan phra thaat*," he told us while pointing to an intricate stupa-shaped design on his upper abdomen, "it helps you have a strong mind for keeping vows."

The master doesn't accept money for doing tattoos. "You can't buy monks, not this one anyway. A plate of flowers, incense and candles is enough."

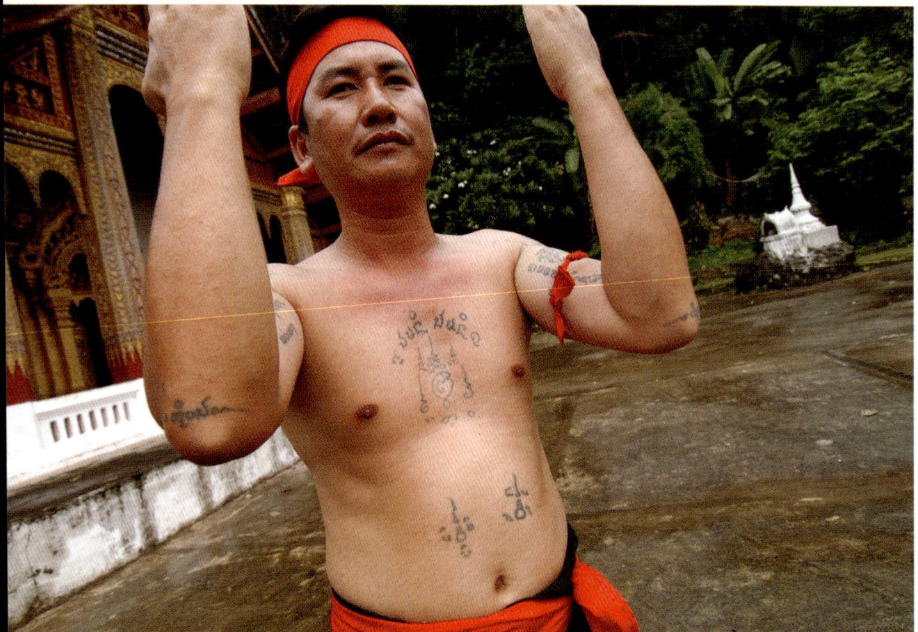

Than Tik teaches Lao martial arts and traditional dance. His *sak yan* came from the late Sathu Ong Ta at Vat Manorom, where he was once a monk.

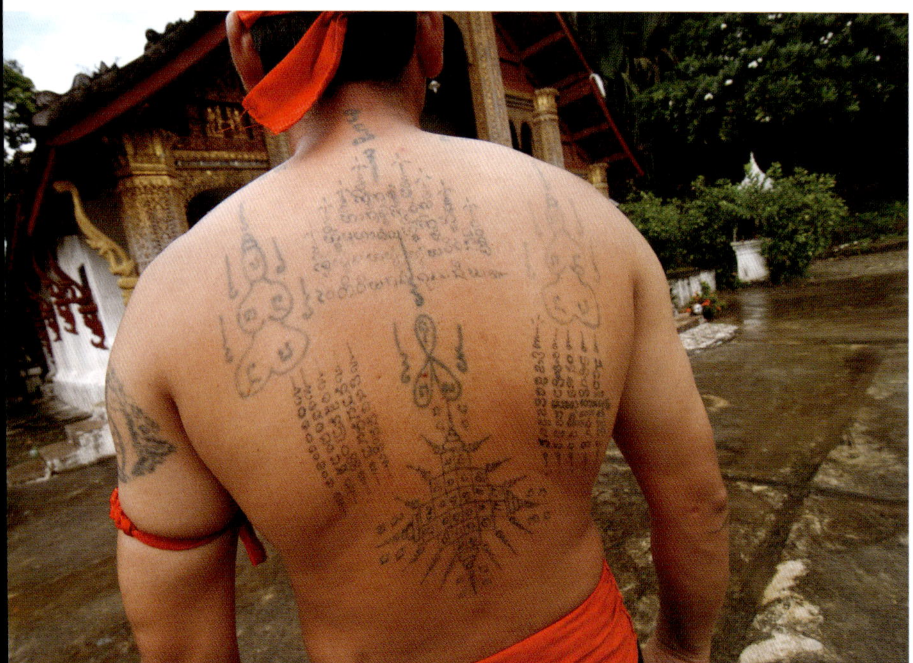

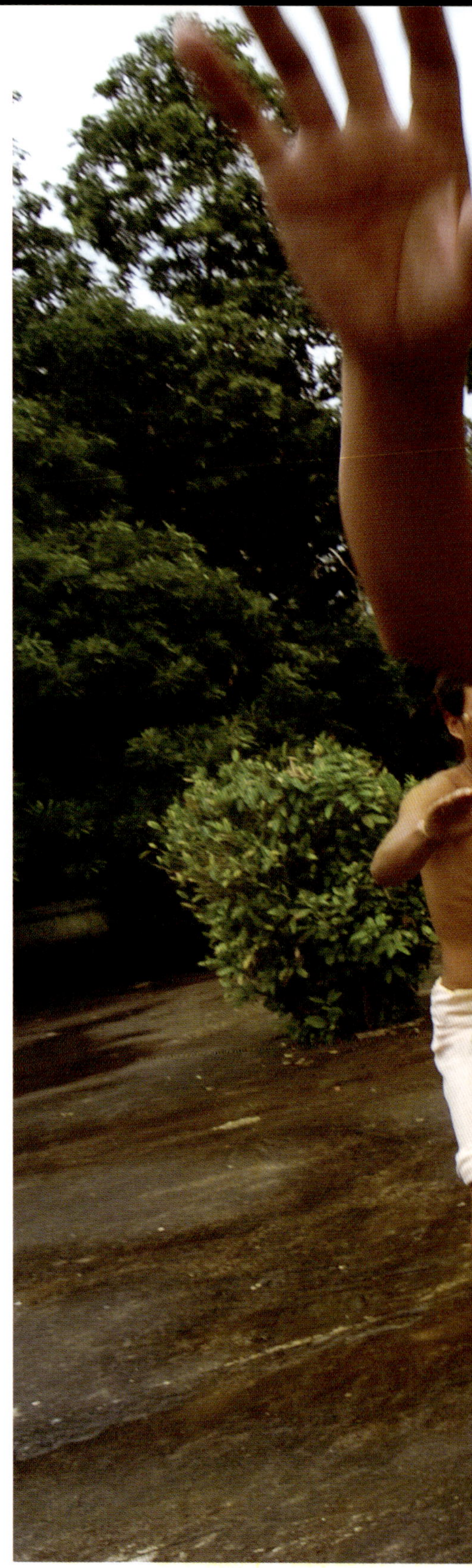

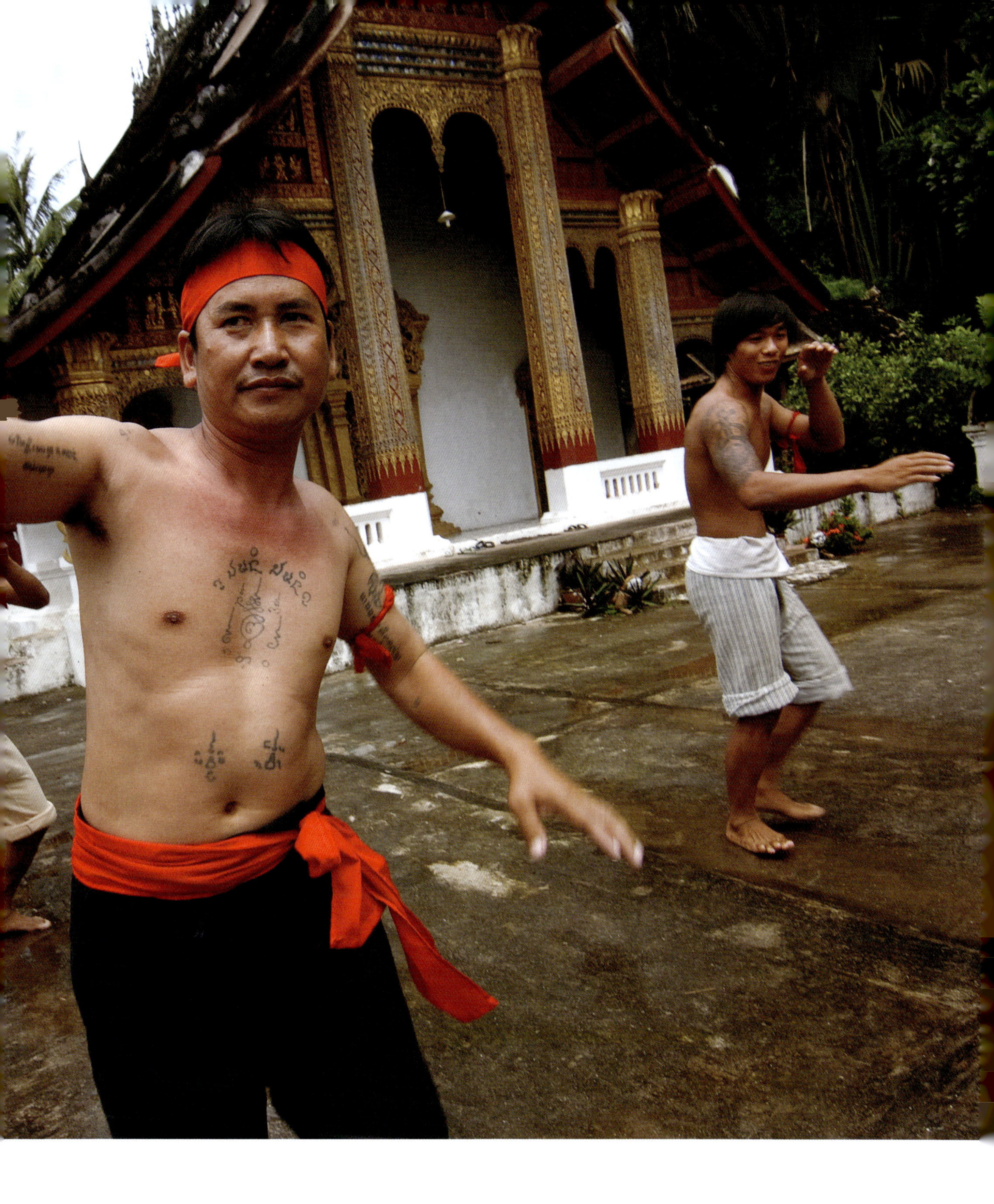

THE KHMER TRADITION

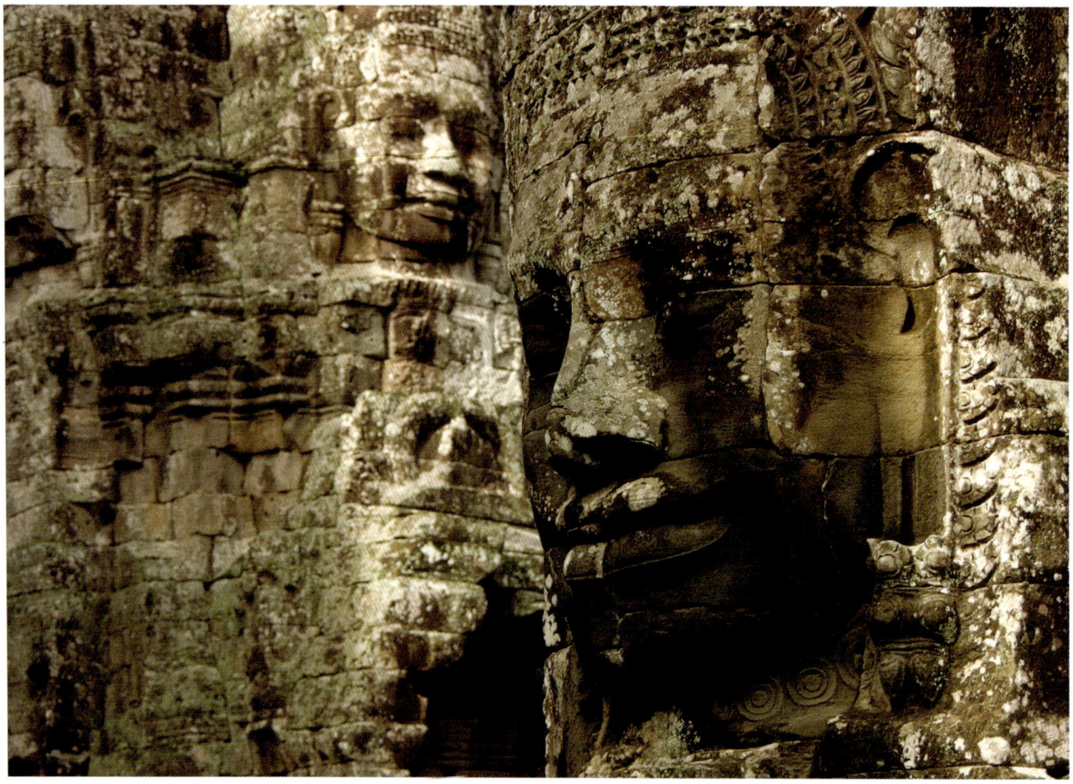

Above: Angkor Thom, Cambodia.

The earliest references to sacred tattoos in Cambodia date to 2nd-century Chinese chronicles describing Funan, a pre-Angkor kingdom based in and around the Mekong Delta from the 1st to 7th centuries. Both soldiers and civilians, the writers noted, wore ink tattoos as protection against possession and sorcery.

Since older, pre-Funan references find sacred tattoo history among Tai groups to the north, and the Khmer word for 'tattoo' *(sak)* is a Tai loan word, it is generally accepted that the origins of the tattoo tradition in Cambodia can be traced to the northern Thais. It is possible that the Brahmanism of Funan – and later the alternating Brahmanism and Buddhism of early Angkor (8th to 13th centuries) – introduced Brahmanist/Buddhist beliefs and symbols to what was primarily an animist tradition, although both religious systems existed in what is today Laos and northern Thailand at the time as well.

After the Thai conquest of Angkor in the 14th and 15th centuries, much of Khmer culture, especially in the spheres of Buddhism, arts and the royal court, fused with existing Thai culture. Even though the Thais had their own alphabet by then, the Khmer script was sometimes preferred for writing Pali passages – and occasionally even for Thai language – after the Angkor conquest.

We have no way of knowing whether Khmer script was used for *sak yoan* (the Khmer term for "*yantra* tattoo") at this time, but since Angkor at the peak of its empire ruled much of what is today Thailand, it is probable that Khmer script was used in many spheres even before the Thai conquest.

Some scholars have suggested that an indistinct engraving found on the abdomen of a 12th-century sculpture of Jayavarman VII (found in Phimai, Thailand) may represent a tattoo, but if so it is the only evidence of a *sak yoan* tradition during the Angkor period.

Many civilians also sought out *sak yoan*, including designs to be tattooed on the legs as protection from landmines.

The first post-Funan literature mentioning sacred tattoos in Cambodia appeared in the French Indochina colonial period (1887–1953). In terms of both design and ritual, the Khmer tattoo tradition by that time had much in common with Thai and Lao traditions.

Oral histories in Cambodia today also parallel what one hears in Thailand and Laos. Most historians and *adjar* (Khmer masters) trace the formulae to Buddhist and Brahmanist origins. As with Pho Kae legends in Thailand and Laos, many Khmer also talk about a lineage descending from hermit sages *(muni ey-sey)*.

As in central Thailand, Khmer masters have used the "round" Khmer alphabet *(aksor mool)*, for the seed mantras *(moun)* associated with each design. Most *yantras (yoan)* tend to be geometrical designs which serve as frames for the written verses *(gatha)*. Animal figures such as tigers and monkeys appear less frequently, but deities are common, particularly depictions of Narayana (Vishnu) and Garuda.

Tattoo rituals *(bidhi sak)* and empowerment rituals *(saek)* resemble those found in other parts of mainland Southeast Asia, as do the required behavioural codes (including avoidance of starfruit and purple gourd) and relationship between master and disciple.

Unfortunately the standard formulae for such practises and relationships have largely been lost in Cambodia since the Cambodian Civil War (1970–75), Khmer Rouge rule (1975–79) and civil conflicts that continued well into the 1990s.

Many *adjar* disappeared during these tortured periods. We could find no written records or first-hand accounts of *adjars* being executed by the Khmer Rouge, although it is likely some were. During Khmer Rouge rule, monks were forced to disrobe, leave their monasteries and work the land as peasants as part of the Year Zero campaign. By the end of the Khmer Rouge's reign of terror, there were no monks active in Cambodia, and most temples were in ruins, so the monastery-based tradition of *sak yoan* had completely vanished. Virtually all *adjar sak yoan* by this time had either fled to Thailand or died, whether by execution or starvation. A few survivors are said to have quit practising magical tattoo arts altogether.

Those *adjar* who continued to practise during the conflicts were in high demand by government troops, who would receive tattoos for power and protection during battle. Many civilians also sought out *sak yoan*, including designs to be tattooed on the legs as protection from landmines. Refugees heading for the border might receive tattoos that prevented them from getting lost in the forest.

Tattoo ink was usually made out of the juice of pounded sugarcane mixed with powdered charcoal

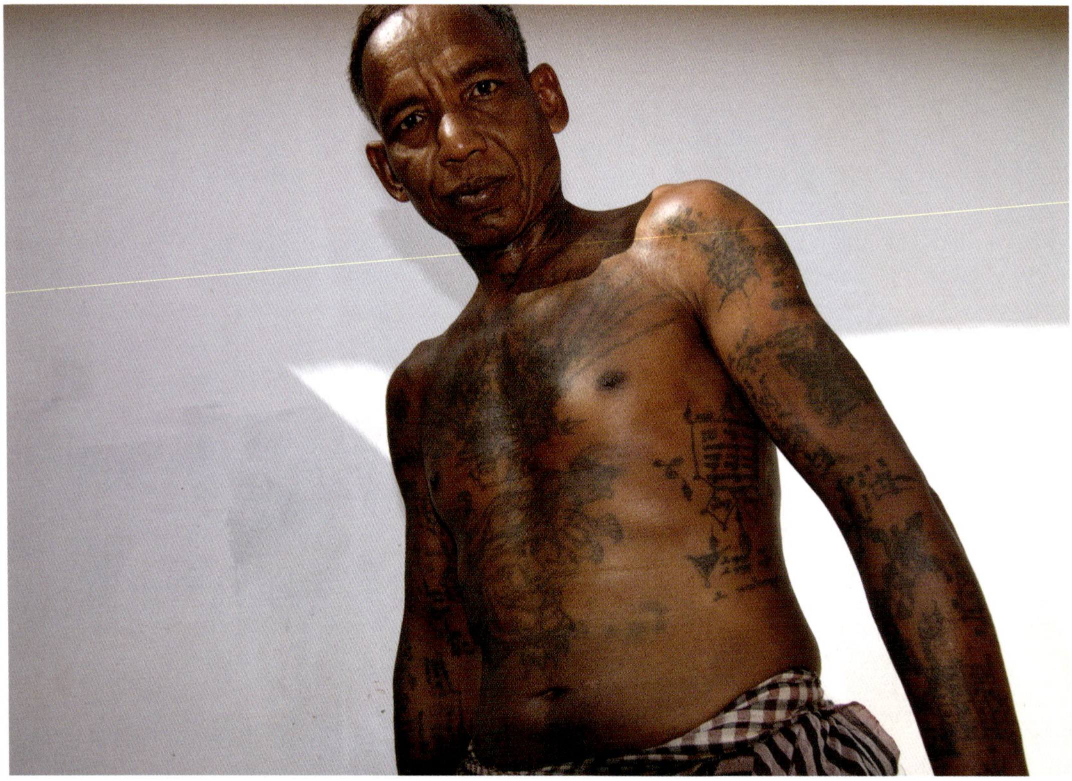

Above: A military veteran of more than one armed conflict in Cambodia says he owes his survival to *sak yoan*.

or, when that was not available, carbon extracted from old batteries.

Major General Lay Virak, a former senior commander in the Khmer People's National Liberation Front (KPNLF) who fought against the Vietnamese-installed People's Republic of Kampuchea (PRK) regime from 1979 to 1993, has confirmed that during extended civil conflict, belief in the power of *sak yoan* and other magic was strong.

"We knew a lot, including magic that prevented you from being tied up or hurt by torture," the general has stated in interviews.

Aksor mool script is still prominently visible along the jawline of Nhek Bunchhai, secretary-general of the royalist Funcinpec party and also a former KPNLF soldier. The design, Nhek affirms, made troops obey his orders. Tattoos on his forearms turned his fists into deadly weapons and those on his chest and shoulders protected him from bullets and other projectiles.

After the Khmer Rouge were overthrown and peace came to Cambodia, interest in sacred tattoos dropped to almost nil. Today many Cambodians associate *sak yoan* with soldiers and war, and it is rare to find anyone bearing tattoos inked after the early 1980s.

Reut Hath, one of the more well-known *adjar sak yoan* during the war years, gave up the tradition in the 1990s. "During the fighting, most of the fighters were powerful – the magic worked," he said in an interview with *Global Post*. "But with peace many came to the cities and starting drink-

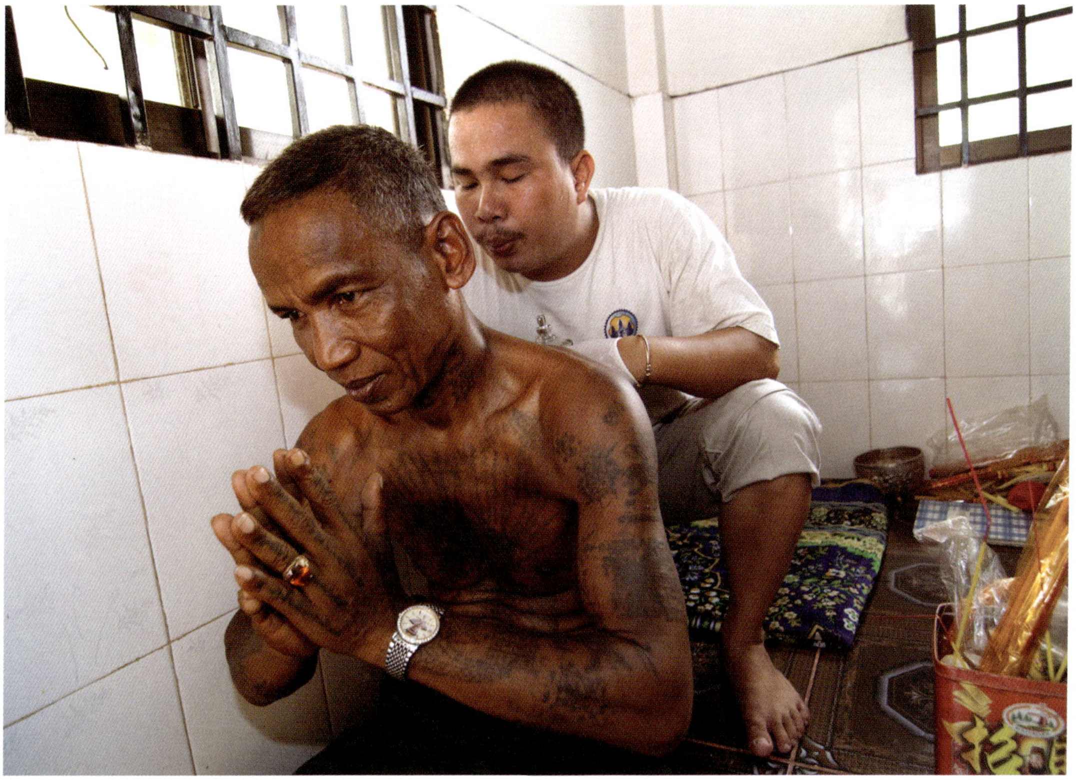

Above: Adjar Darin adds another sak yoan to the ex-soldier's personal repertoire.

ing and sleeping with girls, and the magic has faded away.

"I decided to stop giving the tattoos because I cannot trust the young people these days. If they had tattoos they'd probably fight. Before, we thought about the liberation of our country. We had a good spirit."

Although many Cambodian monks practised the sacred tattoo arts before 1975, today they have either died off or have stopped making tattoos. Some still create *yoan* on cloth, paper or amulets for their disciples instead of using needle and ink, and such objects are commonly seen in homes and shops around Cambodia.

The most recent comprehensive research into Khmer *sak yoan* appeared as *Yantra et Mantra*, a 1998 book by Olivier de Bernon of the École Française d'Extême-Orient. Writing of ritual in the Battambang area, de Bernon noted:

"When the time comes to send his disciple back, Krú Seng Huon recommends that he visit seven venerable monks in seven different monasteries to ask them to practise on him the 'ritual of the aspersion' (Sraôch Toek). This is said to cleanse or purify the body and the spirit."

Bronwyn Sloan, in her *Tales of Asia* blog about attempts to find tattoo masters in Battambang, says that one old monk told her that he required character references from potential disciples, who had to undergo a strict assessment before he would agree to ink tattoos on them.

"There is no war here anymore so now I am

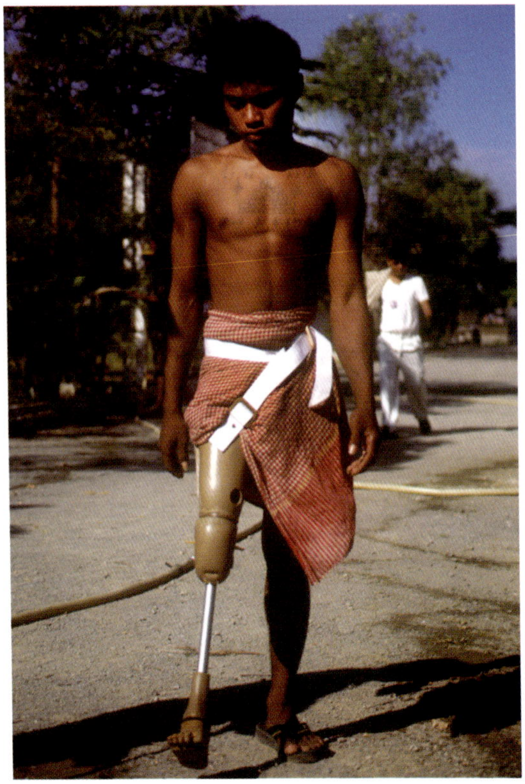

Above: A government soldier who lost his leg to a booby trap or landmine in rehab. On his chest are *sak yoan*.

always asking, 'Why do you need protection? What are you afraid of?'" the monk explained to her. "I always want to know first if it is the law they are afraid of, or if they respect it."

On our own visit to Battambang in search of *adjar sak yoan*, we were unable to find anyone – monk or layman – who could create *sak yoan*. One famous monk, probably the same one Sloan alluded to in her blog, had died just two months before our visit.

SIEM REAP

In Siem Reap, Adjar Darin works out of a modest home behind Wat Thmey. In front of his front gate hangs a sign decorated with the painted head of a demon and the words "Darin Tattoo" in English and simply "Darin" in Khmer. Inside, the artist maintains a beautiful multi-tier altar stacked steeply against one wall and flanked by ceremonial parasols representing the protection and preservation of Buddhist dhamma.

The 27-year-old Siem Reap native, who also goes by the name Prak Sokdaren, told us he had been making tattoos for seven years, but had only started doing *sak yoan* three years ago. He was unable to find anyone to teach him, so he taught himself to make *sak yoan* by studying old illustrated books about the tradition. He learned *gatha* (incantations) from the same books, and devised blessing and empowerment rituals based on accounts from older Cambodians as well as a few written accounts.

About half of Darin's disciples are Cambodian and the other half are foreigners. The master offers the option of having their tattoos inked either by hand or with a modern machine-powered stylus. His traditional stylus, made from a car antenna, has been tooled with screw threads at the end so that modern, interchangeable machine needles can be attached, much like the set-up used by famous Thai master Ajahn Noo Ganpai and a few others in Thailand. He uses unadulterated Chinese ink that has been blessed by local monks. When inking a tattoo, he wears latex gloves to lessen the risk of infection.

Darin seemed happy that someone from outside Siem Reap was taking an interest in his *sak yoan* practice. At the same time, he appeared to be a little nervous as we photographed his designs. Whether he suspected we were going to borrow them for use elsewhere, or simply wasn't confident about his repertoire, we couldn't tell. He was completely open and humble, however, about the auto-didactic nature of his training.

Among the more unique designs we saw in his simple catalog was a figure depicting Narayana standing on a tiger, a *yantra* we saw nowhere else

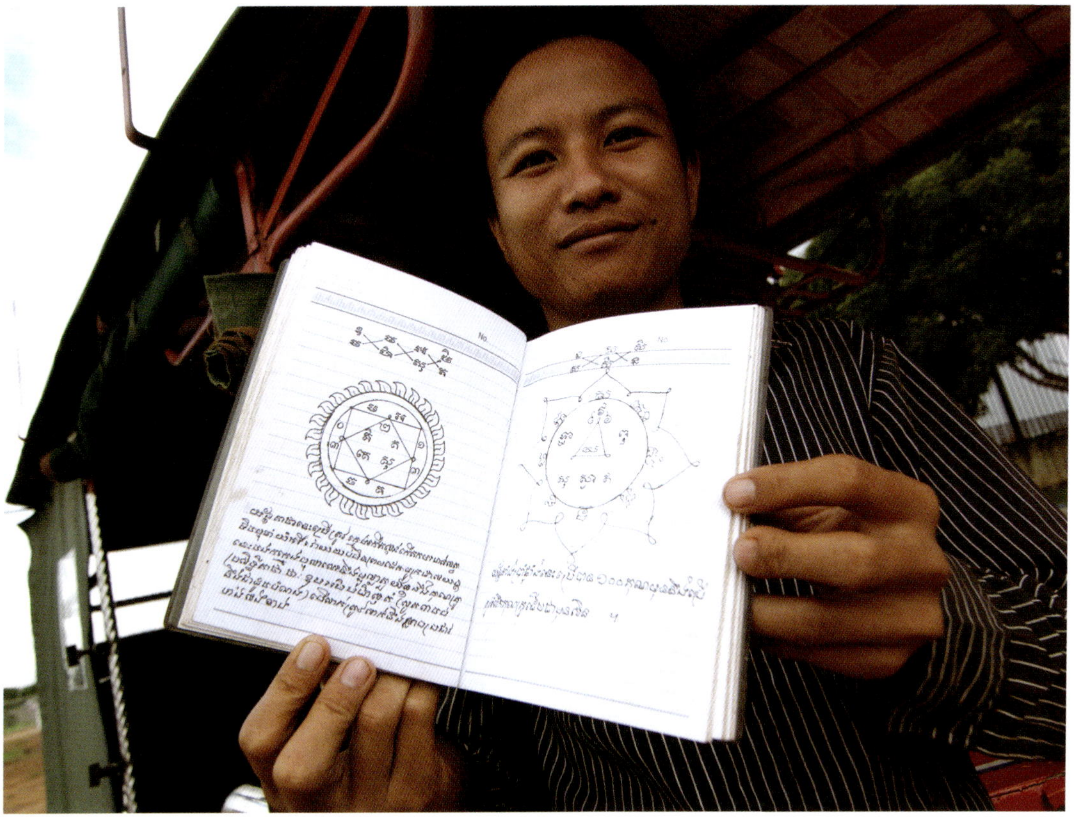

Above: A travelling master in Phnom Penh shows his *yantra* design book.

in our travels. Another design in his "look book" not commonly seen in the world of sacred *yantra* tattoos focused on Dharani, the Hindu-Buddhist earth goddess, standing in a sensuous "S" pose while squeezing water from her long black hair.

While we were interviewing Darin, an older Khmer man came in to receive a tattoo. Lean, muscled and sun-bronzed, he was a former KPNLF soldier who had also fought with Lon Nol in the early 1970s. He already bore numerous *sak yoan* on his chest, back, arms and legs; all, he said, dating to the 1980s. Notable were a huge Narayana on the chest, a dragon on the abdomen, a Hanuman brandishing a victory flag on one shoulder blade and anthropomorphic figures on each thigh, including one that appeared to be an ogress giving birth. One powerful calf sported a lion with bird claws instead of paws.

Darin, dressed in white, performed the rituals and inked the tattoo – a simple geometric *na* at the nape of the neck – with aplomb, in a solemn atmosphere of respect. Despite being self-taught, he is striving to preserve some measure of overall authenticity, balancing magic and artistry.

Meanwhile in the centre of town, amidst rows of shops and tourist guesthouses, another sign offering tattoo services reads "Neng Sinath Tattoo Machine". Inside the small, two-room building, enlarged photos of tattooed clients, underscored by a black-painted silhouette of Angkor Wat. In one corner sits a steel rack with a padded bench, a barbell

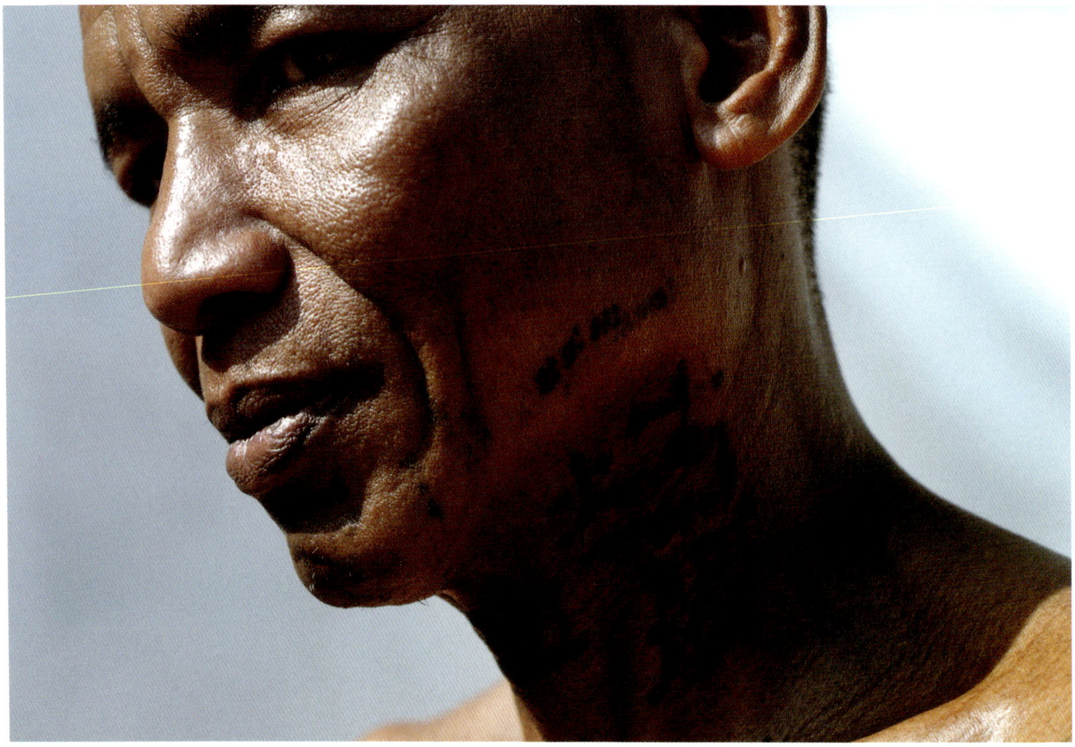

Above: *Sak yoan* along the jaw lends added power to an officer's orders to his troops.
Right: This monk received many of his tattoos while he was a soldier for Lon Nol.

and set of freeweights. A stack of well-thumbed tattoo magazines occupy a low table, along with plastic photo albums containing more photos of Adjar Neng's clients and ink drawings of tattoo designs, both modern and traditional.

Although Neng copies traditional *yantras*, he makes no claims about the power or efficacy of the work in terms of the occult world of *sak yoan*.

"My *yoan* have no magic, because I don't know how to put the magic in them.

I mostly copy from this book," he told us, hefting a thick book with a sky-blue cover lettered in Khmer.

Inside was a virtual encyclopaedia of *yantras*, riddled with Pali syllables in old Khmer script, and accompanied by captions in modern Khmer explaining the proper *gatha* to go with each *yantra*. Around a third of the *yantras* were familiar to us as facsimiles or variations of designs we had seen in Thailand. These included both geometric *yantra* as well as designs composed around mythical animals from the Hindu-Buddhist tradition, particularly those based on elephant, tiger, lion and bird motifs.

Compared to similar catalogues we had seen in Thailand, the book contained a much larger number of sigils with entirely geometric basic forms. Typically these were rectangles or squares filled in with grids of diagonal lines, forming full or broken diamond shapes. Inside each diamond, or in some cases in the middle of broken lines, were single numbers or letters – all variations on the "diamond armour" or "diamond net" *yantras* seen elsewhere

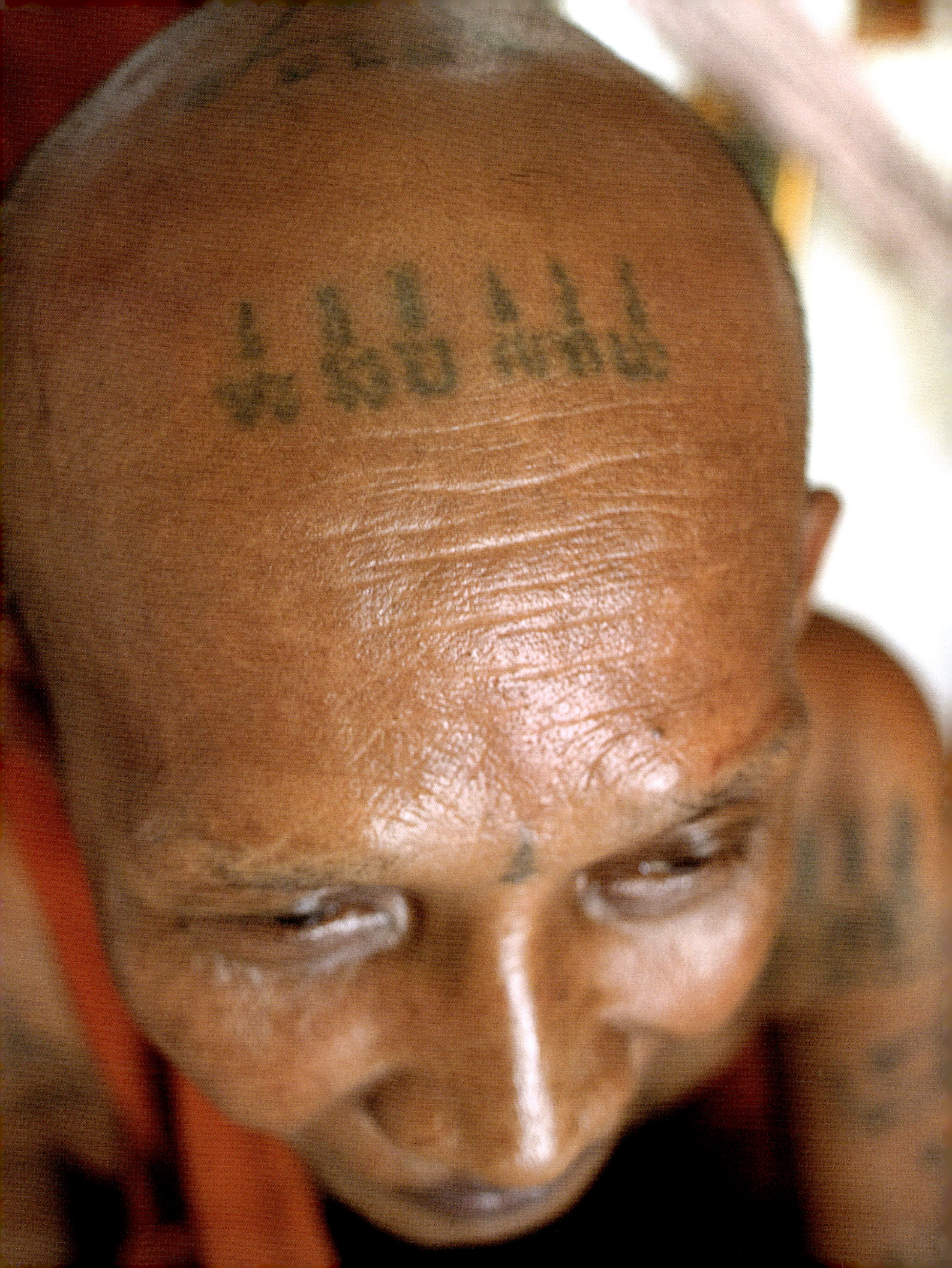

in mainland Southeast Asia. Each *yantra* represents a unique formula carrying numerological and alphabetic import to yield protection from malevolent forces, physical attack and accidents.

A number of the designs carried similar coding that formed anthropomorphic shapes, some of which clearly represented the Buddha (recognised by the prominent bulge on the crown of the head, and by meditation or right-fingertips-to-the-ground, "calling earth to witness", postures) and some of which represented less well-known spirits and deities.

Neng told us that most of the interest in traditional *sak yoan* at his studio comes from international clients. His repertoire also includes elegant designs from traditional Khmer art, including Ramayana characters as well as decorative motifs commonly seen in Khmer temple art. He says that these figures, as well as thickly inked names or slogans written in classic *moul* script, are popular with both international and Cambodian clients. In the case of the latter, it represents "Khmer pride", a trend that began with the repatriation of Cambodian youth who had been deported from the USA for alleged gang activity, mainly in southern California. Among this crowd are a number of hip-hop MCs and DJs who are heavily tattooed in Khmer decorative art and lettering, none of it associated with typical *sak yoan*. In another departure from *sak yoan* tradition, Neng offers full-colour work, and will also cover up old tattoos with new ones upon request.

Neng applies his work using a tattoo machine, changing needles for each client and wearing latex gloves.

EH PHOUTONG

Cambodia's most celebrated kickboxing champion, Eh Phoutong, lives in a simple two-storey shophouse on the outskirts of Phnom Penh. We telephoned ahead to make an appointment. When we arrived on a rainy Sunday afternoon, a powerfully-built man came out to greet us and led us under the shelter of a makeshift roof that formed a porch in front of the shophouse.

Off to one side of the porch, a heavy training bag hung from a chain. Inside the shophouse, a bookshelf sagged under the weight of shiny metal trophies. Most bore Khmer inscriptions but we noticed a few from France and Australia.

Having been born in Ko Kong, an island near the Thai border, the affable Eh Phoutong spoke perfect Thai. He was eager to talk about *sak yoan*, and has been quoted many times in the press saying that the sacred tattoos are partially responsible for his success in *pradal serey* (Khmer kickboxing).

Of the 185 times Eh Phoutong has fought in the ring, he has only lost 10 bouts.

"I fought a lot when I was a teenager, and did well, but I felt I needed more power in my kicks and punches, and that I needed to be bolder.

"So when I was in my early 20s I asked Adjar Ran for *yoan* that would help me become a better fighter. Adjar Ran came from Battambang, which is famous for powerful magic."

In Khmer, Battambang means "disappearing stick", a tribute to a local tale of a legendary Khmer king who maintained power over the region using a powerful walking staff acquired from a great *muni ey-sey*.

"I don't know what happened to Adjar Ran. I think he is still around somewhere."

The 40-year-old Cambodian national hero was wearing a pair of satin boxing shorts, and we could make out the faded lines of tattoos on his back, chest and arm. We asked about the large Narayana on his back.

"That is 'Narayana-changing-form'. It boosts my overall power, and makes it more difficult for opponents to understand my strategies or my stance. And Hanuman here," he indicates the outline of the

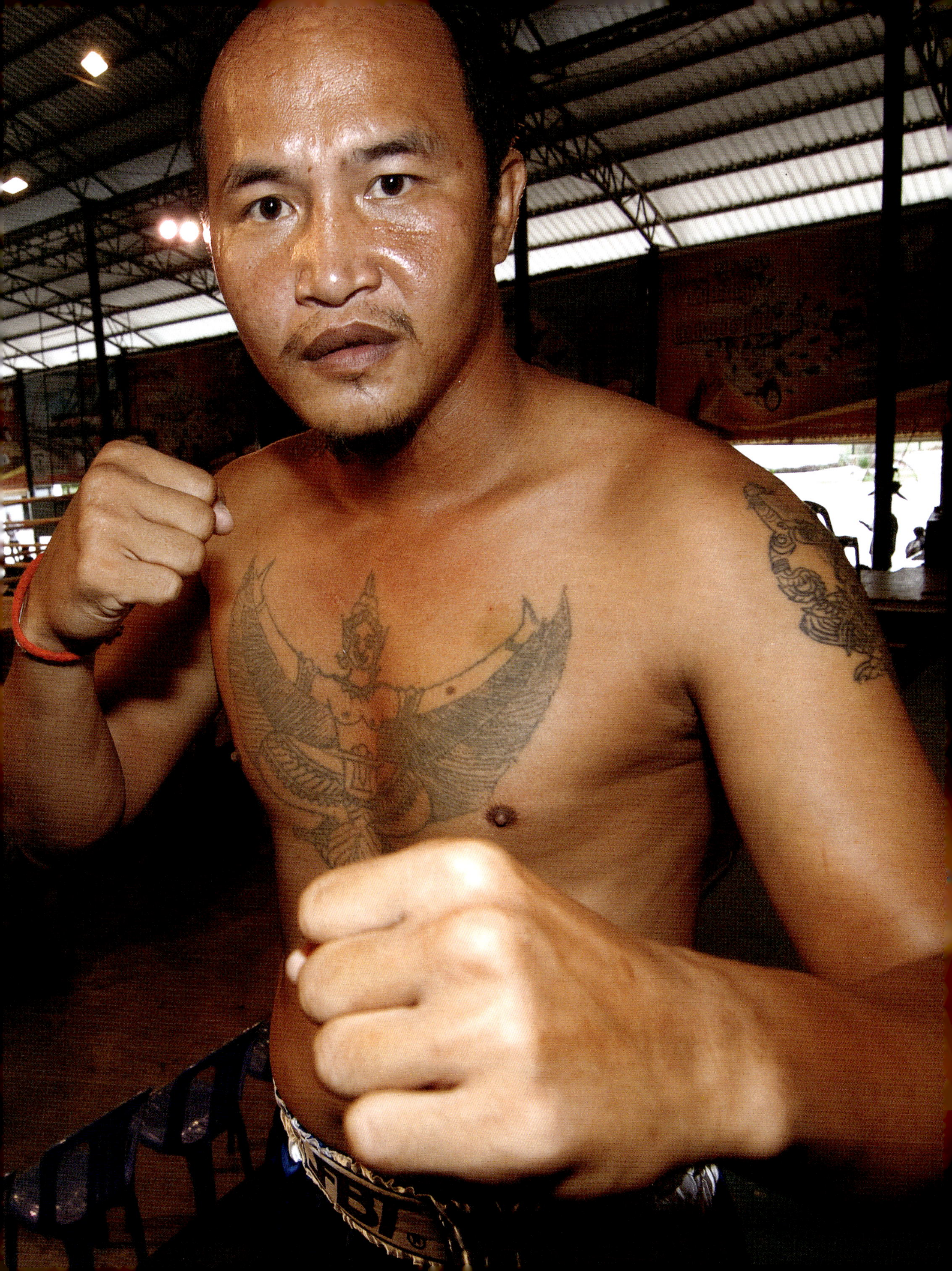

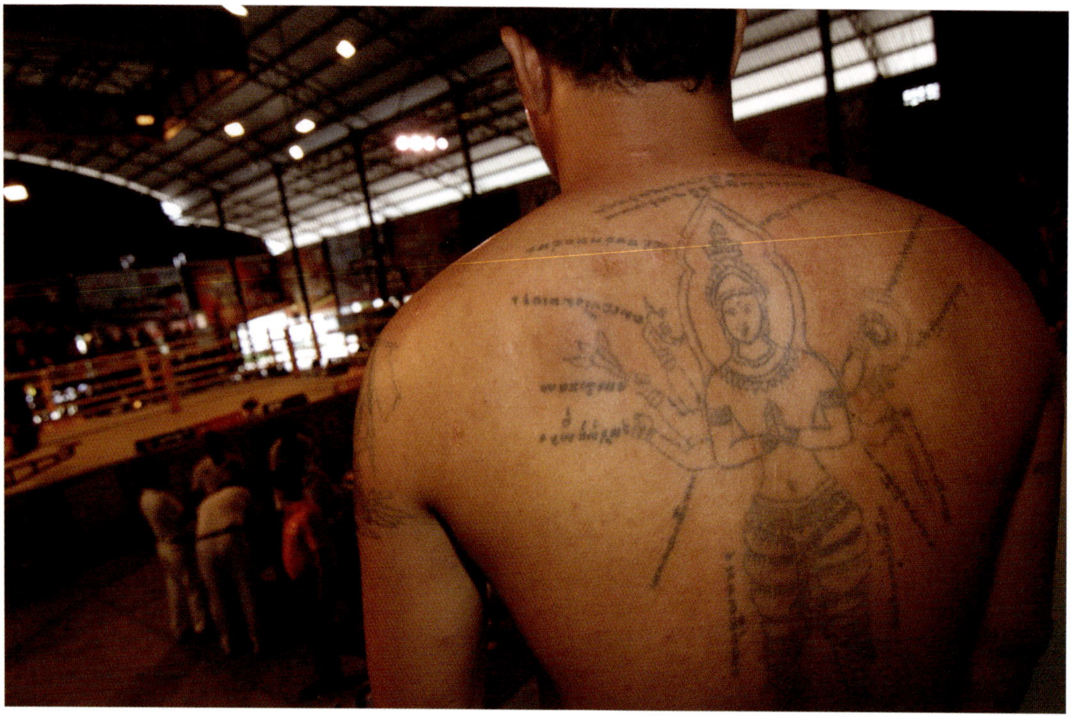

Previous page: Khmer boxing champ Eh Phoutong received the Garuda on his chest from a master in Battambang.
Above: The "Narayana-changing-form" *yoan* makes it more difficult for Eh Phouthong's opponents to understand his fight strategies.
Right: Khmer fighters in action at a ring in Phnom Penh.

monkey god elsewhere on his back, "brings me more agility in the ring. Hanuman is a tricky fighter, and so am I!"

On his right hand and forearm is a series of Pali phrases written in Khmer script. "It says 'Great Weight', and makes my punches heavier, more powerful."

"I don't know how it works, but it does. Of course you have to believe or the power is lost."

These days Eh Phoutong rarely fights but instead has undertaken the training of several promising young fighters. On another visit we followed him to the TV5 boxing stadium where his trainees were to compete in a series of professional matches for the regular Friday night live telecast. Although he was obviously something of a celebrity among the judges and crowd, he avoided being singled out by announcers and spent most of his time behind the scenes coaching his charges.

We asked whether young *neak pradal* (fighters) in Cambodia were interested in *sak yoan*.

"Some of them are, but they can't find any masters to give them tattoos. The masters have pretty much all disappeared in Cambodia.

"A lot of Westerners nowadays show up here looking to get Khmer tattoos. I don't get it; it just seems like a waste of time to me to come all the way to Cambodia when there are plenty of masters in Thailand."

Chuckling softly, the champ added, "Most just want them for decoration anyway. Why don't they just get tattoos in their own language?"

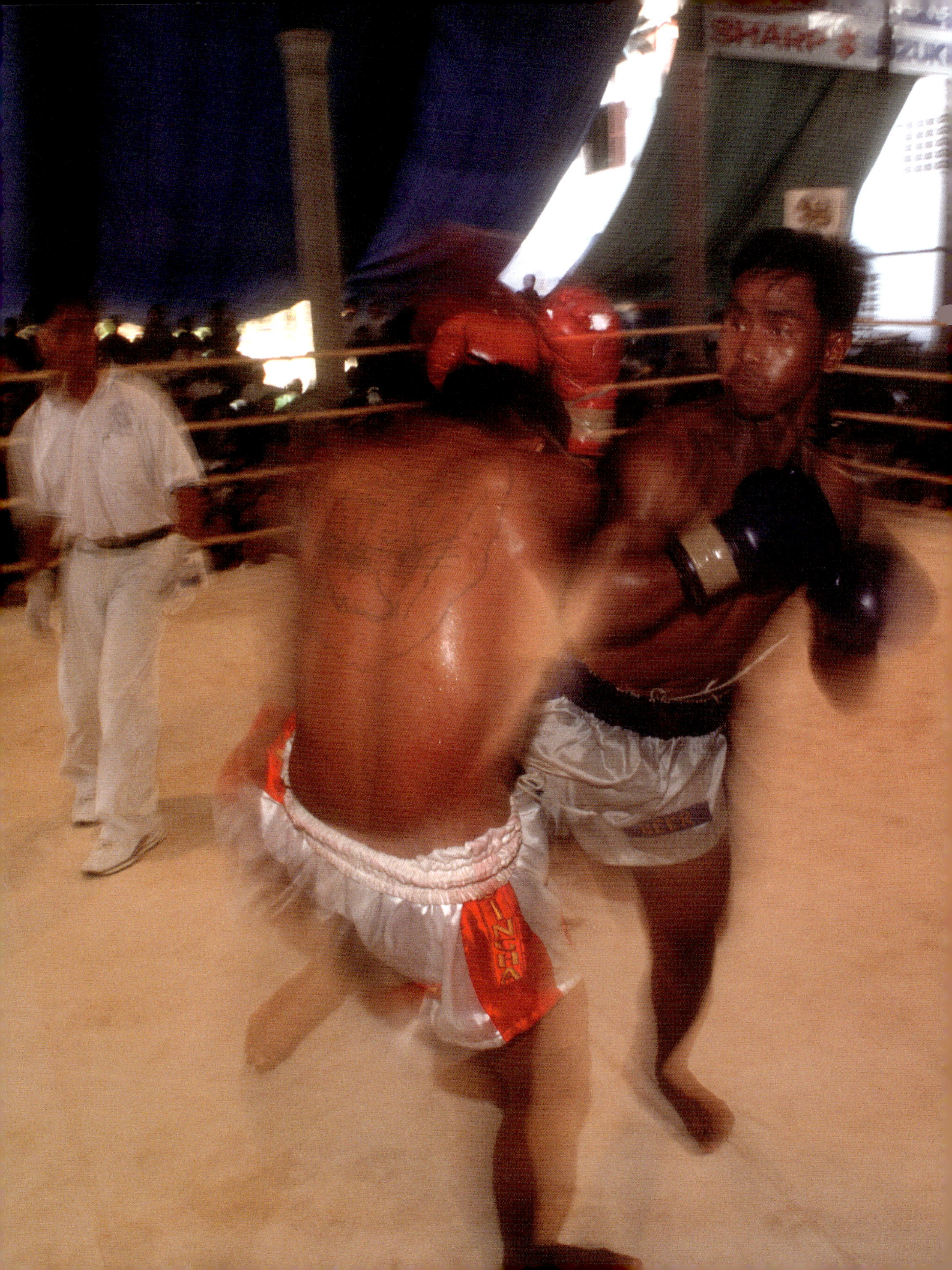
SHARP

WAI KHRU - PAYING RESPECT TO THE MASTERS

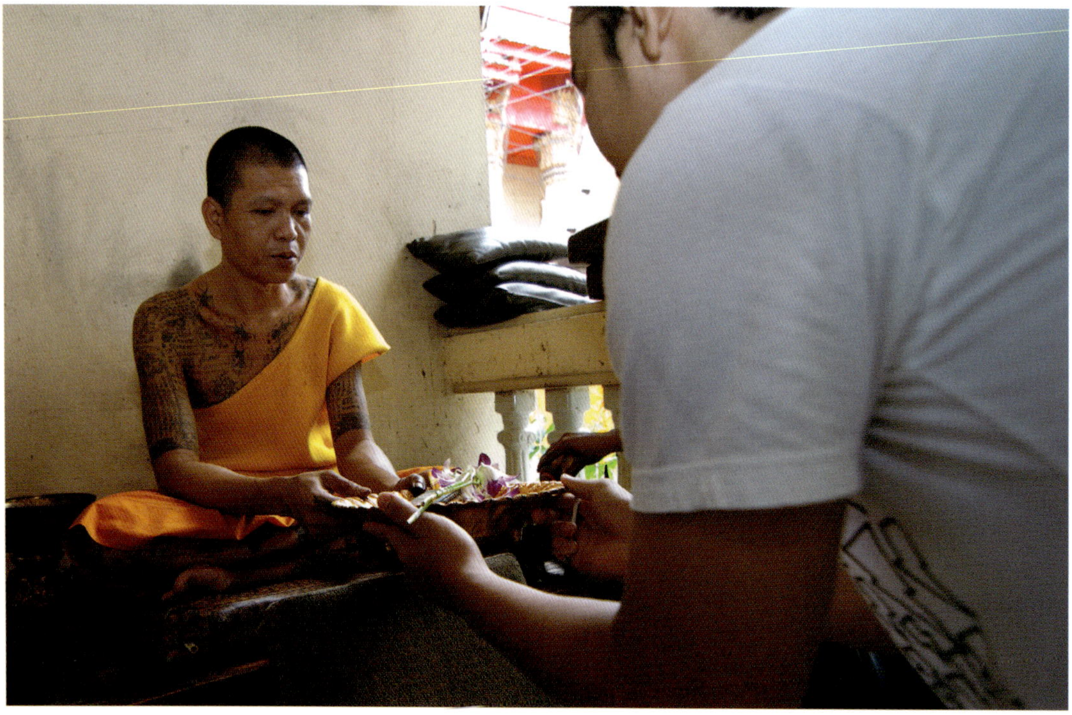

Above: Ajahn Baew receives offerings from a disciple.

Every year on a designated date, a *khru sak* invites all his disciples – all those he has tattooed in the past – to visit him for a series of ceremonies called *wai khru* (paying respect to one's master or teacher). Beyond re-affirming their allegiance and respect to the *khru sak*, the occasion allows the master to re-consecrate all of the *sak yan* previously inked on his disciples.

The day spent with the master also gives his disciples a chance to re-establish the correct moral conduct for maintaining the power of their tattoos. If their adherence to the code has been less than sterling during the intervening year, their tattoos will have lost a corresponding amount of power and efficacy. As explained in the Magic Ink chapter, the code also serves as an invisible layer of power and protection.

The *wai khru* day gives everyone a chance to compare their tattoos, receive new tattoos if they so wish, and seek counsel from the master on problems they may be experiencing in their lives.

The ceremonies begin in the morning with a ritual in which the disciples kneel or sit cross-legged on the floor in front of the *khru sak*, who sits with his back to the main altar of his *samnak* (tattoo centre) or, in the case of monks, a special tattoo altar in the monastery. While the master chants a selection of Pali or mixed Pali and Thai verses, the disciples close their eyes and hold their hands in front of their chests in a prayer-like *wai* gesture. At this time he may also pass a length of consecrated white cotton thread around the backs of the necks of his disciples and through the fingers of their hands to creative a protective circle. He will also splash holy water on the assembly with a reed whisk.

During the chanting and water-sprinkling, some of the disciples tattooed with animal *yantra* may slip into trance, making animal sounds, pawing the floor and rolling their eyes as the power in the designs surges.

At smaller *samnak* the rituals are usually over in an hour or two, after which lunch is served and those who want new tattoos confer with the master while everyone else leaves. At larger centres or monasteries the ceremonies may stretch on all day to accommodate the larger numbers of disciples.

The biggest and most well-known *wai khru* day in Thailand occurs each year in March at Wat Bang Phra. This large Ayuthaya-era temple in a relatively rural area of Nakhon Pathom province owes its *sak yan* lineage to the late Phra Udom Prachanart, more commonly known as Luang Pho Poen.

During the annual Wat Bang Phra *wai khru*, thousands of tattooed disciples gather at the monastery to undergo consecration rituals in a large empty space in front of a huge black statue of Luang Pho Poen. Women on their period are strictly forbidden from entering this area. In front of them on a podium are the temple's tattoo masters, both monks and white-clothed laymen. Directly in front of this podium is a line of volunteer guards chosen for their physical strength.

Hundreds of disciples enter into trance, many of them breaking into a sprint as they throw themselves at the granite base of the statue. The ring of volunteers around the statue catch the

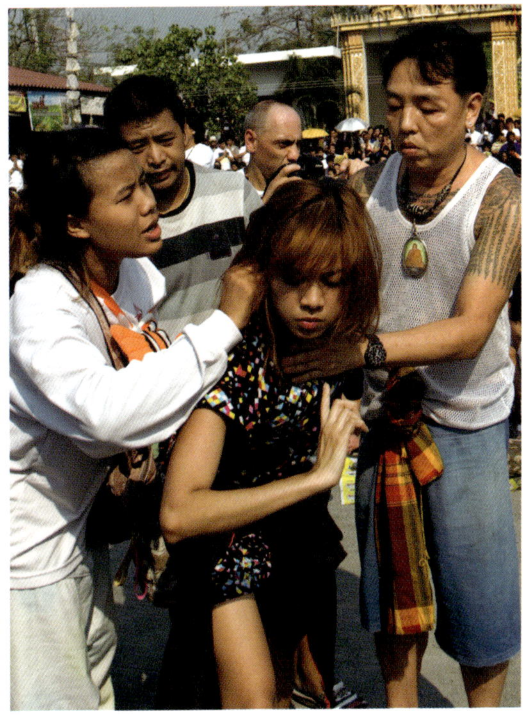

Above: A girl in trance at the huge *wai khru* ceremony at Wat Bang Phra.

wayward disciples, lift them off the ground, and bring them out of trance by grasping their ears and shaking them while whispering soothing words. Once the disciples are out of the trance they calmly walk back into the crowd.

As the ceremony progresses, increasing numbers of people will enter into trance, many of them running towards the podium at the same time. To reach the massive crowds at Wat Bang Phra, the monks use water hoses instead of reed whisks for the water consecration stage of the ceremony. Afterwards, disciples grab the sacred string looped around the entire area to tie sections around their wrists. During the entire ceremony, a monk delivers a lengthy sermon through an outdoor speaker system, reminding the disciples that *sak yan* mean nothing without a firm Buddhist foundation.

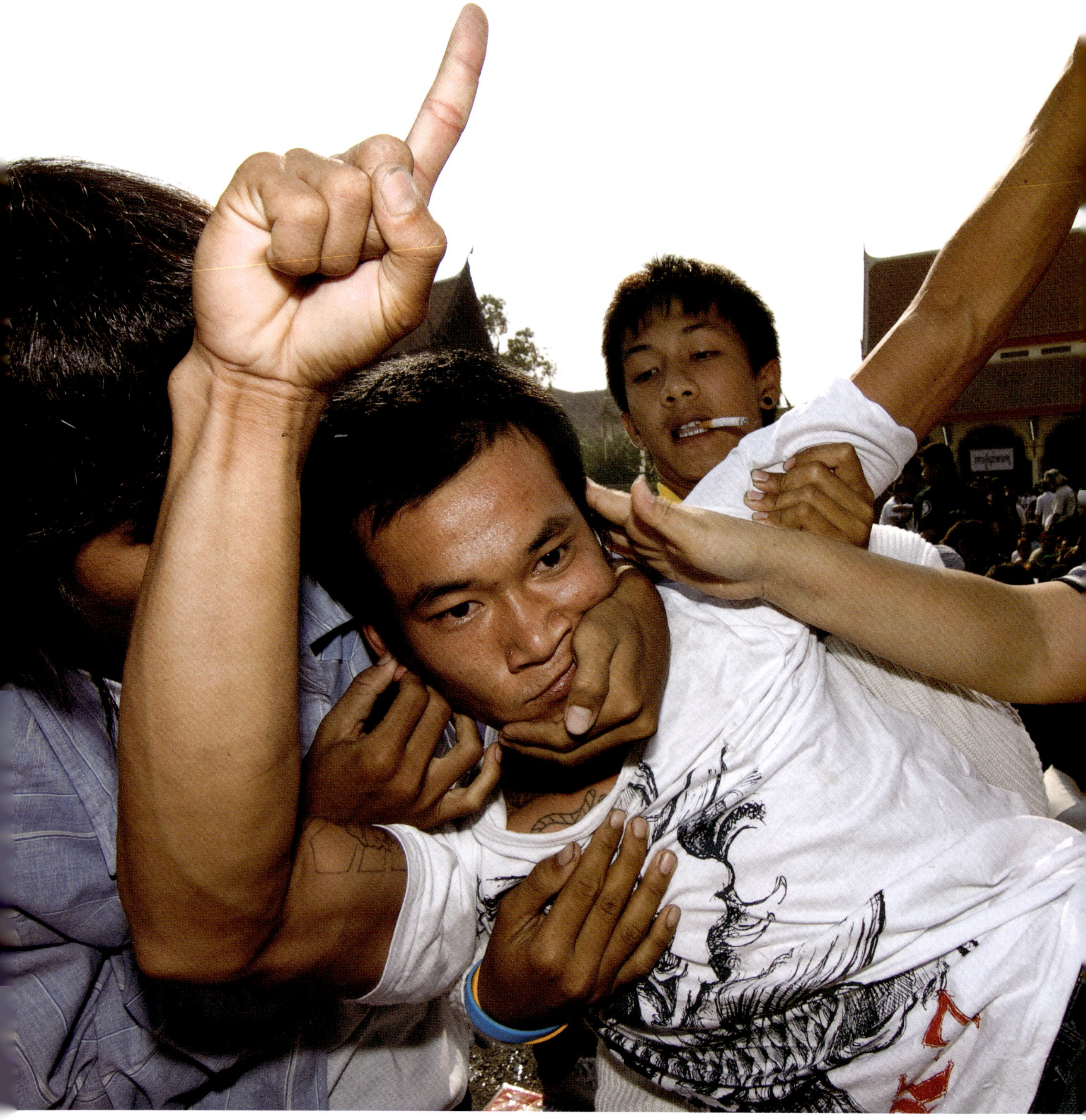

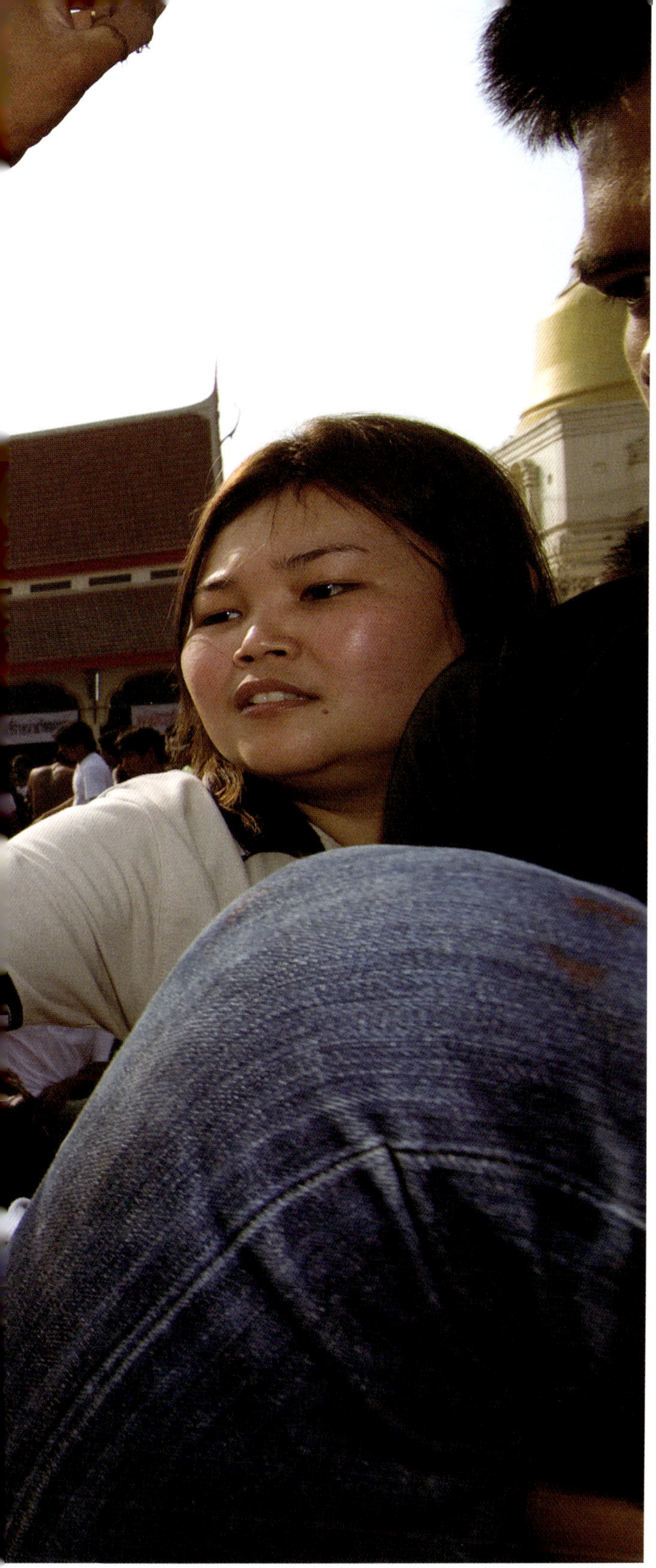

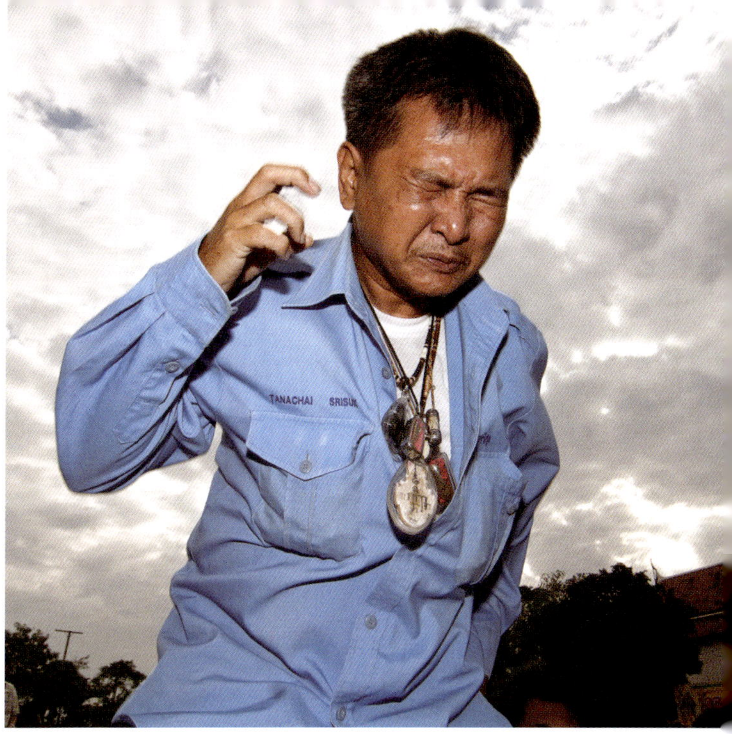

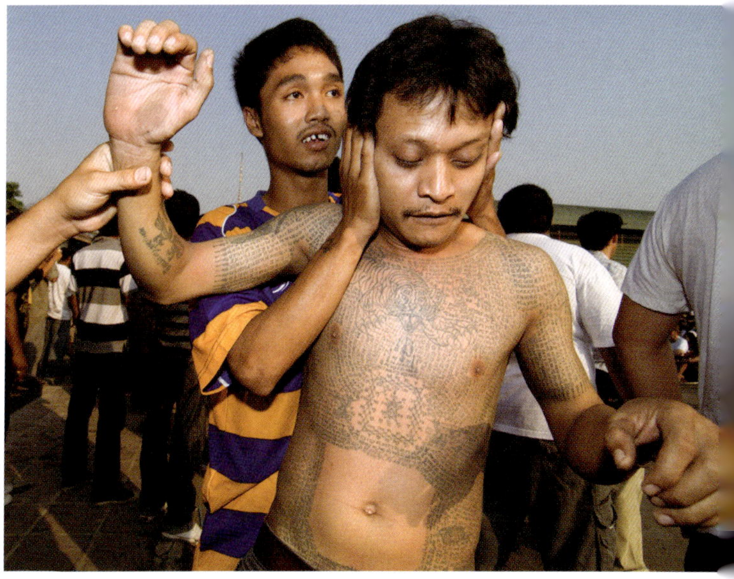

The most common method for bringing someone out of a trance is to rub or grab their ears.

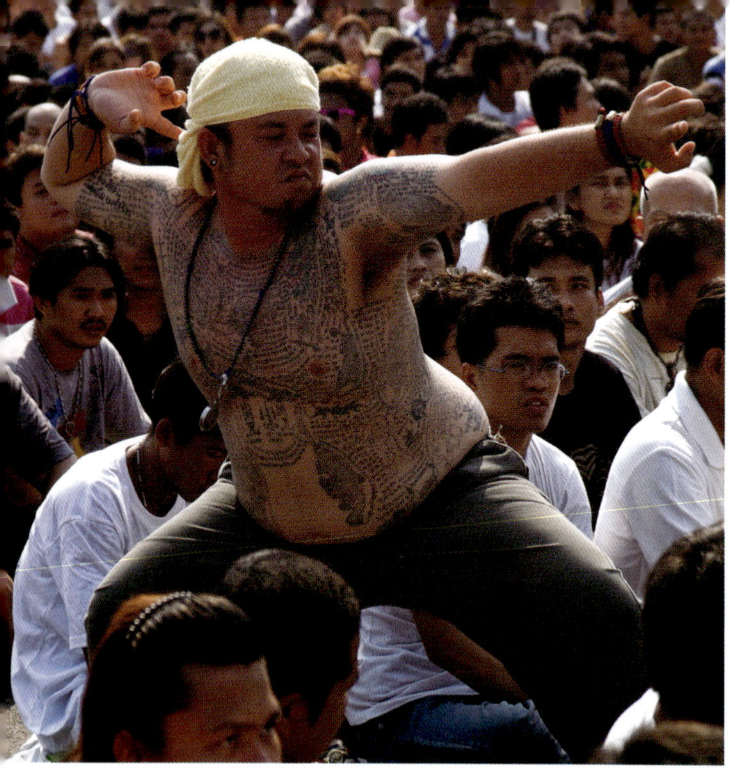

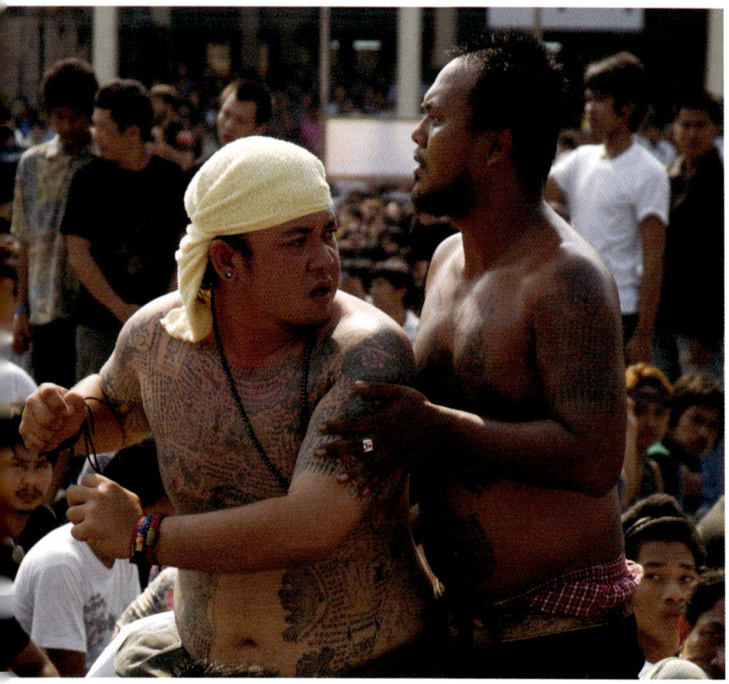

An exuberant disciple in trance.

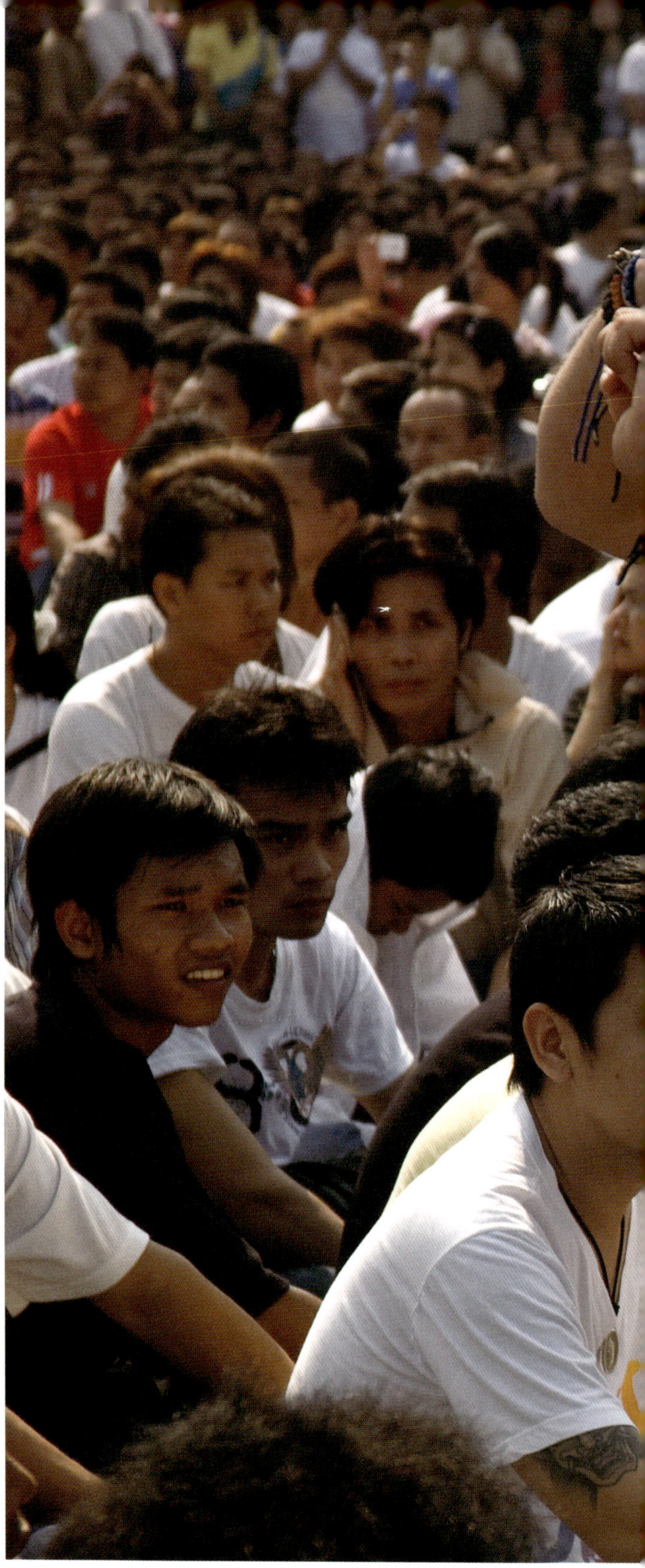

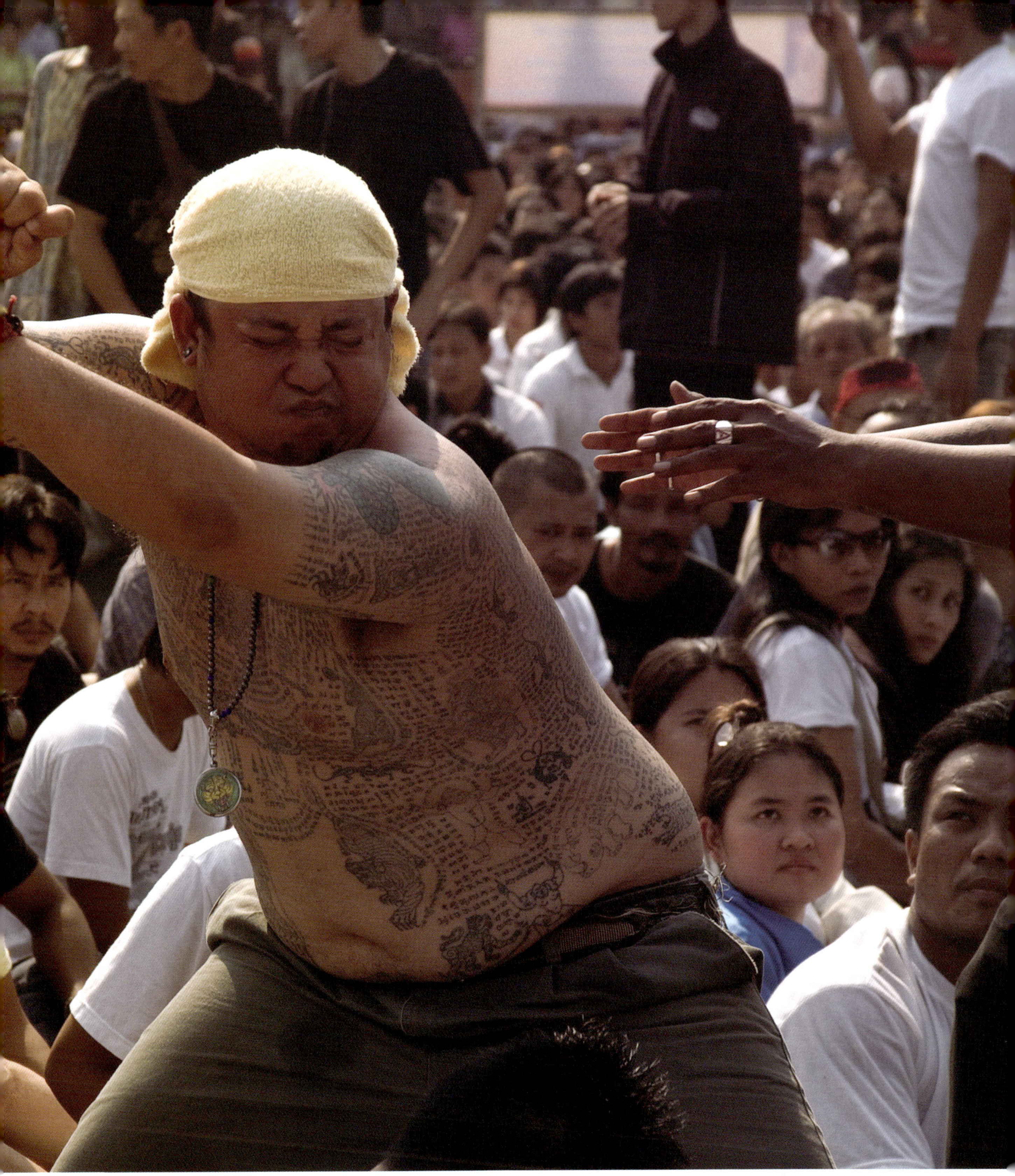

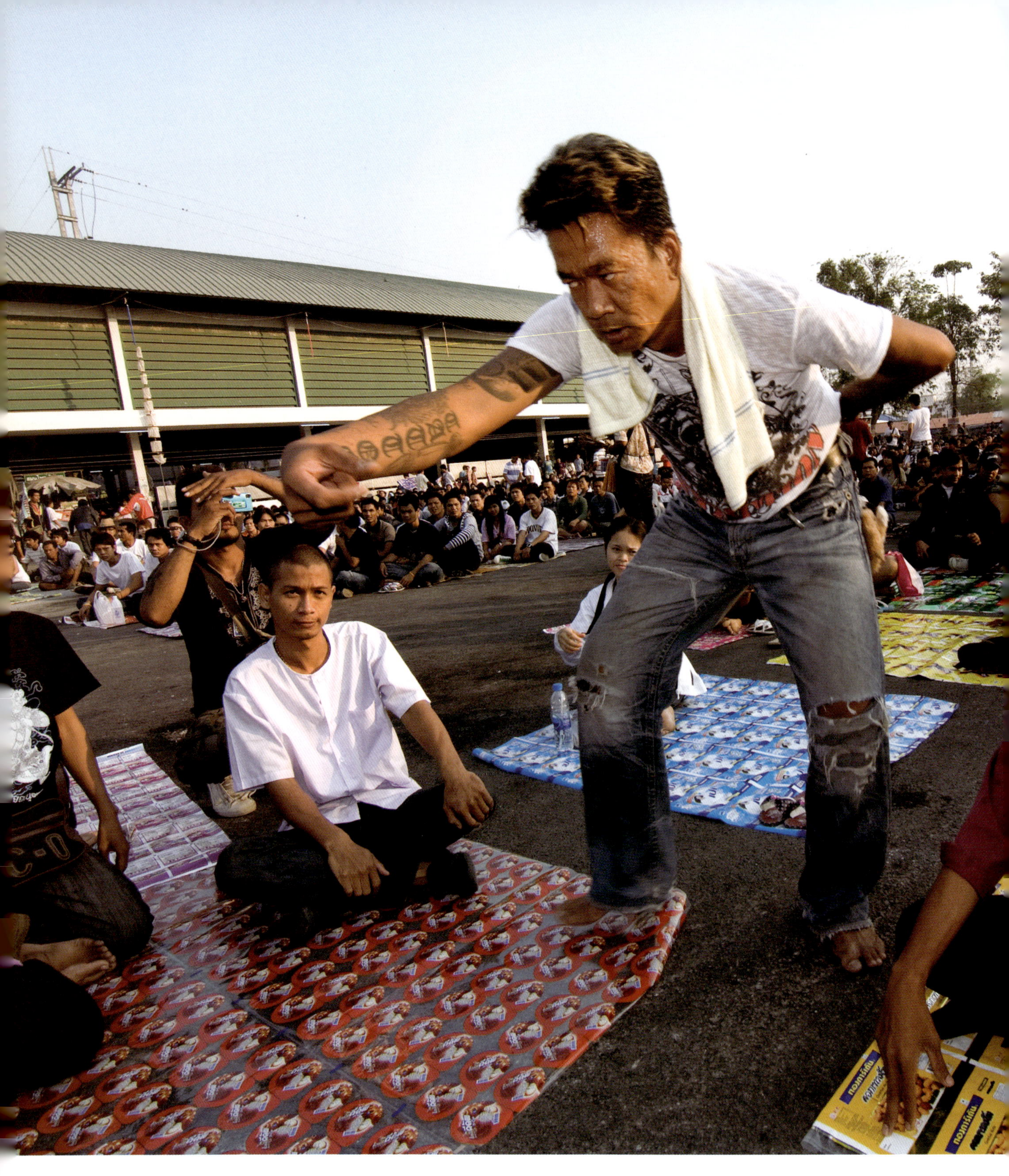

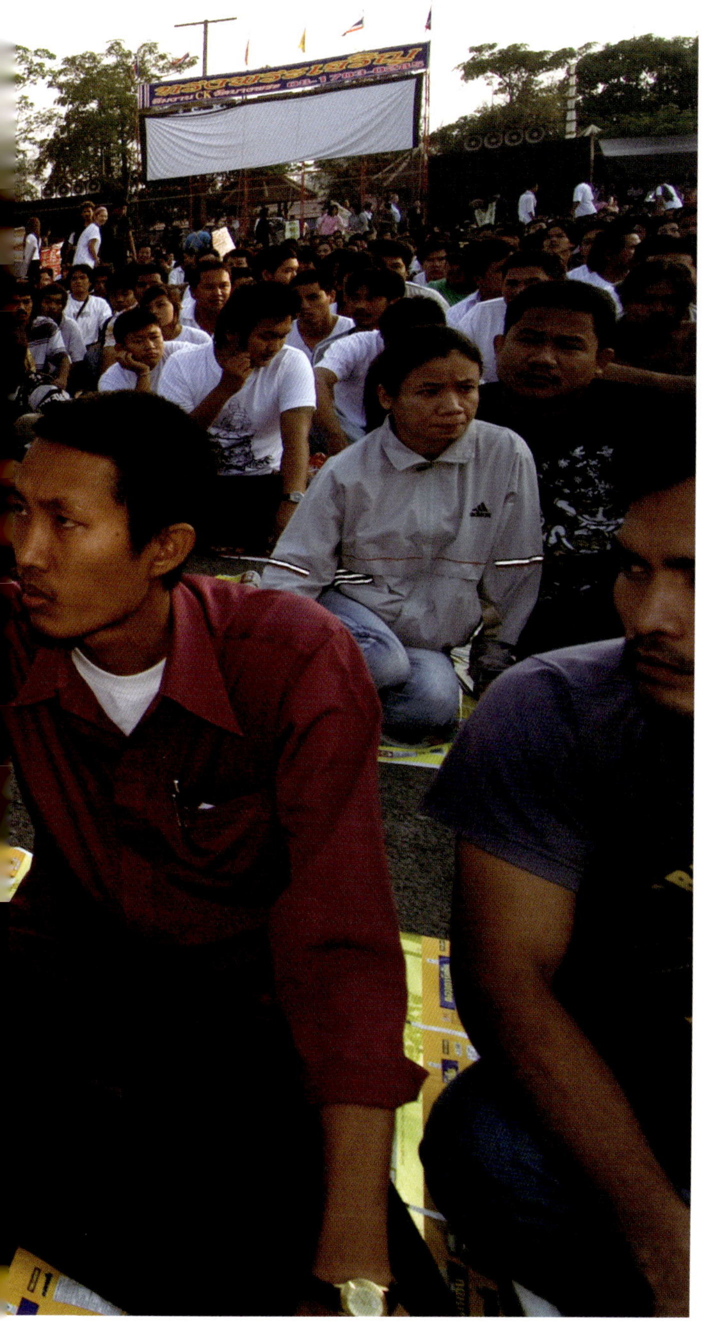

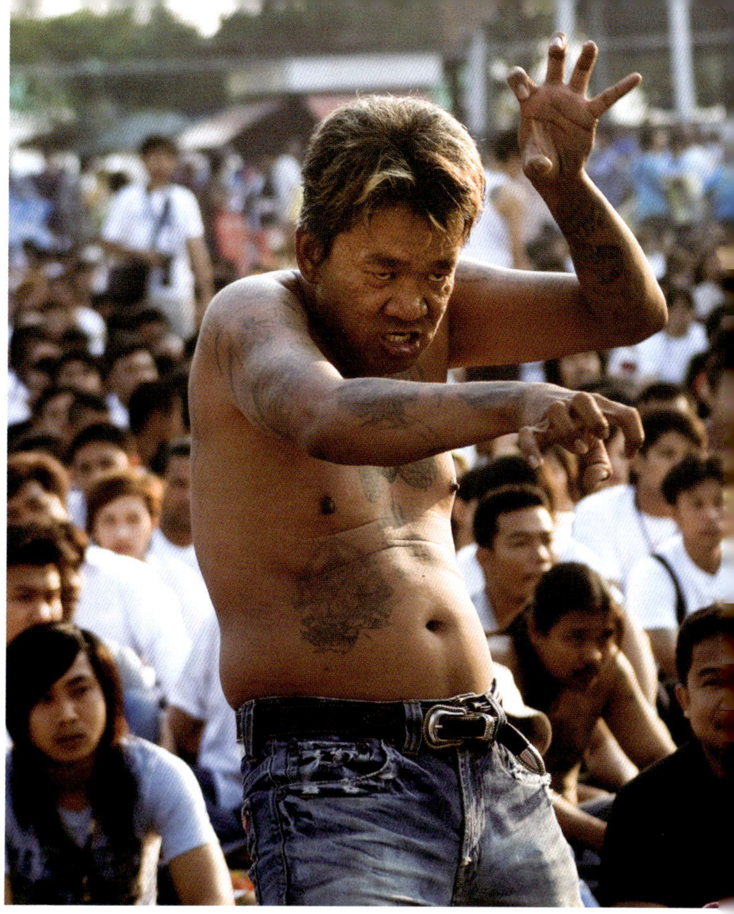

A man in trance imitates the characteristics of a tiger *yantra* inked on his back.

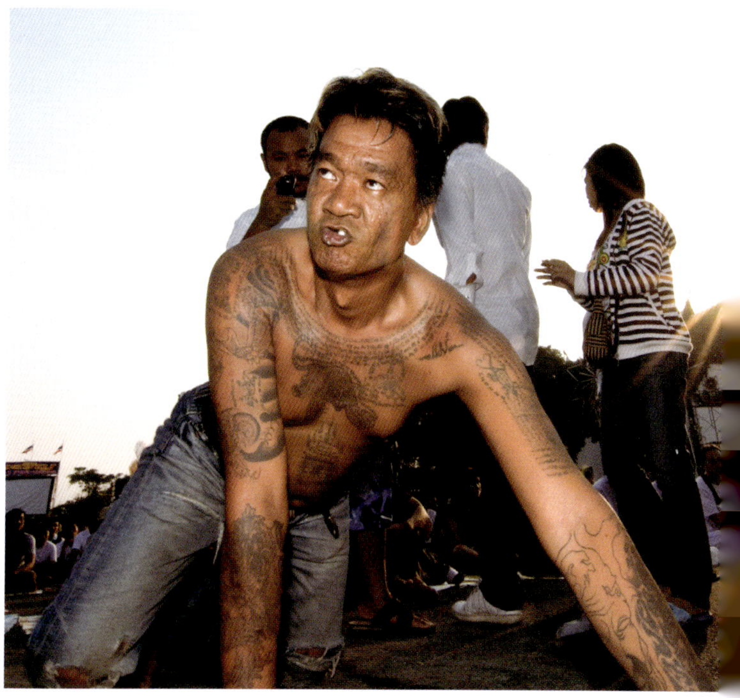

AJAHN TOY

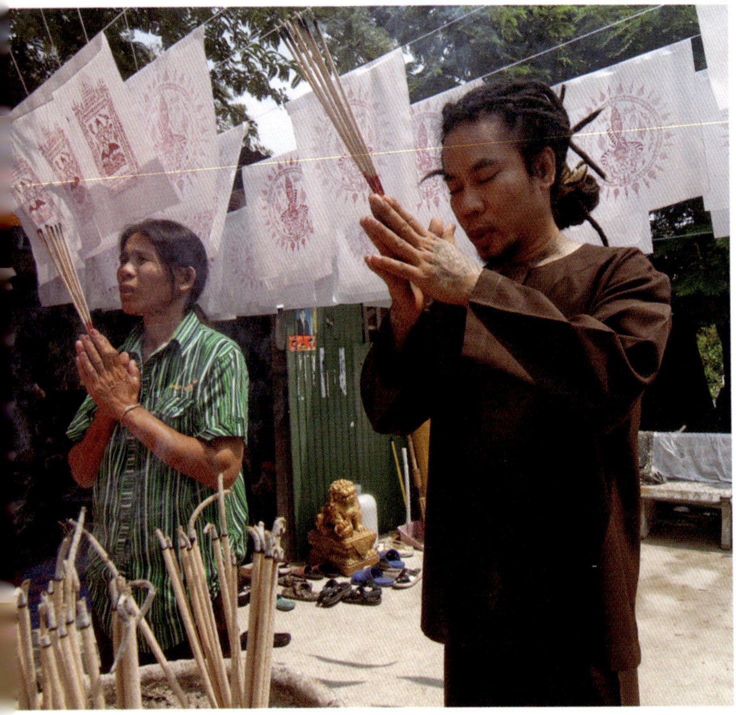

Above: Ajahn Toy pays respect to his Pho Kae lineage on his annual wai khru day.

Right: The spirit of Pho Kae has entered Ajahn Toy, turning him into an old man.

Ajahn Toy's annual wai khru ceremonies take place on 5–6 March. One of the rituals unique to the *reusee* tradition is *krop khru*, during which the Pho Kae mask is placed on the head of the disciple to receive Pho Kae's blessing and protection. Some disciples will enter into trance during this ritual, temporarily possessed by the spirit of the hermit sage. Ajahn Toy himself will enter into an impressive full Pho Kae trance in front of an outdoor altar erected especially for this day. It is one of the only days of the year that 'Pho Kae' ventures outside in Bangkok.

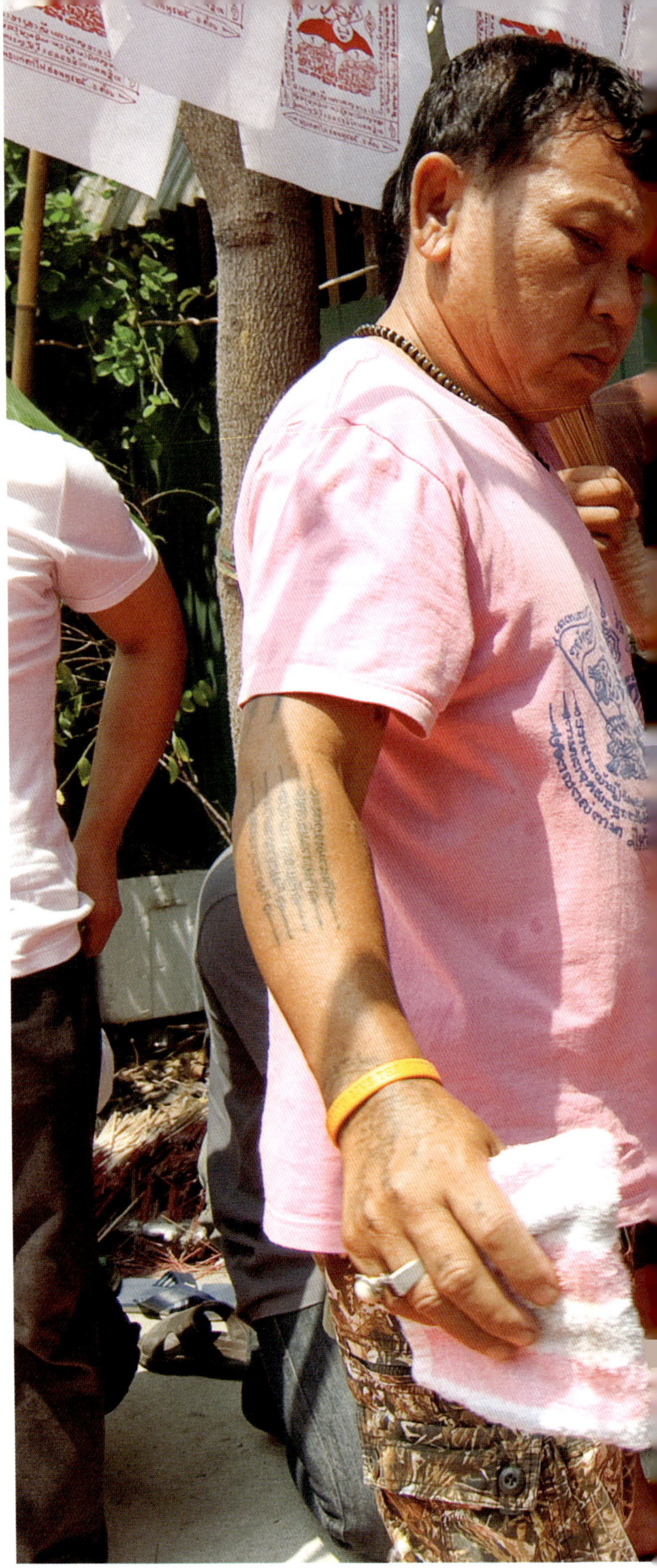

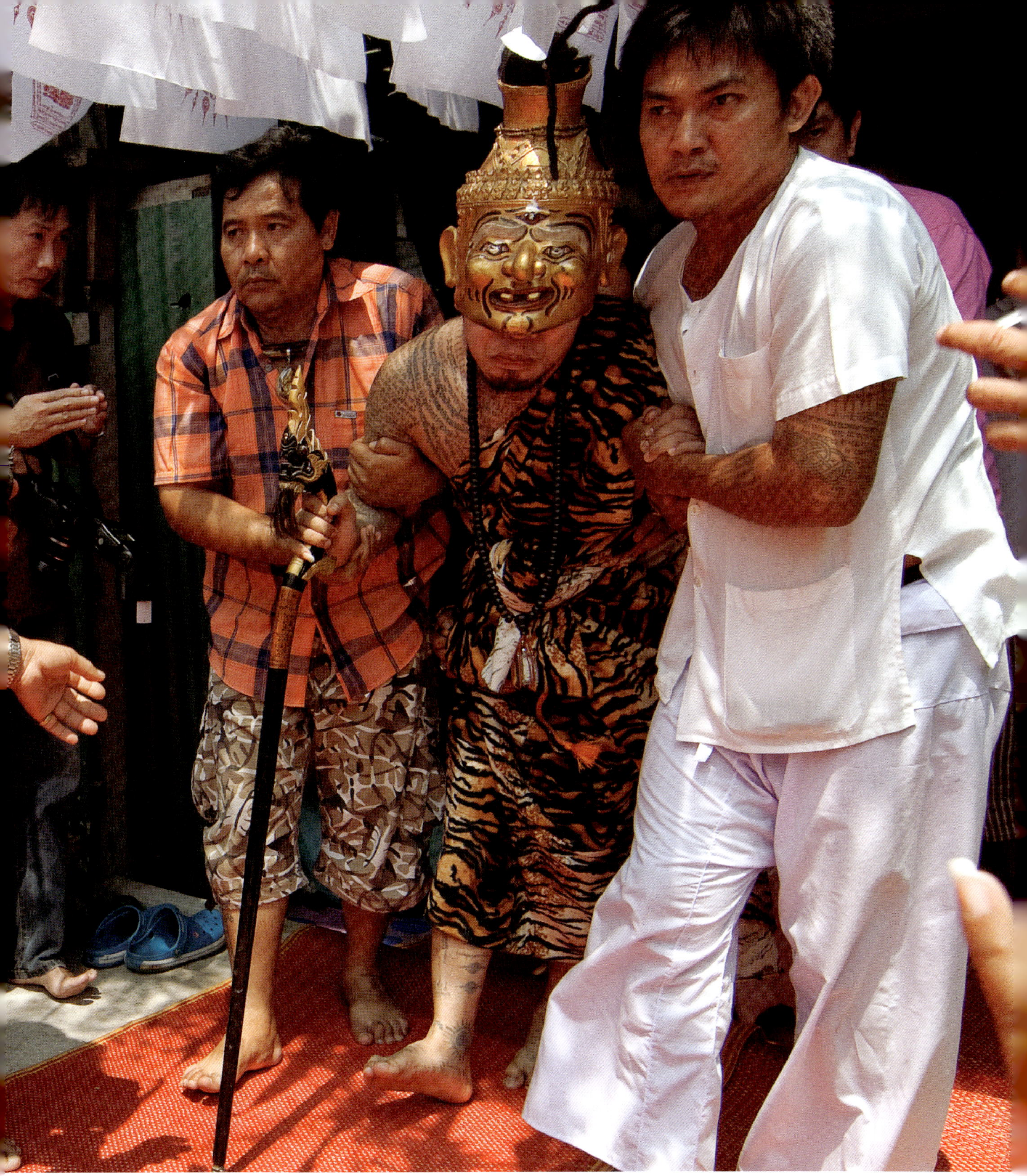

SAK YAN PEOPLE

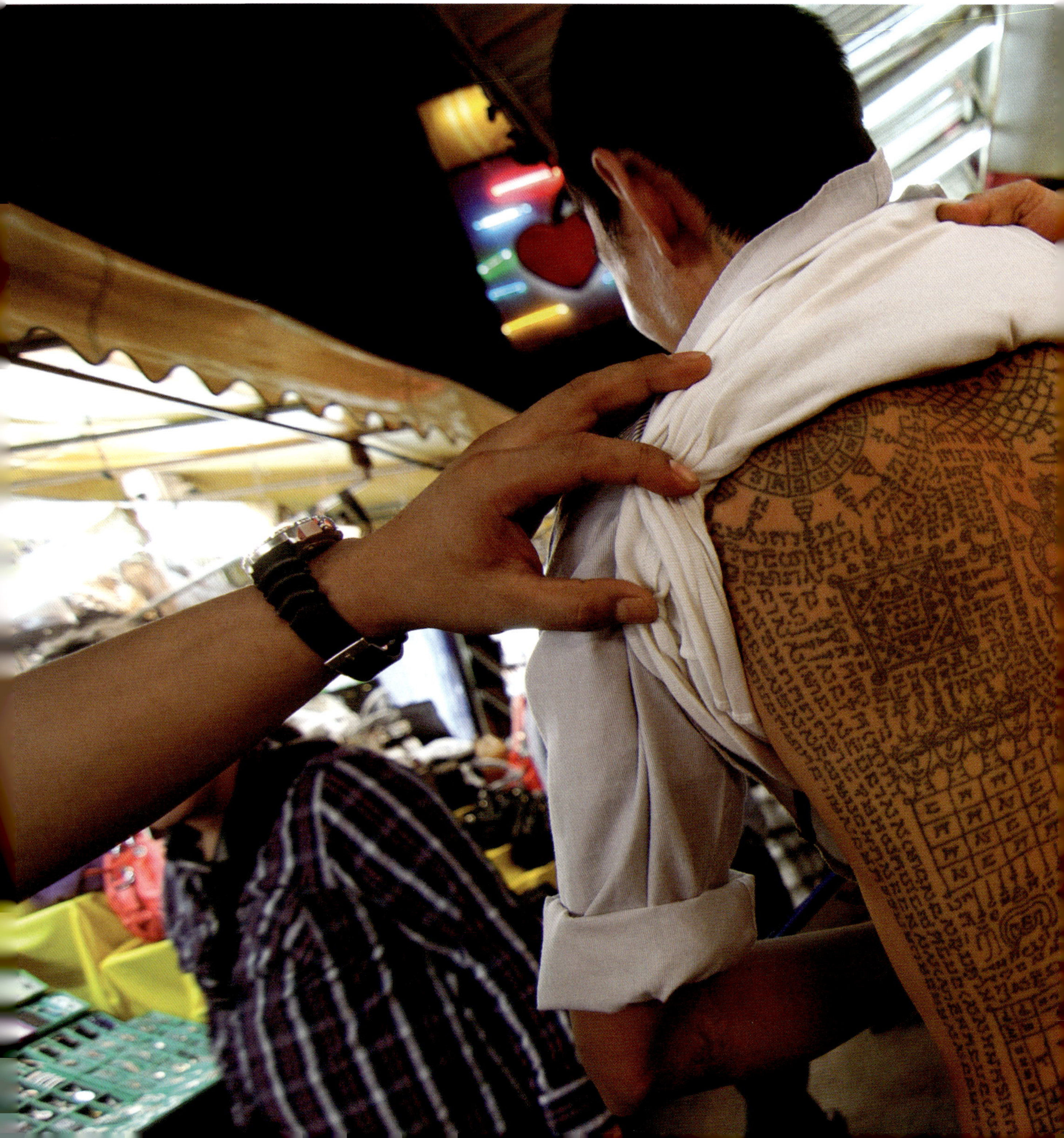

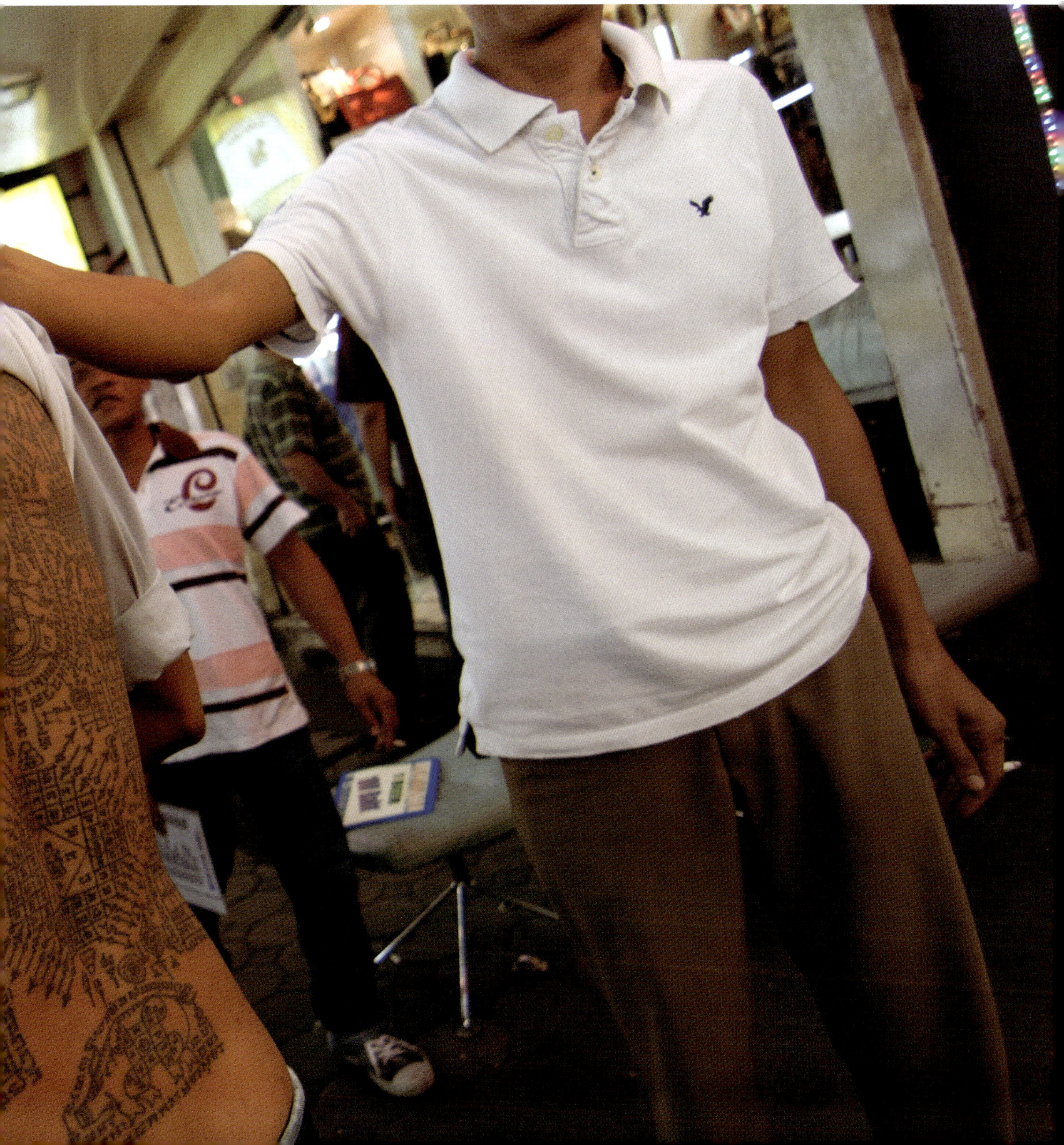

THE MONK

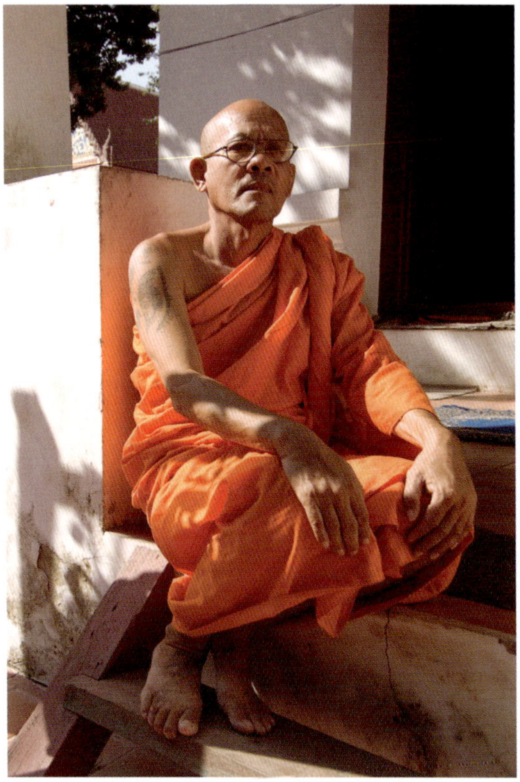

Phra Khao Sanutjitto received many *sak yan* as a young layman. A typical array of *yantras* for prosperity, charisma and disaster evasion graced his broad back, most inked by Luang Pho Poen while the great master was still alive. One day he awoke to find he was almost completely paralysed. As the *sak yan* had apparently failed to protect him, he concluded that he hadn't properly honoured his tattoos. For three days he repeated the *khaathaa* which Luang Pho Poen had taught him, and promised that if he recovered he would become a monk for the rest of his life. The following day the paralysis disappeared; he ordained and has remained in robes ever since.

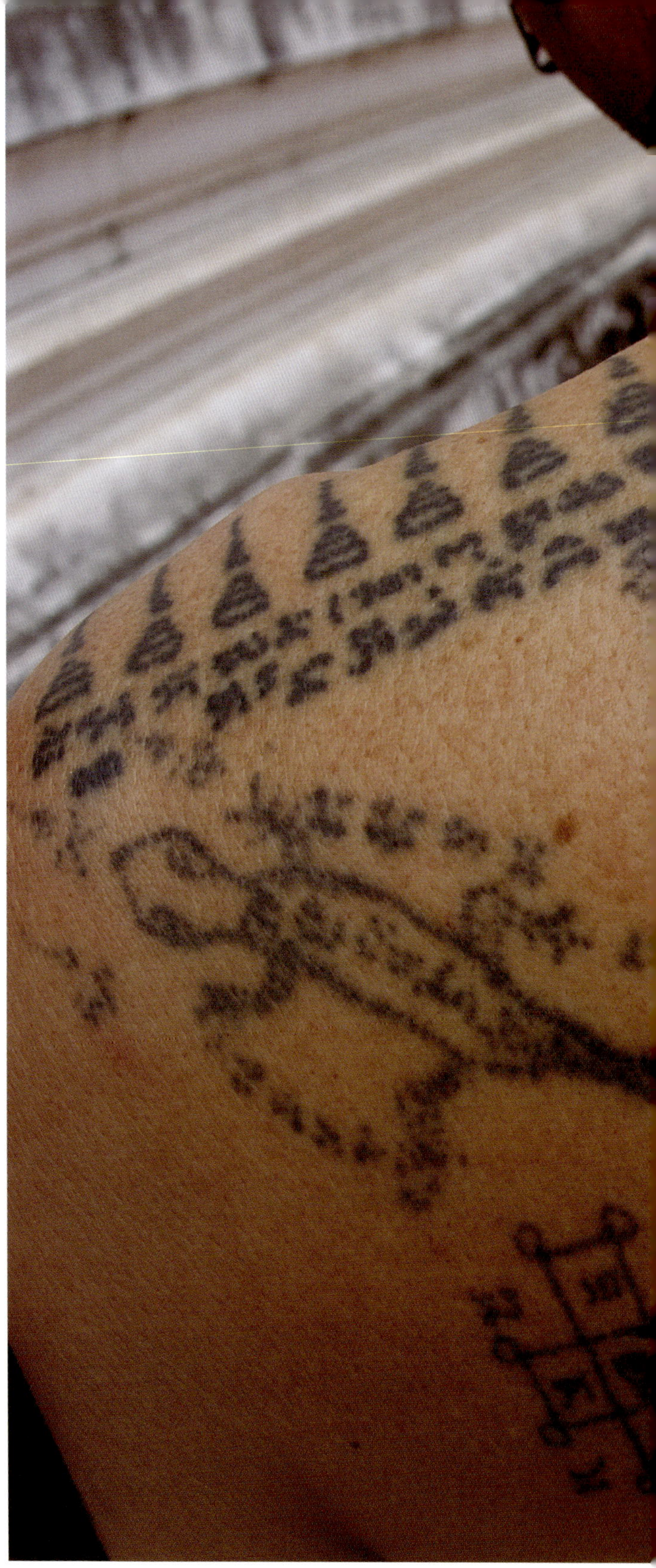

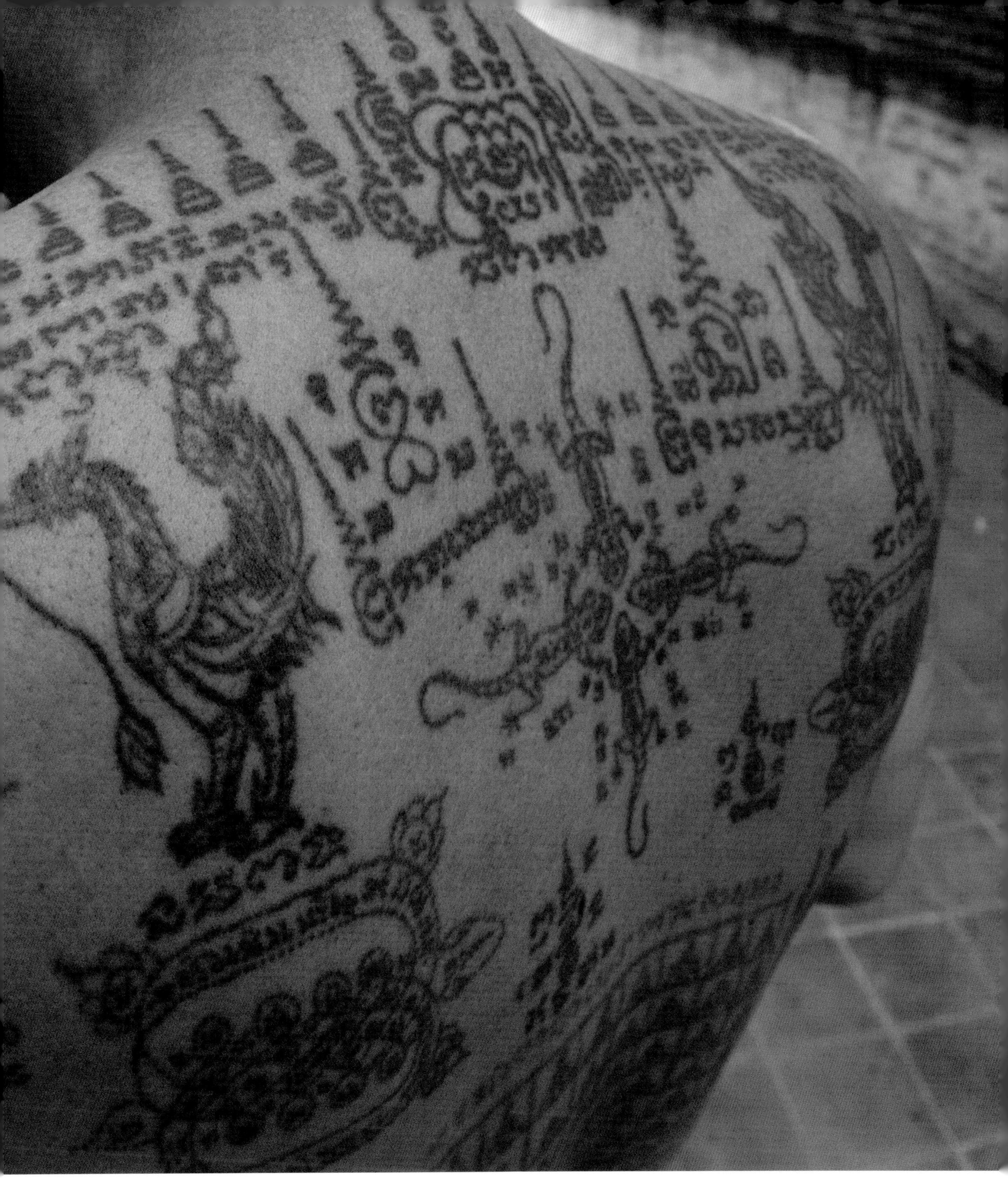

THE DOORMAN

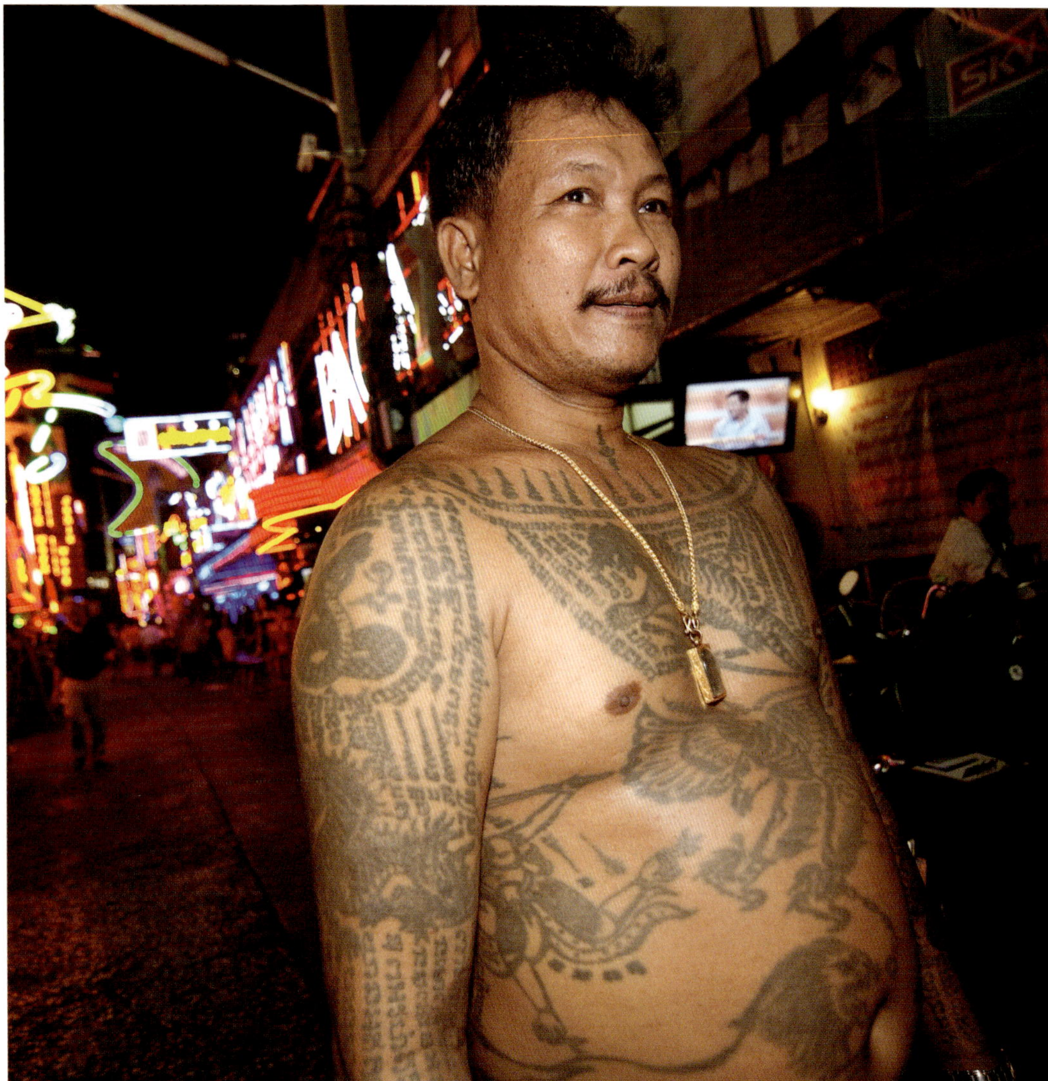

Haw works as a "security manager" for three bars along Soi Cowboy in Bangkok. He originally hails from Buriram, where he worked as a carpenter until 10 years ago, when a relative working in one of the Soi Cowboy go-go bars told him about an opening for a bouncer. Most of his *sak yan* were inked by Ajahn Thong across the river in Talat Phlu, Thonburi. His torso bears several large *yantra* intended to bolster power, including a flying tiger on his chest and an eagle on his left lower abdomen.

THE LECTURER

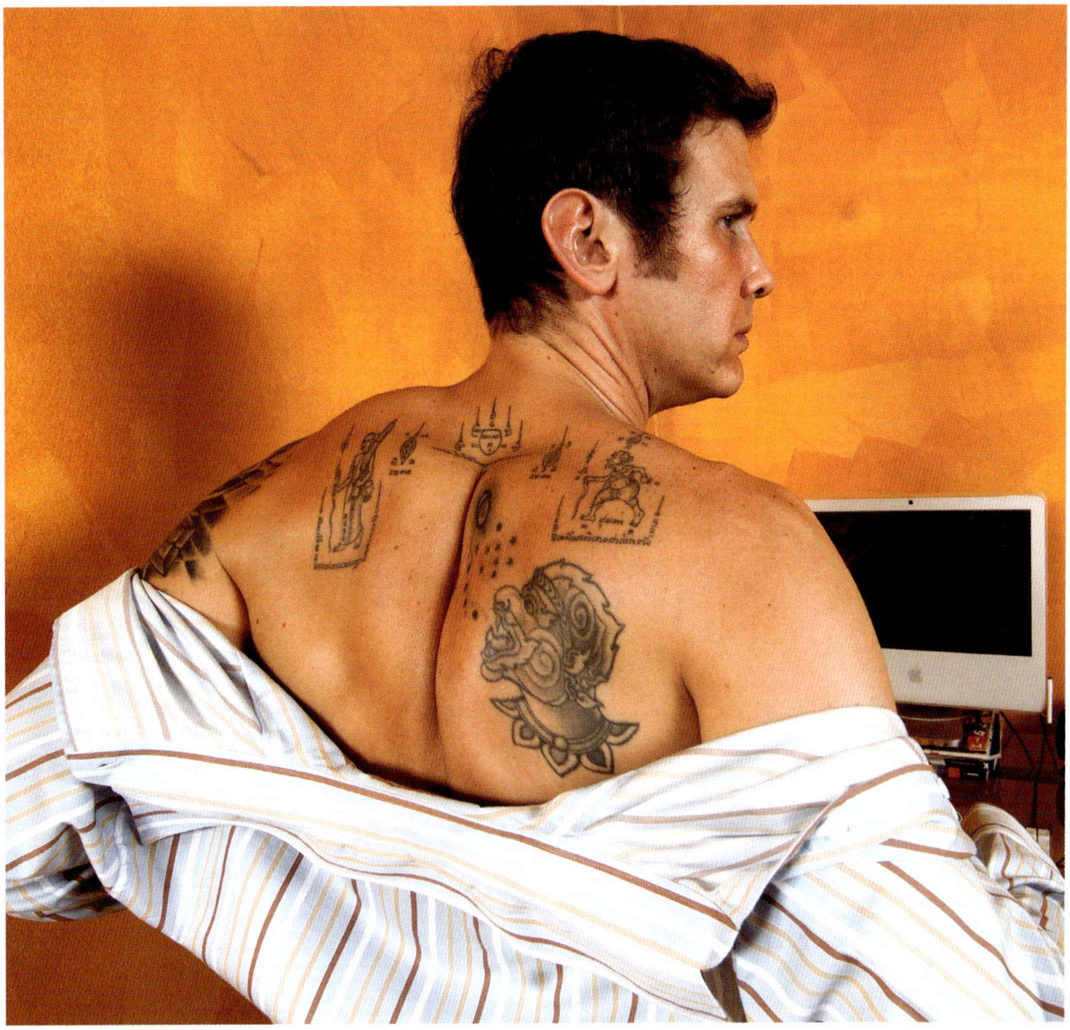

Erich Fleshman worked in Thailand for many years as an actor, film dialogue coach and lecturer in film history at Chulongkorn University. On the advice of a friend, he visited Ajahn Gop in Ayuthaya to ask for *sak yan* that would help boost income and career development. Ajahn Gop placed the figure of Pho Kae (see Lineage of the Hermit Sage earlier in the book), meant to evoke cleverness and power, on his left shoulder blade.

Balancing it on the right is a potbellied Chuchok. A figure from the Vessantara Jataka, the Buddha's penultimate life story, Chuchok (Jujaka in Pali) was a wily Brahmin who had the ability to attract wealth and possessions simply by asking.

THE MUSICIAN

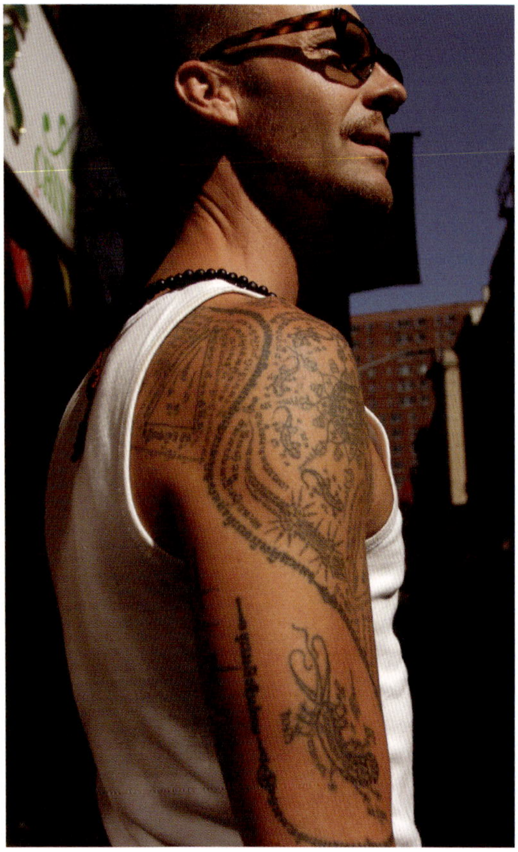

Photo by Paula Neudorf

Ming Roth, a professional drummer who has recorded and toured with many notable musical artists in Europe, America and Asia, has been collecting *sak yan* from various masters in Thailand for the last decade. The *kao yaut* on top of his back came from Wat Bang Phra, while the lotus blessing tattoos and some of the many house lizards on his arms and torso were inked by Ajahn Gop. The *paet thit* (eight directions) in the centre of his back came from a commercial tattoo artist in Pai, Thailand. The large twin tiger design on his lower back was applied at Ajahn Noo's *samnak*.

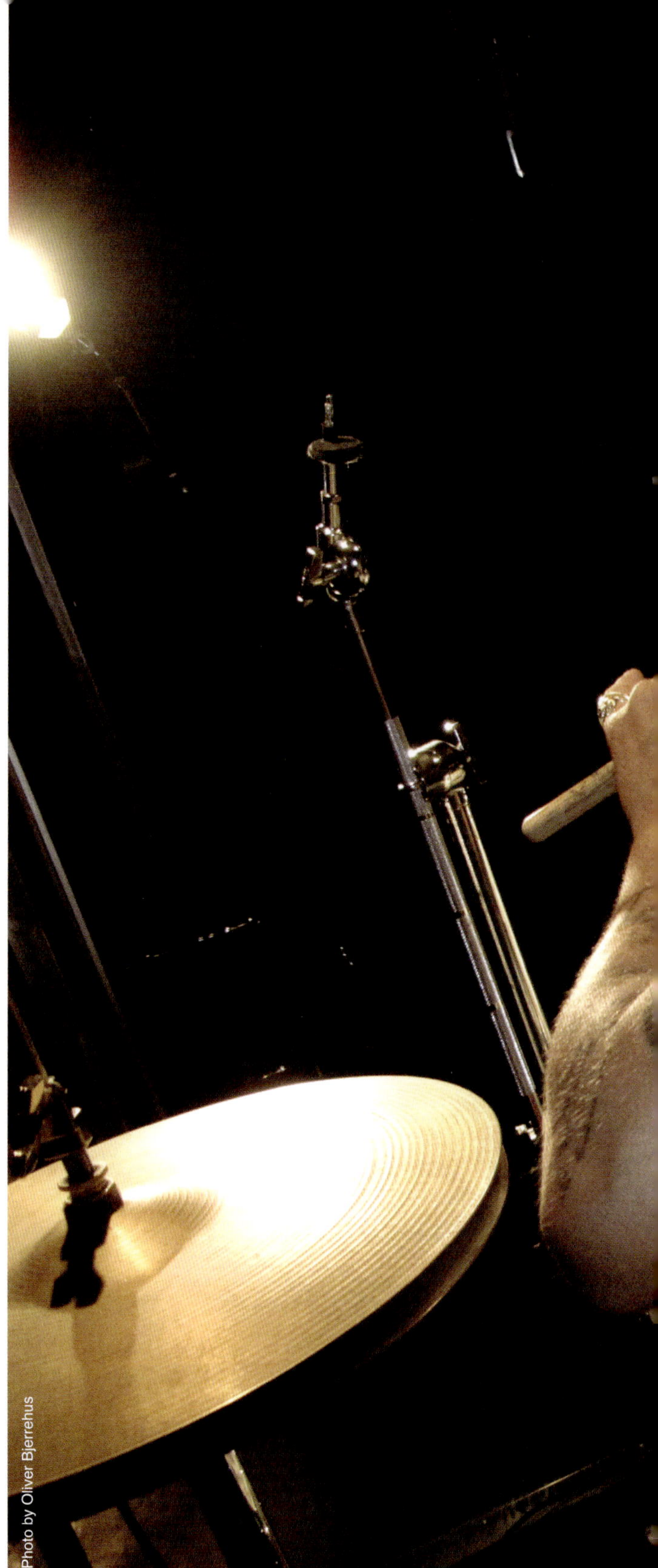

Photo by Oliver Bjerrehus

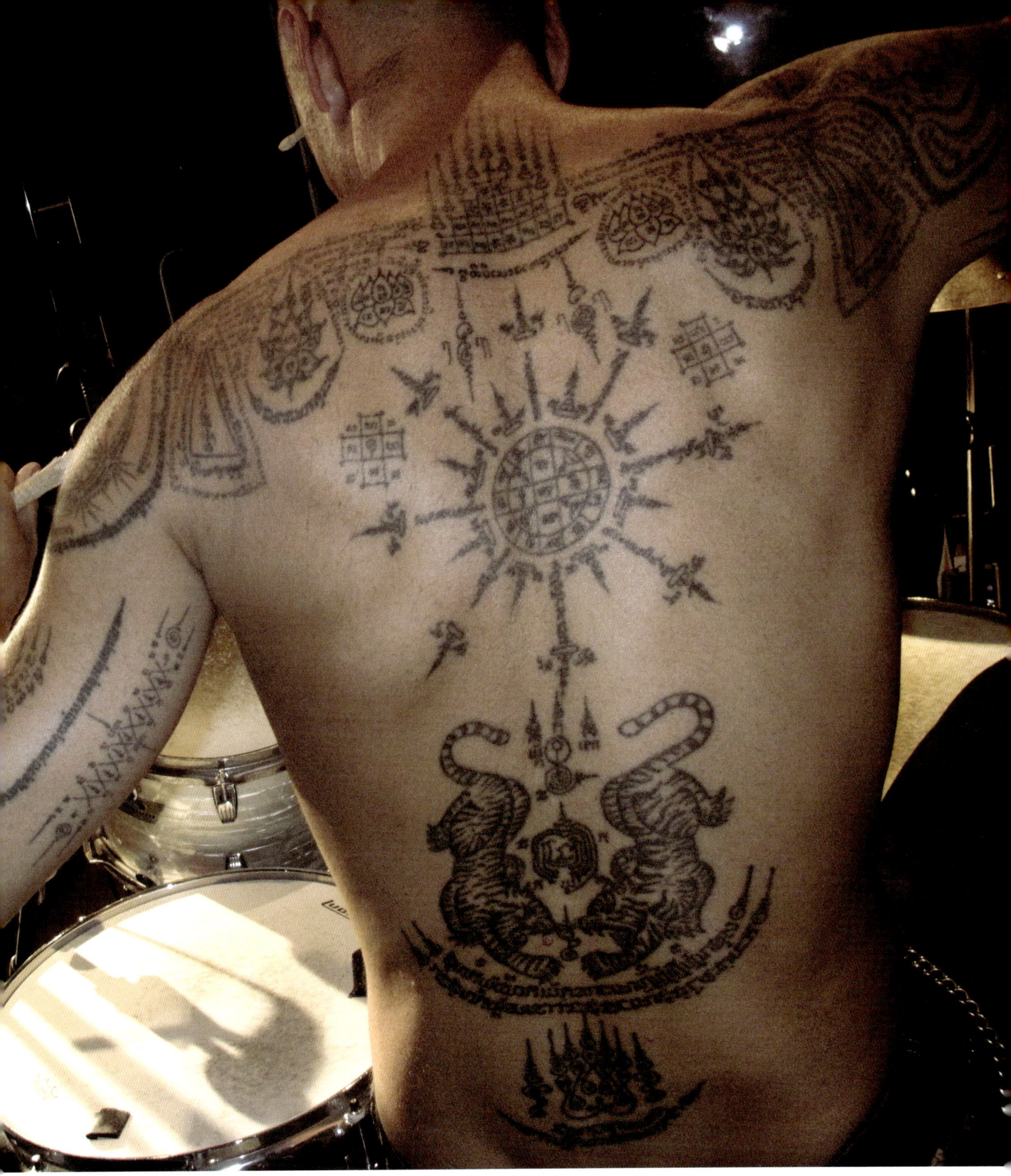

THE DIVING INSTRUCTOR

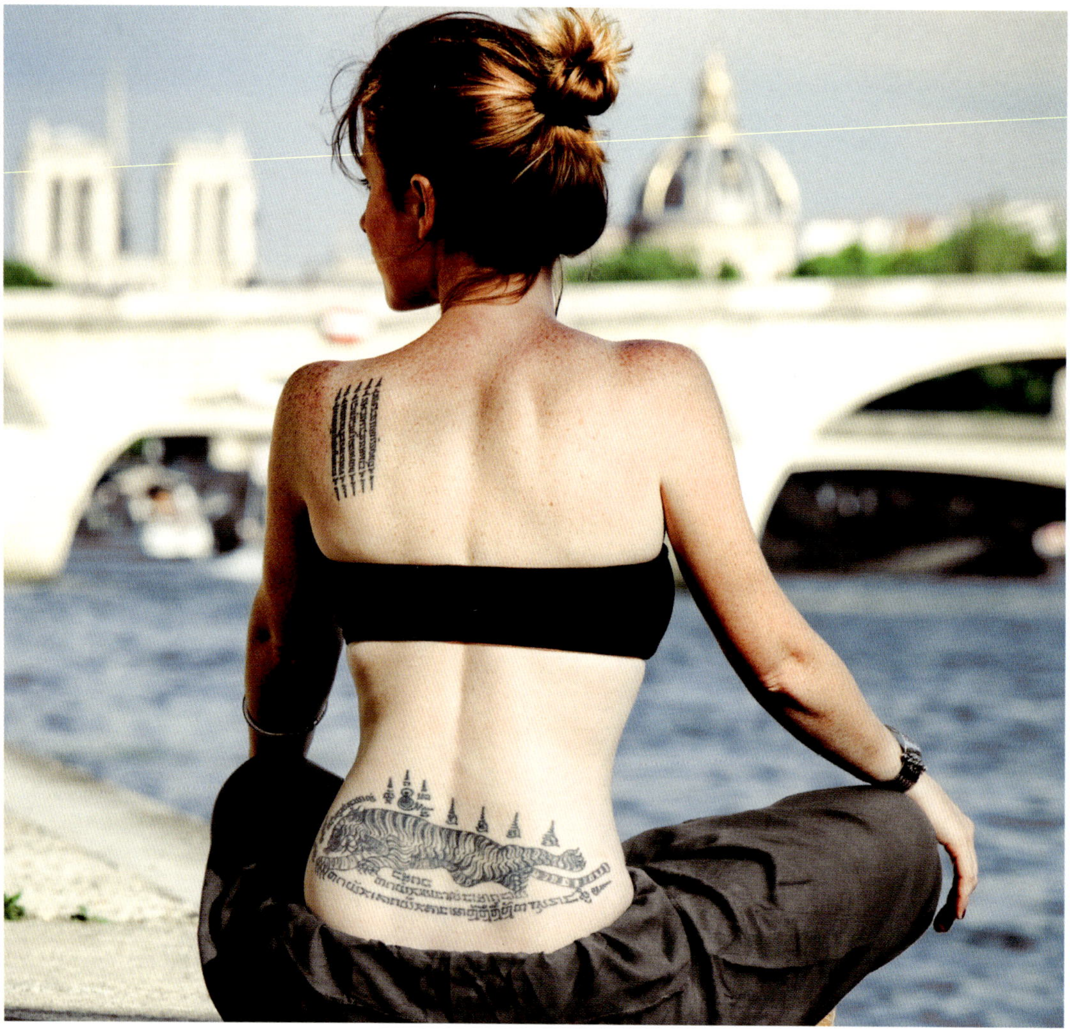

Photo by Sacha Rovinski

Anne Chebanier was inspired to investigate the world of *sak yan* after seeing photos of Angelina Jolie's tiger tattoo in the press, and in 2004 she emailed Joe Cummings to ask if he could help her locate Jolie's master, Ajahn Noo Ganpai. The two travelled to Ajahn Noo's *samnak* in July 2005, and after consulting with the master, Anne decided on a *haa thaew*, placed on her left shoulder blade as is customary.

She later returned on her own for the much larger and more painful leaping tiger inked across her lower back. Around the same time she began taking scuba diving lessons in southern Thailand, a pastime that turned into a passion and eventually her profession.

THE MODEL/ACTRESS

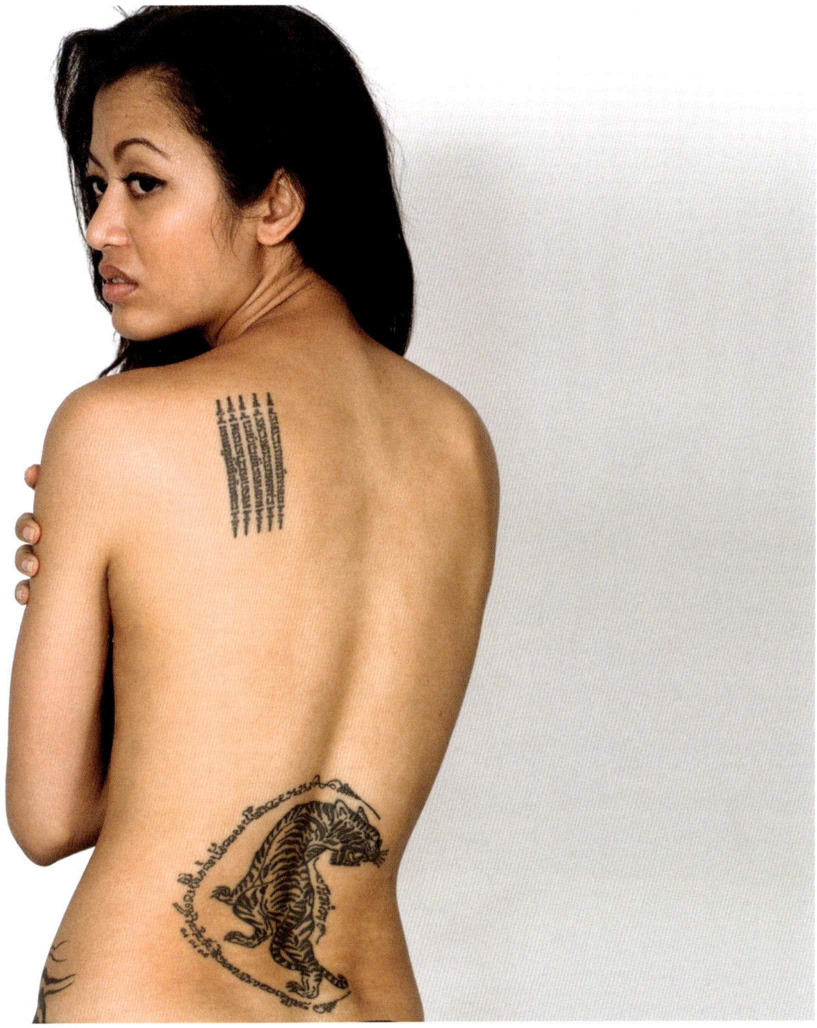

Jan Yousagoon grew up in Pathum Thani, a province just north of Bangkok which also happens to be home to several *sak yan* masters, including Ajahn Noo. Jan works as a model and actress, and originally went to acquire a *haa thaew* from Ajahn Noo in order to better her luck, gain personal charisma and boost her potential for getting ahead in a difficult business. She later returned for a large *seua liaw lang* – "tiger looking back" – on her lower back. This *yantra* evokes great power while at the same time protecting one from rivals or enemies who may be plotting against one. The tiger took six hours to ink, divided into two sessions.

THE DETECTIVE

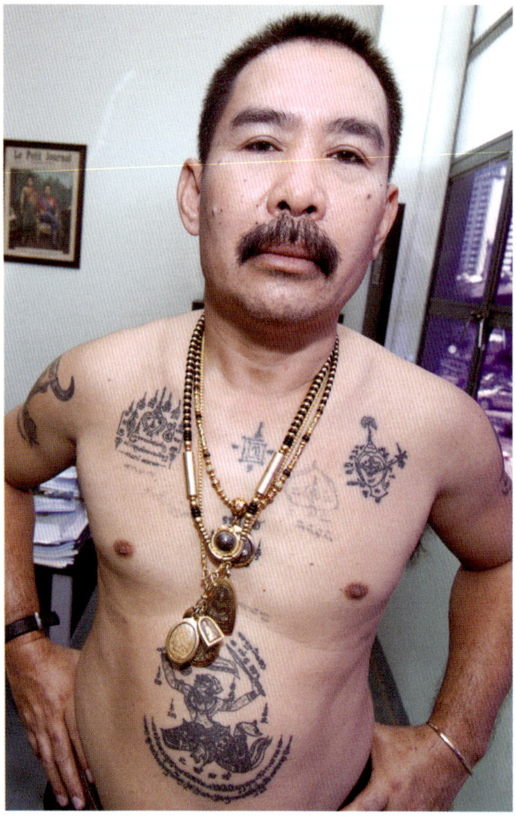

Police Colonel Veerapan Tanjai, a detective for the Central Investigation Bureau, believes that *sak yan* received from a master in Nakhon Si Thammarat have helped him evade injury during gunfights with criminals. He also credits their power for helping him solve crimes. When first arriving on a crime scene he will pray to his *ajahn sak yan*, as well as to the monks who have blessed the several amulets he wears, to help him solve the case. When murder is involved, Col Veerapan places a photo of the victim in his uniform pocket, and asks the departed spirit to help him find the killer. There it stays until the crime is solved.

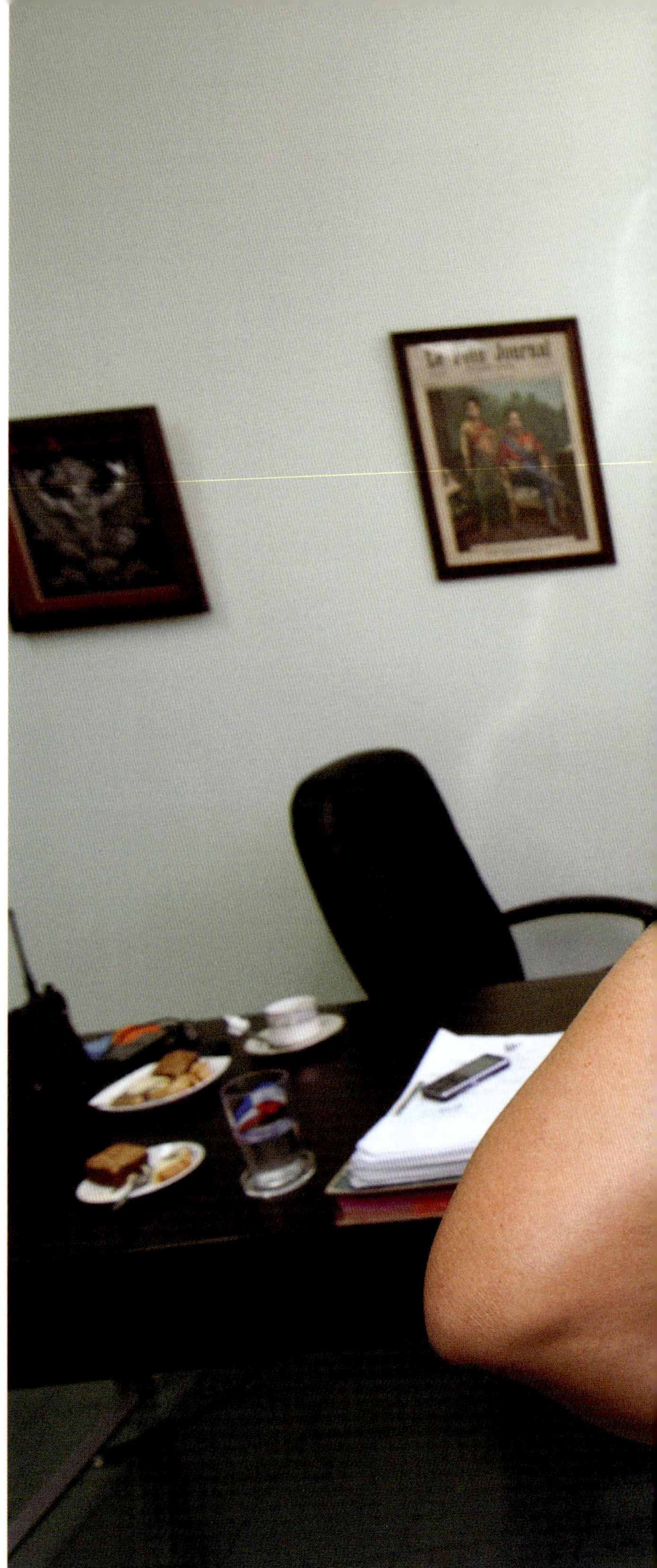

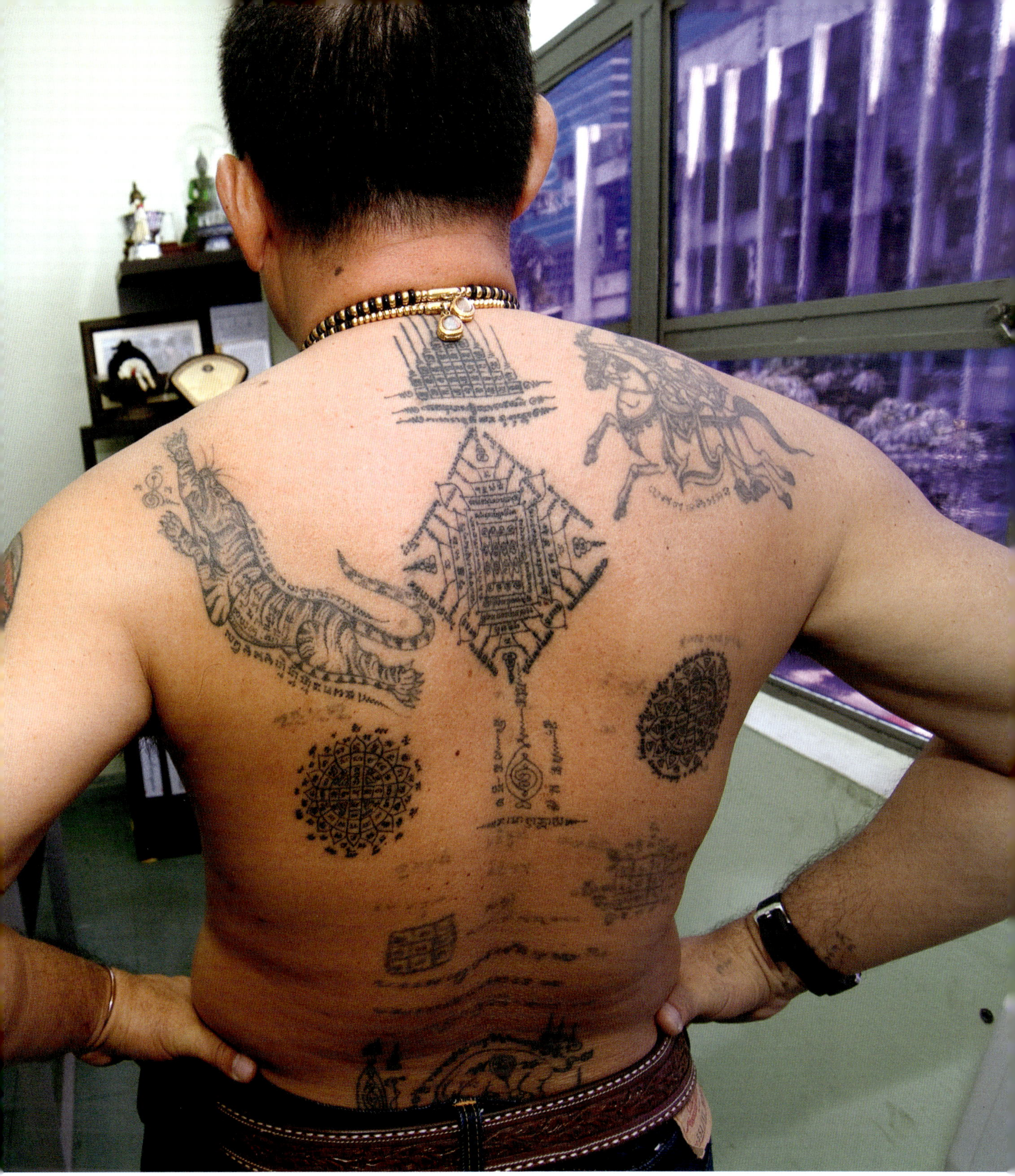

THE FILMMAKER & THE DJ

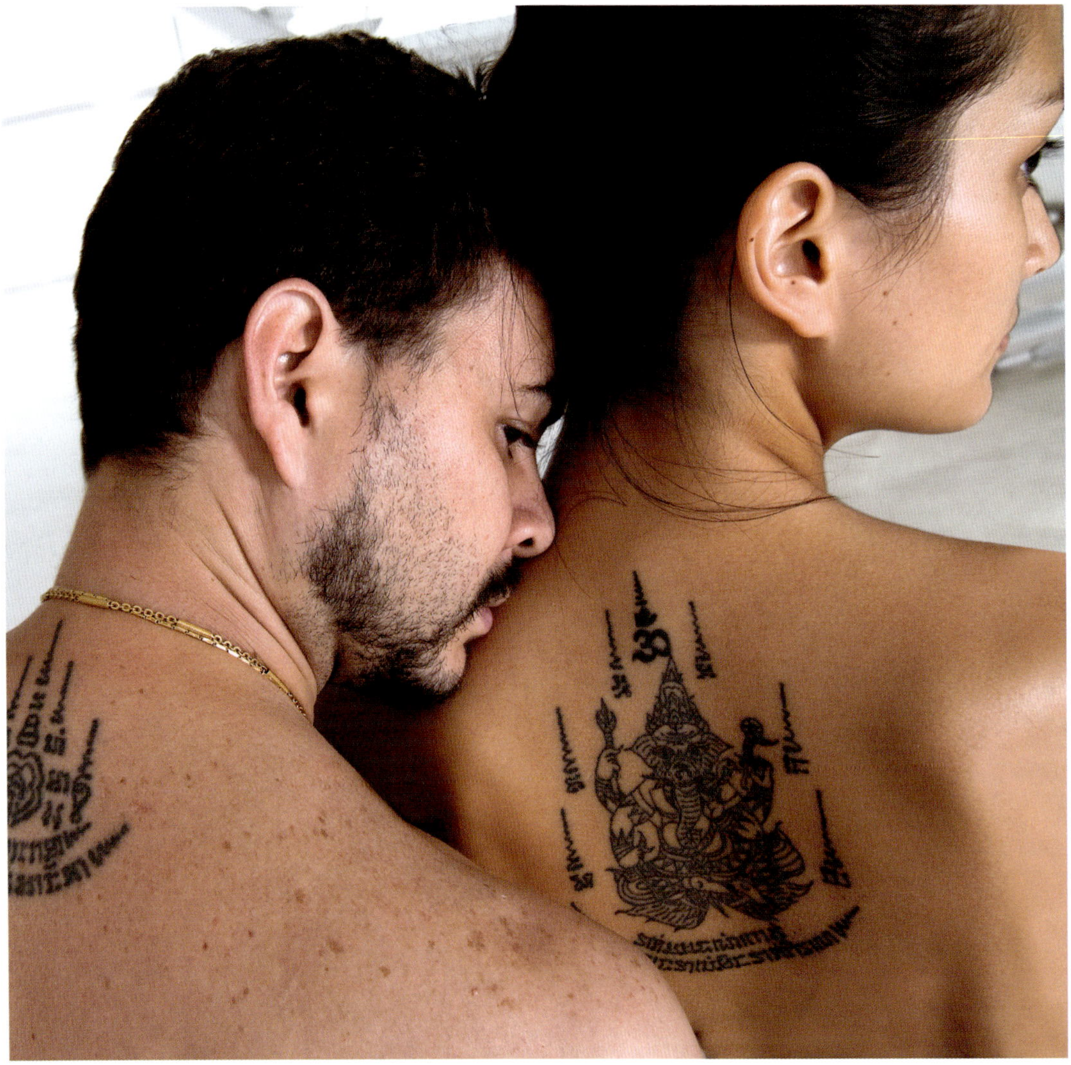

Desho Bernard paid his first visit to a *samnak sak yan* as a videographer for *Guru* magazine's website. He never intended to receive a sacred tattoo, but during the course of taping a short film about Ajahn Noo, he ended up doffing his shirt and getting inked between his shoulder blades by one of Ajahn Noo's disciples. The *yantra* brings luck and prosperity. Later he returned to Ajahn Noo's *samnak* with DJ Mia Lackgren, who received a Ganesh *yantra* in the same spot on her back. Ganesh, an elephant-headed Hindu god and son of Shiva, is believed to be a remover of obstacles in one's path.

THE FISHERMAN

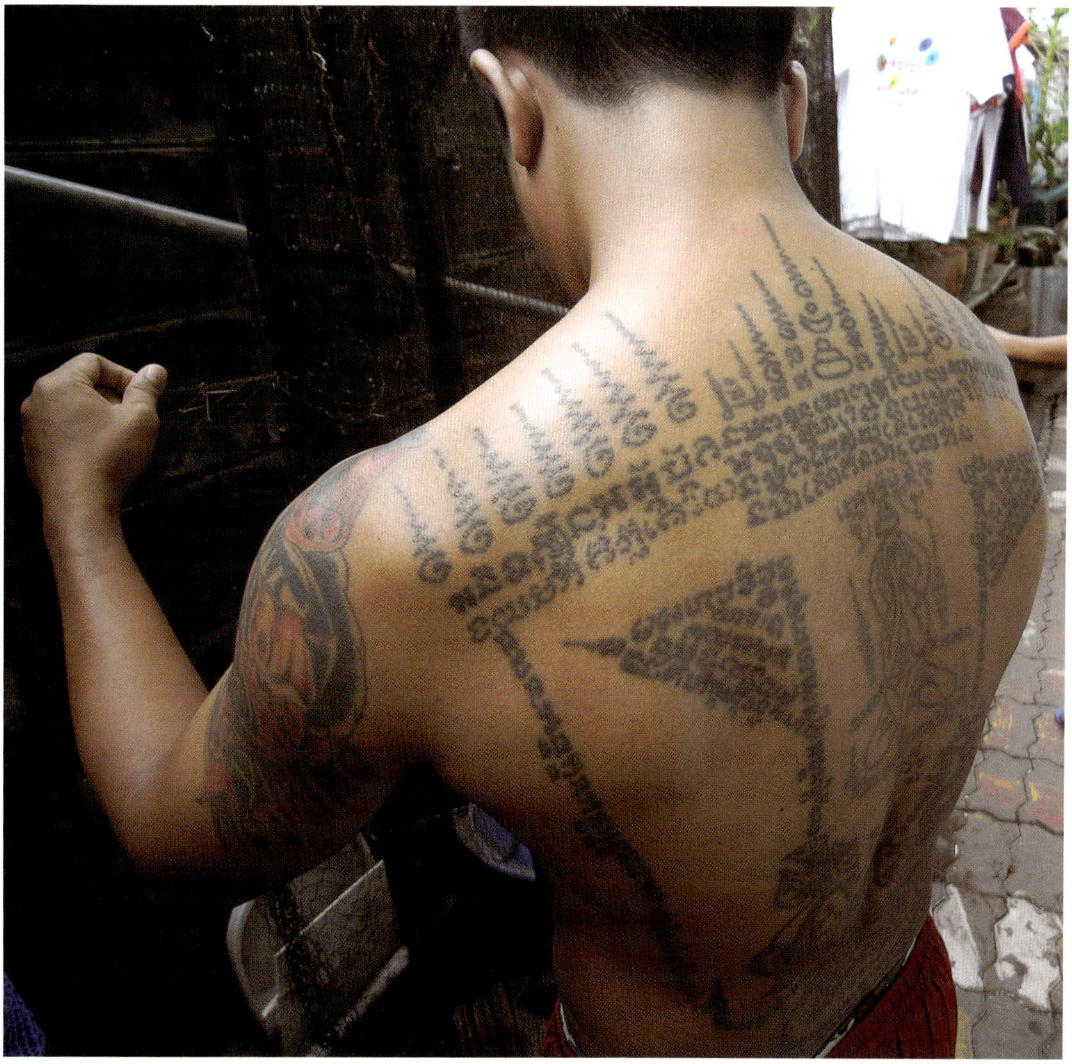

Nung, a 26-year-old resident of Klong Toey, one of Bangkok's biggest slums, sought out *sak yan* as soon as he turned 20, the age of majority. All of his sacred designs were inked by Ajahn Dech, a disciple of Luang Pu Lui from Wat Ratchayotha in Bangkok. Among the larger *yantras* on his torso are a Pho Kae and a Hanuman. Large victory flag *yantras* are tattooed on each side of his spine just below the shoulder blades. Running along the width of his shoulders is a row of *unalom*, one of the most common geometric designs in the tradition, representing unity, strength and concentration.

THE MUSICIAN/AUTHOR

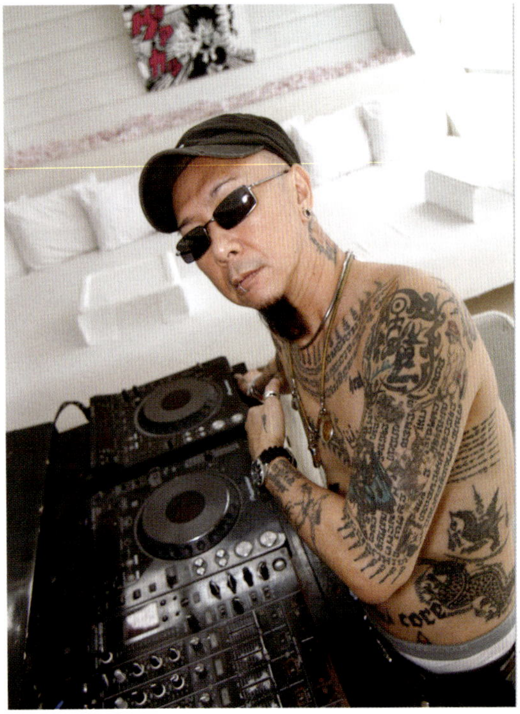

Singaporean media star, writer, filmmaker, DJ, musician and self-confessed "professional griper" Chris Ho – commonly known by his public persona, X'Ho – got acquainted with Thai culture while exploring Golden Mile Complex (formerly known as Woh Hup Complex), home to Thai food, fashion, CDs and even live Thai bands. Founder of Singapore's first punk/new wave group, Zircon Lounge, Ho has received a number of tattoos from Thai masters who visit Singapore. They are mixed in with fashion tattoos, but since starting down the *sak yan* road, he has released several solo albums and written three books, including, *Skew Me You Rebel Meh?*, a collection of essays and social critiques expressing his outrage at hypocrisy and double standards.

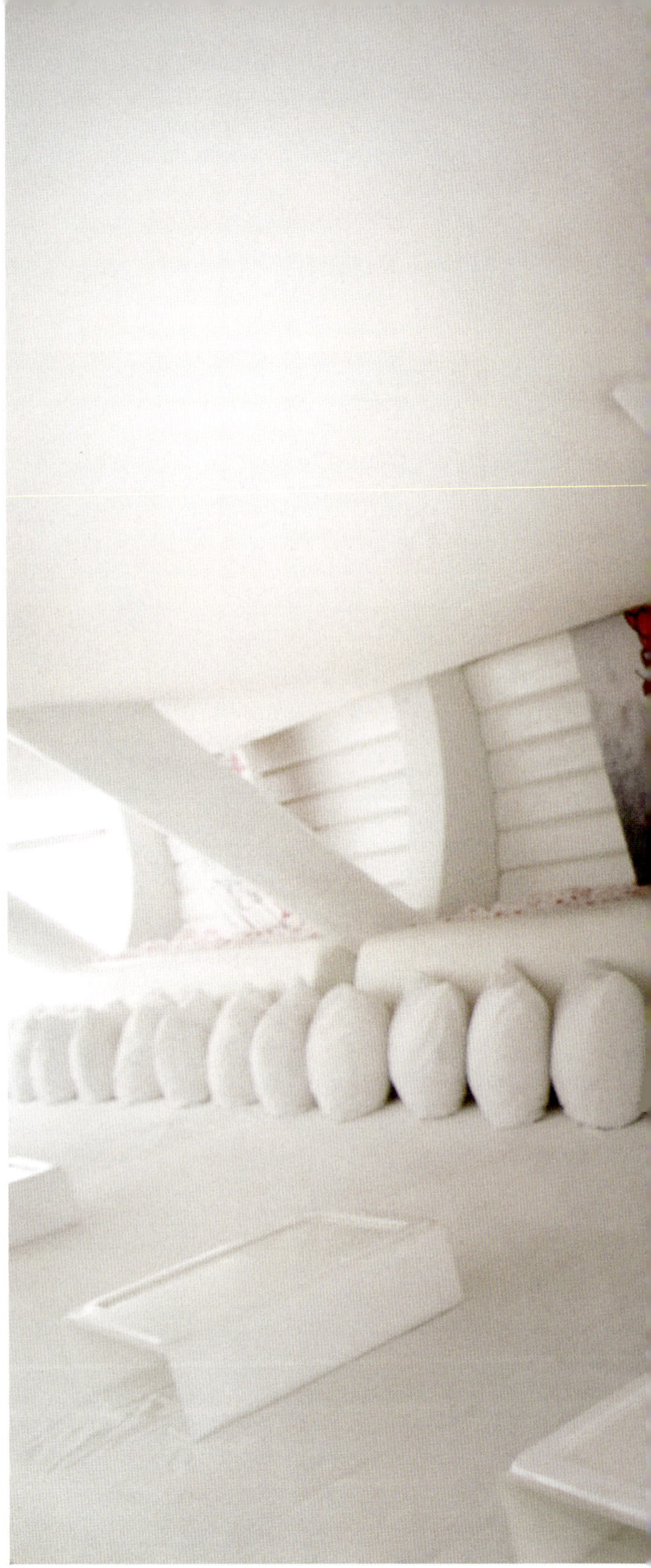

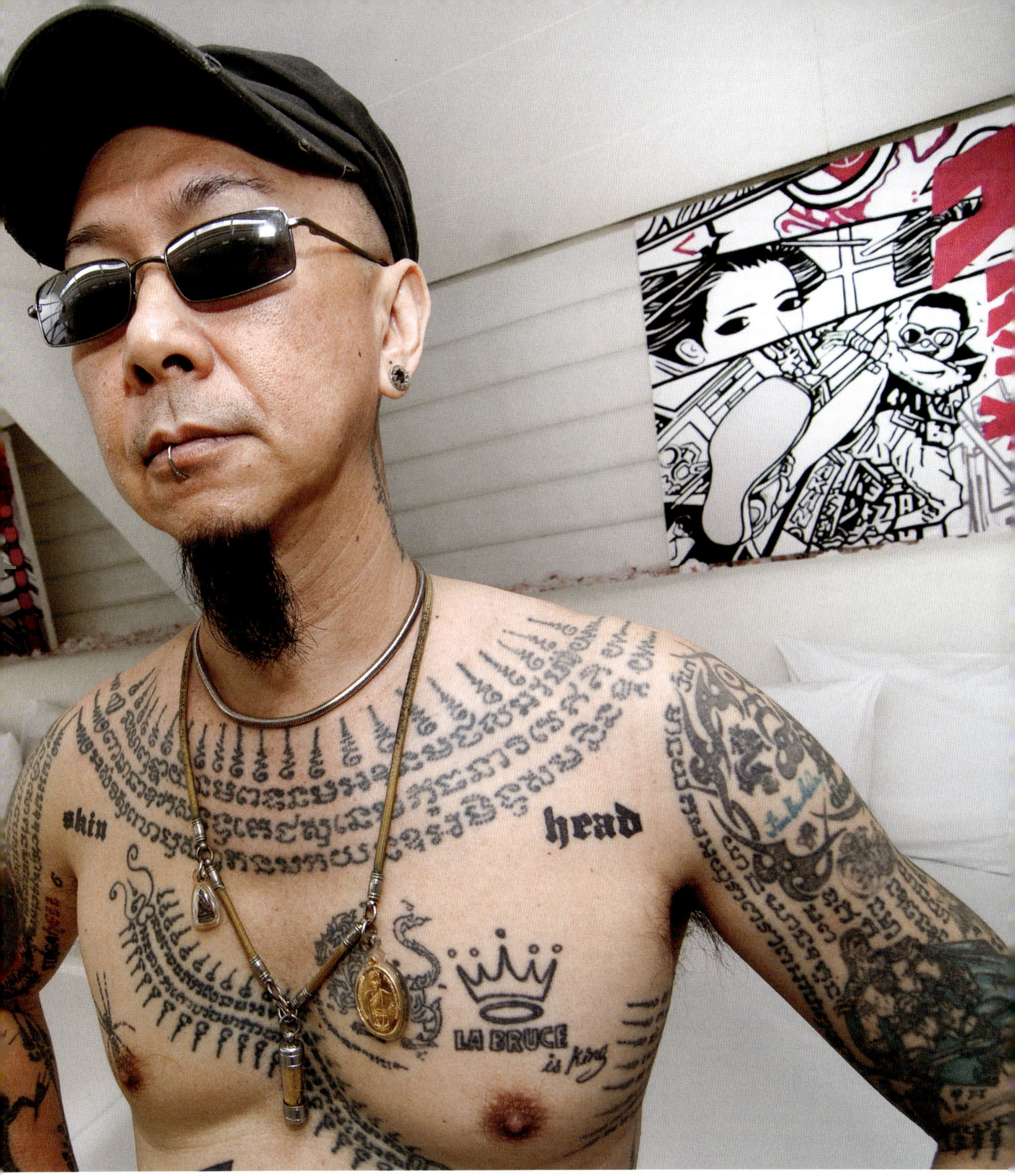
skin
head
LA BRUCE
is king

YANTRAS

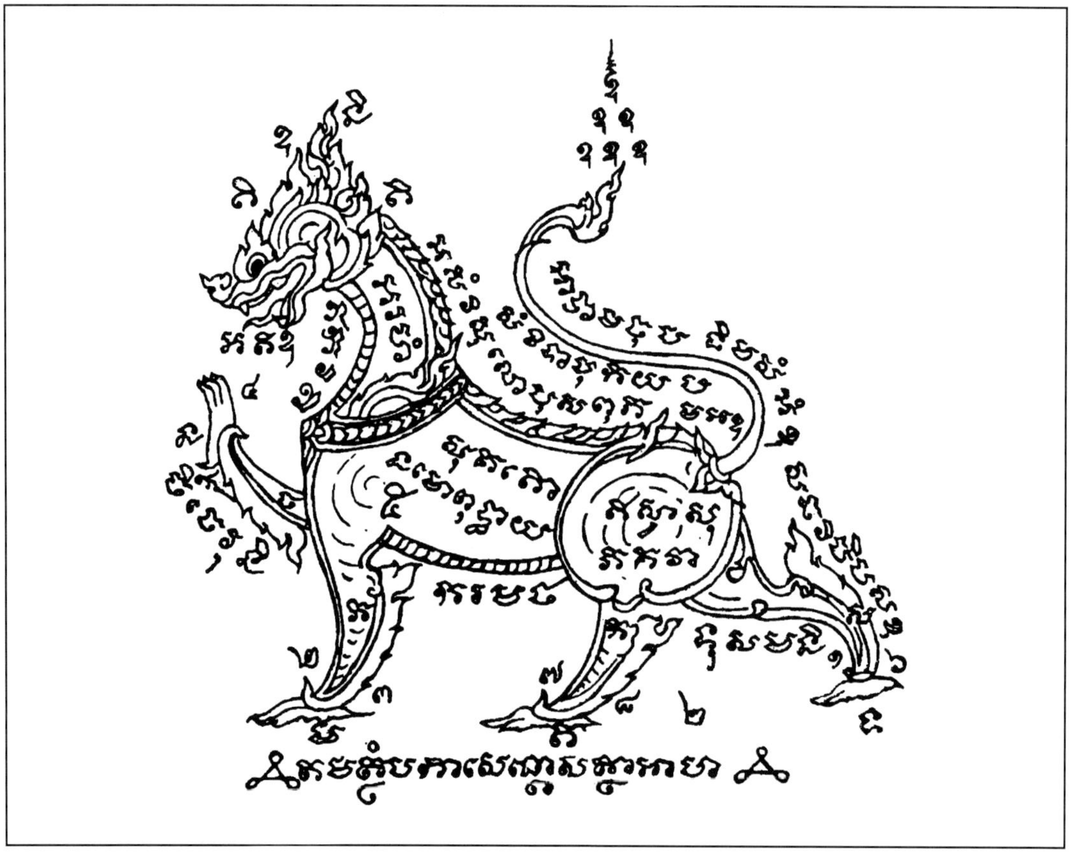

Above: Royal Lion; power and rank. Aside from *sak yan*, may also be applied to a cloth used to wipe one's face.

In the *sak yan* tradition, most *yantras* consist of two basic components, to be applied in consecutive order. The first component to be tapped into the skin is the line drawing. Depending on the *yantra*, this could be a purely geometric matrix (lines, squares, triangles, circles, spirals or any combination of these); an animal figure (such as a tiger, or a mythological Himapan animal such as the *kilen*); a deity (from Hindu-Buddhist mythology); or a sacred plant (for example, the lotus). Some masters refer to the drawing-based component as the *kratuk* (bones) of the *yan*.

The second component of the *yan* to be inked is the associated *akkhara* or script. As explained earlier in the book, the script may be one of several alphabets available to the master depending on his lineage or preference. The *akkhara* adds flesh to the bones, as it were, completing the sacred whole. It represents an abbreviated form of the *khaathaa* (verses) which consecrate the *yantra*, maintaining the magic power which the master has placed into the disciple when all ceremonies are complete.

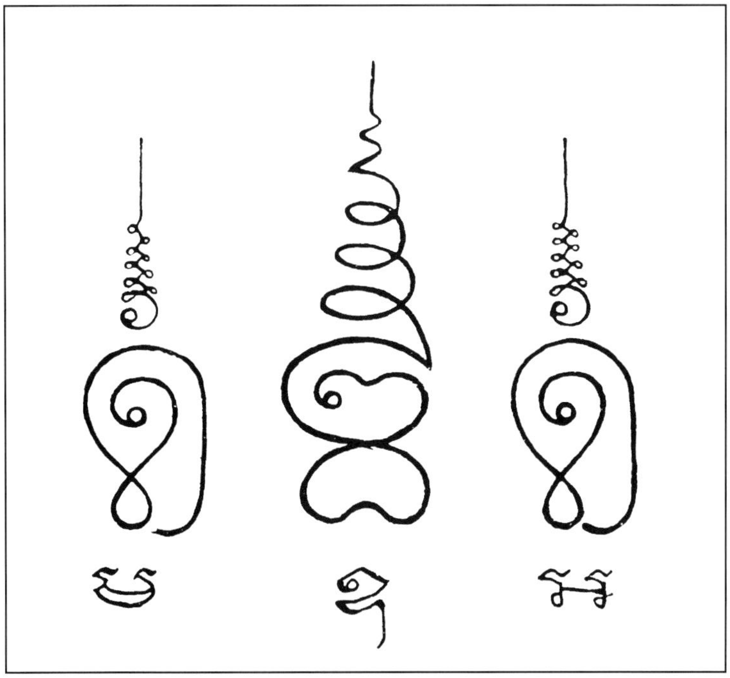

Left: Trinet; protection from enemies.

Below left: Narayan (Vishnu) on tiger back; invincibility and courage in combat. Cambodian *sak yan*.

Below right: Four Buddhas; protection from magic spells and bullets. Cambodian *sak yan*.

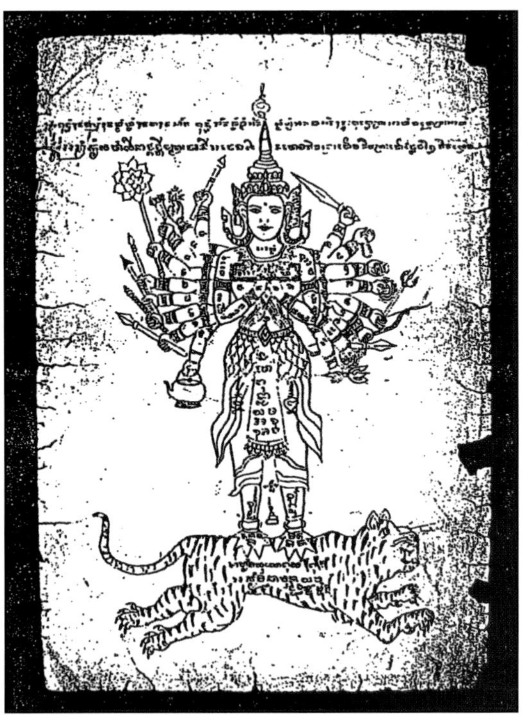

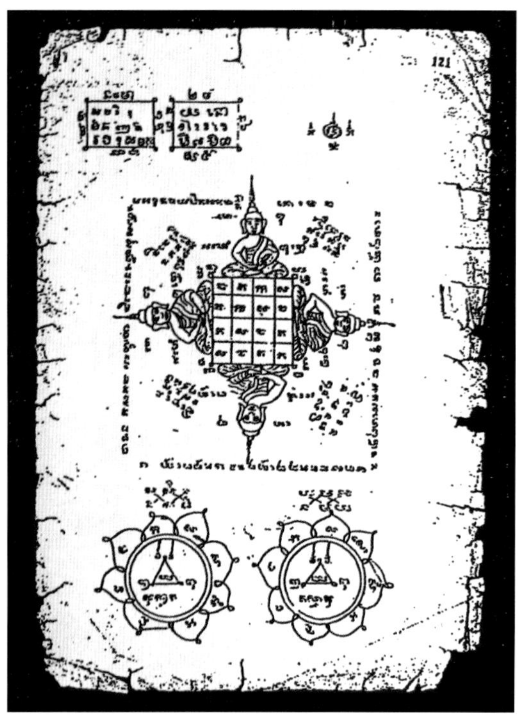

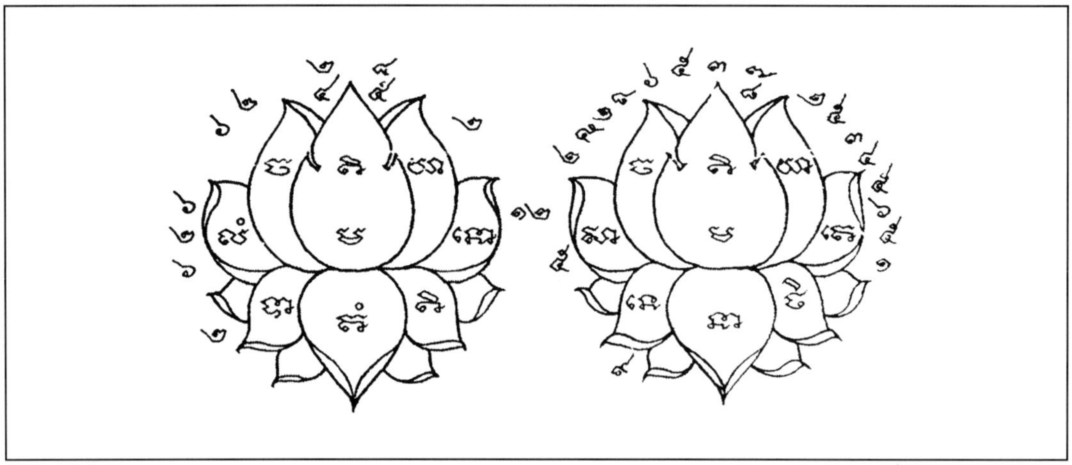

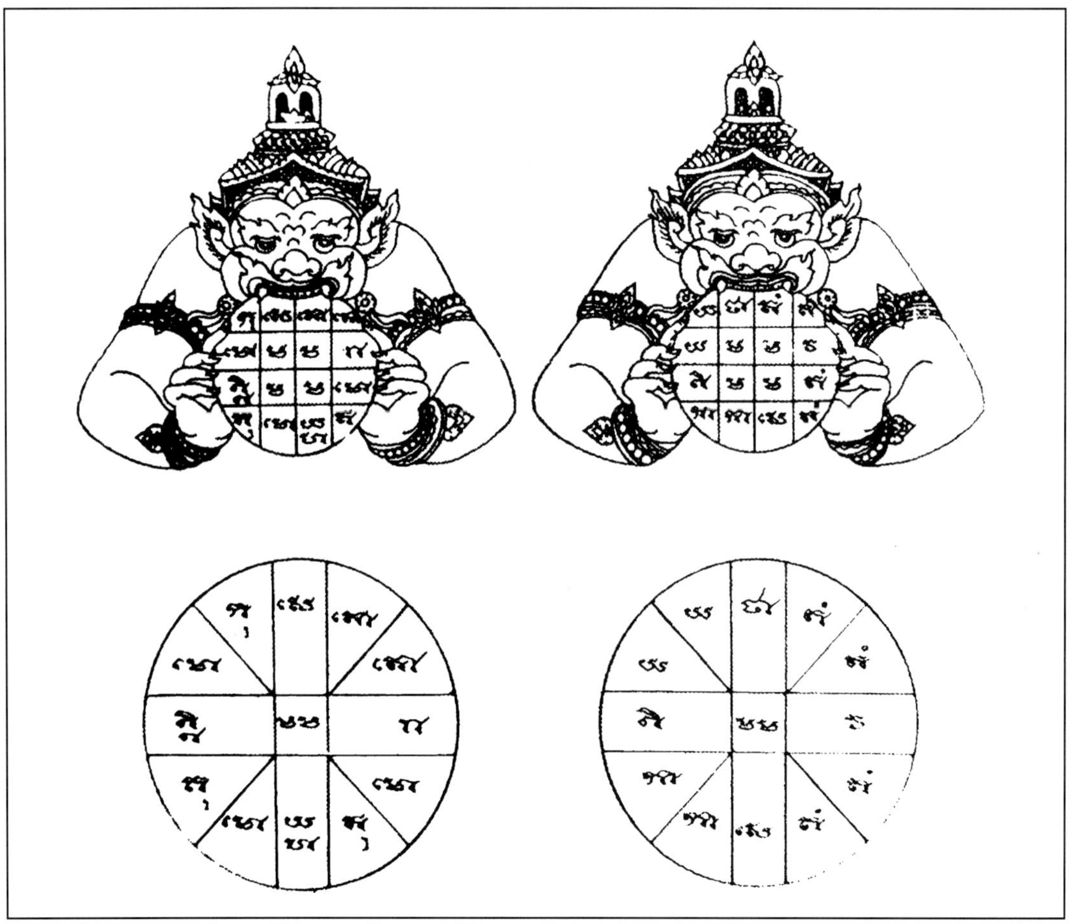

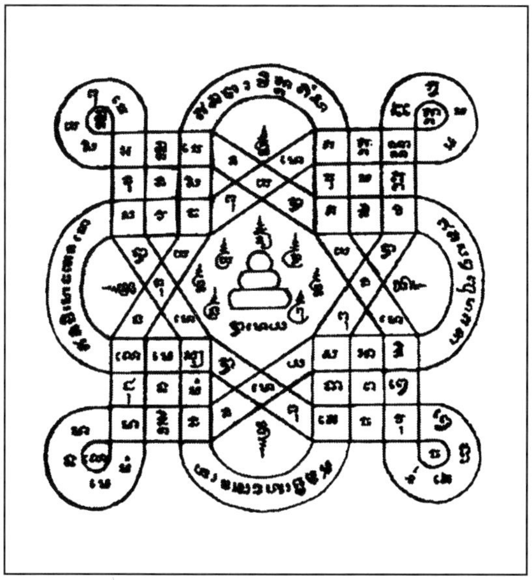

Far left top: Lotus Pair; multi-purpose *yantra* for mishap avoidance, protection from sharp objects and projectiles, and loving kindness.

Far left bottom: Brilliant Sun; wealth and prosperity. Considered one of the most powerful in this category. Should be tattooed as a pair, one on the chest and one on the back, with slightly different *akkhara*. The circular Brilliant Moon *yantras*, below, often accompany the sun pair for added efficacy. The figure 'swallowing' the sun is Rahu, a deity from Indian mythology.

This page, clockwise from top left: Maha Ut; will cause guns to misfire. Middle-of-the-Back *Yantra*; protection from weaponry of all kinds. Buddha Summons Renunciants and Bhikkhunis; protection from evil. Strictly speaking, this is a *na* rather than a *yantra*; may be ink-tattooed on the hand or applied to the forehead through goldleaf. Buddha Metta; general loving kindness.

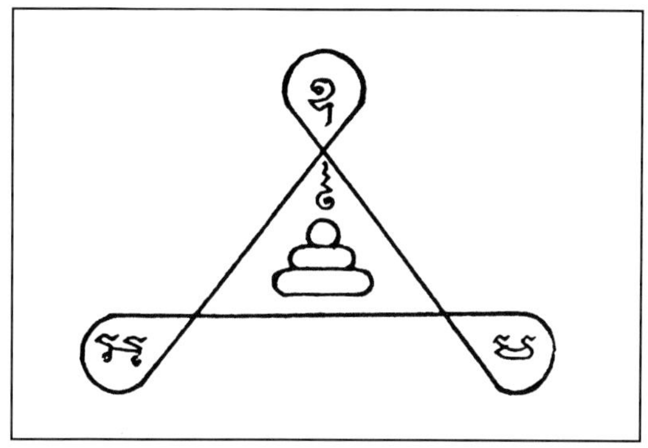

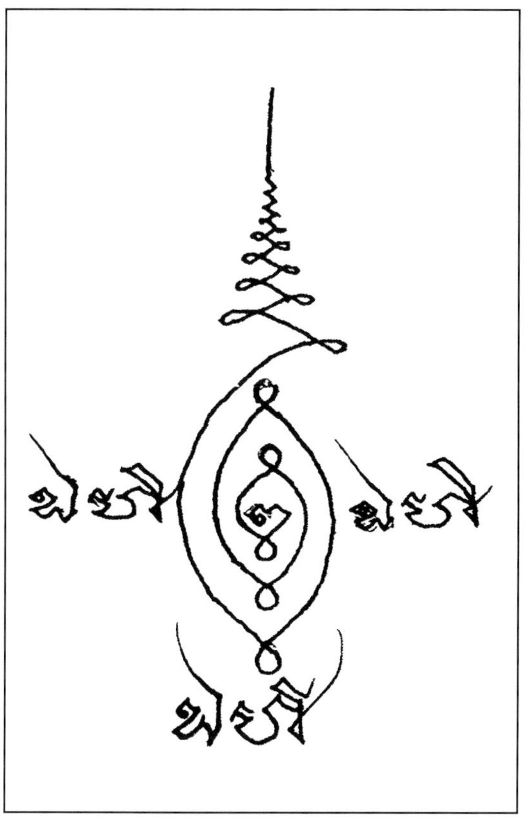

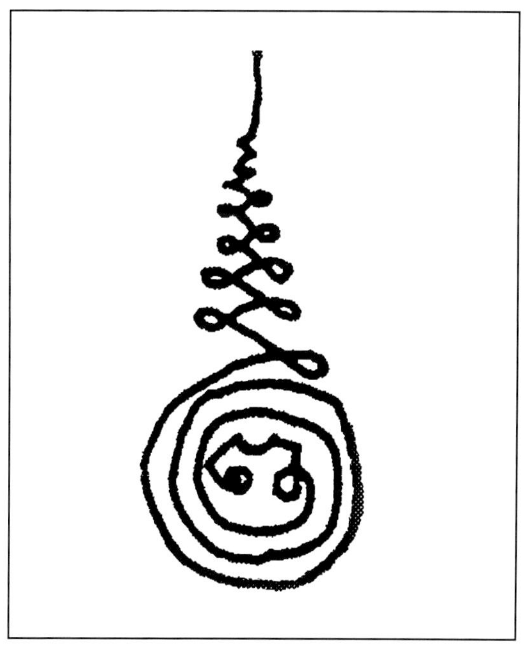

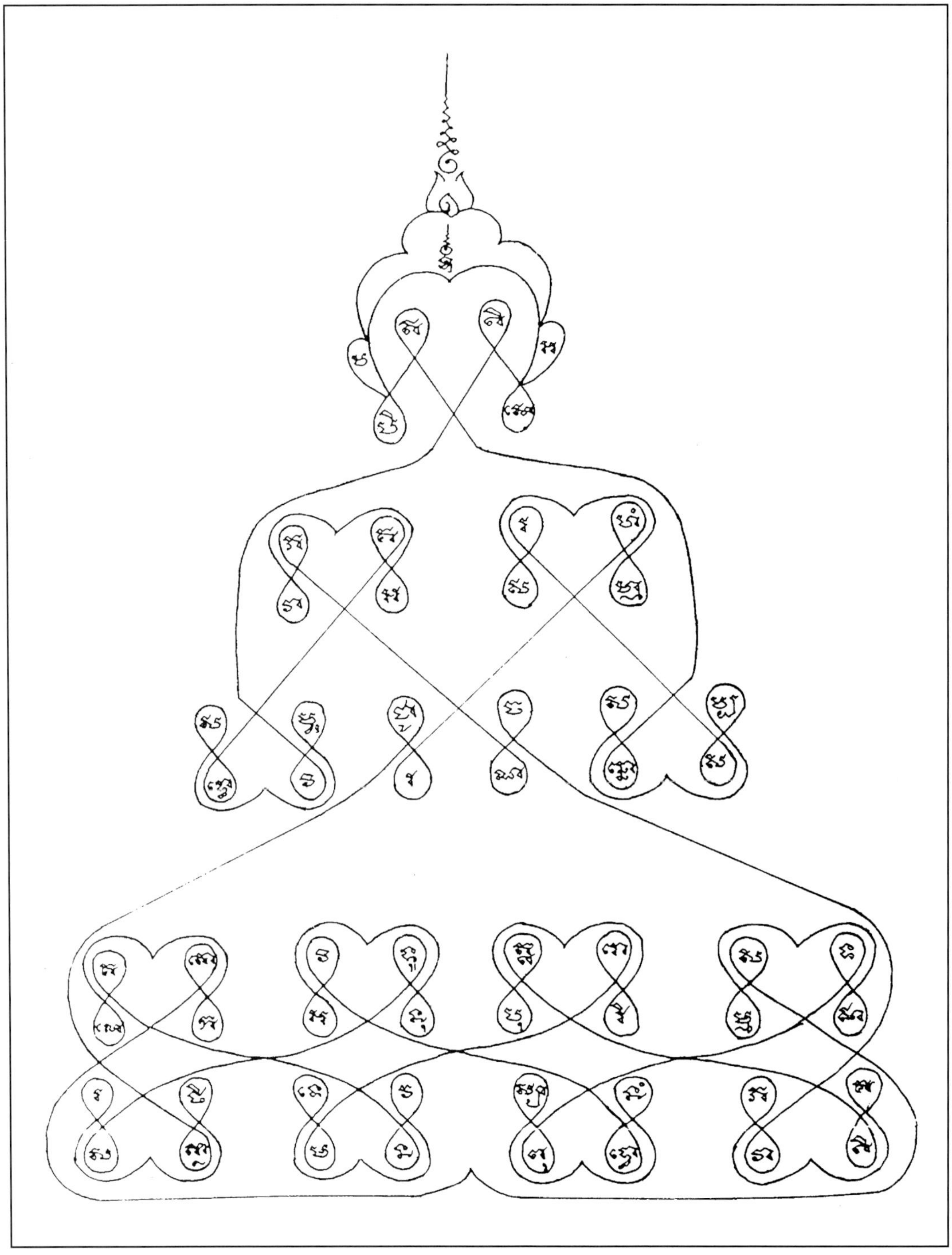

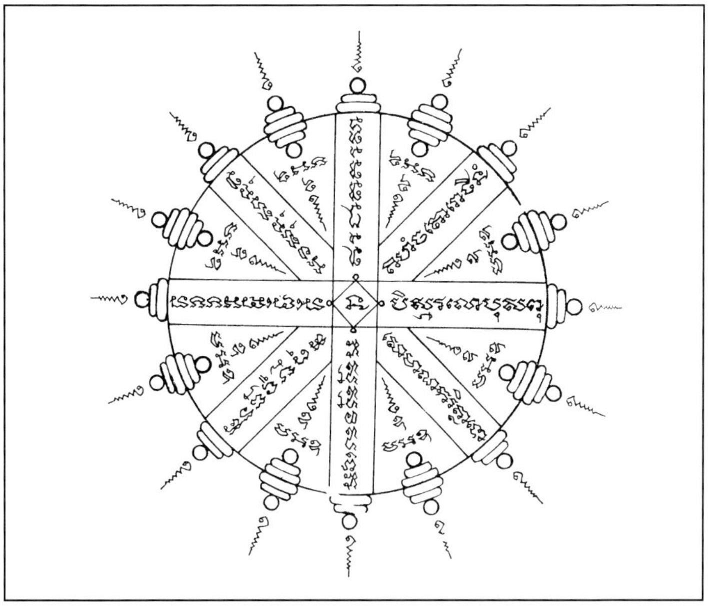

Far left: Buddha Signs; general protection from danger.

Left: Eight Directions; protection from danger in all directions while drawing loving kindness. There are many variations of this same *yantra* from master to master.

Bottom: Hanuman Holding Flag of Victory; general power, also will cause guns to misfire.

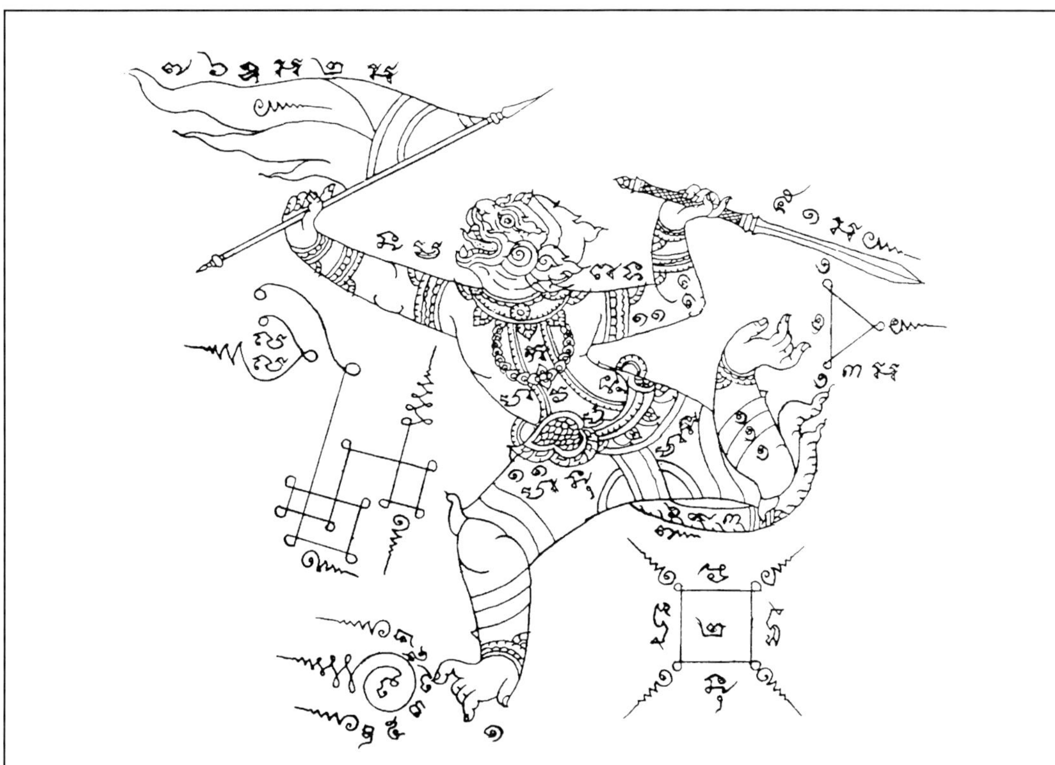

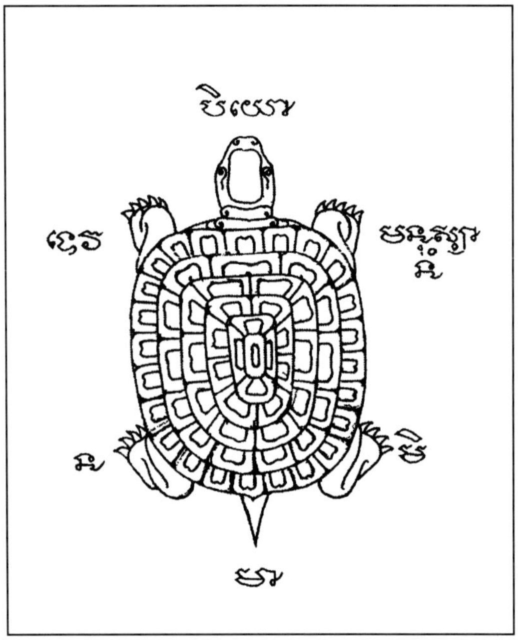

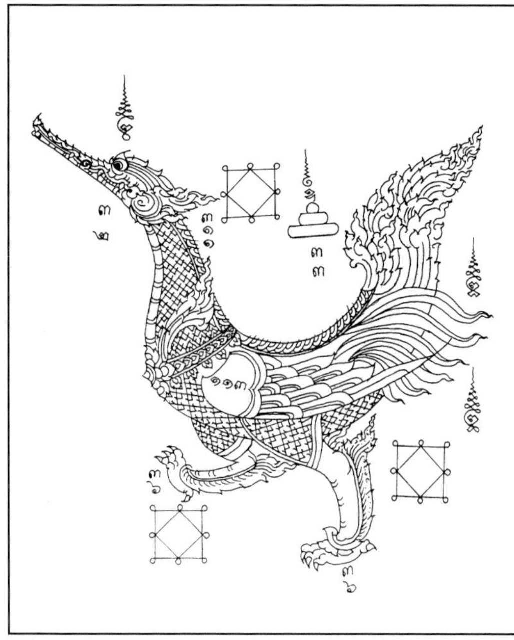

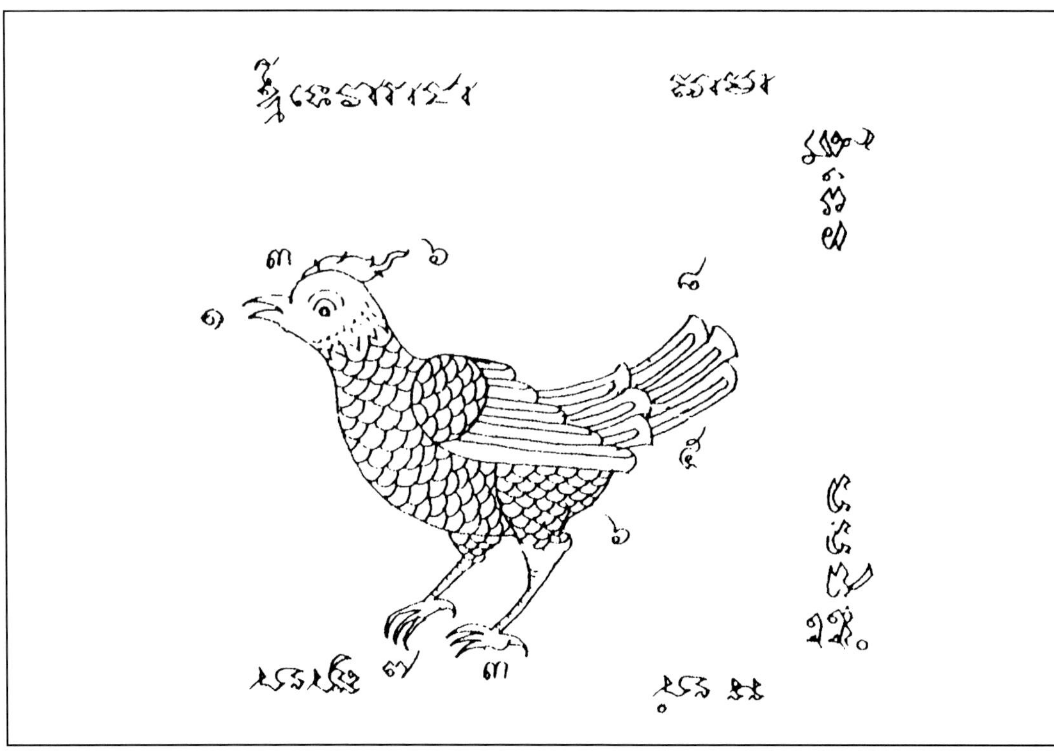

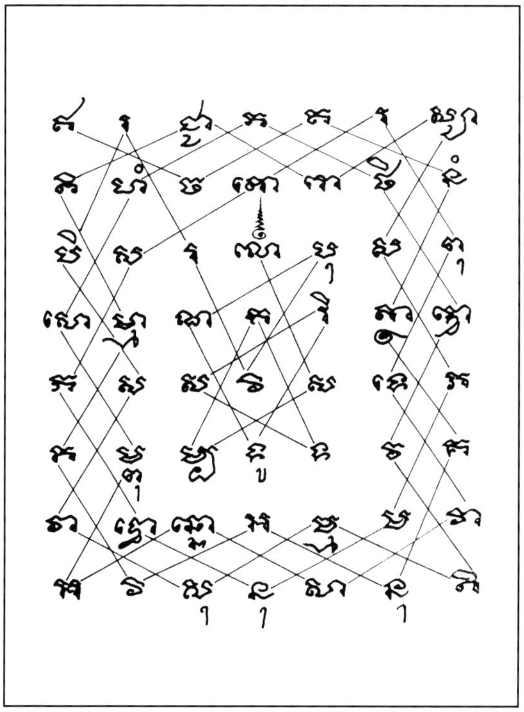

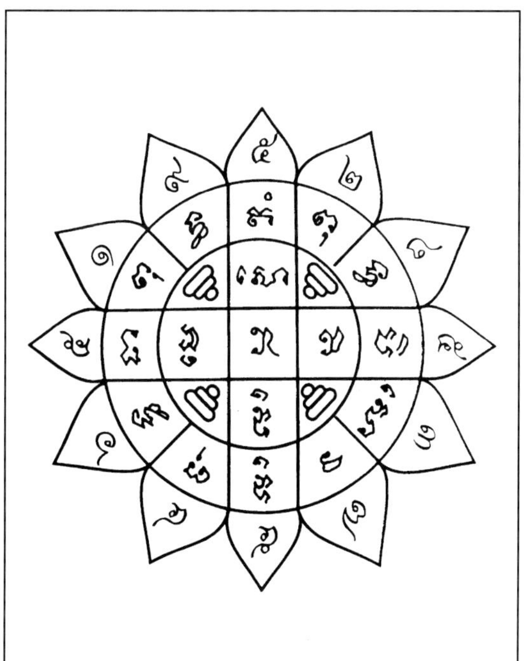

Far left, clockwise from the top: Golden Turtle *Yantra*; for general good luck and turning enemies into friends. Great Golden Swan; charisma and romance. One of the most popular designs in Thailand, the swan (or Brahminy duck, among Mon and Shan cultures) is often tattooed in pairs facing each other on one's upper back, one near the left shoulder blade and one near the right. Sarika; persuasiveness; loving kindness from the opposite sex.

This page, clockwise starting top left: Buddha's Diamond Armour; protection from danger in all directions. Great Blessing; for conserving and increasing material resources. Lord Elephant; attracts wealth while protecting against weaponry. Sukkhitima; mishap avoidance and loving kindness.

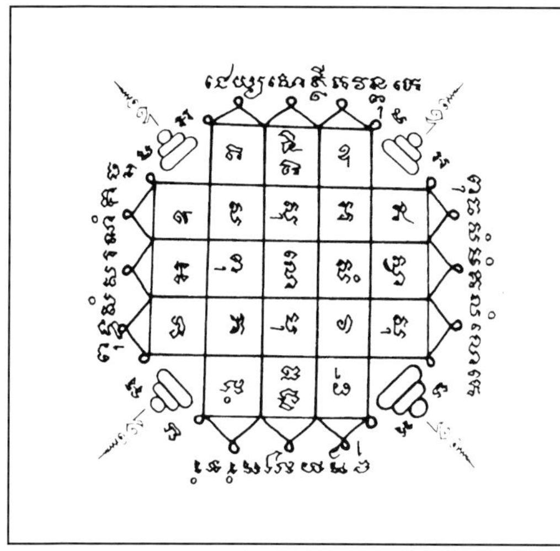

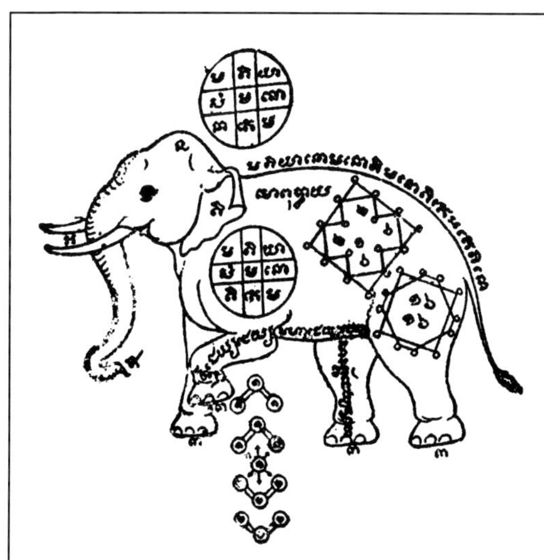

TOOLS OF THE TRADE

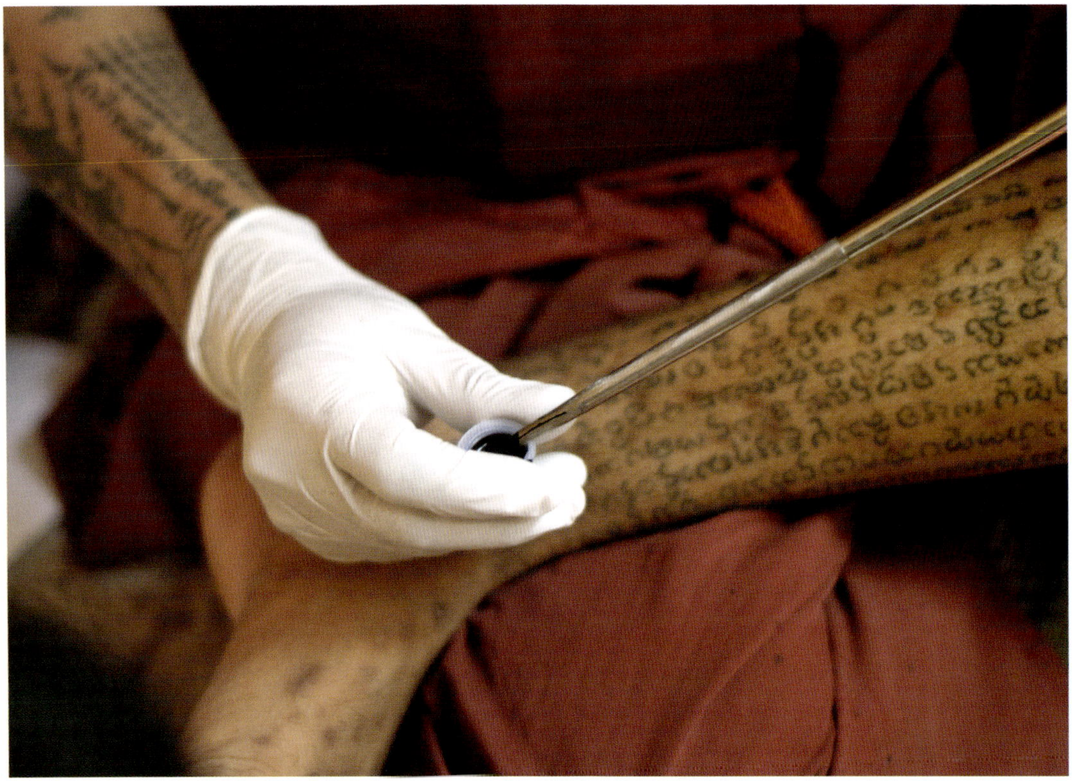

Above: Needle and ink.

KHEM SAK

A master needs only two basic tools to create *sak yan*, the tattoo needle *(khem sak)* and the *yantra* medium, whether ink *(meuk)* or oil *(nam-man)*.

The *khem sak's* shaft, called *mai sak* (tattoo stick) usually consists of a single metal rod measuring 50–75cm, with a carefully sharpened end that is bifurcated in order to hold a few drops of ink. A century ago the *mai sak* would be made of forged metal, often bronze and quite weighty. Nowadays shorter lengths of stainless steel are used, often improvised from television antennae or umbrella shafts.

Other materials, such as wood or bamboo (hence the misnomer 'bamboo tattoo' used in tourist districts), may also be used for the shaft, although metal shafts are the norm.

The divided tip is known as a *paak pet* (duck's bill) if both sides are equal in length or *paak chalaam* (shark's mouth) if slightly staggered. Staggered tips allow the master the choice of applying either thinner one-point lines or thicker two-point lines.

Another type of stylus, *khem mat* (bundled needles), bears a row of two to five sewing needles that have been cut into 2cm lengths and bound with wire to the end of the shaft. The needle tips are arranged to form an angle, so the master can rely on just one or two needle tips for fine lines, or three or more for thicker lines. Rarely, a master will simply bind two sewing needles together, forgoing a handle/shaft altogether.

MEUK

Up until the mid 20th century, when commercial inks became readily available, masters made their own inks from soot or charcoal powder mixed with oil. Today they use bottled printing ink, usually made in China, to which they may add an infusion of herbs as described earlier in Chapter 2.

Black or blue/black are the most common colours used, although some masters employ red ink for specific *yantra*. One master we interviewed preferred red ink for *mettamahaniyom* (loving kindness/charm) designs while another said he used it to strengthen *khong kraphan* (invincibility) tattoos.

NAM-MAN WAAN

Sesame oil infused with herbs can be used in lieu of ink for disciples who don't want visible tattoos. See Chapter 2 for further detail.

RITUAL OBJECTS

Aside from the needle-and-ink basics, masters will keep a variety of objects used in consecration rituals. Among the most common is a reed whisk for sprinkling holy water *(nam-mon)* on the head and tattooed body part after the design has been inked. Some masters will also keep a knife whose blade is engraved with *akkhara*, and tap a disicple's head and shoulders with the flat side of the blade.

More elaborate rituals may require consecrated white thread, looped between the *samnak* altar and the disciples, to transfer power. A helmet-like mask of the forest sage Pho Kae may also be placed on a disciple's head during blessing ceremonies.

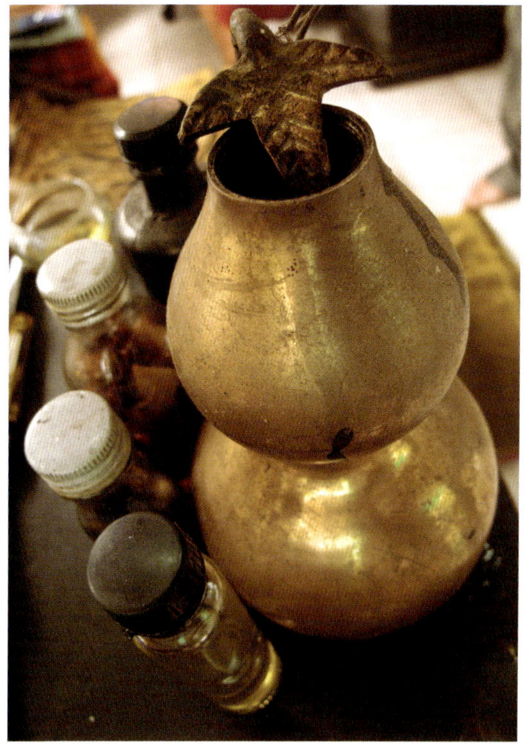

Above: A brass pot containing ink. Below: *Nam-man waan* (sesame oil mixed with herbs) is a common alternative to ink.

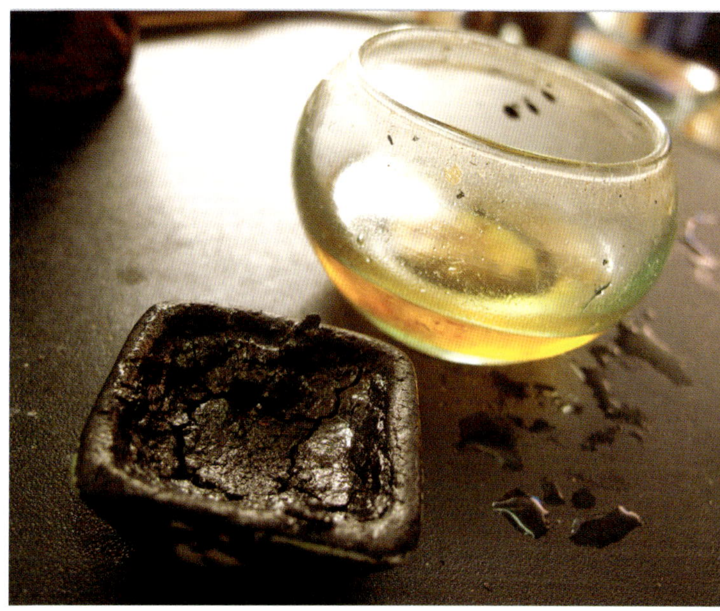

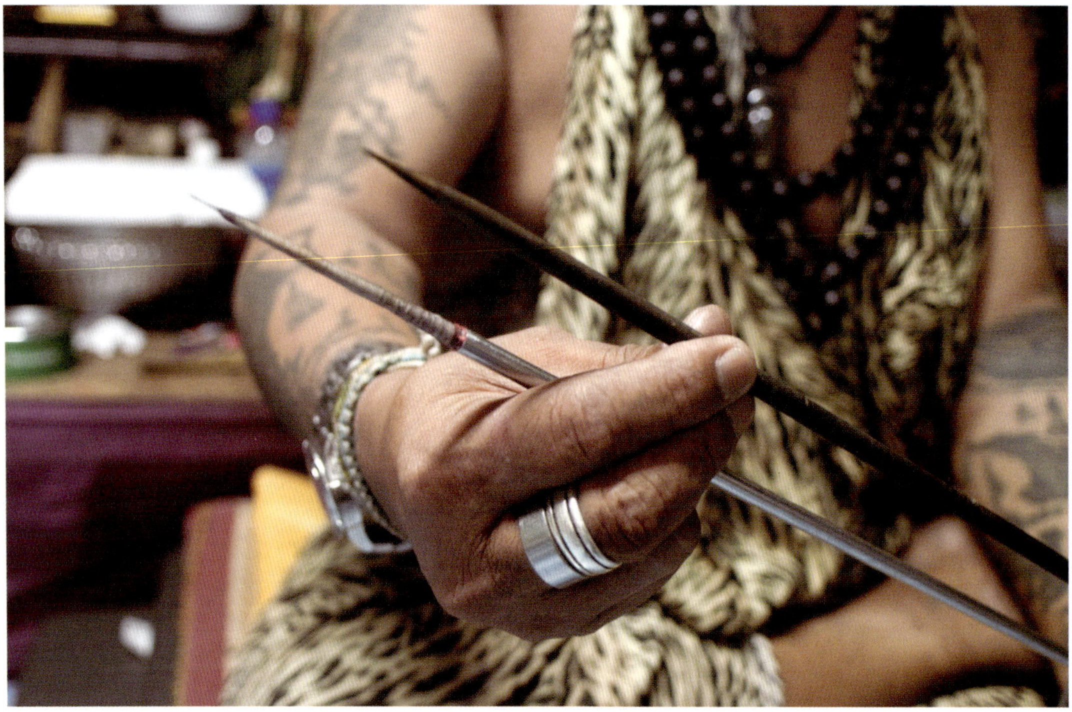

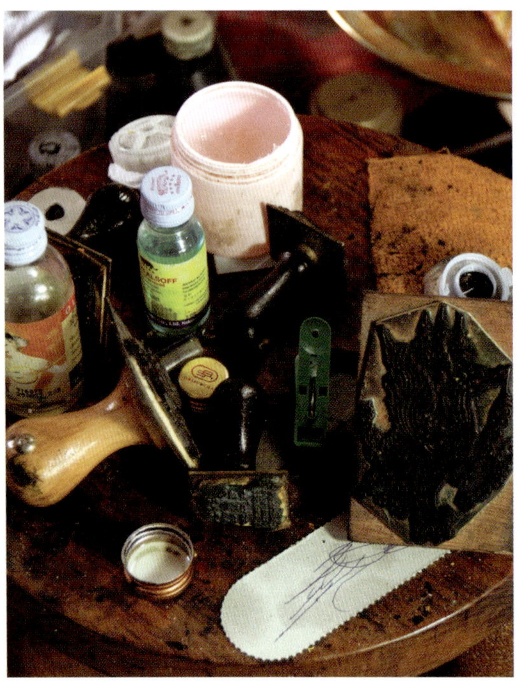

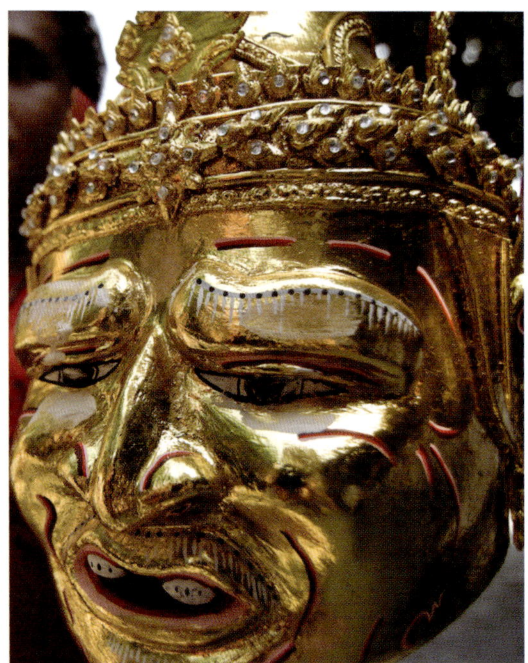

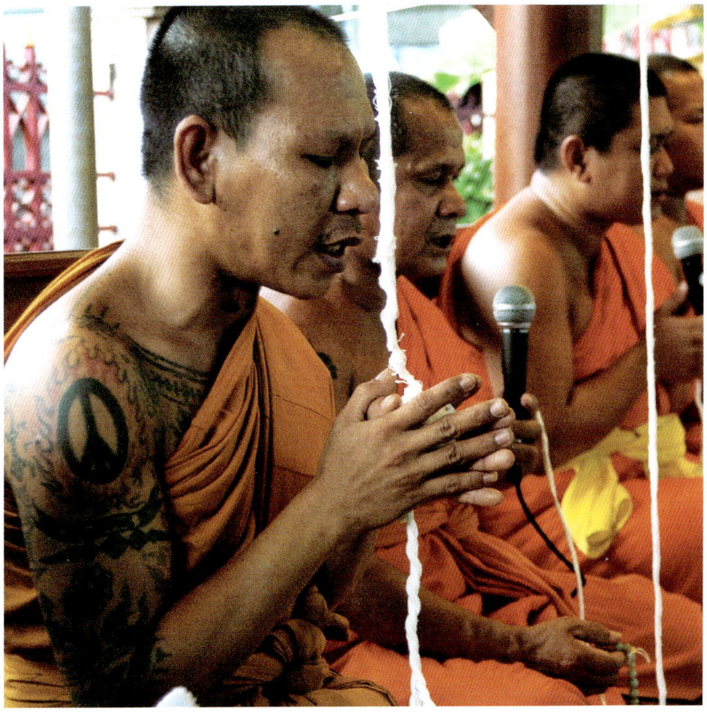

Previous page, clockwise from the top: The needle below is a *khem mat* (sewing needle tips fastened in a row) while the large needle above shows the traditional split end.

Pho Kae mask.

Rubber stamps for guiding the master's work, alcohol for sterilisation.

Left: Blessed string.

Below: Knife with *akkhara* and *na*.

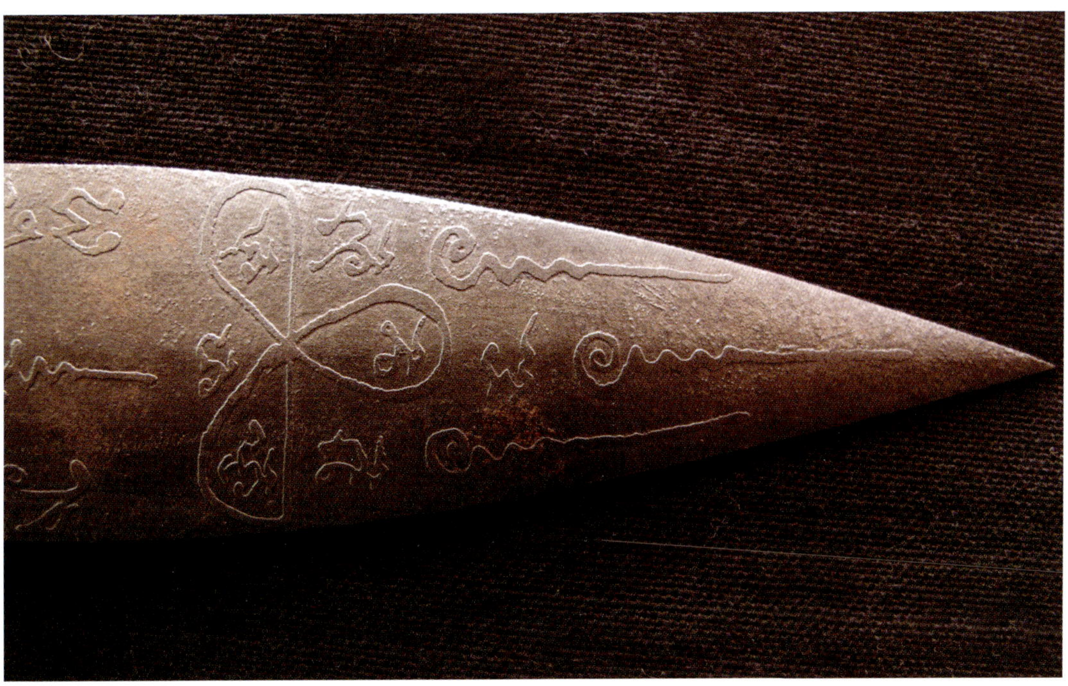

EPILOGUE

Since my first encounter with the *sak yan* tradition 30 years ago, I've seen Thai perceptions of the tradition change significantly. Back then most middle- and upper-class Thais looked down upon *sak yan*. It was the domain of people who needed to protect themselves because they were regularly exposed to violence. People in "polite" society wouldn't consider going to see a *sak yan* master.

With the rise in popularity of tattoos in the West over the last couple of decades, Thais have grown much more tattoo-tolerant. Like blue jeans, tattoos are now a common means of self-adornment. Thai youth who can't afford the high prices charged at Bangkok's trendy tattoo parlours may choose *sak yan* as an inexpensive fashion statement.

Another influencing factor has been a resurgence of pride in things that are uniquely Thai, as kick-started by Thai rock band Carabao when their song "Made in Thailand" became a massive hit in the 1980s. Suddenly Thai tattoos were cool – maybe even cooler than American or Japanese tattoos.

High-society Thais, particularly those in the entertainment industry but also people in the business world, jumped on the bandwagon after superstar Angelina Jolie had herself inked. As a result, *sak yan* is enjoying more inter-class acceptance and popularity than it has for at least a century. In urban Thailand particularly, more Thais than ever before are seeking sacred *yantra* tattoos. Many foreigners visit Thailand nowadays specifically to acquire *sak yan*, and this trend, too, is no doubt affecting how Thais view their own tradition.

Meanwhile a few elite Thai masters regularly visit Singapore and Malaysia, where their work fetches high prices. Just as famous Buddha amulets fetch millions of baht, *sak yan* are becoming increasingly commoditised.

At the same time, sensationalistic accounts of the occult characteristics of *sak yan*, of heavily inked disciples (which is far from the norm) and wild trance states (equally far from the norm) in the Western media often overshadow the cultivation of Buddhist virtues and other positive aspects of the tradition.

Some observers suggest that as *sak yan* is further absorbed by pop culture, and by commerce, its significance as a magico-religious tradition will erode. This presumes that a new generation of disciples will be less likely to respect the moral codes prescribed by their masters.

Yet while attention from Thai celebrities and foreign tattoo aficionados may fuel a temporary trend, it's the rank-and-file disciples who will continue to support the tradition in significant numbers. Common folk who seek counsel from the masters, and who wish to improve their lot in life or turn over a new leaf, still form the backbone of *sak yan* culture, and that's not likely to change much.

Where *sak yan* will be a half century from now is anyone's guess. European interest in the tradition will likely continue to grow. One of the more interesting questions to consider is whether the sak yan renaissance we see in Thailand will catch on in neighbouring Cambodia and Laos.

It's a certainty that the world of *sak yan* will continue to evolve in interesting ways.

ACKNOWLEDGEMENTS

This has been one of the most challenging book projects I've yet undertaken, and one that would never have got very far along without the generous assistance of a number of people along the way.

First and foremost, hats off to the *sak yan* masters who took the time to talk to us, to show us their work and their techniques, and to allow us to photograph them, their disciples and their *samnak*. Ajahn Nuad, Ajahn Toy and Ajahn Gop were particularly helpful in their explanations.

Anyone researching *sak yan* in English today will be aware of the work of Spencer Littlewood, who maintains a number of websites on the subject, including the very extensive Sak Yant Thai Temple Tattoos (www.sak-yant.com). Although we've never had a chance to meet, Spencer and I enjoyed a few telephone conversations, and he was very helpful in making contact with Ajahn Toy in particular.

Dan White faced the difficult task of capturing the action through his lenses while trying to be as minimally intrusive as possible. Often he waited patiently outside the *samnak* in the sun or rain for hours while I chatted with masters and their assistants, carefully building a rapport before asking permission for him to enter with his camera gear. I sometimes wonder if he would have agreed to take this project on if he had known how tough it would be! Dan was a real trouper, a capable travel companion and a valuable sounding board for ideas as well. Thanks to Ben Owen-Browne for leading us to Nung, the Klong Toey fisherman.

Editor Greg Lowe and publisher Marshall Cavendish showed epic patience waiting for me to deliver the manuscript, and agreeing to one extension after another. Designer Mark Soo has done a great job taking everything Dan and I threw at him and turning it into a coherent volume. Like Greg, he had to put up with long gaps of artistic gestation as the baby grew and moved down the birth canal. Thanks guys.

Lastly, thanks to Bongkoj Khongmalai, Anne Chebanier, Chris Ho, Ming Roth, Erich Fleshman, Desho Bernard, Mia Lackgren and Jan Yousagoon for allowing us to photograph their sacred tattoos.

FURTHER READING

Susan Greenwood, *The Anthropology of Magic*. Berg Publishers, 2010.

Mariane Guelden, *Thailand: Spirits Among Us*. Marshall Cavendish, 2007.

Marisa Kakoulas, *Black Tattoo Art*. Editions Reuss, 2009.

Michael McCabe. *Tattoos of Indochina: Magic, Devotion & Protection*. Schiffer Publishing, 2007.

Maarten Hesselt van Dinter, *The World of Tattoo: An Illustrated History*. KIT, 2005

Stanley Jeyaraja Tambiah. *Magic, Science and Religion and the Scope of Rationality*. Cambridge University Press, 1990.

Olivier de Bernon. *Yantra et mantra*. Centre culturel francais de Phnom-Penh, 1998.

GLOSSARY

Abhiseka	Ceremony establishing magical or spiritual power
Ajahn	Master (*adjar* in Khmer)
Akhom	Verse
Akkhara	Script or alphabet
Akkhara lehk yan	"Alphabet, numbers, *yantras*"; a euphemism for the collective lore of *sak yan*
Amnaat	Power
Arahant	Enlightened person
Buddhaguna	Buddhist virtues
Chok laap	Good fortune
Curcuma	Genus of about 80 accepted species in the plant family Zingiberaceae. See *waan*
Dhamma	(Sanskrit: dharma) Buddhist teachings and philosophy
Haa thaew	"Five rows"; a popular *sak yan* that confers five different qualities
Jingjok	A type of small lizard whose form makes an auspicious *sak yan*
Kao yaut	"Nine peaks"; a popular initiatory *sak yan* that evokes the peaks of mythical Mount Meru
Khaathaa	Verses or incantations that impart spiritual or magical power. From Pali-Sanskrit *gatha*
Khai plaa	"Fish eggs"; a name for a traditional tattoo style in which the lines are made up of visible dots
Khaum	Khmer script; also spelt *khom*
Khaung	Literally "stuff"; spiritual content held in the body and spirit of masters and disciples
Khaung kheun	When *khaung* is activated, the state of going into trance
Khem	Needle
Khem mat	Bound needle
Khem sak	Tattoo needle
Khong kraphan	Protection from violence and evil influence
Khru sak	Tattoo master; also *khru sak yan*
Khwan	Spirit entities attached to bodily functions
Kilen	Mythical half-human, half-bird creature
Klaew khlaat	Evading calamity and danger
Kuti	Monastic cell
Lehk	Number
Luang Phee	Venerable Elder Brother, an informal title for respected monks
Luang Pho	Venerable Father, an informal title for respected monks
Luang Pu	Venerable Grandfather, an informal title for respected monks
Luuk sit	Disciple
Maha amnaat	Great power
Mahasaneh	Great charisma
Mai khem	Tattoo shaft and needle (literally "needle stick")
Mai sak	Tattoo shaft and needle (literally "tattoo stick")
Mantra	Sacred incantation
Metta	Loving kindness
Metta mahaniyom	Loving kindness (and) great favour
Meuk	Ink
Meuk boraan	Traditional ink made from charcoal powder or lampblack
Meuk sehk	Blessed ink
Mon	Mantra (*moun* in Khmer)
Muni ey-sey	Khmer term for "forest sage"
Muay Thai	Thai kickboxing
Na	Small *yantra*

Nam-man waan	Blessed oil containing fragrant, medicinal and auspicious herbs
Nam-mon	Blessed water
Na naa thong	*Yantras* applied to the forehead with goldleaf
Nang niaw	"Sticky skin", i.e. skin that has become resistant to injury as a result of *sak yan*
Paak chalaam	"Shark mouth", referring to a tattoo needle with two points offset at an angle
Paak pet	"Duck mouth", referring to a tattoo needle with two even points
Paet thit	"Eight directions", a compass-like *yantra* that confers protection from danger
Phaa yan	*Yantra* cloth
Phee	Spirits or ghosts
Pho Kae	Hermit or forest sage who is believed to have started the *sak yan* tradition
Phra khreuang	Buddhist amulets
Phra thudong	Monk who has taken *thudong* (Pali: *dhutanga*) vows. See *thudong*
Phutthakhun	See *Buddhaguna*
Pluuk sehk	To transfer power or magic to a disciple via *khaathaa* and *sak yan*
Ramayana	Indian epic chronicling the story of Rama and Sita
Reusee	From Sanskrit *rishi*; forest sage
Sai sin	Sacred white cotton string, used in blessing ceremonies
Saiyasaat	The science of magic
Sak	To tattoo
Sak meuk	To tattoo with ink
Sak nam-man	To tattoo with oil
Sak yan	*Yantra* tattoo (*Sak yoan* in Khmer)
Samathi	Concentration, one-pointedness engendered through meditation
Samnak	Room, building or other space dedicated to work
Samnak sak yan	Space dedicated to *sak yan*
Sat himaphaan	Animals from Hindu-Buddhist mythology
Sehk	Empowerment blessing
Seua phen	Leaping tiger
Seup chadaa	Life-extending (ceremony)
Taam khwaam	To cast a spell
Takroot	A metal cylinder filled with *yantra* and *katha* and worn as a protective talisman
Thaay thaut	To "graduate" from the teachings of a master
Tham	Dhamma; dharma
Thudong	(Pali: *dhutanga*) 13 ascetic vows chosen by wandering monks
Vedas	Oldest Brahmanist texts, originally written in Vedic Sanskrit
Vijja	Pali word for "knowledge", pronounced *weechaa* in Thai. In the context of Thai spiritual beliefs, *weechaa* refers to the mastery of magical arts
Vipassana	Insight meditation
Waan	Herbs and roots used in traditional Thai medicinal and magical preparations
Wai	Raising the hands in a palms-together, prayer-like gesture as an expression of respect or devotion
Wai khru	Ceremonies that pay respect to one's teacher or master
Wan phra	Buddhist holy days, occurring every eight days according to lunar phases
Wat	Thai: Buddhist monastery
Weechaa	See "*vijja*"
Yan	Thai word for *yantra*
Yan phra jao haa phra ong	A *yantra* comprised of five Buddha images, along with appropriate verses
Yantra	Geometric designs that confer power, loving kindness and other qualities

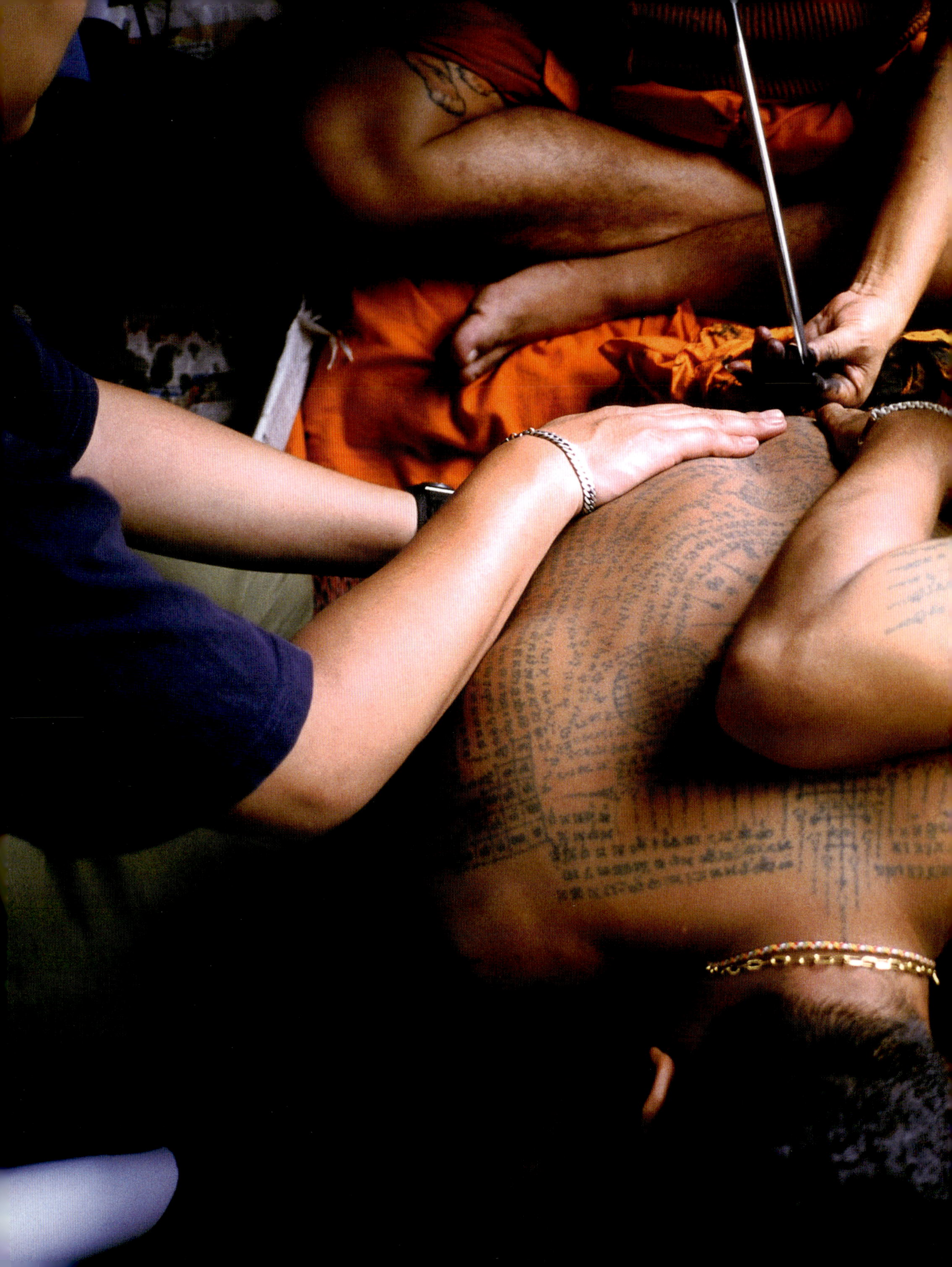

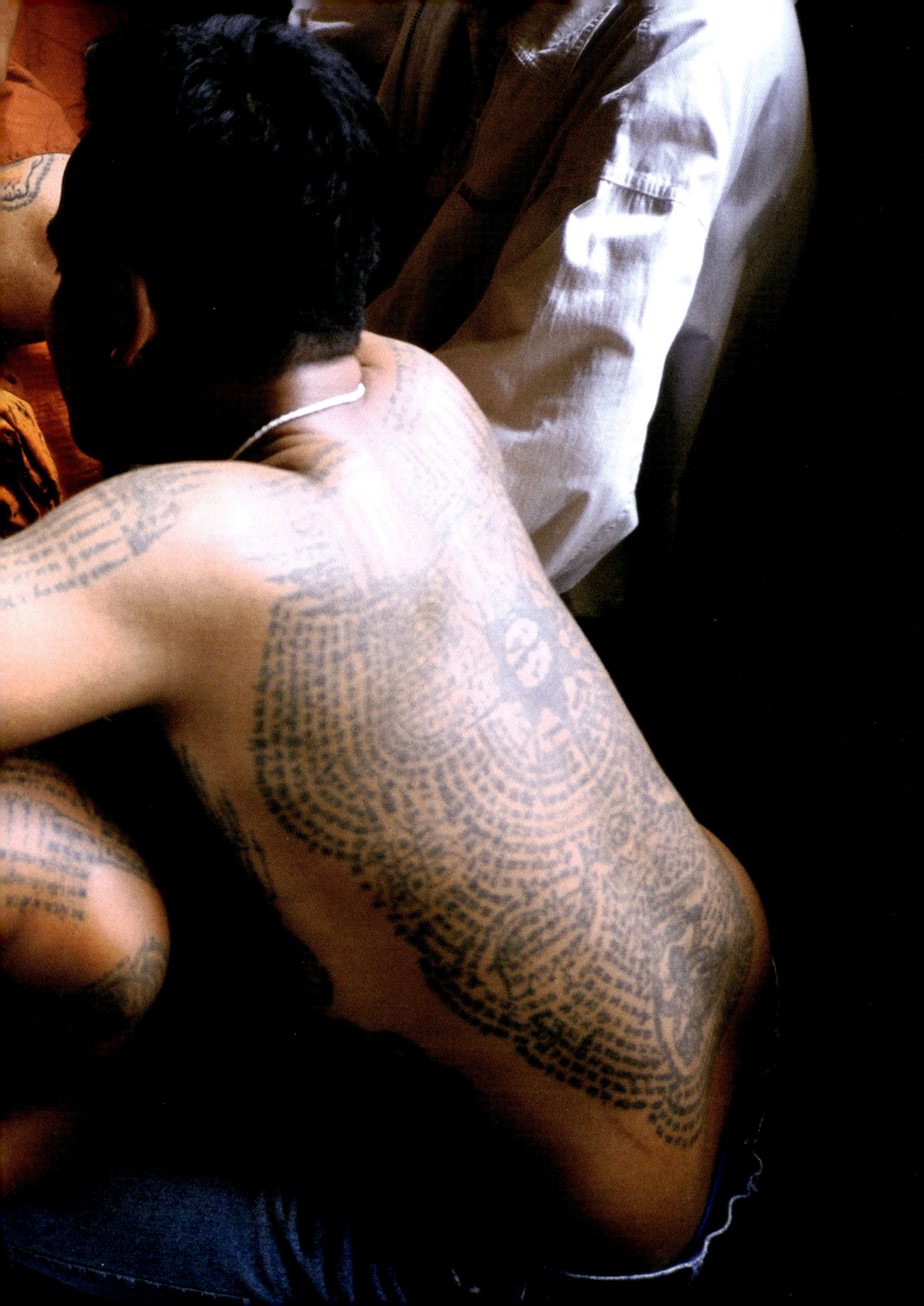

Photo by Joe Cummings

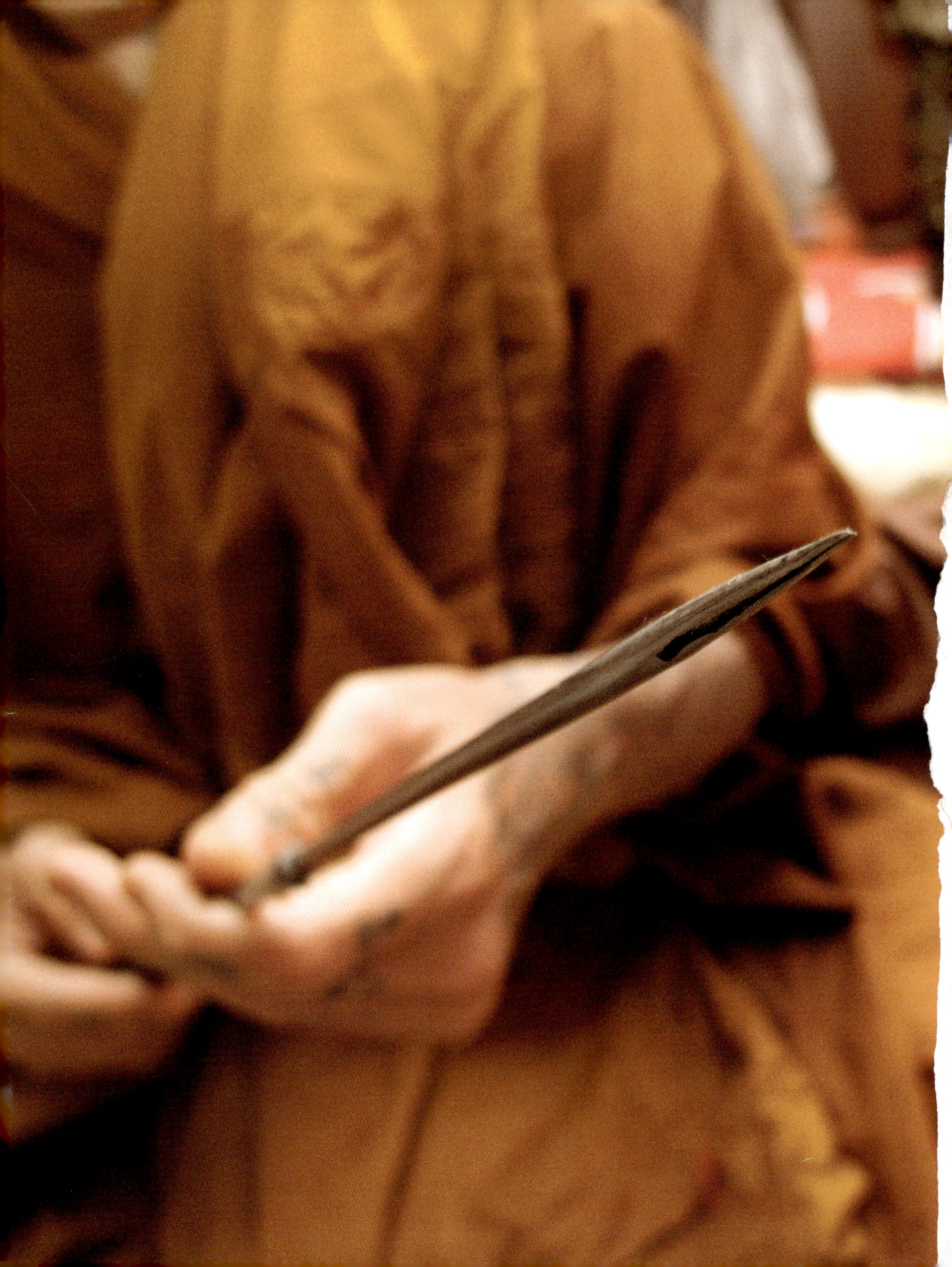